THE AUTHENTIC WILD WEST

THE LAWMEN

OTHER GRAMERCY WESTERN TITLES AVAILABLE

THE
LAWMEN

JAMES D. HORAN

GRAMERCY BOOKS
New York • Avenel

FOR

Gertrude;

in gratitude for her patient assistance on the many rugged trails which finally led to this trilogy.

This 1996 edition is published by Gramercy Books,
distributed by Random House Value Publishing, Inc.,
40 Engelhard Avenue, Avenel, New Jersey 07001.

Random House
New York • Toronto • London • Sydney • Auckland

Printed and bound in the United States of America

Library of Congress Cataloging-in-Publication Data
Horan, James David
        The authentic wild West.
        Bibliography: v.[1], p. 302-308; v. [2],
p. 304-309; v.[3] p. 304-309.
        CONTENTS: v. [1] The gunfighters—[2] The outlaws—[3] The lawmen.
        1. Outlaws—The West—Biography. 2. Peace officers—The West—Biography.
 3. The West—Biography. I. Title.
F594.H79   1976   978'.02'0922   [B]   76-10758
ISBN 0-517-15016-6

8 7 6 5 4 3 2 1

A large portion of this book is based on letters sent to the author, on tape recordings, interviews with persons now deceased, unpublished family reminiscences written to the author at the author's request, and on other personal material, all legally considered not to be within the public domain.

ACKNOWLEDGMENTS

This is the final volume of my trilogy on the Authentic Wild West. Throughout this project, over twenty years in the making, I have tried to uncover material that would help me to present the gunfighters, outlaws, and lawmen who compose our endearing American myth as flesh and blood, and not as the ridiculous, canonized caricatures created by films, television, and legend makers. To accomplish this, I have had the assistance of numerous historical societies, federal depositories, courthouses, and private collectors. I have also made use of my own collection of western Americana, particularly original photographs, put together over many years.

In the previous volumes I thanked those who had assisted me in gathering research material for *The Gunfighters* and *The Outlaws*. Now I wish to thank those who helped me with *The Lawmen*. They include: Arizona Historical Society, Margaret S. Bret Harte, Research Librarian, Lori Davisson, Research Specialist, Barbara J. Bush, Photo Department; The American Film Institute, Audrey Kupferberg, Associate Motion Picture Archivist; Amon Carter Museum, Marni Sandewiss, Curator of Photographs, Ginger Garrison, Assistant to Curator of Photographs; The Bancroft Library, University of California, Berkeley, Susan Rusev, Peter E. Hanff, Coordinators, Technical Services; Archives Nationales, Canada, Abisror Pinas; Chicago Public Library, Stephen C. Smith and his staff, Newspaper Division; The State Historical Society of Colorado, Mrs. Alice L. Sharp, Mrs. Catherine T. Engel, Reference Librarians, Documentary Resources, Judith Kromsdorf Golden, Photograph Librarian; Denver Public Library, Western History Department, Eleanor M. Gehres, Head; Connecticut State Library, Eunice Gillman, Reference Librarian, Archives, History and Genealogy Unit; The Huntington Library, San

Marino, California, Mary L. Anderson, Curator of Manuscripts, Mrs. Valerie Franco, Assistant Curator; Harvard University Library, Theodore Roosevelt Collection, Wallace Finley Dailey, Curator; Iowa State Historical Society, Mrs. Joyce Giaquinta, Manuscript Librarian; Kansas State Historical Society, Nancy Sherbert, Curator of Photographs, Joan Whelan, Newspaper Clerk; The Library of Congress, William Matheson, Chief, Reference Department, Rare Book and Special Collections Division, Bernard A. Bernier, Jr., Head, Reference Section, Serial Division, Patrick J. Sheehan, Katherine L. Wise and Sam Daniel, Reference Librarians, Motion Picture Division, Frank J. Carrol, Head, Newspaper Section, Serial and Government Publications Division, Robert N. Mullin, who for many years did such splendid pioneering research in the history of the West; Museum of Modern Art, New York, New York, Eileen Bowser, Curator, Department of Film; Montana Historical Society, Mrs. Harriett C. Meloy, Librarian, Ms. Lory Morrow, Photo-Archivist; National Archives, Richard Maxwell, National Resources Branch, William T. Murphy, Chief, Motion Picture and Sound Branch, Richard C. Crawford, Legislative and Natural Resources Branch, Ferris E. Stovel, Legislative, Judicial and Fiscal Branch, Lee R. Johnson, Librarian; Oklahoma State Historical Society, R. W. Jones, Director, Museums; University of Oklahoma, John S. Ezell, Curator, Western History Collections, June Witt, Clerical Supervisor, Michael Fife, David W. Coon, Research Assistants; The Panhandle-Plains Historical Museum, Canyon, Texas, Norman Stewart, Archival Research Assistant; Wyoming State Archives and Historical Department, Paula West, Photographic Section, Philip J. Roberts, Research Assistant; Victor Veygel, Little Falls, New Jersey, Photography.

And above all to Gertrude, who accompanied me on this long and rugged trail to track down our Gunfighters, Outlaws, and Lawmen across hills of fading—and at times almost impossible to read—frontier newspapers, in and out of musty courthouse basements and clerks' offices, through the historical treasure houses of the Library of Congress and National Archives, countless historical societies, and, finally, to the tiny dining room of the late Zoe Tilghman where Bill Tilghman came alive.

CONTENTS

THE AUTHENTIC WILD WEST

THE LAWMEN

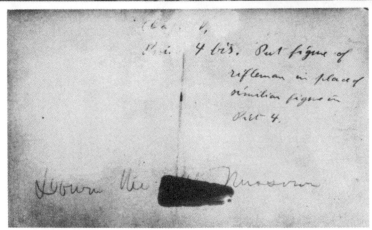

Theodore Roosevelt, deputy sheriff of Billings County, Dakota Territory, guarding the band of outlaws he had chased and captured in March 1886. The future president of the United States took not only Tolstoy's *Anna Karenina* to read on the manhunt, but also his camera to record the action. Roosevelt made the crop marks in ink for the famous frontier artist, Frederic Remington, who did the sketches for the *Century* Magazine article Roosevelt wrote about the manhunt. Remington's sketches also appeared in Roosevelt's book, *Ranch Life and the Hunting Trail*, published in 1897. For TR's incredible sequence of photographs see the Theodore Roosevelt section. This collection of photographs, captioned and cropped in ink by Roosevelt, is published here for the first time. *The James D. Horan Civil War and Western Americana Collection. Copied from the original by Victor Veygel*

INTRODUCTION:
DAY OF THE LAWMEN

THE LAWMAN, ALONG WITH THE GUNFIGHTER AND THE outlaw, played a prominent role in the creation of the legend of the Wild West. There he was—tall, slender, raw-boned—his sombrero pulled down over steely blue eyes surrounded by wrinkles, gazing into the immense distances of the plains. Or he rides into town from the solitary manhunt, the body of the killer wrapped in a yellow slicker, bobbing gently across the saddle of a horse the lawman leads. Always the star gleams on his vest.

Who was this lone courageous man, this symbol of law and order on a lawless frontier? He could have been a rancher elected by his frightened fellow citizens who were plagued by horse thieves, rustlers, desperadoes, or fast-drawing gunmen terrorizing their community. This newly elected lawman could also have been buried very shortly after his election by his sorrowing family while the town hunted for another foolishly heroic man to accept its tin star.

Those who survived were fast with a gun; had the physical strength to control mobs of drunken, dangerous Texas cowhands in from a drive; had the flinty determination to trail a killer or an outlaw band for days, perhaps for weeks, to bring them back to justice; the moral integrity to ignore bribes and resist the pressure of local politicians who could be as corrupt and ruthless as any New York Tammany Hall ward heeler.

1

John Slaughter of Arizona's Cochise County survived. He was a quiet rancher who strapped on his guns at the pleading of his neighbors and drove out the rustlers and outlaws, a task the vaunted Earps failed to do. Another was "Bear River" Tom Smith, a displaced New York policeman who kept Abilene peaceful with iron fists instead of a six-shooter. Chauncey Whitney, a mild-mannered former Indian fighter, became sheriff of Ellsworth, Kansas, at the peak of that cow town's use as a terminus for the Texas drovers. Whitney would act as a peacemaker rather than blow the hot-tempered Texans apart with a shotgun. Whitney and Smith were killed with their guns holstered.

California of the 1870s produced Sheriff Henry N. Morse of Alameda County, one of the West's finest, if not most popular, lawmen. Young, unshaven Morse rode alone into the hills studying the haunts of the outlaw bands who were terrorizing ranchers and communities, including Los Angeles, then a small frontier town. He made friends among ranchers and frightened Mexican sheepherders and studied the general topography of the area. He also corresponded with other sheriffs and the wardens of jails to determine the habits and weaknesses of the territory's most notorious badmen. When he was fully prepared, he obtained warrants, then went in alone to take his prisoners at gunpoint in dance halls, backwoods saloons, or at fandangoes.

In Texas, at the pleading of his friends and neighbors, L. B. Blair left fighting Comanches to become deputy sheriff of Erath County. A cold-eyed man with a pirate's moustache, he efficiently cleaned the county of outlaws. A frontier newspaper noted three murderers and seven rustlers—all captured by Blair—crowding his small jail at one time. Blair doggedly hunted Sam Bass and his gang until, with the Texas Rangers, he cornered Sam at Round Rock where the outlaw was killed.

The good lawmen were determined men, like Colorado's Sheriff Charles Neiman who was beaten unconscious by Harry Tracy, one of the most dangerous men on the frontier and his partner, David Lant, a rustler. Groggy and battered, Neiman saddled up, trailed the pair to Steamboat Springs, then took a stage to head off the fugitives before they could reach the railroad. Two miles out of Steamboat, Tracy and Lant hailed the stagecoach. They stepped in to face Neiman's cocked shotgun.

"Good morning, gentlemen," the sheriff said with a grim smile. "Breakfast is waiting for you back at the jail."

Tracy grunted in disgust as he held out his wrists for the handcuffs. "Who the hell thought a hick sheriff would be up this early?" he asked Lant.

Not all the lawmen of the Wild West wore badges. William Wallace, prosecutor of Missouri's Jackson County, who campaigned for office with a gun on his hip, skillfully and courageously broke up the James-Younger gang. Wallace, who didn't drink or smoke, and read the Bible daily, defied his fellow Democrats and spurned political support for his senatorial campaign by putting Frank James on trial for murder. Wallace is the unsung hero of the saga of Jesse James.

There were also lawmen who worked for railroads, express companies, cattlemen's associations, and private detective organizations hunting outlaw bands, train and bank robbers, rustlers, and killers. Among the best known of these lawmen is William Pinkerton, a huge man with dark brooding eyes, who directed a small army of "operatives" on the frontier. They used horses, mules, wagons, and trains to chase, kill, and capture those outlaws who had selected as their targets clients of the Pinkerton Agency.

The Pinkertons established a crude but efficient rogues' gallery of western outlaws. Sheriffs and marshals propped the bodies of outlaws they had killed against a barn door or a fence and had the local cameraman photograph the corpse—sometimes dug up after a long interment. The print was sent to the Chicago Pinkerton office to be studied by Bertillon experts. The Bertillon system, devised by Alphonse Bertillon, a nineteenth-century French criminologist, was a method of identifying criminals by means of various body measurements, colorings, and markings.

If the dead man was wanted, the Pinkertons closed his file and guaranteed the lawman he would receive all outstanding rewards. The Pinkertons' gallery became the country's most extensive listing of nineteenth-century criminals, including a large number of western outlaws. It was turned over to the government by the agency when the FBI was established, and became an early part of that organization's famous Bureau of Identification.

Both William and Robert Pinkerton, sons of the founder of the agency, often took to the trail themselves. Once William, to save his life, hurled a powerfully built outlaw into the churning wheel of a steamboat. A Pinkerton operative, Charlie Siringo, became the celebrated "cowboy detective" who rode thousands of miles in an unsuccessful attempt to capture Harvey Logan, the deadly Kid Curry of the Wild Bunch. After he retired, Siringo and the Pinkertons became engaged in a series of bitter court battles over his published memoirs.

James B. Hume, John N. Thatcher, and Fred Dodge, Wells Fargo special officers, spent years in the West trailing and capturing stagecoach and train robbers. Dodge joined Wyatt Earp's posse in the hunt for the outlaws who held up the Tombstone stage and killed the driver. General David J. Cook, who founded the famous Rocky Mountain Detective Agency, roamed the West with his deputies, arresting more than three thousand men and women, "including fifty of the West's most desperate killers and outlaws." As his son recalled: "Of all those three thousand, he never allowed one to seriously hurt him, not one of them to get away when taken, and not one to be violently dealt with when in his hands as an officer."

Before he opened his own detective agency, Cook had been one of Colorado's most efficient sheriffs. After his retirement the *Rocky Mountain News* estimated he had recovered $70,000 in lost property. He broke up four organized gangs of train robbers, prevented a serious riot, captured and helped to convict several murderers who were hanged, and located more than three hundred stolen steers and fifty horses. The *News* proudly commented that "not a hoof was lost in Arapaho County" when Cook was its sheriff.

Consider the circumstances under which these lawmen, public and private, fulfilled their duty: the enormous distances, primitive transportation, hostile ranchers, outlaw sympathizers, indifferent fellow townsmen, too few deputies, and economy-minded city councilmen. Posses of businessmen often turned back, leaving the lawman to continue on alone. On the trail his best friends were his horse and his gun. There were no scientific devices to aid him, no fingerprinting, no telephone; the nearest railroad could be a day's journey. Most of the time there were no photographs, only vague descriptions of the wanted men. He was expected to return with the prisoner or his corpse—if he failed too many times he was replaced.

His jail was usually a one-room shack, so flimsy a gang of outlaws could kick it apart to free their friends. His deputy could be a drifter or a jobless cowhand easily intimidated or willing to sell out to a gang planning to rob the bank. The lawman's salary was $50 to $100 a month; if he was a celebrated gunfighter like Wild Bill Hickok, he could command as high as $125.

T. C. Henry, mayor of Abilene, was so desperate to find a lawman who could control the wild Texans gradually taking over his community that he persuaded his four-man city council to pay "Bear River" Tom Smith $250 a month "and half the fees" he collected.

The lawman's work was mostly plodding, routine, dangerous, and seldom glamorous. The sheriff or city marshal—the federal marshal took over when mail became part of the robbers' loot—would round up his posse and pick up the trail of the wanted men. There could be running gunfights or ambushes. If the lawman was killed, his body would be brought back wrapped in a blanket or slicker and tied across the saddle of his horse or put in the back of a wagon. His widow would receive his guns and horse along with the town's temporary sympathy and a few prayers from the local clergyman. There was no pension for the widow and her children; her husband's heroism would probably be forgotten within a few months.

But the wives of western lawmen stoically accepted the death of their men. They knew it was all part of dealing with a violent, majestic and, many times, unpredictable land where men were killed by a loco steer, a herd of cattle stampeded by the dropping of a tin plate, a drunken fool playing badman in a saloon, or the bite of a rabid skunk. Even the weather was their enemy. On the open plains a bolt of lightning reduced a man to a charred crisp, a flash flood could drown him and his horse within minutes. He could also be sucked down by quicksand along the river bottoms, or be crushed by crags of ice released in a sudden spring thaw.

Yet the lawman's job had its advantages. He could own, on the side, a saloon or part of one, its gambling concession or a dance hall—all legitimate occupations in the Wild West. He would probably have an "understanding" with the local livery stable, and his office was a firm base to move into politics. In mining camps, like Tombstone, the sheriff's job was lucrative; he received a percentage of all the taxes he collected—including the tax on whorehouses. William M. Breakenridge, a Cochise County deputy sheriff, claimed in his memoirs the sheriff's post "was worth $40,000 a year, as the sheriff was allowed ten percent for [tax] collections."

In contrast, the Rangers of Isaac Charles "Hanging Judge" Parker's United States Court for the Western District of Arkansas having jurisdiction over Indian territory, now Oklahoma, were paid by the fee system. They received ten cents a mile, one way, serving papers or bringing in prisoners; forty cents a mile for feeding prisoners; and $2.50 "for serving a warrant and the same amount for the commitment of prisoners." The "guardsmen" accompanying a deputy earned $2 a day. The casualty rate among the Rangers was high: 65 Rangers out of a total of 225 died in the line of duty, a record not matched by the Texas Rangers.

The tools of the western lawman were few; he supplied a rifle, six-shooter ammunition, horse, slicker, and blanket. The community provided the jail, board for prisoners, courts, judges, and juries. The local newspaper printed his wanted notices.

Sheriffs, city marshals, deputies, Rangers, and guardsmen, they all lived close to death and violence. The late Mrs. Zoe Tilghman, widow of one of the most famous lawmen in the West, recalled for me: "I never knew what to expect when they called Bill. He would shrug it off as just another job, but a cold shiver would go up my spine when I saw him strap on his gun and look over his rifle. It was then I realized he was going after one or more men who would kill him rather than spend a good part of their lives behind bars."

Ironically, Tilghman, who survived gunfights, ambushes, and countless manhunts for the most dangerous men in the Wild West, was killed by a drunken Prohibition agent.

But not all western lawmen were of Tilghman's breed. There were times when a thin line separated the good from the lawless. Terrorized communities eagerly hired gunfighters, outlaws "on the dodge," or known killers to protect their town. In the end, they found they had to live with the whirlwind they had created.

There was Phil Watson, marshal of Casper, Wyoming, who entered a saloon, walked up to a gunfighter, took his gun, slapped his face, and ordered him to leave town.

A few months later, the citizens who had hailed his bravery were stunned when Watson was arrested as the leader of an organized band of horse thieves. The stolen herds were gathered in Montana and Wyoming, driven to isolated ranches and canyons, and then finally shipped to Casper, where Watson had arranged for them to be sold to eastern markets. He was found guilty and sentenced to five years in Wyoming State Prison.

Henry (Hendry) Brown rode with Billy the Kid during the Lincoln County War and was with the Kid when Sheriff William Brady was ambushed and killed in Lincoln on April 1, 1878. In July, with the posses closing in, Brown left New Mexico to escape the gallows. He drifted north to Kansas, where he found that Caldwell, a cattle town, needed a fast-shooting lawman. He was elected sheriff and soon demonstrated his skill with a gun when he killed two desperadoes trying to take over the town.

In May 1884 Brown was married. Six weeks later he led his deputy Ben Williams and two cowboys in holding up the Medicine Lodge, Kansas, National Bank, killing its president and cashier. The outraged citizens fought back, captured and then lynched them.

In Newton, Kansas, Billy Brooks, cold-eyed and fast on the draw, was elected sheriff; two years later he was hanged as a horse thief.

Watson, Brown and his gang, and Billy Brooks were not exceptions to the rule. There were many more cowardly, corrupt, and drunken lawmen who were either jailed in their own cells, stripped of their badge, or lynched by infuriated citizens. Yet the faithful outnumbered the betrayers.

Good or bad, they were the most colorful of the myths and legends of America's Wild West. Problematic, lionhearted, cowardly, laconic, bullying, occasionally murderous, they were all walking conundrums of the frontier.

JAMES D. HORAN
The Notch, 1980

THE BUFFALO HUNTERS

Some of the best-known lawmen of the Wild West came from the ranks of the buffalo hunters who roamed the plains in the 1870s stalking the huge herds. They supplied meat for the railroads' construction gangs and sold the hides for coats and tongues for gourmet meals in the eastern markets.

The daily kill for skilled marksmen like Bat Masterson and Bill Tilghman averaged about 125. Their friend, Tom Nixon, once accounted for 120 in forty minutes. He quit at 204 when the heat from the heavy-grain powder had destroyed the barrel of his rifle.

The buffalo hunting team was composed of the shooter, the skinner, and the hideman, who pegged the fresh skins to the ground to dry. They had a wagon, food, kegs of powder and lead for balls, and later, thousands of rounds of ready-made ammunition. The Hollywood version of the hunters charging madly at a herd while shooting at a gallop is colorful but laughable. This was a deadly serious business; any wild action would only "spook" the herd. The goal was to kill as many of the big shaggy animals as possible.

When the herd was sighted, the hunter would select his "stand," usually a mound, the peak of a small hill, or a group of rocks. Making sure he was downwind, he would then start shooting methodically; every bullet had to count. After about twenty-four kills he would rest to allow the heavy acrid gunpowder smoke to dissipate.

He usually carried a "Big Fifty"—a Sharps 1875, caliber 50-50. If the rifle overheated, the breech lock would be opened, a canteen of water poured down the barrel, followed by a greasy rag wrapped around a ramrod.

When the army found it expensive and impossible to pin down and defeat the swift-moving Plains warriors, they encouraged the killing of the buffalo, the commissary of the tribes. For centuries the Indians had lived in almost spiritual harmony with the beasts whose bodies supplied them with everything from hides for their tepees to glue.

In 1874 Texas legislators, alarmed at the rapid rate the herds were disappearing, proposed a bill limiting the range of the hunters and the numbers of the animals to be killed. But in Washington General Sheridan thundered: "The buffalo hunters have done more in two years to settle the vexed Indian question than the entire regular army has done in the last thirty years. They are destroying the Indian commissary and it is a well-known fact that an army losing its base of supply is placed at a great disadvantage."

In the end, the hunters not only wiped out the herds but an entire culture. The nomadic tribes of the plains were reduced to beggars who would die at Wounded Knee.

A rare photograph of a buffalo hunter in the 1870s taken by Frank Jay Hayes, who began working as a frontier photographer in 1866. The following year he made a photographic tour of Montana and the Dakota Territory. His negatives are an important visual record of America's frontier. *The James D. Horan Civil War and Western Americana Collection,* hereafter *The James D. Horan Collection*

Cheyenne women dressing buffalo robes. Cow skins were easier for the women to tan, lighter and more pliable than the skins of the old bulls. The thick neck and hump skins, stretched green over a bed of coals to shrink and harden, were used by warriors as shields. *Courtesy National Archives*

A grazing buffalo, one of the millions that roamed the Great Plains of America's West. *The James D. Horan Collection*

A buffalo stampede, by William Jacob Hays. Frontiersmen agreed there was nothing more terrifying than a stampeding buffalo herd. The ground shook for miles, towering walls of dust rose in the air, animals fled from the path. Colonel Richard Irving Dodge, the famous Indian fighter, described how in 1872 stampeding buffalo derailed a train in their path. It was not unusual for hundreds to rush blindly over the edge of a bluff and be killed, or to be drowned in rivers. Hays, born in New York City in 1830, spent all his life in the Missouri River country, painting the frontier. He was one of the fine artists of the western frontier. His works are rare. *The James D. Horan Collection*

Until the middle 1870s, buffalo covered the western plains. John Mix Stanley, one of the most important artists of the early West, painted this vast herd around 1843. Stanley, born in New York in 1814, spent most of his life wandering about the frontier painting Indians, forts, wild life, and portraits. In the fall of 1842 he established a studio at Fort Gibson, Indian Territory (Oklahoma). Frontiersmen, Indians, hunters, explorers, and army officers passed through his gallery. In 1865, his collection of 200 paintings, a life's work, was destroyed when fire gutted a wing of the Smithsonian Institution. Only five of his works survived, along with some published woodcuts. His works are rare. *The James D. Horan Collection*

Wright's and Rath's buffalo hides outside their store in Dodge City, 1873. Bob Wright, one of the founders of Dodge City and a close friend of Bat Masterson, was with Masterson in the Battle of Adobe Walls. Wright and Charlie Rath were among the early and successful frontier businessmen. They started as buffalo hunters. *The James D. Horan Collection*

This is a hunter's kill after his "big 50" had done "five minutes work, "as L. A. Huffman recorded. Huffman, of Miles City, Montana, friend of Theodore Roosevelt, photographed the dying frontier, including the killing off of the last great herds. *The James D. Horan Collection*

The booming of the heavy guns of the buffalo hunters echoing across the empty prairie could alert any war party of painted warriors eager for scalps. That was an accepted risk. But when the hunters were scouting for a herd and wanted to avoid any confrontation they did not light a cook fire but subsisted on pemmican.

This was dried pulverized buffalo meat mixed with hot liquid marrow fat and poured into bags sealed with tallow and then pounded flat. The dessicated meat would last for years without spoiling. "It took a lot of chewing," one old hunter recalled, "and the taste wasn't the best, but you got used to it after a while. In fact you got to like it. And it was better than saying good-bye to your hair."

N. C. Wyeth's painting *How Buffalo Bill Won His Name. The James D. Horan Collection*

A rare photograph of Buffalo Bill taken in Paris in 1889 by the famed French photographer Eugene Pirou. The mounted picture is autographed by Cody. *The James D. Horan Collection*

William Frederick Cody, "Buffalo Bill," was the glorified hero of the buffalo hunters of the Wild West. In October 1867 he signed a contract with Goddard Brothers to supply 12 buffalo a day for $500 a month. According to his biographer, Don Russell, Cody killed 6,750 animals to feed the Union Pacific's construction teams.

Historical estimates of the huge herds which once covered the plains "like a great black cape," as one awed explorer wrote, range from 20 to 60 million. The hunters wiped out all but a few within several years.

The scene of the killing of the last buffalo in Kansas, possibly on the southwestern frontier in the 1880s. *The James D. Horan Collection*

THE CATTLEMEN

The Civil War was over, the proud and still defiant Texans wearing parts of Confederate uniforms returned to their frontier towns, villages, and isolated ranches. There had always been cattle on the plains, but the returning veterans were amazed to find large herds of grazing longhorns untouched by a branding iron.

When the western movement of covered wagons began in the 1840s, resourceful Texans had driven their stock along the Shawnee Trail to markets in Missouri to supply the emigrants with beef. The Shawnee, or Kansas, Trail led from southwestern Texas, crossed the Red River into Indian country, then over the Canadian, Arkansas, and Grand rivers along the Kansas border to veer into Missouri and finally St. Louis.

The most traveled trail after the Civil War, popularly known as the Chisholm Trail, was marked out by Jesse Chisholm, son of a Scotch father and Cherokee mother. His aunt was Sam Houston's wife. In 1832 Chisholm first blazed a wagon road, then in 1864 moved cattle along this trail to Kansas markets. The Chisholm began at the Rio Grande in southwestern Texas, crossed the muddy Brazos into Indian country, where it crossed the Washita, North Canadian, and Cimarron to finally reach Abilene, Kansas.

Texas cattle only trickled north in 1866 but the following year a courageous, imaginative stock dealer named Joseph Geiting McCoy linked the beef-hungry eastern markets with the Texas drovers.

McCoy began his career in the Civil War selling and shipping mules. From his interviews with stockmen he realized there was a demand for a western beef terminal to meet the needs of the Texas cattlemen. McCoy finally selected Abilene, Kansas, and the Union Pacific agreed to pay him $5 for every carload of steers to leave the terminal. He bought 230 acres west of the six-year-old frontier village, built cattle pens, then sent agents across the Southwest posting handbills praising Abilene in saloons, freight offices, and post offices.

A series of rare pictures of Joseph McCoy, who established Abilene, Kansas, as the first major midwestern beef terminal. McCoy was twenty-nine years old when this picture was taken, about the time he persuaded the president of the Union Pacific that cattle could be moved by rail from a midwest terminal to New York and Chicago markets. Earlier, the president of the Missouri-Pacific had quickly ushered McCoy out of his office because of McCoy's dusty coat, worn boots, and battered hat, a gesture the railroad executive would always regret. *Courtesy Margot Gayle, granddaughter of Joseph McCoy*

Sarah Epler McCoy, Joe's wife, who encouraged his dreams of establishing a cattle empire. At twenty-nine McCoy's yearly dealing with one bank was $2,500,000. Mrs. McCoy was about forty in this photograph. *Courtesy Margot Gayle, granddaughter of Joseph McCoy*

In the fall of 1867 the first herd of twenty-four hundred longhorns arrived at McCoy's stockyards, accompanied by forty-four cowboys, "all armed with six-shooters, new repeating rifles, and one hundred cow ponies." Within a year, Abilene was the busiest cattle center in the West, with thousands of steers leaving daily for Midwest grazing terminals or for the beef-hungry East. The steers were valued at $5 a head on the Texas plains and sold for $50 in Abilene.

With the herds came the cowboy, the wild cow towns, the gunfighters, and the lawmen—all to become part of the American legend.

An early Kansas Pacific Railroad flyer advertising its facilities for Texas cattlemen. *The James D. Horan Collection*

Texas longhorns crossing a stream on the way north to the Kansas cow towns, by A. R. Wauld. The muscular longhorns with their wide-spread horns and narrow heads, which gave them a particularly dangerous look, were tough and durable. They could withstand drought, blizzards, insects, and wolf packs. One old cattleman claimed longhorns could walk fifteen miles and make one drink last two days. Colonel Dodge described them as "fifty times more dangerous" to a man on foot than the fiercest buffalo. Alfred R. Wauld was a Civil War combat artist for *Harper's Weekly*. He went west after the war to sketch the building of the Union Pacific, cattle drives, Indians, forts, and the army. *The James D. Horan Collection*

Doan's store on the bank of the Red River, Texas, the last stop for cowboys driving the herds north. *The James D. Horan Collection*

The feared night herder's cry, "Stampede!" would waken any cow camp within minutes. It was the cowboy's difficult and dangerous job, using blankets, shots, and shouts, to "turn the head" of the leaders of the rampaging herd. Men vanished and their mangled remains were buried at dawn. A dropped tin plate, a flash of lightning, or the howl of a wolf pack could "spook" a herd. This painting is by Hy Sandham, an excellent painter and illustrator of books and articles on the West at the turn of the century. *The James D. Horan Collection*

The immensity and majesty of the Great Plains awed many of the early Texas drovers. A few kept diaries, and entries written by the flickering light of a campfire briefly described the immense prairies covered with wild flowers, the banks of streams lined with wild plums, flocks of prairie chickens, and towns of prairie dogs. The vastness of the plains is caught in this photograph made by General John T. Pitman who, for perspective, placed a horseman against a bluff. For more of Pitman's photographs see the Theodore Roosevelt chapter. *The James D. Horan Collection*

A photograph by the noted western photographer C. D. Kirkland of Cheyenne, Wyoming, who made a life's career of photographing the cowboy and the cattle industry. The cow camp's cook makes a pie on a wooden attachment to his mess wagon while an amused cowboy grins at Kirkland's camera. *The James D. Horan Collection*

A Night Herder, by N. C. Wyeth. On the trail north, the night herder patrolled the fringe of the herd, singing softly to the unpredictable animals. Old cowmen claimed the ballad of Sam Bass, the Texas outlaw, calmed most of the longhorns heading to the Kansas cow towns. *The James D. Horan Collection*

A rare layout of sketches of cowboy life from an issue of the *Golden Argosy,* a popular magazine of the 1880s. *The James D. Horan Collection*

On Guard

Noon Time.

Racing

In the fall of 1867 Alexander Gardner, former manager of Mathew B. Brady's Washington studio and a superb Civil War photographer, went west to make a series of "views" along the Union Pacific's Eastern Division. Gardner not only visited the cow towns along the line but made side excursions into the interior, photographing main streets, corral sheds, railroad equipment, bridges, and ferries. He used the wet plate process, the same as he had used following the Army of the Potomac. He made stereoscopic views and whole glass plates, 8" x 10" and 11" x 14" sizes. In 1868 Gardner photographed the historic peace council between the United States and the Arapaho and Cheyenne at Fort Laramie, Wyoming Territory. In this first view Texas cattle are crossing the Smoky Hill River at Ellsworth, Kansas. Joseph McCoy later charged that Ellsworth men rode 100 miles to try to induce the Abilene farmers to drive off the Texas drovers who were starting to use McCoy's pens. But by 1871 Ellsworth had become a cattle boom town and one of the wildest in the Wild West.

Cattle cars at McCoy's corral, Abilene. *The James D. Horan Collection*

Ellsworth, Kansas, Abilene's rival. *The James D. Horan Collection*

Emigrant bull trains moving along Walnut Street, Ellsworth. *The James D. Horan Collection*

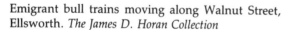

Brown's Hotel, Fort Laramie, Wyoming Territory, attributed to Gardner. *The James D. Horan Collection*

THE HOMESTEADERS

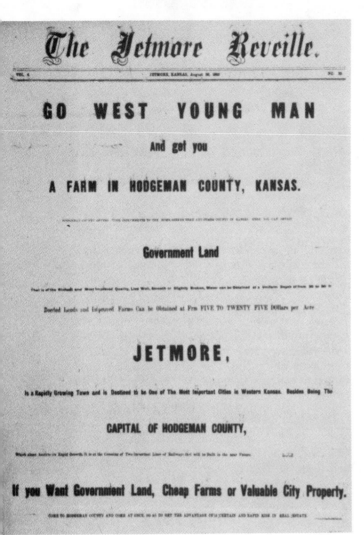

As their rails snaked across the plains, railroads vigorously campaigned to get settlers to leave the eastern cities and move to the West's open spaces. The Homestead Law passed on May 20, 1862, by Congress gave a citizen 160 acres if he stayed and cultivated his homesite for five years. The railroads' campaigns attracted thousands who came west to farm. They clashed with the cattle barons whose cowboys tore down the fences of the homesteader, drove cattle over his fields, and occasionally killed him. But many of the "sod busters" or "nesters," as the cowboys contemptuously called them, stayed, plowed their fields, and helped the lawmen to bring law and order to a wild frontier. This is a typical "Go West" poster. *The James D. Horan Collection*

HOMES FOR THE HOMELESS.

WHAT THE REPUBLICAN PARTY

HAS DONE FOR

THE POOR MAN.

PUBLISHED BY THE UNION REPUBLICAN CONGRESSIONAL COMMITTEE, WASHINGTON, D. C.

A Republican party "question and answer" pamphlet advising homesteaders. *The James D. Horan Collection*

No more important act to the poor man, whom it was intended exclusively to benefit, was ever enacted by Congress than the Homestead Law, which originated with, and was passed by, the votes of the Republican members of the Thirty-Seventh Congress. Enacted during the dark days of the Rebellion, at a time when hundreds and thousands of the laboring men of both sections of the country were arrayed in deadly hostility to each other, it has failed to attract that attention, especially in the Southern communities, which its great importance demands.

The result of the rebellion in the emancipation of the slaves of the South, the enactments of Congress whereby these former bondmen have been made citizens of our great Republic, and the amendment of the original Homestead Act of 1862, so as to confer its benefits on all who may choose to avail themselves of the same, irrespective of race or color, has greatly increased its importance by opening up a channel through which may be reached and permanently benefited a large class of industrious, law-abiding citizens, not contemplated as coming under its benign operations at the time of its adoption. In order, therefore, that this law may become better known and more widely disseminated among that class it is destined to so greatly benefit, it has been thought best to explain its provisions in the form of a simple dialogue, wherein every section and amendment is made so plain that all may learn how to proceed to avail themselves of the benificent offer thus proffered by a still more bonificent government through the votes of the Representatives of the great National Republican Party in Congress.

An 1863 homesteader's application. *The James D. Horan Collection*

Exceedingly rare photograph of a homesteader's family and his sod house, 1870, Kansas Territory. *The James D. Horan Collection*

Pilgrims on the Plains, an 1869 sketch by Theodore R. Davis, famous *Harper's Weekly* Civil War combat artist, who went west for the weekly to sketch life on the frontier. Note the wagons "forted up," prepared for an Indian attack. *The James D. Horan Collection*

The first appearance of "Western Home," later the popular modern ballad. *Courtesy Kansas State Historical Society*

THE KIRWIN CHIEF

Job Office,

East side Public Square,

First door south of the Post-office, Kirwin, Kan.

PLAGIARISM.

The editor of the Stockton *News* has allowed himself to become the victim of an ambitious aspirant for poetical fame. In his issue of Feb. 3d., 1876, he publishes under the head of "My home in the West" a poem, purporting to have been written by Mrs. Emma Race, of Raceburgh, Rooks county, Kansas. The poem in question, with the exception of two words, was written by Dr. B. Higley, of Beaver creek Smith county, Kansas and first published in the Kirwin Cur.. March 21st, 1874. We re-publish article as written by Dr. Higley and ask our readers to compare it with the stolen article from Raceburgh. Bro. Newell must book to his laurels, as he will find plenty of people who are willing to profit by the brain work of others.

Western Home.

BY DR. HIGLEY.

Oh! give me a home where the Buffalo roam,
Where the Deer and the Antelope play;
Where never is heard a discouraging word,
And the sky is not clouded all day.
  [*Chorus*] A home! A home!
Where the Deer and the Antelope play,
Where seldom is heard a discouraging word,
And the sky is not clouded all day

Oh! give me land where the bright diamond sand,
Throws its light from the glittering streams,
Where glideth along the graceful white swan,
Like the maid in her heavenly dreams.
  [*Chorus*] A home! A home!

Oh! give me a gale of the Solomon vale,
Where the life streams with buoyancy flow;
Or the banks of the Beaver, where seldom if ever,
Any poisonous herbage doth grow.
  [*Chorus*] A home! A home!

How often at night, when the heavens were bright,
With the light of the twinkling stars,
Have I stood here amazed, and asked as I gazed,
If their glory exceed that of ours.
  [*Chorus*] A home! A home!

I love the wild flowers in this bright land of ours,
I love the wild curlew's shrill scream;
The bluffs and white rocks, and antelope flocks,
That graze on the mountains so green.
  [*Chorus*] A home! A home!

The air is so pure and the breezes so free,
The zephyrs so balmy and light,
That I would not exchange my home here to range,
Forever in azures so bright.
  [*Chorus*] A home! A home!

An early windmill. Like barbed wire, windmills played an important role in the development of the West. Without them neither the cattlemen nor the homesteaders could have survived. *The James D. Horan Collection*

Busted, the ruins of a Kansas homesteader, October 1873, by Frenzeny-Tavernier. Paul Frenzeny and Jules Tavernier, both young artists, went west for *Harper's Weekly* in the 1870s. *The James D. Horan Collection*

BAT MASTERSON

MOST AMERICANS RECALL BAT MASTERSON AS A FRON-
tier sheriff who wore a derby, had a catchy nickname, a jaunty smile, and a cane
that he used to dispose of his enemies. Unfortunately, the trivialities have
obscured the fascinating story of a young lawman who helped tame the toughest
cow town in the Wild West with courage, humor, understanding—even
compassion, and his skill with a gun.[1]

Masterson spent his early years on the frontier and lived out his time in the
comfortable "catbird's seat" of a sports columnist for the *New York Morning
Telegraph*, a friend of President Teddy Roosevelt, Damon Runyon, Tex O'Rourke,
Frank Ward O'Malley, Irwin S. Cobb, Richard Harding Davis, and other early
twentieth-century celebrities of the sporting, literary, and newspaper worlds.

In his memoirs, Cobb tells how disappointed he was when he first saw Bat.
Instead of the lean, leathery, sun-darkened gunfighter of the western legends, he
saw a "sawed-off and stumpy-legged man with stub nose and a flat-topped
derby." But on closer inspection he also observed the "smooth oval eyes with
flecks of mica glistening in them if he were aroused. But you might not notice the
glint in his eyes unless you looked closely; it came and was instantly gone. And
some of the men who faced him through the smoke fogs of cow town melees
haven't lived long enough to get a good look."

Will Irwin once wrote an article on Bat for the *New York Sun*, describing how he watched the elderly Masterson walk into a rough off-Broadway saloon crowded with young toughs. The place quickly quieted down; only after Bat had left did the noise and clatter rise again.

Incredibly, the buffalo hunter, Indian fighter, cow-town sheriff, and gunfighter did not die of lead poisoning but while finishing his daily column. While he undoubtedly would have been amused at the numerous page one stories reporting his passing, he would also have been enraged at the myth included in some of the obituaries that he had a notched gun to prove he had killed twenty-six men.

"My God!" he once roared when confronted by the legend. "Is anyone fool enough to believe a man would make a mark on his gun to show he had killed another man?"[2]

The opening of the frontier after the Civil War produced the Wild West with its boom cow towns, homesteaders, mining camps and Indian wars. The most thrilling period in American history lasted only a short time, but the men and women who played major roles in it became American legends known to the world from Capetown to the Arctic Circle. One of the most colorful figures was Bat Masterson, whose incredible career included buffalo hunter, sheriff of Dodge City, gambler, gunfighter, deputy U.S. marshal, friend and part-time political adviser to President Theodore Roosevelt, columnist and vice-president of his New York newspaper. For generations it was assumed Bat had been born in Illinois but church records show he was born in Canada. Here are the baptismal certificates from St. George's of Henryville, County of Iberville, province of Quebec, for Bat and his brother Edward, also a western lawman. Bat was called "Bart" by a few close friends, including Roosevelt. *Courtesy Archives Nationales Quebec*

It has been repeated countless times that Masterson was born on a farm in Iroquois County, Illinois. However, documents located in Canada prove he was a Canadian, born November 26, 1853, in St. Georges of Henryville Parish, County of Iberville, Quebec Province. Bat was baptized in the original French, "Bertholomiew," by Father St. Aubon. His brother, Edward, born two years earlier on September 22, was baptized in the same church. Godfather for both was Charles McGurk, probably the brother of Bat's mother, Catherine McGurk Masterson. The godmother was Mary Anne O'Shea.[3]

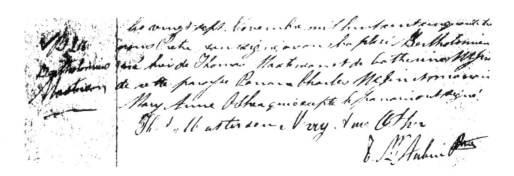

Thomas Masterson, Sr., and Catherine McGurk Masterson, Bat's parents. *Courtesy Denver Public Library, Western History Department*

Little is known about Bat's parents. His father was born in Canada; his mother, Catherine, who may have been born in Ireland, lived in St. Johns where the Mastersons were married.

Not long after Bat was born the Mastersons moved to the United States, finally settling on a farm in Grant Township, Sedgwick County, Kansas, where Bat spent his early years. He and Edward were inseparable, hunting and fishing in the nearby streams and woods.

Bat went to the local one-room schoolhouse. He was never attracted to books. The teacher's droning voice, the sums on the blackboard, the rows of the various grades made him feel confined. In the spring he yearned for the greening woods, in the winter for the herds of deer looking for food in the frozen fields and pastures. As his brother Tom recalled in the 1930s, Bat could never sit in a classroom if he could slip out while the teacher wasn't looking, grab his rifle, whistle for his dog and come home with meat for the table.[4]

The family grew every year. By the end of the Civil War Bat and Edward had three brothers, James P., Thomas, Jr., and George, along with two sisters, Nellie and Emma, whom the family called Minnie.

Bat's first job at seventeen was working with his brother Edward for a subcontractor grading a five-mile section of the roadway for the Atchison, Topeka & Santa Fe then moving across western Kansas. They were defrauded of their wages and left stranded in Dodge City.

Edward returned to Wichita but Bat joined a group of buffalo hunters preparing to move into the Texas Panhandle. His closest friend in the rough party was another young adventurer, Billy Dixon, the famous scout and Indian fighter. Dixon recalled: "He [Masterson] was a chunk of steel and everything that struck him in those days always drew fire."[5]

The following year, 1873, Bat and his brothers became free-lance hunters, selling buffalo meat to construction crews in newly established Dodge City. Bat's reputation as a skilled marksman had been established. Ed and Bat did most of the shooting of the big shaggy beasts while Jim, the youngest, dried the hides by pegging them to the ground, Indian style.

Bat followed the herds deep into Oklahoma and as far south as the Texas Panhandle, using Adobe Walls, about one hundred and fifty miles from Dodge, as his headquarters.

Old Adobe Walls had been built by Colonel William Bent as a trading post for the Comanches, Kiowas, and Prairie Apaches—not for buffalo hides because it was too far from Bent's Fort on the Arkansas River to haul hides, but for horses and mules the Indians had stolen from the Texans. The stock was driven to Missouri and also to the Platte River to be sold to emigrants.[6] By 1848 the post had been abandoned. In 1874 the walls were only about five feet high and the buildings were gone.

In the early spring of 1874, before the buffalo hunters moved out on the plains to intercept the vast herds moving north from their winter grounds, several residents of Dodge City started to build what the hunters would later call "New Adobe Walls."

Fred Leonard and his partner Tom Lyons built a twenty-by-sixty-foot "picket house," and James Hanrahan constructed a sod saloon, erecting a rough bar in the twenty-five-by-sixty-foot room. Thomas O'Keefe, a blacksmith, opened a smithy; Bob Wright, one of the founders of Dodge City and his partner, Charles Rath, set up a sod house trading post; while a young couple, William Olds and his wife, Nancy, opened a restaurant.

All the buildings were built in a row and faced east, with a cottonwood stockade for horses, oxen, and mules at one end. There was no glass for windows, the floors were earth, and the sod walls two feet thick. The roofs were rudimentary; heavy cottonwoods dragged six miles from the Canadian River by mules were used as ridgepoles with slabs of sod and dirt piled on saplings cut from nearby Bent's Creek.

Bob Wright, a Dodge City pioneer and businessman, who was with Bat Masterson in the Battle of Adobe Walls. *The James D. Horan Collection*

Billy Dixon described the Walls of that spring: "It was a little town in the wilderness, a place we could buy something to eat and wear, something to drink, ammunition for our guns and a place where our wagons, so necessary for our expeditions, could be repaired."[7]

Before the buildings were finished, a trail had been opened from Dodge City and freighters made regular trips to the Walls.

After celebrating Christmas Day on the frozen plains, Jim and Ed returned to the Masterson farm but Bat remained in riotous Dodge. In the spring the restless hunters moved out on the plains, but many returned with news that there were no signs of the herds.

The Walls was a busy place with the hunting parties moving in and out, sometimes shattering the night with wild whoops and pistol shots, laughter and songs from Hanrahan's saloon. Nancy Olds, the only woman at the post, cooked for her husband's restaurant. She appears to have been a typical frontierswoman, indomitable but worn out from overwork, hardships, and constant danger. Some men recalled her as slim, brown haired, and attractive and "a woman of some refinement and education." She had been under Indian attack and could handle a rifle as good as she did a skillet.

In early May, Bat and his company moved deep into the Texas Panhandle searching for signs of the herds, but the plains were empty. They returned to the Walls for supplies and again set out. One morning as he stood around the campfire Bat heard the familiar sound—like a number of trains rumbling across wooden trestles. When he and the rest of the company raced to the top of the nearest hill, they could see the solid mass of the herds covering the plains like a vast undulating black woolly blanket.

The buffalo had returned.

Bat ran to get his .50 caliber "needle gun" and the slaughter began. Soon dead buffalo littered the plains with skinners methodically stripping the hides and tossing them into wagons. The wagons were returned to the Walls, where the hides were sold to Leonard and Rath, who piled them in huge mounds behind their sod building. At intervals, freighters brought the hides to Dodge City to be shipped east.

One day two hunters warned the camps there was an Indian uprising. Large bands were roaming the plains and two men had been killed and scalped on Chicken Creek.

Masterson, Dixon, Hanrahan's company, and others moved back to the Walls. All were reluctant to seek the safety of Fort Dodge; the season had not reached its peak, the herds were huge, and, as Billy Dixon warned, the buffalo were getting scarcer every year. Soon there wouldn't be any left.

While they waited for more specific information from the hunters arriving daily, Masterson, Dixon, and the others drank the horrible frontier whiskey in Hanrahan's saloon, ate the tender buffalo steaks cooked by Nancy Olds, gambled, raced horses, and wagered on their marksmanship. Inevitably, it was Billy Dixon and Bat Masterson who won most of the bets. One day Amos Chapman, a scout from Fort Supply, accompanied by a sergeant and four troopers, rode into the Walls to confirm the hunters' warning: an Indian army under Quana Parker, the Comanche chief, was raiding along the frontier and would probably attack the Walls.

Rath and Leonard tried to persuade Olds, the restaurant owner, to send his wife Nancy to Fort Dodge with Chapman and the troopers leaving the following morning. As Chapman pointed out to Olds, Nancy was suffering from an infected tooth and could find an army dentist at the fort. Finally Olds let his wife make her own decision. Without hesitation the frontierswoman told Chapman:

"I came out here with Mr. Olds to make a living and we intend to stay out here. If the tooth gets worse I'll have one of the men pull it out with a pair of pliers."

When Rath hinted at the horrible torture Indians inflicted on white women, she only shrugged and replied:

"I won't run away, gentlemen, and that's that."

Within a few days Nancy would become a frontier legend.[8]

The hunters knew, feared, and respected Quana (Quanah) Parker, the half-white Comanche chief and one of the ablest Indian leaders on the southwestern plains. His mother, Cynthia Ann Parker, had been taken captive at the age of twelve during a raid on Parker's Fort, a small settlement on the Navasota River, Texas,

Quana Parker, the great Comanche chief who led the attack on Adobe Walls. *The James D. Horan Collection*

in the fall of 1835. She later became the wife of Nokoni, leader of the Kwahadis, the wildest and most hostile division of the Comanche nation and a noted raider of Texas border settlements. Cynthia, with a young infant, was later rescued by troops and returned to Texas, where both soon died.

After the death of his father, Quana rose to a position of influence in the tribal council and became a popular war captain. In 1867 the Kwahadis refused to enter into the Medicine Lodge Treaty by which the Kiowas, Comanches, Apaches, Cheyenne, and Arapaho nations were assigned to reservations, and they continued to raid isolated settlements, forts, and wagon trains.

In 1874, when he realized the government had not kept its promise to clear the buffalo hunters from the southwestern plains, Quana persuaded the Comanche and Southern Cheyenne to join his tribe in an attack on Adobe Walls.[9]

On the evening of June 26, 1874, there were thirty-eight men and one woman at Adobe Walls. It was a warm night and most of the buffalo hunters made their beds outside the buildings. Billy Dixon and Bat Masterson spread their blankets near the blacksmith's shop, with Dixon placing his Sharps between their blankets to protect it from the heavy morning dew. Every door was left open; "such a thing as locking a door being unheard of at the Walls," Dixon wrote.

One by one the lights were turned out, Dixon and Masterson talked for a while, making plans to go back to the herds. Dixon later recalled the evening as sultry, with owls hooting in the trees along Bent's Creek. In the early hours of the morning they were awakened by a loud report, sharp as a rifle shot. Dixon and Masterson grabbed their guns only to discover a cottonwood ridge pole had split. The noise woke the camp and repairs were made to the sod roof.

As Dixon pointed out in his autobiography, the providential cracking of the roof pole saved their lives. Curiously, when the pole was later examined the split could not be found.

The sky was tinged red in the east when the task was finished. Dixon and Masterson rolled up their blankets and started to fill their wagons, preparing to leave the Walls, when Dixon's keen eyesight caught an object far off on the plains. He studied it for a moment, then shouted a warning.

Coming toward them was a long wave of warriors. As they drew near, the hunters could see their feathered headdresses rippling in the wind; then came the faint war whoops. As Bat and Billy ran for Hanrahan's sod saloon, Quana Parker's warriors thundered across the plains now in full sight of everyone at the Walls.

They were the finest of the Plains: superb horsemen, armed with guns, feathered lances, heavy shields of thick buffalo hide, their bodies painted like snakes, glittering with silver ornaments and beads. Behind them was the rising sun, tinging the air blood-red as the hordes of warriors seemed to ride out of a hole in the earth.

The Battle of Adobe Walls had begun. It would signal the beginning of the Red River uprising of 1874–75, the bloodiest chapter in the military conquest of the southern Great Plains.

There have been many estimates of Quana Parker's Indian army. Shortly before he died in October 1921, Masterson, in a letter to Olive Dixon, Billy's wife, insisted a "thousand" warriors had stormed Adobe Walls. Dixon agreed Bat's figure was too high and judged there had been seven hundred, but probably the most accurate figure was made by Fred Leonard while the Walls were under siege.[10]

Asking a friend in Dodge City to send them reinforcements, in a letter published in the *Leavenworth Times*, Leonard estimated two hundred warriors had attacked the tiny settlement in waves and had suffered from twenty-five to thirty casualties. He reported the attack came at dawn with Parker's horsemen sweeping up to the doors of the sod house for over three hours. Four of the defenders were killed, including two freighters who had been caught in their wagons outside the Walls in the first few minutes of fighting. Among the dead was William Olds, Nancy's husband, who had accidentally shot himself.

Leonard's vivid dispatch went on.

Fred Leonard's letter, published in the *Leavenworth Daily Times*, July 10, 1874, giving the first account to the outside world of the Battle of Adobe Walls. *Courtesy Kansas State Historical Society*

FROM THE FRONTIER.

Five Days Fighting on the Canadian, and Twenty-Five Red Skins Killed.

Hunters Corralled--Herders Driven in--Stock Run Off--Bridges Burned--Men Murdered.

The Latest and Most Reliable News from the Seat of the Indian War.

Yesterday the mails from the South brought full and complete particulars from the scene of the Indian troubles. Not only have the infernal red skins been skirmishing along the Kansas border, but they have skipped out of the Territory on both sides, and on the Canadian, in the Texas Pan Handle, they have been giving the hunters a lively game. Over a hundred hunters and teamsters have been corralled there since the 27th of June, and have been fighting the red devils tooth and nail. The first of the week a courier reached Dodge City bearing dispatches from the imprisoned men, and also an account of the killed and wounded. The letter was addressed to Mr. A. C. Meyers, partner of one the imprisoned men and reads as follows:

ADOBE WALLS, Texas, July 1, '74.

DEAR MYERS:—We have been attacked by Indians, and corralled since June 27th. The attack was made early in the morning, and the battle lasted about three hours. Ike Shadler and brother, Billy Tyler and Mr. Olds, were killed. The latter shot himself accidentally.

The hunters are all sick of hunting, so they say, and are apt to leave without a moment's warning; but I am willing to stay if I can get enough men to guard the place. The bastions and corral were useless to us; we had to do our fighting from the store. About 25 or 30 Indians were killed—we found 11. I have put the place in a state of seige. If you can get an escort of 50 men, send Anthony's or all the horse teams you can get. If things quiet down so that the boys will stay, I will send a dispatch. Indians in sight all the time. All the hunters are in except about 30, and we are expecting them to-night. The corral is full of horses; we have 38. We are well armed, and can stand off 500 Indians. There were 200 of them. We were completely taken by surprise. Our men behaved like heroes. If the Indians had come one hour later, we would all have been killed, as Dixon and Jim Hanrahan and their men would have been started on a hunt, leaving the place with only 17 men, and only half armed. I killed one Indian that I know of, and I don't know how many more, as I was shooting at them with my 40 at from forty to sixty yards, for twenty shots. I took one scalp. Fred Myers killed two Indians; they rode around up to the corral and got off their horses, and fought as brave as any men I ever saw. We had 150 Indians around our place at one time. Their intention was to take the place, and probably the hunters as they come in. All the men are of the opinion that the Indians are waiting for reinforcements, and then give us another rattle, but we are fixed for them.

FRED LEONARD.

The Dodge City *Messenger* also states that on Thursday evening last, at about 7 o'clock, a herder was driven in to Cimmaron station, 25 miles west of Dodge City, by the Indians. They chased him about two miles and within 500 yards of the station—two of their shots hitting the building. After firing their last shots they turned and fled—the soldiers at the station not having horses, could not follow the Indians. A short time after the Indians left, a smoke was discovered some distance west of the station, and the soldiers thinking that they had camped, took a hand car and rolled off towards the supposed camp. It was soon discovered that instead of a camp, the smoke came from a railroad bridge that had been set on fire, and was burning briskly. The Indians were seen, but nothing could be done with them, as the soldiers were not mounted. The only thing they could do, was to carry water in their caps and canteens and put out the fire. The bridge was about 60 feet long. A portion of the cross-pieces were so much damaged as to cause new ones to be put in. The upright timbers were somewhat damaged, and four lengths of the rails were bent and twisted badly. The bridge was repaired in ten hours' time.

On Saturday, near Granada, a man and boy while herding cattle—they being some little distance apart—a gang of Indians suddenly appeared and surrounded the boy. The man started to go to the assistance of the boy, when he saw another party of Indians going for him. The boy called and begged that he might not be left alone, but the man could render no assistance against such odds, and, having a good horse, made his escape. The boy was found shot and scalped, and his body naked.

The next day, while a man was out after a load of wood, he was shot through, killed and scalped. His body was found the next day in the wagon, about six miles from Granada, with the axe sticking in his head. He must have been shot while riding, as a bullet had penetrated both sides of the wagon-box.

On Friday afternoon, twelve Indians made a raid on some stock, near Syracuse, and run off six head belonging to Fotey, six from Prairie Dog Dave, and one from Lawrence. Dave threw some hot lead after the savages, but could not get a scalp.

We have reliable information of the arrest of six white men at Granada, for horse stealing. They run a herder, who was riding one horse and leading another, into Sargent. Being hard pressed, the herder left the lead horse, when it was captured by the thieves, who started for Granada, where the horse was soon recognized by the owner, who had employed the herder to take care of his stock. The thieves at first refused to give up the horse, saying that it was their property, that they had "shot an Indian and took his horse"—but finally concluded to yield. They were arrested, and at last accounts were still under arrest.

FROM KANSAS.

'errible Indian Massacre—A Station Destroyed—Mail Coaches Plundered and Burned—Six Passengers Killed.

[Special Despatch to the Chicago Tribune.]

LAWRENCE, Dec. 1.

One of those horrible massacres, altogether of too ·quent occurrence lately, occurred at Downer's tation on the Smoky Hill route on Sunday. The tation was attacked by Indians, and one of Butrfield's express coaches was burned, together ith all the goods and buildings at the station. ix passengers were killed. One passenger sucseded in killing three Indians, but was afterward illed by them, who cut out his heart and buried s body. They are supposed to be the Dog Soldiers f the Arapahoes, Cheyennes and Apaches on their ay south, who recently interrupted travel on the latte Valley route.

CRIME.

ERIOUS CHARGE AGAINST GEN CUSTAR

E IS ACCUSED OF MURDER

Important Statements.

The Leavenworth *Conservative.* of Thursday, the h, states that on Wednesday General George A. ıstar and Lieut. W. W. Cook were put upon prelimiry examination there, for the alleged murder of ıarles Johnson, private in Company K, 7th United ates Cavalry.

Capt. R. M. West, of Company K. first testified. We ridge his statement:

Custar was Lieutenant Colonel of the regiment and ook a First Lieutenant in it; Johnson died near Fort 'allace on the 19th or 20th of last July. Up to 2 P. . of the 7th he was on duty as private in witness' mpany. At that time six men were seen leaving e camp. Two mounted parties were ordered by en. Custar to pursue and bring none of them in alive. Government wagon returned bringing three men ho had been shot, one of whom was Johnson. He as very feeble, and seemed to be suffering very much om a wound in the head. The wound which seemed affect him most was a pistol wound entering the de of the head near the right temple and ranging wnward, coming out near the left side of the windpe. He had another wound in his body, and one in s arm. He was shot in the Territory of Colorado, ly 7th, 1867. Witness applied to Gen. Custar for edical attendance for the wounded men, and was ld that they were deserters, and a deserter was not titled to any consideration. Witness urged that the ounded men receive surgical attendance, which was lowed after some further conversation. Witness did t see the shooting, but heard the firing. Lieutenant ook was in one of the pursuing parties. He told itness he had done some of the shooting, and hoped ne of the wounded would die. Johnson was hale d hearty before the shooting. A detail of his comny buried him, and witness read the Episcopal rial service at the grave.

On cross-examination witness remembered to have nversed with General Custar about Johnson's being desperate that he would not be brought back witht a fight, and about Johnson's being so resolute at he might offer resistance. Major J. H. Elliott mmanded one of the pursuing parties, and Lieut. Jackson the other, and they were gone an hour, or hour and a half. Witness *did not hear the order not bring any in alive*, and cannot say if Cook heard it. ard Custar say something to the effect to go after em and not bring any in alive. Was not at the exact ot where the parties rode off, but was in hearing stance. The medical attendance was ordered at the ne it was applied for, after the conversation.

THE INDIAN WAR.

GEN. AUGUR'S EXPEDITION.

From Our Special Correspondent.

OMAHA, Neb., May 21, 1867.

I have arrived at this place, and my first step was to seek the headquarters of Gen. Augur, and learn from him personally whether there was any authority for the conflicting statements concerning his intended expedition to the headquarters of the Yellowstone River, and I found there was not any particle of truth in it. He stated that, until the turn of affairs which Gen. Hancock had made in burning the Indian village, he had intended to take a force of 2,000 men, mostly infantry, to defend our northern posts against any future aggressions of the red men. But now his whole attention must be given to the Platte route—the Union Pacific Railway. Dispatches arrive daily at his headquarters, announcing some new depredations. This morning he received a dispatch stating that 100 herd of stock had been taken from the neighborhood of Julesburg, and three herdens had been killed and scalped. Troops are being hurried along the Union Pacific to defend the posts most liable to attack. Custer is still at Fort Hays, and his men are slowly recovering from the attack of Samroy. Fresh provisions are being rapidly hauled to his command, and other posts are being plentifully furnished with provisions, thus providing against any contingencies that may arise. The Indians who are at war are encamped on Turkey Creek, about 25 miles from this city. Gen. Augur will probably undertake his expedition next Fall. He has engaged some 250 Pawnees as Indian scouts. Gen. Hancock at present is at Fort Leavenworth.

BY TELEGRAPH TO THE TRIBUNE.

ON THE PLAINS.

The Last Indian Scare—The Country and the Crops.

TOPEKA, Kansas, June 7, 1868.

The Cheyennes are on the warpath in the Kaw reservation. Nearly 250 warriors in full feather entered the Kaw territory a few days ago it was supposed for the purpose of avenging the death of some of their tribe killed by the Kaws last summer. The Cheyennes made their appearance near Council Grove, fifty-five miles south of this place, creating a panic among the white settlers in that vicinity. Indeed, the alarm reached this point to a certain extent, but upon my arrival here I found the reports exaggerated. Governor Crawford, however, after appealing to Fort Riley for troops, which were not furnished, for some reason, started for Council Grove to allay the fears of the whites, where he still remains. The warriors rode through the streets of the village of Council Grove and were met three miles out on the plain, near the Indian agency, by a band of three hundred Kaws, who received them with a galling fire. After three hours' hard fighting the Cheyennes were driven back through Council Grove disorganized. The settlers nearly all left their homes in terror, but many of them have since been induced to return. The Indians on their retreat west attacked and gutted the houses of R. B. Lockwood and a Mr. Polk. Citizens of Emporia, Council Grove and other points went out after the Cheyennes· but being an unorganized body and without any ostensible commander, I have not learned that they accomplished anything. It is rumored that there were some Sioux warriors and Arrapahoes with the Cheyennes. This is not certain, but what is far more likely is the report that the attack was instigated and shared in by some unruly whites and half-breeds. The Kaw reservation is coveted by these classes, who would be glad to see the Kaws driven off. The Cheyennes were

PRICE FOUR CENTS.

THE INDIAN WAR.

BY TELEGRAPH TO THE TRIBUNE.

ST. LOUIS, June 24.—Gen. Sherman has issued a circular in substance as follows:

First: That the treaties with the Indians must be preserved, but that Indians who have gone beyond the Reservations, and are committing crimes, will fall under military control, &c.. and are subject to punishment by the civil powers.

Second: The Military Division is divided into three departments, viz.: Dakota, commanded by Gen. Terry; the Platte, commanded by Gen. Augur; the Missouri, commanded by Gen. Hancock.

Third: If each State or Territory will organize a battalion of mounted men, they will be called for by the Department Commander in case of any emergency, to be mustered in in accordance with the law, and will await an appropriation by Congress for their payment.

Fourth: Gives direction to the civil authorities to be prepared to pursue at all times with horse, thieving bands of Indians who are endeavoring to avoid the military.

Fifth: When stolen stock is traced to Reservation, a demand should be made by the Agent, and if the tribe is entitled to annuities, such annuities should be chargeable with the value of the stolen property. The Governments of the States and Territories interested are requested to communicate with the Department Commander, and appeal only to Gen. Sherman.

The steamboat W. Brooks, lying at the levee, was robbed of $8,000, a gold watch, and other valuables, yesterday morning.

RAILROAD WORKMEN ATTACKED.

A dispatch from the present terminus of the Kansas Pacific Railroad says the Indians have driven the railroad grading parties into Fort Harker; also, that two railroad men and two residents were killed near Bunker Hill, about 20 miles west of Fort Harker, on Saturday, and a considerable amount of stock had been driven off. Efforts were being made to procure arms for the railroad employés, many of whom have already left their work, and it is feared all will leave unless they are better protected. The excursion party from Fort Wallace arrived at Salina to-day, all in good health.

WORK ON THE RAILROAD SUSPENDED.

LAWRENCE, Kansas, June 24.—The grading parties on the Pacific Railroad within 20 miles of Bunker Hill, were attacked by Kiowa Indians on Saturday last. Three men were killed and the remainder were driven off, All work on the road is suspended beyond Wilson's Creek, and unless strong measures are taken by the military, the progress of the road must be greatly retarded.

As matters now stand the lives and property of the people on the border are totally unprotected.

Gov. Crawford is making an effort to obtain arms and ammunition from the military to arm the railroad employés in the disturbed district.

ATTACK ON FORT DODGE—NINETY-TWO HORSES CAPTURED —THE INDIANS LED BY SANANTA.

LEAVENWORTH, Kansas, June 24—10 p. m.—A letter from Frot Dodge, Kansas, on the Santa Fe road, says that on the 30th ult. a band of Indians, numbering 150, led by Satanta, Chief of the Kiowas, who lately made treaty with Gen. Hancock, dashed up within 400 yards of the fort and captured 92 horses belonging to Company B, 7th Cav. Only two men were on guard, one of which escaped, but the other had five arrows shot into his body. The garrison rescued him in a dying condition. The Indians escaped with the stock. During the same night two men came into the fort, closely pursued by Indians, and stated that the Kiows were murdering settlers and stealing stock 30 miles west. Company I, 37th infantry, and once put in six mule wagons and sent in pursuit, but up to the 16th inst. nothing had been heard from them. The railroad employés west of Fort Harker were attacked and driven in. Many Mexican trains on the Santa Fe road are in great danger. The letter states that the borders settlers are fleeing to the military forts, leaving property behind them. The citizens of Colorado have raised a large fund, and offer $20 each for Indian scalps. Over 200 men have taken the field in small parties to obtain scalps.

GEN. SHERMAN AND THE COLORADO VOLUNTEERS— SIX COMPANIES ORDERED NORTH.

From Our Special Correspondent.

FORT SEDGWICK, Col., June 14, 1867.

At an interview with Gen. Sherman this morning, during which I asked him whether he was willing that volunteers should be employed to pursue the Indians, he said: "Certainly; I have no objection. They have a right to punish and kill Indians as they would punish and kill white men, were any found committing depredations and killing innocent people. The Governor has a right to call volunteers out to defend the Territory from hostile tribes. But they are too slow for me; I wanted them last Sunday to pursue some Cheyennes, but they were not forthcoming. I offered them 40 cents per day; they refused it because it was not enough. That is all Government will allow me to pay them. I expect I will have to do without them."

MORE INDIAN DEPREDATIONS BETWEEN LARAMIE AND DENVER—THE UNION PACIFIC RAILROAD ALL SAFE—THE BLACK FLAG RAISED IN COLORADO.

FORT SEDGWICK, June 17, 1867.

The following circular appeared in the morning papers at Central and Denver the 8th inst.:

"WOODWARD, De[illegible]

"Five thousand dollars have been subscribed this morning, to be paid for scalps with the ears on, at twenty dollars each. MANY CITIZENS."

A montage of clippings from various frontier newspapers giving accounts of the Indian wars. *The James D. Horan Collection*

THE RED DEVILS.

THE WILD AND HUNGRY CHEY-ENNES.

COMMIT MURDER AND ARSON.

SEVERAL HERDERS MURDERED.

A HOUSE BURNED DOWN.

Wholesale Stealing of Horses.

AN INDIAN FIGHT.

THREE SOLDIERS KILLED AND THREE WOUNDED.

THE BORDER WILD WITH EX-CITEMENT.

STRAGGLING BANDS OF INDIANS RAIDING EVERYWHERE.

Another Indian Skirmish.

AN INDIAN KILLED—A SOLDIER WOUNDED.

Immigrant Trains Robbed.

FOUR COMPANIES OF CAVALRY ORDERED TO DODGE.

DODGE CITY UNDER ARMS.

There has been great excitement all week over the news brought in almost hourly of murder and depredations by the straggling bands of Northern Cheyenne Indians. Reminiscences of early Indian troubles are recounted and the old plains-man appears in high humor when gossip-ing over the dates of times more critical than these.

The Indian Wars were page-one news in Bat Masterson's day.

We have endeavored to gather all truth-ful news. Some of it is reliable and some of it may be exaggerated. But there is no mistaking the fact that strolling bands of Indians are traversing the entire fron-tier on the south, and some of these red devils have come within sight of Dodge City.

Our account of the ravages of these wild and hungry Indians is made up from the best information we can gather.

Wednesday the excitement was at its highest pitch in Dodge City. The fre-quent arrival of couriers and messengers from off the plains, bringing accounts of the Cheyenne murder and stealing, threw the people of Dodge City into the wildest tremor, when it was reported that the Indians were seen within a few miles of the city. The ringing of the fire bell at 2 o'clock, calling upon the people to as-semble at the engine house, added zest to the already highly inflamed patriot heart. A call was made on the Governor for arms. All the pistols and guns in Dodge were made available, and everybody was ready to fire the savage breast

At this time flames were seen issuing from the house of Harrison Berry, on an island 4 miles west of this city. It was at once rumored that the Indians had fired the house.

A locomotive loaded with citizens was

THE INDIANS.

Hancock's Expedition.

St. Louis, April 22.—The *Democrat's* correspondent, with General Hancock's Indian expedition, gives an account of a council held at Fort Larned on the 12th, between General Hancock and fifteen Cheyenne chiefs. The council amounted to nothing, only a part of the chiefs of the tribes being in attendance. The next day General Hancock moved toward the Chey-enne camp, and when about half way was met by over 300 chiefs and warriors, who professed peace, but during the night the whole tribe abandoned their village, leaving their wigwams, but taking everything of value. General Custer's command was sent in pursuit, but had not returned when the letter was closed.

Indications point to a confederation between the Cheyenne and Sioux for evil purposes. General Hancock intended burning the Cheyenne village on the 14th.

Denver, Cal., April 20.—Lookout Station, two hun-dred and seventy miles east on the Smoky Hill route, was destroyed by the Cheyenne Indians last Monday. Three employees of the United States Express Com-pany were killed and scalped and eight of the Com-pany's horses stolen. General Hancock had reached Fort Learned and attempted to treat with the Indians, but was unsuccessful.

He then surrounded their camp, but before com-mencing an attack sent forward a messenger propo-sing to treat. The camp was found deserted and most of their property abandoned. General Hancock supposed they were now on the war path. About 1,000 warriors passed Downer's Station going north, probably the same that burned Lookout.

A Letter from Adobe Walls

Indians in sight all the time. All the hunters are in except about thirty and we are expecting them tonight. The corral is full of horses. We have thirty-eight. We are well armed and can stand off five hundred Indians. We were completely taken by surprise. Our men behaved like heroes. If the Indians had come in one hour later we would have been all killed as Billy Dixon and Jim Hanrahan and their men would have started a hunt, leaving the place with only seventeen men and only half armed. I killed one Indian that I know of and I don't know how many more as I was shooting them with my .40 at forty to sixty yards for twenty shots. I took one scalp. Fred Meyers killed two Indians. They rode up to the corral and got off their horses and fought as brave as any men I ever saw. We had one hundred fifty Indians around our place at one time. Their intention was to take this place and probably take the hunters as they came in. All the men are of the opinion they are waiting for reinforcements and then give us another rattle but we are fixed for them.

At the height of the attack above the crash of the guns the besieged hunters were amazed to hear a clear urgent bugle call. Through the firing loopholes they watched amazed as the painted braves wheeled and swung into formation, answering the bugler's command as precisely as a trained regiment of troopers.

Fortunately two of the hunters had served in the cavalry and knew the calls. Bat Masterson recalled what followed.[11]

The Indian Bugler at Adobe Walls

We had in the building I was in [Hanrahan's saloon], two men who had served in the United States Army and understood the bugle calls. The first blown call was a rally which our men instantly understood. The next was a charge and that also was understood, and immediately the Indians came rushing forward to a fresh attack. Every bugle call he blew was understood by the ex-soldiers and was carried out to the letter by the Indians, showing the bugler had the Indians thoroughly drilled.

The bugler was killed late in the afternoon of the first day's fighting as he was running away from the wagon owned by the Shadler brothers both of whom had been killed in the same wagon. The bugler had his bugle with him at the time he was killed by Harry Armitage. Also, he was carrying a tin can filled with sugar and another filled with coffee, one under each arm. Armitage shot him through the back with a .50 caliber Sharps rifle, as he was making his escape.

The hunters were divided among the buildings with Bat and Billy Dixon in Hanrahan's saloon. By noon the ammunition was getting low, so Billy and Hanrahan made a run for Charles Rath's store, where there were thousands of rounds brought from Dodge City for the hunters. They reached the store to find "the group in good shape." There was a major worry: Nancy. Rath's store held the smallest number of defenders and as Dixon wrote, "If the Indians learned there was a white woman there, there was no telling what they might attempt, and a determined attack by the Indians would have meant death for everybody in the store, for none would have permitted themselves to be taken or have permitted Mrs. Olds to be captured.[12] It was the unwritten law of the frontier:

defenders of any post, fort, or stockade fought to the death rather than face the terrifying tortures of an Indian camp, and the last bullets were always saved for the women.

Hanrahan returned to the saloon and Billy Dixon remained at Rath's because of his superior marksmanship. As the attacks increased in fury, the warriors reached the buildings, pounding on the doors with their rifle butts and using the Indians' favorite trick of backing their ponies against the doors. After the first attempts, the hunters piled bags of grain and flour against the doors, "making them the best breastworks imaginable, the Indians having no guns that could shoot through it." Fire arrows were useless against the dirt roof and the two-foot-thick walls.

For most of the first day the Indians recklessly rushed the buildings shouting taunts, waving the bloody scalps of the two freighters they had killed and risking the deadly fire of the hunters to drag away their dead, dying, and wounded. Dixon remembered: "A man's mouth gets dry and his saliva thick and sticky when he fights hour after hour, knowing that if he goes down his death will be one of torture, unless he should be killed immediately."

In his autobiography, Bob Wright described how one warrior, his war bonnet flattened by the wind, charged the buildings "straight as an arrow" to fire his six-shooter through a porthole. As he ran for his horse he was shot again and again. He continued to stagger but finally fell down, "deliberately drew another pistol from his belt and blew out his brains." [13]

Quana Parker finally withdrew his army, but small bands continued to harass the Walls for about six days. After the attack, Bat, Billy Dixon, and several hunters dragged off the dead Indians, now becoming bloated and stinking in the hot July sun. Two large groups of hunters hauling hides to Dodge arrived and were astounded to hear of the raid. They were not aware an Indian war was sweeping across the plains. Other groups arrived until there were about a hundred armed men crowding the Walls.

One young hunter, about nineteen, was introduced to Bat as an excellent marksman.

"This is Bill Tilghman, Bat," Dutch Henry, another hunter, said. "And I bet he can beat you shooting."

Bat carefully studied the slender, dark-eyed youth with the quizzical blue-gray eyes and slow smile. They shook hands.

"We'll have to have a shooting match someday, Bill," Bat promised.

Many years later Tilghman, like Bat, a famous frontier lawman, recalled that meeting and the beginning of a friendship that lasted until their deaths.

Tilghman remembered Bat at the time as a "handsome young fellow with a devil-may-care look" who already was a noted shot and an Indian-wise plainsman.

Now groups of hunters moved out, cautiously searching the empty plains for signs of war parties. On San Francisco Creek they found and buried the mutilated body of a hunter and the pair who had been killed on Chicken Creek.

Then Jim Hanrahan selected Bat, Billy Dixon, and several other experienced hunters to alert Dodge. They arrived to a tremendous welcome but learned Dodge already knew of the attack. Tom Nixon, Bat's friend and former employer, had recruited a relief party of forty hunters and were on their way to raise the siege of Adobe Walls. Bat and Dixon, avoiding the main trail, had missed them.

Some of the survivors who began drifting into Dodge now decided "they had enough of Indians to last them a lifetime and went straight to the depot and bought tickets for their homes in the East." One who stayed was the new widow, Nancy Olds, heroine of the Battle of Adobe Walls, who, legend has it, opened a restaurant in Dodge.

Details of the battle were telegraphed to Fort Leavenworth. Troops under General Nelson A. Miles arrived in Dodge during the first week of August to launch a campaign to subdue the tribes.

Bat Masterson and Billy Dixon were hired by Miles as scouts and attached to Lieutenant Frank D. Baldwin's command. Their first mission was to ride to Adobe Walls.[14] When they neared the Walls, Bat was sent on ahead "to tell the boys the troops were coming." It was a month since the battle had been fought but Bat found more than a dozen hunters still occupying the sod houses. They had kept their horses and mules in the corral—there were Indian skulls stuck on the posts—and had cut hay from the creek bottom.

The next morning Bat and Dixon accompanied Baldwin on a tour of the battlefield. The early quiet was suddenly shattered by the crash of rifle shots. Two hunters who had gone to gather wild plums were galloping across the valley chased by a number of Indians. One brave, whipping his pony with a quirt, drew alongside one of the hunters and plunged his lance through the man's body. He swayed, threw up his hands, and slid out of the saddle. The riderless horse continued running while the second hunter, bent low in the saddle, frantically tried to outrun the brave, who finally swung around to join his band.

Bat and the others gave chase, but the braves had vanished in the sand hills of White Deer Creek. In a few hours another grave had been dug in the makeshift cemetery of Adobe Walls.

The following day, the post's last survivors joined Bat, Dixon, and Baldwin's troop to rendezvous with Miles's main command at Cantonment Creek. This was the last time the buildings were occupied. A year later Dixon found them destroyed by the Indians.

As Miles's long column of troopers snaked across the scorched, staked plains of Texas, Quana Parker's Indian army sullenly retreated, leaving behind many dead and scalped settlers. Parker would keep his people on the plains for two years until he finally surrendered. On September 10, 1874, a band of Cheyennes under Stone Calf and Gray Beard trapped John German (also spelled Germain) and his family several miles east of Fort Wallace. The warriors killed German, his wife, Lynda, their twenty-year-old son, Stephen, and two daughters, Joanna, fifteen, and Rebecca Jane, twenty. Catherine Elizabeth, seventeen, Sophia, twelve, Juliana (Julie), and five-year-old Nancy (Addie) Adelaide were taken captive.

Later Julie and Addie were left on the plains to die; Catherine and Sophia were taken south by Gray Beard. Miraculously, the younger children survived for more than three weeks on the desolate prairie. Once they came upon an abandoned homesteader's cabin with an apple tree, but a burro had eaten all the

34
°

The German sisters rescued
by Lieutenant Baldwin's
scouts. *Courtesy Kansas State
Historical Society*

Billy Dixon, the famous Indian scout who
fought at Adobe Walls with Bat Masterson
and who won the Congressional Medal of
Honor for his bravery at the Battle of Indian
Wallow. *The James D. Horan Collection*

Cheyenne braves and their
families. The warriors
enlisted as scouts after the
Cheyenne surrendered in
1877. This photograph was
taken by Christopher
Barthelmess, the frontier
Indian photographer. *The
James D. Horan Collection*

fruit within its reach. Julie caught the animal and tied a rope about its neck.
While Addie held on to the rope, Julie climbed on the burro's back and threw
down a number of apples. However, a few days later they were discovered by
Stone Calf's tribe and again taken captive.

In early November Baldwin's troopers attacked Stone Calf's camp and rescued
Julie and Addie hidden under a pile of buffalo robes. They were first taken to
Fort Supply, Oklahoma, and then to Fort Dodge. In February 1875, the other two
sisters, Catherine and Sophia, were turned over to Miles by Stone Calf and Gray
Beard when they surrendered with sixteen hundred warriors, women, and
children.[15]

44TH CONGRESS, } HOUSE OF REPRESENTATIVES. { EX. DOC.
1st Session. } { No. 59.

CATHARINE AND SOPHIA GERMAIN.

LETTER

FROM

THE SECRETARY OF THE INTERIOR,

PRESENTING

A further communication from the War Department upon the subject of the destitute condition of Catharine and Sophia Germain, two Cheyenne captives.

JANUARY 12, 1876.—Referred to the Committee on Indian Affairs and ordered to be printed.

DEPARTMENT OF THE INTERIOR.
Washington, January 5, 1876.

SIR: Referring to letter from this Department, dated the 20th ultimo addressed to the Speaker of the House of Representatives, upon the subject of the destitute condition of Catharine and Sophia Germain, and inclosing certain papers from the Indian Bureau in relation thereto, I now have the honor to present a further communication from the honorable the Secretary of War upon the same subject, together with copies of the papers referred to by him, and, in accordance with his request, earnestly recommend the subject to the favorable consideration of Congress.

I have the honor to be, very respectfully, your obedient servant,
Z. CHANDLER,
Secretary.

The SPEAKER *House of Representatives.*

WAR DEPARTMENT,
Washington City, December 22, 1875.

SIR: I have the honor to invite your attention to the inclosed copy of letter from Col. Nelson A. Miles, of the Fifth Infantry, requesting that the Government make the same provision for Catharine and Sophia Germain. captured by the Cheyenne Indians, and rescued by the military authorities, as was made for their sisters by the last Congress, (18 Stat., part 3, page 424.)

Inviting your attention to the indorsements upon the said letter, I beg to request that you will earnestly recommend this matter to the favorable consideration of Congress.

The issue of one ration a day to each of the children has been authorized until Congress makes some provision for their support.

Very respectfully, your obedient servant,
WM. W. BELKNAP.
Secretary of War.

The Hon. SECRETARY OF THE INTERIOR.

2 CATHARINE AND SOPHIA GERMAIN.

HEADQUARTERS FIFTH INFANTRY,
Fort Leavenworth, Kans., December 1, 1875.

SIR: I have the honor to bring to your attention the case of Catharine and Sophia Germain, the eldest two of the four children who were rescued from captivity among the Cheyennes by the operations of the troop s in the Indian campaign of 1874-'75 in the Southwest.

As they were left orphans and destitute by the action of the hostile Indians, I would respectfully submit that the General Government may properly make some provision for their support, and that as they were rescued during active operations, it would seem that they are entitled to the same considerations as prisoners of war pending action of the Government in their case. I would therefore earnestly in their behalf request that rations be issued to them until the necessary legislation be had in their case.

The honorable Secretary of War will remember that this case was brought to his personal attention at Des Moines, Iowa, when the above request seemed to meet with his favorable consideration.

Very respectfully, your obedient servant,
NELSON A. MILES.
Colonel Fifth Infantry.

The Hon. SECRETARY OF WAR.

(Through office of Assistant Adjutant-General, Department Missouri, Division of the Missouri, and of the Army.)

HEADQUARTERS FIFTH INFANTRY.
Fort Leavenworth, Kans., December 2, 1875.

SIR: In behalf of two most unfortunate and helpless orphans, Catharine and Sophia Germain, who have suffered everything but death at the hands of the hostile Cheyennes, and who were recovered by the force of military operations in the Department of the Missouri, I would earnestly request that the Government make the same provisions that were made by the last Congress for their sisters, in the act a copy of which is herewith inclosed.

Very respectfully, your obedient servant,
NELSON A. MILES.
Colonel Fifth Infantry.

The ADJUTANT-GENERAL,
U. S. Army, Washington, D. C.

(Through office of Assistant Adjutant-General, Department of the Missouri, Division and of the Army.)

HEADQUARTERS DEPARTMENT OF THE MISSOURI,
Fort Leavenworth, Kans., December 9, 1875.

These papers are respectfully forwarded and are fully concurred in. Attention is invited to my communication of November 30, 1874, on which and the indorsements on it the appropriation for the two younger Germain children was made.

At the time, the two elder children were still in the hands of the Indians, and it was not known whether they would be recovered alive.

They were fortunately surrendered alive, but in a terrible condition, and they have needed constant care and attention ever since. They were rendered destitute and their natural supporters and guardians

CATHARINE AND SOPHIA GERMAIN. 3

were murdered by the Cheyenne Indians, and it seems only proper that a moderate provision be made for them out of the money appropriated for the subsistence of the Indians who reduced them to such a state.

I hope, therefore, that the application will be urgently presented to Congress.

Colonel Miles has accepted the guardianship of these children, but of course is without the funds needed for their actual support.

Until Congress acts upon the case, the War Department should authorize the issue of one ration to each of the elder children at least.
JOHN POPE,
Bvt. Major-General U. S. A., Commanding.

WAR DEPARTMENT,
Adjutant-General's Office, Washington, December 14, 1875.

Respectfully submitted to the Secretary of War with previous papers relative to the Germain girls, including General Pope's communication of November 30, 1874, referred to in preceding indorsement.
E. D. TOWNSEND.
Adjutant-General.

WAR DEPARTMENT.
December 17, 1875.

Respectfully referred to the Commissary-General for remark.
By order of the Secretary of War.
H. T. CROSBY.
Chief Clerk.

OFFICE COMMISSARY-GENERAL SUBSISTENCE.
December 18, 1875.

Respectfully returned to the honorable Secretary of War, with the recommendation that authority be granted to issue one ration per day to each of the within-named children (Catharine and Sophia Germain) until some provision for their support be made by Congress.
R. MACFEELY,
Commissary-General Subsistence.

WAR DEPARTMENT.
December 22, 1875.

Recommendation of Commissary-General approved.
By order of the Secretary of War.
H. T. CROSBY.
Chief Clerk.

○

War Department communications on the rescue of the German sisters. Secretary of War Z. Chandler used the spelling "Germain." *The James D. Horan Collection*

In the winter of 1874 Bat killed his first man in a stand-up fight in the raw frontier town of Sweetwater, Texas, where the star of the Lady Gay, a local dance hall and gambling spot, was dark-haired, attractive Molly Brennan. She had been the girl friend of Sergeant Melvin A. King, attached to Fort Elliott's Company H, Fourth Cavalry, but when the handsome Masterson appeared she promptly forgot King.

The owner of the dance hall liked Bat and gave him an extra key so he and Molly could have a few drinks in private after closing hours.

On the night of January 24, 1876, Bat and Molly were sitting at the rough bar, laughing and talking in the dim light of an oil lamp, when someone knocked on the door. Bat, thinking it was a late customer, opened the door and stepped back. King, gun in hand and shouting curses, filled the doorway. Witnesses later testified he had been drinking heavily all day and brooding over his lost romance.

Molly jumped in front of Bat and, according to early accounts, cried: "Don't shoot—you're drunk!"

King fired, the slug tearing through the girl's abdomen and shattering Bat's pelvis bone. As Molly screamed and fell, Bat fired, his one shot instantly killing King.

Legend has Ben Thompson, the Texas gunfighter, leaping on a table and holding off a crowd of King's friends with his six-shooter. It makes a stirring scene, but unfortunately there is nothing to document it but repeated telling.[16]

Masterson left Fort Elliott's hospital in the spring of 1876 to return to Dodge, where he worked for a short time as deputy marshal under Wyatt Earp. In the early summer he joined the hordes of gold seekers hurrying to the Black Hills.

King's bullet had left Bat with a slight limp, and he used a cane the mythmakers described as his second best weapon and which gave him the nickname of "Bat." The facts once again shot down the legend: Masterson was known as "Bat" for some time before the Sweetwater shooting. Some of his close

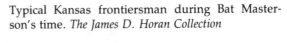

Typical Kansas frontiersman during Bat Masterson's time. *The James D. Horan Collection*

General George Crook, called "Three Stars" by the warriors and chiefs he fought, led the Indian Fighting Army of the West in the 1870s. In this extremely rare glass plate photograph taken by General John Talbot Pitman at Fort Abraham Lincoln, Dakota Territory, Crook is seated at the left with Territorial Governor Fasler, and Major Warner, a noted Indian fighter. For additional glass plates by Pitman see the Theodore Roosevelt section. *The James D. Horan Collection.*

Dodge City's first depot was these two Santa Fe boxcars in Bat Masterson's time. *The James D. Horan Collection*

Dodge City in 1876, looking southeast from Boot Hill. The building with the black roof is a government warehouse and the two-story frame building with the outside staircase on the right was located on the corner of Front Street and Second Avenue. This is Dodge City as Bat Masterson, Wyatt Earp, and Bill Tilghman knew it. *The James D. Horan Collection*

Dodge City during the time when Bat Masterson was sheriff of Ford County. Note the sign: "The carrying of firearms Strictly Prohibited," a law Masterson strictly enforced. *The James D. Horan Collection*

The first building on the town site of Dodge City, built in 1871 by H. L. Sitler. Standing in the doorway is Tom Nixon, a buffalo hunter and Masterson's friend. Nixon raised a party of Dodge City volunteers who marched to raise the siege of Adobe Walls. While assistant city marshal, Nixon was killed in a gunfight with "Mysterious Dave" Mathers on the evening of July 21, 1884. *The James D. Horan Collection*

friends, including President Theodore Roosevelt, at times called him "Bart"—for Bertholomiew—and from that came "Bat."

In the Black Hills Masterson soon decided that swinging a pick and shovel and hoping for a strike was not as lucrative—or easy—as gambling, so he opened a faro game in a Sydney, Nebraska, saloon. Wyatt and Morgan Earp met Bat there on the way to the gold camps and tried to persuade him to join them. But Masterson told them he had enough of Nebraska and the Black Hills and intended to return to Dodge City.

Both Earps urged him to run for Ford County sheriff, pointing out that just before they left Dodge, Sheriff Charlie Bassett had announced he would not run again.

"But I'm not even twenty-three," Bat protested.

"You're as much of a man as you'll ever be," Wyatt replied.

Bat spent part of that winter with his family in Wichita before returning to Dodge. The following June he became involved in a brawl with Dodge City's marshal, L. E. Deger, a huge man weighing over three hundred pounds, who Bat insisted was abusing a smaller prisoner. The court fined Bat $25 but Ed Masterson, Bat's brother, then one of Dodge's deputies, promptly rearrested the original prisoner and the court fined him $5. It had been rumored for weeks that

Bat would campaign for the sheriff's job—Deger was already a candidate—and as the *Dodge City Times* reported, "politics" was behind the fight.[17]

A few weeks later Bat bought an interest in the Lone Star dance hall, probably part of his campaign to show that as a local businessman he had a stake in the community.

The Dodge City law enforcement agencies appear complex at this time: Bat was running for Ford County sheriff but at the same time was a county deputy with Wyatt Earp under retiring Charlie Bassett. Then in September, before the election, he was appointed Dodge City's policeman.

Masterson took his duties seriously. When two fast-talking confidence men bilked his old friend Bob Wright out of a wagonload of supplies, he headed a posse that captured the pair and "persuaded" them to pay for the stolen merchandise.

Visiting cowhands who had made the long drive from Texas were stopped before they could infiltrate the town. Bat was genial but firm: no more shooting at lamps and signs, all damages were to be paid for immediately, and guns had to remain in holsters during their visit. Records of the Ford County district court reveal both Wyatt Earp and Bat worked efficiently as lawmen during the summer of 1876. On October 10 the city council authorized Sheriff Deger to pay Bat $25— or $2.50 a day—for his services.

Bat and the huge Deger despised each other; it was probably political pressure which forced Deger to hire Bat. After he had been paid by the city council, Masterson published a formal notice in the *Dodge City Times* alerting Dodge and

Eddie Foy, the celebrated vaudevillian, who played in Dodge City's *Comique*. He later described Bat Masterson, then sheriff of Ford County, as a "trim, good-looking young man with a pleasant face and carefully barbered mustache . . . and two big-silver-mounted ivory-handled pistols in a heavy belt." Foy was on the *Comique's* stage when the dance hall was sprayed with bullets. In his autobiography Foy said he was "impressed" by the way Masterson and Doc Holliday "flattened out like pancakes on the floor." *Courtesy of The Library of Congress*

Busy Topeka's depot in the days of Bat Masterson and Wyatt Earp. The carriages and "hacks" are probably waiting for the Santa Fe to arrive. In the winter of 1879 Sheriff Masterson, accompanied by Michael (Mike) Sutton, Ford County's prosecutor, and Undersheriff Charlie Bassett, arrived at the Topeka depot. Later that day Bat was sworn in as deputy U.S. marshal. *The James D. Horan Collection*

A diamond-stack engine and train, the type held up by Dave Rudebaugh's gang on January 17, 1878, at Kinsley, Kansas. Bat and a posse of former buffalo hunters captured the gang twelve days later in a driving snowstorm. *The James D. Horan Collection*

the county he was running for Deger's job as sheriff. The notice was brief, without the usual nineteenth-century bombast of frontier politicians. Bat refused to make promises or predictions about his future.[18]

"I have no pledges to make, as pledges are usually considered before election, to be merely claptrap," he wrote.

A week before Election Day, Bat's Lone Star Dance Hall was the scene of a gunfight between his brother Ed and two gamblers, Bob Shaw and "Texas" Dick Moore. Shaw had gained the drop on Moore but Masterson, as the *Dodge City Times* wrote, "gently tapped him on the back of the head with his shooting iron, merely to convince him of the vanities of this frail world and to teach him that all isn't lovely even when the goose does hang high."

As he went down, Shaw spun around and shot Masterson, shattering his right arm, but the law officer did a "border shift" and fired with his left hand, rendering Shaw "hors de combat," as the *Times* reported.[19]

Ed, severely wounded, returned to Wichita to recover, and Bat temporarily took his brother's post as deputy marshal.

On November 6, 1877, Bat Masterson was elected sheriff of Ford County, beating Deger by only three votes. As the *Hays Sentinel* commented, Dodge now had a sheriff who was a "bad man with a pistol."

On January 14, 1878, Bat Masterson began his two-year term. A political deal had probably been made with Charlie Bassett, who was prevented by law from running again, and Bat appointed him his undersheriff.

A few weeks later Bat strapped on his six-shooters, slid his rifle into its boot, and led a posse to run down an outlaw gang which had attempted to hold up a train at Kinsley, Kansas. The four-man bandit team bungled the robbery; for some reason during their escape they stopped to blacken their faces and broke up

Dodge City's famous "Cow-Boy" band in Bat Masterson's day. The eighteen members, including a drum major and color bearer, wore sombreros, blue shirts, silk scarfs, leather leggings, cartridge belts, and Navy Colts. "Professor" Eastman, the director, who used a six-shooter to direct, was once asked by a reporter for the *St. Louis Globe-Democrat* why he used a gun. "To kill the first man who strikes a false note," was the professor's solemn reply. *The James D. Horan Collection*

In October 1877 Bat Masterson ran for sheriff of Ford County, which took in Dodge City. The *Dodge City Times* praised Bat as a "young man of nerve and coolness in danger" and published Bat's letter formally declaring his candidacy. *Courtesy Kansas State Historical Society*

Sheriff of Ford County Bat Masterson. *Courtesy Kansas State Historical Society.*

into two parties, one headed by Dave Rudebaugh, later to ride with Billy the Kid.

Bat and his posse captured Rudebaugh and another bank robber, Edgar West, near a cow camp. After sitting out a blizzard in a sod hut with his handcuffed prisoners, Bat returned the pair to Dodge's crude jail, then to Kinsley for trial.

Bat and his men unsuccessfully scoured the frigid plains for the other two holdup men. When they returned to Dodge he distributed a description of the fugitives to the merchants, warning them to be on the lookout for the pair, who he predicted would come in for supplies. Two months later the bandits confirmed Bat's hunch; they slipped into town late one afternoon. But the owner of a general store alerted Masterson, who took them at gunpoint.

Dodge City now knew it not only had a vigorous, competent law officer in the twenty-four-year-old Bat Masterson but undoubtedly the best-dressed man in all the cow towns.

Bob Wright recalled in his autobiography that a stranger once asked a resident of Dodge where he could find Bat Masterson. A lawyer who overheard the question broke in and said: "Look for one of the most perfectly made men you ever saw, as well as a well-dressed, good-looking fellow and when you see such a man call him 'Bat' and you have hit the bull's-eye." [20]

Bat had been in office only four months when he was touched by the cow town's violence. The herds had started to move north and bands of cowboys, hungry, dirty, eager for excitement after weeks on the drives, were riding into Dodge City. Bat, determined to keep the peace, patrolled the streets nightly, visiting the saloons, bordellos, and dance halls, always with a smile or quick quip that took the sting out of his brisk orders to any cowboy starting to slide a six-shooter from its holster.

Late on the night of April 9, 1878, shots rang out on the south side of the railroad tracks. Marshal Ed Masterson and his deputy, Nat Haywood, hurried to the spot to find six drunken cowboys who had just arrived from Texas with a herd, singing, laughing, and dancing about. One of the six, John (Jack) Wagner, was carrying a gun. Masterson disarmed him and gave the six-shooter to A. N. (Alf) Walker, who the *Times* reported was foreman of the group.

Later Masterson and Haywood encountered Walker and Wagner outside of the Gay Lady Dance Hall. Wagner again was carrying his gun. When Masterson began to disarm Wagner, Walker drew, pointed his six-shooter at Haywood's head, and pulled the trigger—but the gun misfired. Haywood ran, leaving Masterson to face the cursing pair. There were shots and Masterson staggered back against the building. A number of accounts have Bat running up and killing both cowboys. Then he carried his brother to a room over Bob Wright's store, where Ed died. Bob Wright's romantic version described Bat as getting the details from his dying brother of who shot him; then, bidding Ed "an affectionate farewell he hastily departed to avenge his brother's death; and I have no doubt he made the murderers pay the penalty." [21]

This does not agree with the accounts in the *Dodge City Times* and the *Ford County Globe*, which picture Ed Masterson staggering across the street into Hoover's saloon, whispering to George Hinkel, the bartender, "George, I'm shot," and sinking to the floor. Hinkel then extinguished the small fire in Masterson's coat started by Wagner's shot fired at close range. When Bat rushed in, he and several others carried Ed to his rooms, where Ed died.

Wagner, badly wounded, made his way into Peacock's saloon and clung to Ham Bell, a former deputy sheriff, crying, "Catch me, I'm dying." But Bell pushed him off and told him, "I can't help you now."

Wagner staggered a few feet backward and fell. Cowboy friends carried him to "Mr. Lane's rooms," where he died the following morning after he had confessed he shot Masterson. The following day, April 11, he was buried in Dodge City's Boot Hill, probably the last to be interred there.

Walker, who had been hit three times, once in the right lung, and had his right arm "horribly shattered," as the *Times* reported, did not die in Dodge as many accounts insist. Eleven days after he had been shot the *Times* told its readers the young cowboy would probably recover "if mortification can be prevented." On May 11, the *Times* noted the arrival of Walker's father, "who is attending his son." On June 1, Walker was taken to a Kansas City hospital and from there slipped into oblivion.

Stuart Lake's much distorted version of the gunfight has Walker dying of pneumonia in Texas. There is no documentation for this statement nor is there any for the story that Bat killed Walker and Wagner. It is logical to assume that

Ed Masterson, a fearless and efficient lawman, shot both cowboys while he was still on his feet and before his brother arrived on the scene.

The Dodge City saloons, gambling halls, and business houses closed in respect for the death of the popular lawman, with the city council and various civic groups "passing resolutions of respect." Then after the largest funeral the territory had ever seen, Bat took his brother to Fort Dodge to bury him in the cemetery there "because there was only Boot Hill and no respectable cemetery in Dodge." Bat was the only relative attending. Tom Masterson and his wife could not come from Wichita. When the last words had been spoken by the post's chaplain, Bat returned to Dodge to once again patrol its noisy, dangerous streets.

Cowboys still filled the saloons but the loud laughter, curses, and singing died away when Bat pushed through the swinging doors, nodded to the bartenders and gamblers, surveyed the smoky rooms and left. The wildest of the Texans wisely kept their guns holstered. There was no bluff or brag in the grim young lawman, and if they went for their guns they knew they had to be prepared to die in a stand-up fight.

In November 1879, Bat's younger brother, Jim, who had been with him during the "buffalo days" and Neil (Neal) Brown, Bat's friend, a quiet but deadly gunfighter, were appointed marshal and assistant marshal.

Dodge by now had gained a reputation as a wild, open frontier town, "a wicked little town," as the *Washington Evening Star* described it in the winter of 1878. An invisible "deadline" was established running east and west, south of the railroad tracks to separate the "good people" of Dodge from what Bob Wright called "the vicious character of certain citizens." There was a recognized 9 P.M. curfew and any tenderfoot who broke that curfew and crossed the line "was like to become a creature of circumstances," possibly lassoed by a drunken cowhand, tossed into a horse trough "to cool off," or made to dance with six-shooter slugs raising the dust about his toes.

Dodge's fierce reputation enhanced rather than damaged its image in the East. Major newspapers sent correspondents to write feature stories about the "wicked little town," while burlesque troupes and comedians played in Ben Springer's Comique Hall. One of the most popular was the nationally known entertainer Eddie Foy, who never forgot his first meeting with Bat Masterson.

One evening Ben Thompson, the Texas killer, "two-thirds drunk," as Foy recalled, spotted the entertainer backstage, drew his gun and called out:

"Getcher head outa the way, I wanta shoot out that light." Thompson was aiming at an oil lamp near Foy's elbow. When Foy refused to "because of a drunken bum like Thompson," the Texan aimed at Foy's head and swore to shoot him.

Then Masterson appeared, pushed the muzzle of Thompson's gun aside and "partly by coaxing and partly by shoving got him out."[22]

In the two years he served as sheriff of Ford County Bat established a good record for capturing fugitives. One day the Fort Lyons sheriff telegraphed Dodge he was seeking a horse thief named Davis. He failed to include a description, although he did reveal that Davis had taken an eastbound train.

Bat spotted a lone passenger and on a hunch called out, "Hello, Davis, how do you do?"

The man's face brightened as he looked up and held out his hand only to be met by Bat's cold smile over his six-shooter. The fugitive was returned to Lyons and a long prison term.[23]

A short time later Bat and Wyatt Earp traded shots with a quartet of Texans who had come in off the trail to terrorize Dodge. Bat wounded one cowhand. His leg was amputated, but he died a month later of infection.

That summer Dodge made an attempt to become respectable. In August the City Council passed an ordinance banning gambling and prostitution within city limits. The *Dodge City Times* applauded the action as the first move to end the city's reputation as the most sinful community west of the Mississippi. However, after a few days the gamblers returned with their "layouts" and the brothels and cribs unlocked their doors.

One of the favorite Dodge City legends is the confrontation between Clay Allison, the Texas gunfighter, and Bat in July 1878. Some versions have Allison, guns strapped to his thighs, arriving in the cow town while Bat is pictured fleeing at the first sound of the hoofbeats of Allison's horse.[24]

The reason for this dramatic meeting was supposed to be Allison's determination to avenge the death of his cowboy friend, George Hoyt, who with some friends, decided to riddle Ben Springer's Comique Variety Hall as they were riding out of town. Wyatt Earp was leaning against a post outside the front door and Bat was inside listening to Eddie Foy recite his favorite poem called "Kalamazoo in Michigan." Earp, intent on the entertainment, didn't notice Hoyt until the young cowboy started to blaze away.

Bat ran outside and with Earp chased Hoyt. They caught up with him on the Arkansas River Bridge and, in an exchange of bullets, Bat shattered the boy's arm. He was brought back to Dodge, and as the *Dodge City Times* reported, "Doctor Tremaine amputated the limb in a very skillful manner." However, blood poisoning set in and Hoyt died. The legend has Clay Allison in Texas hearing of his friend's death and vowing to kill Masterson.

Earp was all for meeting Allison in the street, but Bat as sheriff insisted on a more subtle strategy: confront the Texas killer with enough firepower to make him back down in front of the whole town and leave with his reputation as the invincible gunfighter badly tarnished.

Earp agreed and Dodge held its breath as Bat slowly walked down the main street in the classic Wild West tradition to meet Allison. As the killer approached Bat he suddenly saw the town's plaza ringed with Bat's deputies and Earp, all armed, their guns pointed at him, while Charlie Bassett, Chalk Beson, Bill Harris, and Luke Short, shotguns cradled in their arms, impassively stared out at him.

As Bat and Allison came abreast, the Texan mumbled something to Masterson and continued down the street. He wanted no part of Dodge that hot afternoon; he had seen what shotguns could do to a man's body.

The files of the *Dodge City Times* and the *Ford County Globe* tell a different story. The Texans riding past the Comique in the early hours of July 26, 1878, impulsively decided to riddle the dance hall. The bullets shattered the clapboard walls but passed over the heads of the dancers. Earp, then an assistant marshal, and Jim Masterson, a city policeman, ran to the scene and with "several citizens" began firing at the fleeing cowboys. Hoyt fell from his horse at the bridge and was removed to the doctor's office where the amputation took place. He died on August 21.

For many years Earp claimed he had killed Hoyt, but it was anyone's guess whose bullet from that crowd of lawmen and indignant citizens had really wounded Hoyt.

Another romantic legend, but this time true, has Bat rescuing Billy Thompson, brother of Ben, the Texas gunman, from a hangman's noose in Nebraska. Billy, who became homicidal when he was drunk, had killed Sheriff Whitney in Ogallala and the townspeople were waiting for him to recover "so he can be well enough to hang," as the Ogallala newspapers put it.

Ben sent Bat a telegram asking him to rescue his troublesome young brother. He explained he couldn't go himself "because I got into a mess some time ago and they'll be laying for me with a warrant. . . . They would be sure to give us a double hanging."

Bat, who didn't like the younger Thompson, agreed to go "even though he doesn't deserve it."

Bat convinced Billy's guard he should help him get the young Texan out of town. The plan was for Bat and some friends to start a sham battle near a local dance hall. While the shots attracted a crowd, Thompson would be slipped out of the hotel and put aboard a train. The plan worked. Billy recovered from his wounds at Buffalo Bill's ranch, then Bat drove him in a wagon to Dodge, where he met Ben.[25]

Bat also took part in the hunt for James Kennedy, son of Captain Miffin Kennedy, a partner of Richard King, in the famed Texas King Ranch. Young Kennedy, who had a reputation as an arrogant rich man's son who had accompanied many of his father's cattle drives to Dodge, got into a drunken fight with James "Dog" Kelley, whom legend has winning his nickname from handling General Custer's hounds. Kelley, a tough former buffalo hunter, was not intimidated by Kennedy's guns or his reputation. The fight took place in the Alhambra saloon and gambling saloon, partially owned by Kelley. After he had given the younger man a terrible beating he dragged him out of the saloon and lodged a disorderly behavior complaint against him.

In Texas, the Kennedys were cattle barons, men who made their own justice. For young Kennedy to be thrown into jail was unthinkable. After he paid his fine, Kennedy went to Kansas City and bought the best and fastest horse he could find.

In the meantime Kelley was taken sick and removed to the Fort Dodge Hospital. His quarters in a shack behind the Comique and the Western House were taken over by two dance-hall girls, Fannie Keenan, known in Dodge as Dora Hand, star of the Variety Theater's show, and Fannie Garretson, featured at the Comique. There are the usual sentimental legends about Dora's beauty, her extraordinary singing, dancing talents, and kindness of heart. The truth is, she was an ordinary cow-town entertainer who sold her charms after the dance hall was closed for the evening.

The *Dodge City Times* story of the incident has the raging Kennedy, out for revenge, riding into Dodge at four o'clock in the morning, stopping outside the wooden house and firing two shots into the bedroom formerly used by Kelley. The second slug passed over the head of Miss Garretson, pierced two quilts and the plaster wall separating the bedrooms, to finally strike Dora in the right side, killing her instantly.

Miss Garretson's screams roused the town and a doctor pronounced Dora dead. Suspicion immediately focused on Kennedy. Masterson quickly got up a posse consisting of Wyatt Earp, Bill Tilghman, William Duggy, and Charlie Bassett—"as intrepid a posse as ever pulled a trigger," as Robert Wright called them in his autobiography.

They camped at Meade City where they knew Kennedy had to pass on his way to his father's ranch. When he appeared, Masterson shouted a command to surrender but Kennedy whipped his horse with a quirt and rode off, confident he could outride the man hunters. But he had misjudged their marksmanship. All fired, Kennedy was shot in the shoulder, and his horse was killed. In the fall, the animal pinned Kennedy to the ground.

Back in Dodge Bat told Wright how he had pulled Kennedy free. "He said he had hold of the wounded arm and could hear the bones craunch [sic]. Not a groan did Kennedy let out of him, although the pain must have been fearful. And all he said was, "You sons of b------, I will get even with you for this."

In Dodge Doctors McCarty and Tremaine removed four inches of the shattered bone in the arm, making it useless. When Kennedy finally came to trial, the cow town's rage had gradually cooled and it was agreed the cattle baron's son had been punished enough. His father hired the best attorneys in the territory and their defense was successful. Kennedy was freed and returned to Texas.[26]

Wright reported that although Kennedy's one arm couldn't hold a six-shooter, "he used the other as well to kill several people afterwards, but finally met his death by someone a little quicker on the trigger than himself. . . ."

However, in his memoirs, *A Frontier Doctor*, Dr. Henry F. Hoyt, who knew Billy the Kid, claimed Kennedy died of his wounds a year and a half after he returned to Texas.

At the beginning of his second year as Ford County's sheriff, Bat was ordered by the county prosecutor to bring Henry Borne, alias Dutch Henry, a notorious horse thief and killer, back to Dodge to stand trial.

There were complications in getting legal hold of Dutch. Not only did Colorado want him, but the state of Nevada was offering $500 to anyone who delivered Dutch Henry back there to be tried.

Bat secured the custody of the fugitive, with the *Dodge City Times* hinting it might have been done through political blackmail. "Bat mentioned a few of the unmentionables and got him (Dutch Henry) for nothing," the *Times* said slyly.

The outlaw was returned to Dodge by Bat but his efforts were in vain. Dutch Henry retained a top criminal lawyer who persuaded the jury that the horse thief was an honest citizen framed by his enemies. The appearance of Dutch undoubtedly helped his attorney. The handsome killer and horse thief always dressed conservatively in a black suit, freshly laundered white shirt, and a white pocket handkerchief in his jacket pocket. He was soft-spoken, intelligent, and, as the frontier newspapers reported, looked more like a cattle baron on his way to church than a wanted man.[27]

In mid-January 1879, shortly after he returned from Colorado, Bat was appointed a United States deputy marshal. In March he took part in Colorado's "railroad war" when the Denver and Rio Grande fought the Atchison, Topeka and Santa Fe to be the first to lay tracks to the silver boom camp of Deadwood. In his new capacity as a federal officer, Bat deputized thirty men and led them to Canon City to keep peace between the warring companies. He stayed until March, then returned to Dodge with his small army. But in June he was back in Colorado with fifty gunslingers, cowboys, and former buffalo hunters to prevent a threatened shooting war from breaking out between workers of both roads. Bat and his men stayed in the Pueblo Roundhouse until Bat surrendered to a superior force armed not only with guns but also a court writ. Bat and his men returned to Dodge with the *Times* reporting, "our boys didn't smell any powder." [28]

Bat now had gained a reputation on the frontier as a fearless, dedicated lawman. Rather than draw on the wild young cowhands who rode in to "capture Dodge," or the gunfighters who hoped to gain a reputation by killing him, Masterson either used the barrel of his six-shooter as a club or his fists to subdue his prisoners "hors de combat" as the *Times* called it. One night he waded into three "badmen" who tried to ambush him on Main Street. After the battle was over he dragged the badly battered trio to the lockup. The next day they were fined and ordered out of town.

"Dodge City is hard to take," the *Times* solemnly declared, and described Bat as the "best sheriff in Kansas."

During his campaign for reelection Bat was charged with fraud, but it was discovered one of his employees had been forging vouchers used for the expense of escorting prisoners to the state penitentiary. Robert B. Frey, editor of the *Speareville News* hinted at the charges and then a few days before election, charged Bat with threatening to shoot him "through the g-ts." Frey told his readers he could not support Masterson, "a law breaker himself."

Political advisers advised the raging Masterson not to answer Frey in print and Bat accepted their advice. The Election Day returns proved how wrong their advice had been: George Hinkle, the former bartender, had swept all six of the counties' voting districts and won by one hundred and thirty-six votes. Frey, it appeared, had convinced many voters that Bat was not fit to serve as sheriff for another term.

On November 15, 1879, Bat answered Bob Frey in the columns of the *Dodge City Times.*[29]

Bat Masterson Answers Bob Frey

TO THE EDITOR OF THE TIMES:

In answer to the publication made by Bob Frey of the *Speareville News* asserting that I made threats that I would lick any s-- of a b---- that voted or worked against me the last election, I say it is as false and flagrant a lie that was ever uttered; but I did say this: that I would lick him, the s-- of a b----, if he made any more dirty talks about me; and the words, s-- of a b----, I strictly confined to the Speareville editor, for I don't know any other in Ford County.

W. B. Masterson

When a resident notified the *Times* editor that Frey had showed him a "self-cocking revolver" he said he intended to use on Bat, the *Times* slyly suggested, "Better hitch yourself to a cannon, Bob."

Our merchants report business fair, and the impression is that we will have a good winter trade. The prospects are becoming bright for Dodge City, when we shall have a combination of interests.

———————

To the Editor of the Times.

In answer to the publication made by Bob Fry of the Speareville News, asserting that I made threats that I would lick any s— of a b— that voted or worked against me at the last election, I will say it is as false and as flagrant a lie as was ever uttered; but I did say this: that I would lick him the s— of a b— if he made any more dirty talk about me; and the words s— of a b— I strictly confined to the Speareville editor, for I don't know of any other in Ford county.

W. B. MASTERSON.

———————

STRAYED OR STOLEN,
From the undersigned at Lakin, Kearney county, Kansas, on the evening of October 26, 1879, Two Work Horses; one a sorrel

Bat Masterson's "s-- of a b----" letter to the *Dodge City Times*, Saturday, November 15, 1879, threatening Bob Frye, editor of the *Speareville News*, who had opposed Bat in his bid for reelection as sheriff of Ford County. *Courtesy Kansas State Historical Society*

In the winter of 1880, Bat Masterson, buffalo hunter, gunfighter, and former sheriff of Ford County, turned to cards and the faro bank to earn a living. He was a skillfull gambler and this skill earned him thousands of dollars during his life.

His friend Wyatt Earp had left Dodge for Tombstone and Bat was tempted to try his luck there, but the silver strike in Leadville made that camp a gambler's delight. In the winter of 1880 Bat was in Leadville bucking the faro banks and testing his skill at poker, keno, cassino, and chuck-a-luck.

A year later he joined Wyatt Earp in Tombstone, where Bat worked at the Oriental as a faro dealer for $25 a day. Shortly after he arrived he stepped between two friends from Dodge City, Charlie Storms and Luke Short, who had drawn guns and were about to engage in a shooting match.

Bat escorted Storms to the street and "advised him to go to his room and take a sleep." He then returned to the Oriental to explain to Short how Storms "was a decent sort of man," when suddenly he heard a noise behind them. Bat turned to discover Storms armed with a six-shooter and cursing Short. Both men drew their guns but as Bat later recalled, "Storms was too slow. Although he succeeded in getting his pistol out, Short stuck the muzzle of his own pistol against Storms's heart and pulled the trigger. The bullet tore the heart asunder and, as he was falling, Short shot him again. Storms was dead when he hit the ground . . ."

Bat testified Short had fired in self-defense and the gambler was freed.

In March the celebrated Tombstone Wells Fargo stagecoach robbery took place and Bat rode with Wyatt Earp's posse. After many days of hard riding the posse returned without prisoners.

In the mining camp tensions slowly began to build as lines were drawn between the Earps and the so-called cowboy element. The gunfight at the O. K. Corral, one of the most savage shootouts in the history of the Wild West, was not far off.

One can only wonder what role Masterson would have played during those bloody thirty seconds if he had not been advised when he returned to Tombstone that a telegram was waiting for him.

It was from an anonymous friend in Dodge City who advised Bat his brother Jim was about to be killed by A. J. Peacock, Jim's partner in a dance hall, and their bartender, Al Updegraff.

Jim, who was city marshal of Dodge from November 1879 to April 1881 had entered into a partnership with Peacock, owner of the cow town's well-known Lady Gay saloon and gambling hall. Their bartender, Updegraff, was Peacock's brother-in-law. The bartender was an alcoholic who consumed a large amount of the saloon's profits and this irritated Jim. The partners quarreled bitterly and guns had been drawn. At this point Bat's friend sent him the telegram.

Bat met Peacock and Updegraff at the Dodge City railroad station and a gunfight took place. Updegraff was shot in the lung and A. B. Webster, the city's mayor, arrested Bat. The next day he was fined $8.[30]

Some of Dodge's leaders and citizens were infuriated over Bat's actions. They pointed out in letters to the *Times* that bullets fired during the shootout had shattered store windows and narrowly missed residents. They also protested the small fine, recalling Updegraff had been near death from his wound and the wild shooting melee had damaged the reputation of Dodge at a time when the town was struggling to become respectable.

Staid, hypocritical Dodge City was becoming distasteful to Bat. After the

Updegraff shooting he moved to Trinidad, Colorado, where he opened a gambling concession in one of the large saloons. It was in Colorado that he gained the reputation for having killed twenty-six men, "not counting Indians or Mexicans."

The story began in the depot of Gunnison, Colorado, in the fall of 1881, when a New York doctor named W. S. Cockrell was saying good-bye to his friend, a Mr. Brown. As they waited for the train, Brown nudged his friend and told him to look at Bat, who was sitting nearby.

"Who's that?" Cockrell asked.

"Bat Masterson, the killer," his friend replied. Then straight-faced he continued on with a wild tale of how Bat had killed twenty-six men. He embroidered the tale by describing how Bat had once killed two Mexican bandits, then to prove he had the right men and collect the $1,000 reward, he cut off their heads and put them into a gunnysack to bring back to Dodge. However, the blazing desert heat decomposed the heads so badly they could not be identified and Bat lost the $1,000.

The *Ford County Times,* tongue in cheek, picked up the story Cockrell had given to the *New York Sun,* and the wild tale, like many tales of the Wild West, soon became fact from repeated telling.[31]

In April 1882 Bat was appointed city marshal of Trinidad. The following year, Masterson was back in Dodge with Wyatt Earp and Mysterious Dave Mathers, who had been with him at the Battle of Adobe Walls, to help Luke Short from being harassed by Mike Sutton, Dodge City's crusading prosecuting attorney. Short had left Tombstone to return to Dodge City, where he bought the gambling concession in the Long Branch Saloon.

Sutton had revived the old gambling ordinance and threatened to run the gamblers out of town. When Bat, Earp, and Mathers appeared, guns strapped to their hips, the frightened city officials wired Colonel Thomas Moonlight, adjutant-general of Kansas, asking for help. Moonlight hurried to Dodge and acted as an arbitrator. From the news accounts in the Dodge City and Ford County newspapers, the trio of now-famous sheriffs and gunmen won a reprieve for their old friend.

In a few days Short and the other gamblers reopened their games. Mike Sutton, the vigorous prosecuting attorney who started it all, had taken to a "storm cellar," as one paper told its readers, and emerged only after Bat and the others had left.

Bat's involvement in Dodge City's anti-gambling crusade gained him a bitter enemy. His onetime supporter, the *Dodge City Times,* now never missed an opportunity to denounce Masterson, whom its editor had once called the best sheriff in the state.

In the winter of 1883 Bat escorted an Iowa sheriff and his prisoner to the Trinidad, Colorado, depot but the account in the *Times* had Bat trying to free the prisoner, a murderer, by first showing false papers, then trying to wrest the fugitive from the sheriff. When Bat read the *Times* he was furious and wrote a reply to the *Ford County Globe* denying the charge, explaining he had been "solicited by a deputy sheriff of Chaffee County, Colorado, who had a warrant for the arrest of the prisoner on the charge of murder committed in Chaffee

County two years ago." He denounced the editor of the *Times* for his "scurrilous attack," and the "political machinery" of Dodge he called "that delectable burg." [32]

The following year Bat returned to Dodge, "that delectable burg," this time to establish the *Vox Populi* to support his candidates and to lash back at his old enemy, the *Times*. The paper lasted only one edition but Bat's charges left Dodge City and the *Times* "howling" long after the elections were over and Masterson's party had carried all public offices. [33]

However, Bat's feud with the *Times* didn't prevent him from being selected as Dodge City's "Most Popular Man." He was given a dinner, a great many speechmakers praised him as the best lawman Dodge had ever had, and at the peak of the evening he was presented with a gold-headed cane which he carried until his death.

For the next few years Bat moved from town to town in the West, owning or operating dance halls, burlesque houses, and gambling halls, following the last of the herds moving to the northern cow towns or the crowds flocking to the latest gold strike. The circle of men who knew the early frontier and Indian attacks, who had witnessed the rise and fall of the cow towns, was beginning to get smaller. There was a fierce esprit de corps among them; a call for help was immediately answered. Their one rigid rule was never broken—always be loyal to a friend.

When Luke Short was arrested for killing Jim Courtright in Fort Worth, there was talk of lynching him. Courtright, a former Indian scout and trooper, had been the city's best sheriff during the trail-herding days and was Fort Worth's living legend.

Luke Short, Dodge City gambler and gunfighter. Bat witnessed the gunfight between Short and Jim Courtright, a notorious killer, on February 8, 1887. Short killed Courtright in Short's White Elephant saloon and gambling hall in Fort Worth, Texas, after Courtright tried to extort money from him. *Courtesy Kansas State Historical Society*

Bat Masterson in his Dodge City days. *Courtesy Kansas State Historical Society*

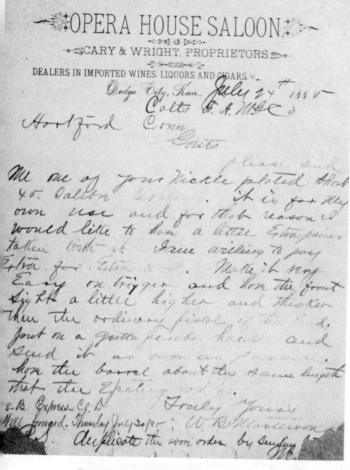

Bat Masterson's friend "Mysterious Dave" Mather, buffalo hunter, Dodge City gambler, gunfighter, and lawman. Bob Wright recalled in his memoirs that Mather was a man "who had more dead men to his credit at that time than any man in the West." Mather killed Deputy City Marshal Tom Nixon in a Dodge City gunfight, July 21, 1884. During his buffalo hunting days Mather killed the only white buffalo. One animal, sold to Wright for $1,000, was stuffed and exhibited across the West. *The James D. Horan Collection*

Bat Masterson's letter to the Colt Arms Company in Connecticut, written on the stationery of the "Opera House Saloon" in Dodge City, ordering a revolver which had to be "easy on the trigger." *Courtesy Connecticut State Historical Society*

BAT'S. BULLETS.

A Talk With the Frontiersman Who is "On His Third Dozen,"

OR AT LEAST IS SAID TO BE

Bat Masterson is Referred To—Some of His More Tragical Exploits.

The gentleman who has killed his man is therefore a ubiquitous individual in this city, and may be met at every corner. He is usually quiet in demeanor, sober and thoughtful in aspect, somber in dress, and the last man on earth one would suspect of having notches on the butt end of his pistol. He may take a drink occasionally, but seldom gets drunk. He plays a game of pool at times, but never quarrels over the game. He perhaps goes down to West Kansas and tackles the tiger, but when there are loud words over the cloth of green he is not the man who utters them. He is quiet—fatally quiet. Your gentleman who has dropped his man is a blue eyed or gray eyed man in nine cases out of ten, and his hair and beard are brown, unless grizzled or whitened with the frosts of the many winters which have come and gone since the glories of the old Santa Fe trail began to wane.

Masterson leaves the city to-day, but will return in a few days and make a brief sojourn here. Whether he has killed twenty-six men as is popularly asserted, cannot be positively ascertained without careful and extensive research, for he is himself quite reticent on the subject. But that many men have fallen by his deadly revolver and rifle is an established fact, and he furnishes a rare illustration of the fact that the thrilling stories of life on the frontier are not always overdrawn.

a blue eyed or gray eyed man in nine cases out of ten, and his hair and beard are brown, unless grizzled or whitened with the frosts of the many winters which have come and gone since the glories of the old Santa Fe trail began to wane.

Your gentleman who has dropped his man is, therefore, no uncommon individual, but when you see a man who has entered upon

HIS THIRD DOZEN,

it is about time to be civil, for he may begin to fear that material is about to run out, and may have an uncontrollable desire to hurry up and finish that third dozen. Such a gentleman was introduced yesterday evening to the iron-clad reporter of the JOURNAL, and the person referred to is none other than the famous H. B. Masterson, of Dodge City—known, by those whom he has not shot, as "Bat" Masterson. Mr. Masterson

In answer to a very leading question, Masterson said he had not killed as many men as was popularly supposed, though he had "had

A GREAT MANY DIFFICULTIES"

and had in fact been tried four times for murder in the first degree and acquitted each time.

"How about shooting some Mexicans, cutting off their heads, and carrying the gory trophies back in a sack?"

"Oh, that story is straight, except that I did not cut off their heads," replied Bob. He

In the summer of 1881, a Dr. W. S. Cockrell began the legend that Bat Masterson had killed twenty-six men. It was printed in a New York newspaper and then picked up by daily and weekly newspapers in the West. Here is the Kansas City *Journal's* interview with Bat, November 15, 1881. The story erroneously had Jim Masterson dead along with A. J. Peacock and Al Updegraff, who took part in the celebrated Dodge City shootout, April 16, 1881. Peacock was wounded but Updegraff, who had traded shots with Bat, was not. There is no evidence Jim Masterson took part in the shooting. Bat's heavy toll of dead men soon became a legend. *Courtesy Kansas State Historical Society*

After being acquitted for killing two Mexicans in New Mexico, Courtright had returned to Fort Worth and insisted that Short hire him as a special guard in his large gambling hall. Short refused and Courtright threatened to drive him out of town.

In their shootout Short killed Courtright, who had been regarded as a skillful gunfighter. Bat, who witnessed the fight, later recalled:

"As usual Short's [bullet] spoke first and went crashing through Courtright's body. The shock caused him to reel backwards; then he got another and still another, and by the time his lifeless form had reached the floor Luke had succeeded in shooting him five times."[34]

After Courtright's funeral rumors spread through the town that a mob would march on the jail and lynch Short.

All that night Bat sat in Luke's cell prepared to kill the first man who entered the jail carrying a gun. He stayed in Fort Worth until Short was formally released by the court, which recognized the traditional law of the frontier that a man had the right to defend himself against a drawn gun. Bat returned to Denver, then one of the great sporting towns of the West, to open a combined dance hall and gambling house. Meanwhile, his brother Jim strapped on his guns in the winter of 1889 to join Bill Tilghman; George Bolds, a young surveyor who had ridden as a posseman in Dodge City; and several other former lawmen who had been hired to protect the rights of the town of Ingalls during the County Seat Wars of Kansas.[35]

By 1885, Masterson, restless and footloose, was back in Dodge City working the faro tables in the Long Branch saloon. He briefly served as a deputy sheriff to disperse a wild-eyed mob determined to tar and feather Albert Griffin, an ardent prohibitionist who had vowed to shut down Dodge City's saloons.

After a year in Dodge, Bat was again on the move. He became a familiar face in the gambling halls and saloons of Trinidad and Denver, Colorado, Reno and Las Vegas, Nevada, and New Mexico. There were streaks of gray in his dark hair. He was heavier, wore a moustache, a black derby, and in winter, a sealskin-trimmed chinchilla ulster that almost reached to the tops of his patent-leather shoes.

He had also become a pugilistic expert, acting as a timekeeper, referee, or as a second to many heavyweights. During this period he met two young brothers, Alfred (Hank) Henry and William E. Lewis. William was a correspondent for the *New York Sun;* his brother was a free-lance writer. Both would help to shape Bat Masterson's future.

Sometime in the 1880s, Bat was back in Denver still making a living at gambling, putting together heavyweight fights, and generally drifting about the frontier. Occasionally he wore a deputy's star or rushed by train, stagecoach, or horseback to aid a friend. He was, as the *New York Times* would call him, "one of the best-known men on the western frontier."

Denver at the time was not only a "sporting man's town" but an important stopover for the best of Broadway's variety shows, Shakespearean companies, and vaudeville acts. One of Bat's favorite theaters was the Palace Variety Theatre and Gambling Parlors owned and operated by two of Bat's gambling friends, Ed Chase and Ed Gaylord. The bar and gambling hall were the finest in the West.

A sixty-foot mirror reflected the flashing lights of hundreds of glass prisms dangling from a huge chandelier. The theater could hold over seven hundred patrons. There were private, curtained boxes, striking wall murals, and luxurious suppers. Some of the best New York and London actors and performers appeared on the Palace's stage, among them Eddie Foy, Bat's old friend from Dodge City.

In the late 1880s, Bat bought out Chase and Gaylord and became owner of the Palace. Many beautiful women passed through his establishment but only one captivated him. She was the petite, blond Emma Walters, a singer and dancer from Philadelphia. After a short courtship Bat and Emma were married in Denver on November 21, 1891.

A short time after they returned from their honeymoon, Bat left for Creede, scene of the big silver strike, to manage Watrous & Benniger's big gambling house and saloon. Photographs taken at the time show Bat to be aging. Instead of the slender, trim dandy of the early Dodge days, a pudgy, round-faced man with thinning hair stared back at the lens. There was one familiar note: the hard, gray-blue eyes.

Creede was a wild mining camp with thirty or more saloons open day and night. The usual band of whores, pimps, gamblers, outlaws, gunfighters, and drifters—the backwash of the dying frontier—poured into the place. The population boomed until ten thousand—one newspaper estimated there were a thousand whores—men, women, and children jammed the narrow streets, rickety shacks, and tents.[36]

In this brawling community Bat Masterson was a model of decorum, a conservative businessman, pleasant, smiling, affable. Bat's reputation as a gunfighter was never questioned. Outlaws and men with a price on their heads went out of their way not to meet him. The graying man in the lavender-colored corduroy suit still made them look the other way.

Creede, for all its noise and bluster, soon bored Bat. He told the correspondent of the *Denver Sun* that the camp was too quiet and warned that the quiet usually comes before the storm:

"It only needs a break to raise Cain here . . . the same thing happened in some of the other notorious camps. . . . It seems as though there must be a little blood-letting to get affairs into proper working order."

Violence did break out in Creede when Ed O. Kelly, a cowboy who yearned to be known as a killer, stalked into Ford's Exchange, run by Bob Ford, "the dirty little coward who had laid poor Jesse in his grave." Kelly fired both barrels of his shotgun, instantly killing Ford. He was arrested and spent ten years in the state penitentiary at Canon City. Two years after his release he was killed by an Oklahoma deputy who refused to be impressed by his boast that he was the most dangerous man in the West.

Bat impassively watched the brawls and the killings, refusing to get involved; it seemed the wheel had made a full turn. When Jefferson Randolph Smith, better known to frontier history as Soapy Smith, came to Creede to take over the gambling establishments, Bat warned him not to include the Watrous and Benniger establishment he was managing. Soapy, more of a cheap confidence man than a gunfighter, forced the merchants and owners of the brothels, saloons, dance halls, and gambling halls to pay tribute to his gang of enforcers. There was only one exception: Bat Masterson's establishment. Soapy refused to challenge the quiet man as he strolled among the tables. He could intimidate the others but he knew Bat would kill him without hesitation if he dared to swagger into Watrous and Benniger's gambling hall—no matter how many thugs and gunfighters followed at Smith's heels.

When Bat finally became disgusted with Creede's squalid surroundings and tinhorn gamblers, he returned to Denver and Emma. She remains only a patient, long-suffering shadow in his life. The only photographs of her were taken in her late years. They show a bland, stolid-looking woman with no trace of the blond beauty who had enchanted the handsome young gunfighter and gambler in the days of the Palace Theatre. Until they settled down in a modest apartment on New York City's West Side, Emma always appears to have been waiting for Bat to return from a frontier town, boom mining camp, or a far-off high-rolling poker game. There are no extant love letters nor did Bat, in his writing on many subjects—from his philosophy of life to the art of gunfighting and the "old buffalo days"—once mention her. Yet they were very close, although Emma admitted in a letter to her niece, Bat "was very peculiar in some ways."

The late Zoe Tilghman, widow of the famous frontier lawman, recalled: "Bill always said Bat was not a demonstrative man. He was not one for throwing his arms around an old friend he had just met on the street. Rather it would be a quiet but very warm handshake and the friend would know instantly how Bat felt about him. He also knew Bat would go to the very gates of Hell for him. Those frontier men were all like that; friendship and loyalty were very important to them.

"In his letters to us, Bat always mentioned Emma and how they talked of the old days and how much Bill meant to them. Although they were together a long time, we never heard of any trouble between them, even though Bat was not the easiest man to have for a husband. You know, he was that restless type, always ready to see what lay beyond that next hill. Bill was like that, but after he put down roots in Oklahoma he stayed close to home. But then he had his lawman's work and his ranch while Bat was a born gambler—and they always follow the cards."

On July 7, 1889, Bat was in Jake Kilrain's corner when Kilrain lost the championship to John L. Sullivan in New Orleans after a battering seventy-five rounds, fought with bare fists. Bat later disclosed he had "gone broke" backing Charlie Mitchell when Mitchell fought "Gentleman Jim" Corbett. And he was wrong when he predicted to the *Rocky Mountain News* that Corbett would knock out Bob Fitzsimmons.

Bat contemptuously dismissed Fitzsimmons—"He's a pudding"—to the *News* but the tall, swift Australian easily knocked out Corbett in Carson City, Nevada.

In September 1896 Bat was in Corbett's corner when Gentleman Jim fought John L. Sullivan. Masterson cleaned up a small fortune in bets when Corbett finally cut down the once great champion. Two years before, Bat and Australian heavyweight Jem Hall acted as Charlie Mitchell's seconds when Mitchell fought Corbett. That time Bat was a loser when Corbett knocked out Mitchell in three rounds.

In February 1894 the *Illustrated Sporting West* had a feature story on Bat, describing him as "one of the best judges of pugilists in America," and predicted he would pick nine out of ten winners in any major bout.

Whenever he backed a losing contender and left the arena with empty pockets, Bat returned to gambling to make a living. His skill with a six-shooter once sent him to New York City to act as a bodyguard for George Gould, son of Jay Gould, the railroad baron, after the family had received extortion letters.

During this busy period Bat also found time to write a sports column for *George's Weekly,* a small Denver newspaper, and open the Olympic Athletic Club in a former Salvation Army barracks, where he promoted fights and acted as referee.

In the winter of 1896, Bat participated in the bizarre and often hilarious Fitzsimmons-Maher heavyweight championship bout. The event began with an announcement by fight promoter Dan Stuart, Bat's friend, that the citizens of El Paso, Texas, had raised a $10,000 purse with the understanding that a series of fights would end in a bout between Fitzsimmons and Peter Maher. "Gentlemen Jim" Corbett had retired as undefeated champion and had named Maher as the new holder of the heavyweight crown, a decision the backers of Fitzsimmons and many fight fans vigorously protested. This bout was to settle who *really* was the champion.

Texas governor Charles A. Culberson immediately announced no prizefights would be allowed in the sovereign state of Texas. Stuart ignored the governor's warning and issued a statement that both fighters had agreed to stage their bout, "in or near El Paso."

Weeks before the date of the fight, gamblers, high rollers, confidence men,

BAT MASTERSON TALKS AGAIN OF CHEAP SPORTS IN DENVER

Bat Masterson, a fashion-plate gambler. *The James D. Horan Collection*

Bat Masterson never forgave Denver for being escorted out of town after he went on a "high lonesome," touring the city's saloons with a six-shooter. In December, the *Denver Times* picked up Bat's column published in the *New York Morning Telegraph* in which he denounced Denver's "cheap sports" and the city's lack of boxing talents. *Courtesy Colorado State Historical Society*

A typical column written by Bat Masterson in *George's Weekly,* a popular sporting newspaper published in Denver in the 1880s.

pickpockets, thieves, outlaws, and fugitives streamed into El Paso. Flimsy gambling halls were hastily erected, promoters staged fights, rodeos, and bullfights. Prices for ringside seats to the heavyweight championship bout soared to the unprecedented price of $25.

Maher set up training quarters at Las Cruces, New Mexico, forty-five miles northwest of El Paso, while Bob Fitzsimmons showed up at Juarez with a pet lion he called Nero.

In Orange, New Jersey, Thomas Edison, the famous inventor, told the New York newspapers his new Kinetoscope, the first moving picture machine, was being rushed to completion to film the fight. Edison boasted the machine could take as many as forty pictures a minute.

An outraged Governor Culberson ordered the Texas Rangers into El Paso to enforce his ruling and to stop the fight. Then the Southwest was electrified by the news Bat Masterson was on his way to El Paso with a small army of gunfighters to make sure the fight would go on. In Washington, Tom Catron, New Mexico's delegate, leader of the "Sante Fe ring" and Billy the Kid's deadly enemy, rushed a bill through Congress forbidding prizefights in any United States territory.

Adjutant General Mabry, surrounded by Texas Rangers, also appeared in El Paso. On the steps of the depot he announced to a crowd of fight fans he had come with the Rangers to make sure the fight would not be held. A few days later another company of Rangers, headed by the tough and very efficient Captain William McDonald, rode into the town. McDonald said very bluntly no prizefight would be held in El Paso and he and his men were there to make sure Dan Stuart understood the governor's ruling.

Stuart at "fight headquarters" calmly replied he would never break any laws in the sovereign state of Texas, but the fight would still be held.

Bat Masterson finally appeared, not with a small army of hard-eyed gunfighters as he had done in Colorado's "railroad war" but simply as a bodyguard to New York gambler Tom O'Rourke, who Stuart had entrusted with the $10,000 purse.

When a rumor spread that the fight would be held in San Simon, Arizona, the governor of that state promptly dispatched a company of National Guardsmen to San Simon while the *Tucson Citizen* protested he was only wasting the taxpayers' money by sending his troops "to chase jackrabbits up and down San Simon Valley."

El Paso was now the liveliest town on the border. Hotels were jammed and saloons and gambling halls were opened twenty-four hours a day.

At the nearby railroad, siding lumber and canvas for the ring were loaded into boxcars along with Edison's mysterious Kinetoscope machine.

On February 20, the day of the fight, it was announced Maher had an eye infection and the event would be postponed a few days. The crowds in El Paso grew restless. Maher and Fitzsimmons were shadowed by state detectives. Bat Masterson shadowed Tom O'Rourke. They in turn were shadowed by Stuart and the group of El Paso citizens who had raised the $10,000 purse.

Finally, one afternoon Dan Stuart posted a notice at his fight headquarters advising all ticket holders to catch a special train leaving the town for a secret rendezvous. The cost of a round-trip ticket to the mysterious spot "will not exceed twelve dollars."

The announcement came at an excellent time. Saloon keepers and the "sporting crowd" had protested to the mayor that the tough-looking Texas Rangers patrolling the streets were ruining their business. The mayor and El Paso city council agreed and passed a resolution condemning Governor Culberson for sending the Rangers into their town.

Adjutant General Mabry answered for the governor and promptly blamed Bat Masterson. He told reporters: "When I saw in the newspapers that Bat Masterson was bringing in a hundred men and have them at ringside, the inference was that these men were going to violate the law. This is what brought me and my men to El Paso."

But now Dan Stuart's notice broke the tension. Fight fans emptied the hotels, saloons, and gambling halls and rushed to the station where the "fight special" was puffing away. The depot was soon jammed with gamblers wearing embroidered vests, spats, and glistening top hats; cowboys in their best boots and Stetsons; and a few Indians stolidly watched the excited white man pushing, shoving, and cursing to get to the ticket window.

General Mabry, Captain Bill McDonald, and his Rangers were first on board, then three hundred fans packed the cars, with many more picked up along the way.

The secret rendezvous turned out to be Langtry, where "Judge" Roy Bean had announced for years that he was the only law west of the Pecos. The judge gave the crowd a hearty welcome and pointed to the sign above his Lillie Langtry saloon—named after the famous English actress—which read: "Ice Cold Beer and Law West of the Pecos."

After the fans had filled Bean's cash box to overflowing and had been well fortified by numerous rounds, they were guided by the judge to the nearby Rio Grande, where a pontoon bridge had been built. On the Mexican side a ring had been hastily erected. With a straight face Dan Stuart informed General Mabry and Captain McDonald that all the fans wanted to do was visit Mexico, and under the law they could not prevent them. Mabry and McDonald knew they had been outwitted by Stuart; there was no way they could prevent a prizefight held on foreign soil. By the time they contacted the Mexican governor the fight would be over. They stood by and watched the fans stream across the bridge, led by a grinning Dan Stuart, Bat Masterson, and Tom O'Rourke, who kept a tight grip on the canvas bag containing the $10,000.

Only one thing irritated Stuart—a large crowd of nonpayers perched on the cliffs and rocks on the Texas side were getting a fine, free view of the contest. And among them were Mabry, McDonald, and his Rangers.

A short time later the gong sounded and the championship fight began. Maher, a 180-pound giant, towered over the slight, tall Fitzsimmons. Maher swung a sledgehammer blow which Fitzsimmons gracefully avoided.

Then after only one minute and twenty-five seconds of the first round, Fitzsimmons found his opening. He hit Maher on the jaw and the giant slowly collapsed, rolled over, and was counted out.

The operators of the Kinetoscope frantically worked on their machine but it didn't take a picture.

The knockout happened so quickly that one spectator recalled he had turned to his friend to light his cigar and when he looked back at the ring, Maher's seconds were carrying the fighter back to his corner.

Flanked by Dan Stuart and Bat, Tom O'Rourke paid off Fitzsimmons and they all returned to Judge Roy Bean's Lillie Langtry saloon to toast Lillie and wash the alkali dust from their throats. Even the Texas Rangers who had watched the bout from the crags agreed it had been worth it to see "Old Fitz" in action.

Bat returned to Denver to write his weekly column and promote fights at his Olympic Athletic Club. He began feuding with Otto Floto, sports editor of the *Denver News,* after their brief partnership in another boxing venture they called the Colorado Athletic Club. But Floto eased Bat out of the club and Masterson vowed he would get his revenge. Bat also used his column to denounce the Colorado's matches as "fakes" and "jug-handled matches." Floto, of course, never missed an opportunity to scoff at Masterson's efforts at the Olympic Club, which he insisted belonged in a mining camp rather than in a sporting town like Denver.

The citizens of Denver watched the feud grow and eagerly waited for its climax. It finally took place on the corner of Sixteenth and Champa streets when Bat met the sausage-shaped Floto coming out of Bert Davis's cigar store.

Gene Fowler, the Denver journalist, novelist, and screenwriter was ten years old when he witnessed the meeting, and recalled it in his book, *Timberline.* "They advanced like any charcoal burners of the Black Forest," he wrote, "and began kicking each other in the groin. . . . The wild blows swung by both men stirred up more wind than the town has felt since the blizzard of 1883."

Bat started to beat Floto with his gold-headed cane, the one presented to him by the grateful citizens of Dodge City. As the *Denver Times* gleefully reported, Bat used his cane "to good advantage." The heavy Floto began running down the street with Bat, still swinging his cane, at his heels.

"I thought I was a good runner," Bat gasped after a short chase, "but that fellow started to pull away from me on the jump. He is the best runner I ever saw."[37]

The battle with Floto wasn't the only street fight Bat encountered in Denver. A gambler Bat offended in his column hired a thug to help him ambush Bat. One night the pair jumped Masterson, who promptly knocked out the hired killer, grabbed his six-shooter, and jammed the gun into the gambler's stomach.

"Don't kill me," the man begged.

Bat hesitated. Then, instead of pulling the trigger, he stepped back and, as the *Dodge City Times* usually reported, Bat "rendered him hors de combat" with the barrel of the gun.

After his defeat in the Battle of Sixteenth Street, Otto Floto stepped up his attacks on Bat's Olympic Club. Bat's top attraction, Normal (Kid McCoy) Selby, left for the East. He was followed by Patrick "Reddy" Gallagher, who had headed many of the "cards" in Bat's club. Finally the Olympic was on the verge of collapse. Bat, bitterly disappointed, left with Emma for Hot Springs, Arkansas.

A short time before they arrived at the spa and gambling town, Bat's friend, Bill Tilghman, had captured Bill Doolin, the outlaw leader, while he was "taking the baths."

Emma and Bat stayed only a short time. While Emma visited her family in Philadelphia, Bat went on to Chicago, Cheyenne, and other frontier towns to buck the faro banks or sit in on big poker games. In the fall of 1900 he and Emma returned to Denver where he sold his interest in the Olympic Club to a gambler named Joe Gavin. A *Denver Times* reporter caught up with Bat and in an interview Bat denounced the town he had once admired. Denver was now "the worst in the country. . . . The bootblacks in Chicago have more sporting blood in their veins than the whole push of Denver sports."

However, Bat and Emma were back in Denver two years later. Bat took his voting privilege seriously and never failed to vote in a local, state, or national election. In the spring of 1902 he was challenged at a voting booth by a poll watcher, a young woman. As Bat told the story many years later, he protested that he had been voting at the same spot for years. The young woman answered with a blow with her umbrella. It was then, Bat insisted, that he decided he would never again return to Denver.

But William MacLeod Raine, the western novelist and historian who knew Bat in Denver, published another version of why Bat left the city. In his *Guns of the Frontier*, published forty years ago, Raine claimed he obtained this story from an unpublished manuscript about the incident written by Harry Lindsley, then the district attorney of Denver.

During his last trip to Denver, Lindsley wrote, Bat went on what Calamity Jane always called "a high lonesome," a prolonged drinking binge. Bat, never a hard drinker, began visiting saloons and drinking heavily from morning until night and insulting anyone who did not accept his opinion of Denver.

Word finally reached Lindsley, who feared there would be gunplay if Bat continued drinking. He went to see Hamilton Armstrong, Denver's chief of police, who confirmed what Lindsley had heard about Bat's drinking and conduct in the saloons. Armstrong told the district attorney, "I should have Bat arrested but he's sore as a boil and won't stand for it without a fight. I hate to give the job to any of my boys because two or three of them are likely to get killed."

At that moment the telephone rang, it was a long-distance call from Jim Marshall, sheriff of Cripple Creek and a friend of Masterson since their "buffalo days."

Armstrong suggested to Lindsley that they ask Marshall to get Bat out of town. Marshall was reluctant but "was under obligation to Armstrong and since someone had to arrest Bat he thought he had better do the job."

Marshall arrived in Denver and got the drop on Bat as he raised a glass in a saloon. Marshall gently suggested he had worn out his welcome in Denver and should be on "the four o'clock Burlington" when it pulled out from the depot. Bat left that afternoon, jauntily swinging the gold-headed cane he had used on Otto Floto and giving a thin good-bye smile to the two detectives who had arrived at the depot to make sure Bat caught the train.

Bat never forgave Denver. "I don't want to hear about that burg," he would growl to anyone who mentioned the city. "The hell with Denver."

After a brief visit to Chicago, Bat and Emma arrived in New York in May 1902, but Manhattan's reception was anything but warm and friendly for a living legend of the Wild West. Bat had been in town only a few days when he was arrested by a police captain and charged with grand larceny.

As the captain explained in the West Forty-seventh Street precinct, Masterson had been identified by George H. Snow, an elder of the Mormon Church, as one of the men who had defrauded him of $16,000 in a faro game on an eastbound train.

Bat was stunned. He had never seen Snow and had not been on the train. In a face-to-face confrontation in the precinct, Snow, son of the president of the Mormon Church, hedged on his identification of Bat as one of the crooked gamblers. Bat, "white with anger," denounced the New York police in an interview with a *New York World* reporter," describing the arresting detective as a "mush head." When he demanded that Snow explain why he had him arrested, Snow told Bat, "I don't know you at all, sir." According to the reporter, Bat snapped, "Well, you ought to know me, you've caused my arrest."

A delegation of well-known New Yorkers rushed to the precinct when they heard Bat had been arrested. George Considine, manager of the Metropole Hotel, one of the best known in the city, and Tom O'Rourke, the Fitzsimmons-Maher Bout purse holder, persuaded the precinct's commander to set station-house bail for Bat at $500. The *World* reported "the sporting crowd" quickly put up the bail and Bat was freed.

Three days later Snow's charges were dismissed in the Tombs' magistrate court but the police still charged Bat with carrying a concealed weapon.

Bat protested he had carried a six-shooter all of his life and he needed the weapon to protect the large sums of money he carried when he managed gambling concessions. The magistrate listened patiently but still found Bat guilty and fined him $10. To Bat's indignation, the police refused to return his gun. Bat stormed out of the courthouse fuming, vowing he'd had enough of New York and would return to the West where a man could defend himself against false charges.

However, Masterson stayed on and became an important part of Manhattan's night life of the early 1900s. He loved the vitality of Broadway during that lusty period. He became well known in Longacre Square—Times Square—a stocky man with a graying moustache, flinty eyes, embroidered vest, highly polished boots, and a gold-headed cane. When Emma joined him they rented an apartment at 300 West Forty-ninth Street, where they lived for many years. Bat at last had found roots and, as he boasted to his friends, he never missed having lunch with Emma.

The President and the Gunfighter

Theodore Roosevelt never forgot the West. From the first brisk October morning in 1883 when he entered the new frontier town of Little Missouri— "Little Misery" to the natives—until his days as a cattleman in the Dakota Territory, Roosevelt had been an enthusiastic westerner.

He had a special love for the land. The vast empty prairie, the silent brooding buttes, the craggy immensity of the Dakota Badlands—"Hell with the fires out," as General Alfred Sully, the famous Indian fighter, called them—had helped him to accept, if not understand, the tragic, almost simultaneous deaths of his mother and young wife.

His valued friends were cowboys, hunters, sheriffs, ranchers, painters, and writers of the Old West. But incredibly, the favorite of the twenty-sixth president of the United States was a gunfighter, killer, gambler, saloon and dance-hall owner, fight promoter, and New York sports columnist—Bat Masterson.

Their friendship lasted for years, with Bat always a welcome guest at the White House. As president, Roosevelt appointed Bat U.S. deputy marshal in New York, and Bat reciprocated with political opinions based on his contacts with western leaders, warnings of unrest or dissatisfaction in TR's Progressive party, and introductions to sporting figures he knew Roosevelt admired. Both men respected each other. Bat never took advantage of his friendship with one of the most popular figures of his time.[38]

They made an odd couple in history. In the oval office of the White House, Roosevelt listened, enchanted, to the stories Bat told of the Wild West. There was the thrilling Battle of Adobe Walls, and Dodge City, when the herds came in and wild Texans tried to take over the town. There were also tall tales of the Earps and how they had faced down the Clantons and McLaurys in the street fight of the O. K. Corral. And of course Bat made his friend Ben Thompson, the most dangerous man on the frontier, come alive when he spun the tale of how Ben's drunken brother killed Sheriff Whitney. This led to the story of how Bat had rescued Ben's brother Billy from the outraged citizens of Ogallala, Nebraska, who had a noose ready for Billy when he recovered from his wounds.

The affairs of state stopped when Bat began his storytelling. Roosevelt never stopped him. The *New York Times* reported that the president of the United States kept an important foreign visitor waiting until Bat finished a story of his experiences in the Wild West.

Roosevelt, in turn, spun his own tales. He undoubtedly told Bat how he headed a posse to capture a band of horse thieves and had photographs he took to prove it. Or how his neighbor in the Dakota Territory, the incredible Marquis de Mores, had bushwhacked three frontiersmen who threatened to kill him.

Roosevelt may have met Masterson through Bat's old friends the Lewis brothers. Alfred Henry, or "Hank" as he was called, was now a well-known writer and editor of *Human Life*, a popular magazine of its time.

In 1903 Hank Lewis wrote a fictionized biography of Bat.[39] Surely the former cow-town sheriff cringed at some of the characters, among them a "sister" of Billy Dixon who Lewis pictured as a Boston society girl. Ruth, her empty-headed fictional sister, was wooed by a hand-kissing French count. In the book Lewis described Bat as "bronzed of brow, cool of eye, alert, indomitable." Ruth, the novel's heroine, always called Bat, "Mr. Masterson." Their romance took place at Adobe Walls with Quana Parker's Indian army about to attack.

But Lewis had Ruth finally realizing the Wild West was not for her and she returned to Boston with her count, leaving Bat, Billy, and the other brave souls at Adobe Walls to fight off the charging Indians. Somewhere in this horrible novel, the homicidal Billy Thompson emerged as Bat's friend and adviser. Unfortunately there is no extant comment from Bat on Lewis's literary effort.

Lewis's brother, William, editor of the raffish *New York Morning Telegraph*, gave Bat a job in the paper's editorial department. Bat immediately took to the paper's very informal city room where copyreaders on the horseshoe shaped desk played poker in between writing the paper's headlines. Heywood Broun recalled there were always chorus girls sitting on desks waiting for their reporter boyfriends, while press agents, actors, gamblers, or policemen wandered in and out of the city room or joined the never-ending poker game.

Bat first joined the general assignment staff covering the regular run of the news. In 1906 he was assigned to the famous Chester Gillette murder trial, the case which inspired Theodore Dreiser to write his classic *An American Tragedy* and gave him his first popular recognition. When the novel was dramatized in 1925 it became one of the most sensational hits in New York's theatrical history.

Bat was convinced that Gillette was not guilty of murdering his pregnant girl friend. His inflammatory stories denouncing the prosecution led to his arrest, along with Lewis and Henry Cary, the *Telegraph*'s publisher. The trio was charged with contempt of court and, after a hearing in Utica, Bat and Cary were found guilty and fined $50 each. Lewis, who was ill, escaped the hearing and the fine.

A year later Roosevelt offered Bat the post of U.S. Marshal of Oklahoma Territory. Bat refused, pointing out to the president he had hung up his guns for good and had no desire to be forced to kill some drunken young fool who wanted a reputation as the gunfighter who killed Bat Masterson.

On another occasion Roosevelt invited Bat to attend a presidential reception for army and navy admirals and generals. Bat refused on the grounds that surely he would be out of place among such glittering heroes. Teddy insisted, and at last Bat consented to attend the reception.

Masthead and excerpts from the magazine *Human Life,* edited by Alfred Henry Lewis, a close friend of Bat Masterson. Lewis, a popular novelist of his time and noted for his "Wolfville stories," persuaded the former Dodge City sheriff to write a series of articles for *Human Life* on the famous gunfighters he had known. In 1907 Masterson wrote about Bill Tilghman, Luke Short, Doc Holliday, Ben Thompson, Wyatt Earp, and Buffalo Bill. *The James D. Horan Collection*

50 Cents a Year   July, 1907   Five Cents a Copy

Human Life

THE MAGAZINE ABOUT PEOPLE
EDITED BY ALFRED HENRY LEWIS

Human Life for July, 1907   11

Famous Gun Fighters of the Western Frontier

Fifth Article. "Billy" Tilghman

By W. B. (Bat) MASTERSON

NOTWITHSTANDING the discovery of gold in California in 1849, and at Pike's Peak, Colorado, ten years later, the civilizing of the West did not really commence until after the close of the Civil War. It was during the decade immediately following the ending of the conflict between the North and South that civilization west of the Missouri River first began to assume substantial form.

It was during this period that three great transcontinental lines of railroads were built, all of them starting at some point on the West Bank of the Missouri River. The Union Pacific from Omaha to Ogden, Utah, was completed during these years, also the Kansas Pacific, from Kansas City to Denver, Colorado, and the Atchison, Topeka and Santa Fé from Atchinson, Kansas, to Pueblo, Colorado. In twenty years from the day the first railroad tie was laid on the roadbed of the Union Pacific at Omaha, our Western frontier had almost entirely disappeared. There has been no frontier in this country for a good many years. The railroads long ago did away with all there ever was of it. Railroad trains, with their Pullman car and dining-car connections, have been reaching almost every point in the West of any consequence for the last twenty years.

On what was once known as our great American plains, which, a generation ago, furnished a habitat for the wild Indian, the buffalo, the deer and the

EDITOR'S NOTE.—Mr. Masterson's previous articles, on Ben Thompson, Wyatt Earp. Luke Short, and "Doc" Holliday appeared in the January, February, April and May issues. He will, from month to month, tell the stories of other western characters, once famous among the hard-riding, quick-shooting chivalry of the plains.
Mr. Masterson himself has witnessed stirring times, and stood for years a central and commanding figure in a dangerous day that has gone. He has been buffalo hunter, Indian trader, and scout for Miles under the great Ben Clarke—in the Indian war of 1874. Later, Mr. Masterson was elected sheriff of Ford County, Kansas, with headquarters at Dodge City. Dodge then was reckoned the roughest camp on the border. That day is now past and Mr. Masterson is no longer a queller of "bad men," but a resident of New York and a contributor to the press. Also he is a warm personal friend to President Roosevelt, who caused him to be named a Deputy U. S. Marshal for the southern district of New York.

The Indian, besides destroying the hunter's buffalo hides and carrying away his provisions and blankets while he was temporarily away attending to the day's hunting on the range, was often known to have added murder to his numerous other crimes, so that an Indian off his Reservation got to be viewed with apprehension by the hunters. It was a well understood thing among the buffalo hunters whose camps were located close to the Reservation line, that any time a hunter could be taken unawares by the Indians he was almost sure to be killed, if for no other reason than to secure his gun and belt of cartridges the Indians had, in prowling around the country one day, come upon Billy Tilghman's camp and, after cutting up what hides he had staked out on the ground

"We will move away from here," said Billy Tilghman in his characteristically deliberate manner, "after I get even with those red thieves for the damage they have done us."

Billy Tilghman, although a mere boy at the time, was the master-mind of that camp, and what he said was law.

"Ed," said Billy to one of the partners, "go and hitch up the team and drive to Griffin's Ranch and get a sack of flour, some coffee and sugar and a sack of grain for the horses and get back here before daylight in the morning, and Henry and I will unload those hides and peg them out to dry. Don't forget to feed the team when you get there and let them rest up for an hour or two, as you will have plenty of time to do that and get back here by daybreak."

Griffin's Ranch was fifteen miles north of Tilghman's camp on the Medicine Lodge River and the only place nearer than Wichita, which was one hundred and fifty miles farther east, where hunting supplies and provisions could be obtained.

Ed was soon on his way to Griffin's Ranch, which only took about three hours to reach. While Tilghman and Henry were busily engaged in fleshing and staking out the green hides, Billy remarked that if those thieving Cheyennes came again around his camp for the purpose of destroying things, there would likely be a big pow-wow take place among the Indians as

Famous Gun Fighters of the Western Frontier

Third Article. Luke Short

By W. B. (Bat) MASTERSON

THE subject of this narrative might have "died with his boots on," for he had many chances—but he didn't. The fact that he lived to die in bed, with his boots removed, as all good folk like to do when the end has come, may have been due to good luck, but I hardly think so. That he was the quickest at the critical moment is, perhaps, the best answer.

When the time came for Luke Short to pass out of this life—to render up the ghost as it were—he was able to lie down in bed in a home that was his own, surrounded by wife and friends, and peacefully await the coming of the end.

There was nothing in his wan and drawn features, as he lay on that last bed of sickness at Fort Worth, Texas, to indicate that luck had ever been his friend. He was aware that his time had come, and was reconciled to his fate. Every lineament in that cold, stern face, upon which death had already left its impress, showed almost be heard to say: "Death! You skulking coward! I know you are near; I also realize I cannot defeat you; but, if you will only make yourself visible for one brief moment, I will try!"

That he was willing to try, no matter how great the odds might be against him, was the one trait in his character that was ever conspicuously present.

Was Known as a "White Indian"

Luke was a little fellow, so to speak, about five feet, six inches in height, and weighing in the neigh-

EDITOR'S NOTE.—Mr. Masterson's previous articles, on Ben Thompson and Wyatt Earp, appeared in the January and February issues. He will, from month to month, tell the stories of other western characters, once famous among the hard-riding, quick-shooting chivalry of the plains.

Mr. Masterson himself has witnessed stirring times, and stood for years a central and commanding figure in a dangerous day that has gone. He has been buffalo hunter, Indian trader, and scout for Miles under the great Ben Clarke—in the Indian war of 1874. Later, Mr. Masterson was elected sheriff of Ford County, Kansas, with headquarters at Dodge City. Dodge then was reckoned the roughest camp on the border. That day is now past and Mr. Masterson is no longer a queller of "bad men," but a resident of New York and a contributor to the press. Also he is a warm personal friend to President Roosevelt, who caused him to be named a Deputy United States Marshal for the southern district of New York.

among the noble red men of the Sioux reservation.

The military commander at Omaha soon had a company of United States cavalry after Short, and, as he had no notice of such a move being made against him, he was soon a prisoner in the hands of the government authorities. He was alone in his little dugout, cooking his dinner, when the soldiers arrived. He was told that he was a prisoner, by order of the government, for having unlawfully traded whiskey to the Indians.

"Is that all, gentlemen?" said Luke, as he invited the officer in command of the soldiers to sit down and have a bite to eat with him.

"There will be no time for eating," said the officer, "as we must reach Sidney by tomorrow morning, in time to catch the Overland train for Omaha. So get together what things you care to take along,

less little adventurer, who really did not seem capable, even if so disposed, of committing a crime of any sort; and for this reason did not have him either handcuffed or shackled, after placing him aboard the train for Omaha.

Sidney, Nebraska, was a very small place in those days. The permanent population in all probability did not exceed the thousand mark. Sidney, following the custom of all small hamlets, however, would turn out when there was anything unusual going on. And the sight of a company of United States soldiers lined up at the railroad station was enough to arouse her curiosity and cause her townsfolk to turn out in a body and investigate the cause. Luke Short's partner was among those who came to see the big show at the depot, and his surprise can well be imagined when he discovered that no less a person than his partner was responsible for the big event. It did not take Luke and his partner long to fix up a code of signals by which they could communicate with each other. Luke could say a few things in the Indian language that his partner could understand, and to which he could make comprehensible reply.

Short Escapes from the Soldiers

"Skidoo" and "Twenty-three" were terms familiar to Short, even in those days. But they were conveyed by the sign language instead of being spoken as now.

Luke made his partner understand that he would soon be back in Sidney, and to have everything in

Before daylight the following morning, Ed was back in camp, having carried out his instructions to the letter. After breakfast that morning, Tilghman informed Ed and Henry that they would have to hunt without him that day, as he intended to conceal himself nearby the camp, so as to be in a position to extend a cordial welcome to the pillaging red-skins when they showed up. Billy, as a precaution, planted himself before the other boys left for the hunting ground, so that in case the camp was being watched by the Indians, they could not tell but what they had all left camp as they had done the previous day. About noon, and just as Billy was commencing to despair, one lone Indian made his appearance. He rode up very leisurely to the top of a little knoll where he could get a good view of the camp, and, after a careful survey of the surroundings, and discovering nothing to cause alarm, proceeded to make the usual Indian signals, which is done by circling the pony around in different ways. Tilghman, who was crouched down in his little caché, was intently watching the Indian, understanding as well as the red-skin did, the meaning of the pony's gyrations. Directly six other Indians rode up alongside of the first and proceeded to carefully make a mental note of everything in sight.

They soon concluded that there was no lurking danger and all rode down to the camp and dismounted. This was exactly what Billy had been hoping they would finally conclude to do. Now if they will only all dismount, said Billy to himself, as he saw the Indians riding down to camp, I will kill the last one in the outfit before they can remount. He got his wish, for they all hopped off as soon as camp was reached. Billy, however, waited for awhile to see if they intended mischief, before opening up on them with his Sharp's big fifty buffalo gun that burned 120 grains of powder every time it exploded a shell. He did not have long to wait, for no sooner had one big buck hit the ground than he ran over to the sack of flour and picked it up and threw it across his pony's back, while some of the others started out, as Billy supposed, to cut up the freshly staked hides.

The big Indian who had swiped the sack of flour had scarcely turned around before Tilghman dropped him in his tracks with his rifle. This, as might be supposed, caused a panic among the other Indians, who little suspected that there was an enemy nearer than the hunting ground, until they heard the crack of the gun. In an instant Billy had in another cartridge, and another thieving Cheyenne was sent to the happy hunting-ground. The first Indian that succeeded in reaching his pony had no sooner mounted him than he was knocked off by another bullet from

state that, though of small build, it required a 7½ hat to fit his well-shaped, round head. At the time he left his father's ranch in western Texas, where he had been occupied as a cowboy in the middle seventies, for the Red Cloud Agency in North Dakota, he was nothing more than a white Indian. That is, he was an Indian in every respect except color. And, as nearly all of our American Indians living west of the Missouri River in those days were both wild and hostile and on the war path most of the time, a fair idea of Luke Short may be gleaned from this statement. Luke had received none of the advantages of a school in his younger days; he could hardly write his name legibly. It was, indeed, doubtful if he had ever seen a schoolhouse until he reached man's estate. But he could ride a broncho and throw a lariat; he could shoot both fast and straight, and was not afraid.

He had no sooner reached the northern boundary line of Nebraska, hard by the Sioux Indian Reservation, than he established what he was pleased to call a "trading ranch."

His purpose was to trade with the Sioux Indians, whose reservation was just across the line in North Dakota. Instinctively he knew that the Indians loved whiskey, and as even in those days he carried on his shoulders something of a commercial head, he conceived the idea that a gallon of whiskey worth ninety cents was not a bad thing to trade an Indian for a buffalo robe worth ten dollars. Accordingly Luke proceeded to lay in a goodly supply of "Pine Top," the name by which the whiskey traded to the Indians in exchange for their robes was known.

Uncle Sam Objects to His Business

He was not long in building up a lucrative business; nor was it long before the Indian chiefs of the Sioux tribe got on to him. Drunken bands of young bucks were regularly returning to their villages from the direction of the Short rendezvous, loaded to the muzzle with "Pine Top," and, as every drink contained at least two fights and as it usually took about ten drinks to cause an Indian to forget that the Great White Father abode in Washington, the condition of those who had found entertainment at the Short ranch, when they reached their camp, can better be imagined than told.

The Indian agent in charge of this particular branch of the Sioux tribe with whom Short had been dealing soon got busy with Washington. He represented to the Department of the Interior that a band of cutthroat white men, under the leadership of Luke Short, were trading whiskey to his Indians, and that he was powerless to stop it, as the camp of the white men was located just across the reservation line, in the State of Nebraska, which was outside of his jurisdiction. He requested the government to instantly remove the whiskey traders and drive them from the country. Otherwise, said he, an Indian uprising will surely follow. The government, as was to be expected, forthwith instructed the post commander at Omaha to get after the purveyors of the poisonous "Pine Top," who were charged with causing such havoc

Tails, shiny black shoes, a tie, and a starched white shirt were prepared for Masterson. At the last moment he disappeared. A few hours later Roosevelt's secretary brought a telegram to the president. It was from Bat in Baltimore. It read: "I ain't going to attend any reception. Am heading east. Bat Masterson."

In 1907 Hank Lewis persuaded Bat to write a series for his *Human Life* on the famous gunfighters he knew in the Wild West. Over a period of several months Bat's stories of Ben Thompson, Doc Holliday, Wyatt Earp, Luke Short, Bill Tilghman, and even Buffalo Bill, appeared in the magazine accompanied by rare photographs Bat owned.

Legend has Lewis writing the series, but it is evident from the details and the prose Masterson wrote every article. He had a simple, direct style and the vivid details could only have come from a man who had either witnessed or had been a participant in the exciting incidents.

Although Bat's stories were colored by an occasional lapse of memory and his strong tie of friendship, he never covered himself with glory in the series.

Lewis corrected this in an article with a typical Lewis headline: "King of the Gun-Players." It was a fairly factual account of Bat's life on the frontier but with the fictional Clay Allison–Bat Masterson confrontation included. In the article Lewis disclosed that Bat's yearly salary on the *Telegraph* was $10,000.

Lewis finally gave Bat a column and the former gunfighter and cow-town sheriff soon became one of the most popular columnists in the city. His column, which appeared three times a week, was devoted to Bat's first interest, boxing, but he also discussed his friends, Manhattan's night life, politics and politicians, the declining society, and even Chinamen.

"The Chinese, as a race," he wrote, "are said to be the most honest people in the world. But in the name of common sense who would want to be a Chinaman?"

Bat still remembered that Chinamen, like Indians, stood on the last rung of the ladder in frontier society.

During the period Bat was writing his column, his friend Theodore Roosevelt had become one of the most popular presidents in his nation's history. In the 1904 election, a landslide vote returned him to the White House. At the peak of his popularity Roosevelt appointed Bat a U.S. deputy marshal attached to the New York U.S. attorney's office.

Here, in this extraordinary letter delivered to the Delavah Hotel at Broadway and Fortieth Street, owned by Bat's gambling friend, Tom O'Rourke, the president of the United States cautions the former gunfighter, gambler, and frontier sheriff to be always kind, courteous, polite, and efficient.[40]

DEAR BAT:

It was a pleasure to me to get you this appointment as deputy marshal. Now, you have doubtless seen that there has been a great deal of hostile comment on it in the press. I do not care a snap of my fingers for this but I do care very much that you shall not, by any act of yours, justify this criticism. I want you not only to be a vigilant, courteous, and efficient officer, always on hand, always polite to everyone, always ready for any duty that comes up, but I also want you to carry yourself so that no one can find in any action of yours cause for scandal or complaint. You must be careful not to gamble or do anything while you are a public officer which might

A cartoon in the *Kansas City Journal*, February 7, 1905, when President Roosevelt appointed Masterson deputy U.S. marshal in New York. *Courtesy Kansas State Historical Society*

WHEN BAT MASTERSON LANDS IN NEW YORK AS NEW MARSHAL.

"Bat"—"Now, Knick, you be good!"

Bat Masterson when he looked and dressed more like a banker than a columnist on the raffish *New York Telegraph,* a sporting and theatrical newspaper. *Courtesy Kansas State Historical Society*

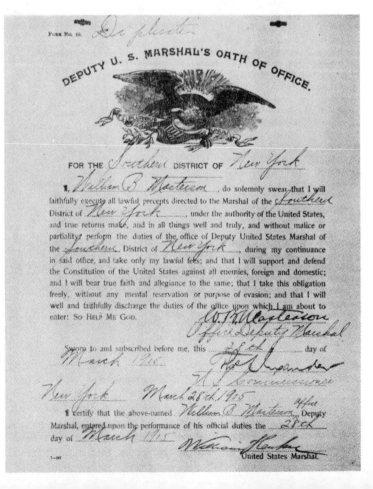

Bat Masterson's oath of office as deputy U.S. marshal, March 1905. *Courtesy National Archives*

afford opportunity to your enemies and my critics to say that your appointment was improper. I wish you would show this letter to Alfred Henry Lewis and go over the matter with him.

Sincerely yours,
Theodore Roosevelt

Earlier in December Masterson had written a confidential letter to Roosevelt from Washington's Raleigh Hotel ("Absolutely Fireproof, European Plan") advising him that Colorado's Senator Teller would oppose the confirmation of Ben Daniels, a former Dodge City lawman, who had been appointed to a federal post by Roosevelt. Daniels, Bat's friend from "the buffalo days," had charged up San Juan Hill with Teddy's Rough Riders and was a favorite of the president. He had also spent some time in a western penitentiary.

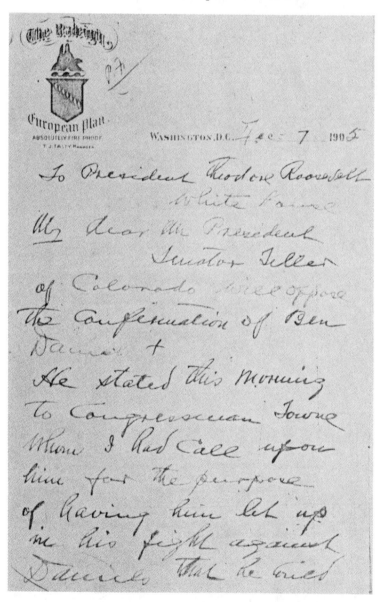

Bat's letter to the president advising him that a senatorial fight was shaping up over Roosevelt's federal appointment of Ben Daniels, a frontier lawman who had spent some time in prison. *Courtesy Library of Congress*

Bat's letter to Roosevelt enclosing a letter written to the *Telegraph* by former Ford County prosecutor, Mike Sutton. Sutton had been in office when Bat was county sheriff. In later years Sutton became a powerful Republican boss of the Southwest. *Courtesy Library of Congress*

OFFICE OF THE
ADVERTISING MANAGER
The Morning Telegraph
LONG ACRE BUILDING
BROADWAY, 43D AND 44TH STREETS
NEW YORK

Dec. 21, 1911.

20.

Col. Theodore Roosevelt,
The Outlook,
New York City.
My dear Mr. Roosevelt:-

I enclose you herewith a page of The Morning Telegraph on which you will find a letter written to me by Judge Sutton of Dodge City, Kansas. Judge Sutton, in my opinion, is one of the best posted men, politically, in the west. He has lived in Kansas since the buffalo days and has always been a consistent and aggressive republican. I think highly of Judge Sutton's opinion.

With best wishes for a Merry Christmas and a Happy New Year, I am,

Sincerely yours,

W. B. Masterson

March 4th 1913.

ear Bat:

    I am much interested in Mr Bernard's letter, but I
ardly like to advise when necessarily I cannot know all
he facts. I wish that Democratic progressives could be
aken in as well as Republicans, and I think it would be
uin for the Progressives to make an alliance with any of
he old gang of the Big Steve and Archie crowd. I wish I
ould answer you more definitely.

                    Faithfully yours,

                    T. Roosevelt

r W. B. Masterson,
    The Morning Telegraph,
        Long Acre Square, New York.

A letter from Roosevelt to Bat Masterson from the
White House. Bernard was the Colorado leader of
the Bull Moose Progressive League and a well-
known western politician. He had asked Bat to act
as his emissary to the former president. *Courtesy
Library of Congress*

Bat Masterson's note to Roosevelt requesting an
appointment for him and Tex Rickard, the famous
fight promoter, to advise the former president on
how to organize his proposed regiment of "outdoor
men" to fight the Germans in World War I. *Courtesy
Library of Congress*

THE MORNING TELEGRAPH
EDITORIAL DEPARTMENT
W B MASTERSON

                                May 14, 1917.

Col. Theodore Roosevelt,
Metropolitan Magazine,
432 Fourth Avenue,
New York City.

My dear Col. Roosevelt:-

    I wish you would arrange for an appoint-
ment with Tex Rickard and myself to meet you
at your office when convenient. We want to
tell you how to organize your European
expedition and how to win your battles when
you get there. You know Tex and I are wonders
in matters of this kind. Anyway, I would like
to have you make a date for us.

    With kindest regards, I am,

            Sincerely yours,

            W B Masterson

The former president's reply asking Bat to meet
with him and Rickard. *Courtesy Library of Congress*

                    May 15th, 1917.

ear Mr. Masterson:

        With reference to your letter of May
4th, will you call at the Metropolitan Magazine
ffice, with Mr. Rickard at about 12 o'clock noon,
aturday next, May 19th?

                    Sincerely yours,

r. W. B. Masterson,
he Morning Telegraph,
ew York.

Bat told the president that Teller's excuse was "pressure from his Colorado constituents." However, he pointed out to Roosevelt: "In view of other remarks made by the senator this morning I am disposed to believe that it is not so much his Colorado constituency that is bothering him as it is a desire on his part to take a slap at the President of the United States who he claims incorporated some good Sunday School doctrine in his message while he was appointing ex-convicts to the important federal positions."

Bat also disclosed to Roosevelt he had spoken to his friend Congressman Towne, and "I think Mr. Towne will take the snide statesman from the Rockies in hand again and may succeed in inducing him to say as little as he can against Ben."

He continued: "I imagine Ben is not anxious to have that penitentiary matter exploited again in the press as well as in executive session."[41]

What the letter reveals is that Masterson had used his influence with a friendly congressman to muzzle a Colorado senator's opposition to a presidential appointment. After all, Washington politics were not very far from the rough and tumble political wars of Dodge City, Tombstone, and Denver.

Bat held the $2,000-a-year job for four years. When Roosevelt refused to run for a third term, Taft won the White House. In April 1908 Charles DeWoody, a Department of Justice "examiner," turned Bat's name in to the newly appointed United States attorney for the Southern District, Henry A. Wise, along with others who were to be fired from their political patronage jobs.

Wise advised the attorney general he had no need for Bat's "services" and he suggested Bat be let go. In turn, the attorney general notified President Taft on June 23 that Masterson's $2,000 salary was higher than that received by any of the other deputies except two. Taft replied on June 29, ordering Masterson discharged.

Bat asked U.S. Marshal William Hinkel to intercede for him in Washington. In July Hinkel reminded the attorney general that Bat had been appointed by Roosevelt, but hastily added, undoubtedly trying to keep his own job, he could take over Bat's trivial duties as an escort and guard for federal grand juries.

Bat then turned to Hank Lewis, who wrote a strong recommendation to Taft, who turned the letter over to the attorney general without comment. Traditionally, all United States attorneys' offices were swept clean when a new administration took over Washington, and Bat's case was no exception. On July 12, 1909, J. J. Glover, chief, Division of Accounts, recommended to the attorney general that Bat be severed from the federal payroll.[42]

Bat finally turned to Roosevelt, suggesting that if the U.S. attorney's office in New York didn't need him perhaps he could get an appointment as a deputy in the federal prosecutor's office in New Mexico.

In the summer of 1908 Roosevelt disclosed to Bat that Hinkel would be reappointed as marshal, then cautiously referring to Bat's suggestion, he wrote: "The Mexican matter stands on another footing. I do not know when the term of the present incumbent expires. However, I am not quite sure as to how New Mexico would feel as to having an outsider appointed. This is something I will have to consider."[43]

Roosevelt apparently "considered" and turned Bat down.

Instead of New Mexico, where the guns of Billy the Kid could still faintly be heard, Bat remained in cosmopolitan midtown Manhattan where the thugs in Hell's Kitchen stepped aside when he passed. He continued to write his daily column, covering important fights and attending the nightly gatherings in the various saloons and restaurants along Longacre Square. His friends were fast-talking fight promoters, drifters, gamblers, writers, press agents, actors, and his fellow newspapermen. But he never lost contact with the former president.

The year 1911 was a busy one for Masterson. In a series of columns he exposed the attempts of Frank Ufer, a western coal and oil man, to build up Carl Morris, an Oklahoma railroad engineer, as the only "white hope" to defeat Jack Johnson, the black heavyweight champion.

Bat bluntly described Morris as "a big lumbering slob." Ufer then held a press conference and told the gathering of reporters that Bat had made his reputation as a western gunfighter "by shooting Mexicans and Indians in the back."

A livid Masterson immediately filed suit for slander against Ufer and the *New York Globe*. By the time the trial came to court two years later, Morris had been beaten so badly he had returned to operating a locomotive in Oklahoma.

Bat's witnesses in New York Supreme Court virtually composed a living history of the frontier West. Indian scouts, former cow-town sheriffs, gunfighters, and cavalry officers from the Indian Fighting Army testified to Bat's courage, integrity, dedication to the law, and his skill with a gun. The court decided Masterson had been slandered and awarded him $3,000 in damages.[44]

During Christmas week, 1911, when Roosevelt was on the verge of announcing his candidacy for a third presidential term, Bat sent him a copy of a long letter written to him by Mike Sutton of Dodge City on the midwestern political climate.

Bat wrote to Roosevelt: "Judge Sutton, in my opinion, is one of the best posted men, politically, in the West. He has lived in Kansas since the buffalo days and has always been a consistent and aggressive Republican. I think highly of Judge Sutton's opinions."[45]

Bat knew Roosevelt would eagerly seek out Sutton's opinion. For years the Dodge City attorney, a veteran Republican, had been the political boss of the Southwest, and as Bob Wright put it in his autobiography, "had the great Southwest in his vest pocket."

Sutton had hung up his shingle in Dodge City in 1878 when it was still what the *Washington Star* called "the wicked little town in the West."[46] With Wright's support, Sutton was elected county prosecutor. He and Masterson, then sheriff, became close friends. Wright recalled "their motto was not Scare 'em and Catch 'em but Catch 'em and Convict 'em."

In 1883 Sutton and Bat became enemies when Bat, Wyatt Earp, and a group of gunfighters arrived in Dodge to help Luke Short, who was then being harassed by Sutton in his drive against gamblers. But as the years passed, the feud cooled and they resumed their friendship. Sutton became a judge, then one of the state's leading attorneys, and finally a powerful southwestern political leader.

Bat received a fast reply from Roosevelt. The former president called Sutton's letter "interesting" and asked Masterson to see him, presumably about Sutton.[47]

In June, on the eve of the Republican convention in Chicago, Bat requested Roosevelt grant him "a few moments time." He wrote: "It seems to me that the only place in which you have not slugged the bosses over the ropes is right here in New York, but you'll get to them in time and when I see them taking the count, maybe I won't laugh."[48]

Roosevelt's secretary promptly replied, telling Bat to come that afternoon to the office of *Outlook,* the popular magazine which listed Roosevelt as a contributing editor.[49]

The former president won in the Republican primaries but when denied the nomination in the Taft-controlled convention, he and his followers bolted to form the Bull Moose party.

In the summer of the tumultuous campaign Masterson wrote Roosevelt asking for a meeting "to consider a matter of more or less importance in connection with the Progressive campaign this fall." Once again he received an immediate appointment. It is not known what "matter" the former gunfighter wanted to discuss with the presidential candidate.[50]

Roosevelt survived an assassination attempt to run second in the three-way race that was easily won by Woodrow Wilson, the Democratic candidate.

In 1913 Roosevelt was preparing for the first of his expeditions into the Brazilian jungle. Before he left, Bat wrote to him at the *Outlook* office on Fourth Avenue, enclosing a letter sent to him by Franklin Bernard, one of Roosevelt's strongest supporters in Colorado.

From Denver, Bernard disclosed there was "a great deal of dissatisfaction among all Republicans in the West, progressive and otherwise, who have one view in mind and that is the defeat of the Democratic Party and at the same time are trying to get away from the machine methods."

Bernard wrote that he had been asked by a number of Bull Moose leaders and Roosevelt supporters to contact Bat so he could "communicate with the colonel and to present to him the exact conditions here."

Bernard and the other members of the Bull Moose League wanted to alert Roosevelt that "organizations of clubs" would clash with the objectives of the league "because they are simply formed in the interest of political aspirants and we all know that if harmony does not exist in our ranks we can't very well succeed."

Bernard asked Bat to intercede with Roosevelt as leader of the Bull Moose League to make the "Progressive League be the Authority through, from, and by which all things in the conduct of our campaign for the success of our party be done."

Bernard concluded with the hope that Bat could convince Roosevelt "the persons who present plans and suggests [sic] are prompted only by a desire to succeed in party efforts, with no dark alleys attached . . . and if you will hand the enclosed to the Colonel and go over the same with him."[51]

Once again Masterson received a quick reply. Roosevelt wrote that while he had found Bernard's letter interesting and informative he hesitated to advise the western Bull Moose leaders because he did not "know all the facts." However, he asked Bat to send on his wish to Bernard that Democratic Progressives could be taken into the Bull Moose party "as well as Republicans, and I think it would be ruin for the Progressives to make an alliance with any of the old gang."

In September, Bernard wrote again to Bat, who advised Roosevelt just before he left for South America that Bernard was "having trouble in keeping the politicians and office seekers of the Progressive Party in Colorado, in line."

He praised Bernard as a "sincere and conscientious worker for the Progressive Party and knowing the character of the general run of Colorado politicians as I do, I can well imagine the trouble Mr. Bernard is having in holding the Progressives together."

Mr. Bernard, he suggested, wanted Roosevelt "to lay the law down for the Colorado Progressives."[52]

The following morning Roosevelt's reply was delivered to Bat's office at the *Morning Telegraph*, advising him he did not want to "lay down the law anywhere at present" but would "take the matter up with the heads of the Progressive Service." He then told Bat he was about to leave for South America but would "get in touch with you on my return."[53]

In June 1914, when Roosevelt returned from Brazil, Masterson asked to see him at the *Outlook* office and his request was granted immediately. In July he dropped by Roosevelt's office but didn't see him because the former president was "quite busy with personal affairs." On July 6 he wrote asking for an appointment to see Teddy at the headquarters of the Progressive League "in the Forty-Second Street building." This meeting was to introduce "Captain Donnelly of Nevada, a western pioneer and excellent citizen" who had met Roosevelt during his western campaign swing "and would be delighted to renew the acquaintance."[54]

Bat was told by "Mr. Grant," Roosevelt's secretary, to bring along Donnelly. It is assumed the "western pioneer and excellent citizen" renewed his "acquaintance" with Roosevelt under Masterson's beaming approval.[55]

There is a three-year gap in the exchange of letters between Bat and Roosevelt. Based on their past relationship there is little doubt they were regularly seeing each other.

In April 1917 when Roosevelt returned from South America, Bat was on hand to welcome him home. Apparently he had forwarded a letter from a "Mr. Price" asking Bat to help get his son a position in the Progressive party. Roosevelt asked Bat to inform Price "I have his letter at hand, I will bear his son in mind and will put the letter before my headquarters 'people.'"[56]

August 1917 saw the outbreak of World War I, which Roosevelt had foreseen. He distrusted the German emperor, whose imperialistic attitude had given him many anxious hours during his presidency. He saw earlier than other leaders in Washington that the United States could not remain untouched by the spreading conflict. His country, he said, could see France, Great Britain, and their allies win, but could not afford to let Germany score an armed peace.

The sinking of the *Lusitania* led Roosevelt to launch a furious attack on the Wilson administration. Once more Roosevelt appealed to the American public and stirred it as he had never done before. His bitterest enemies now joined him. He was put forward as a candidate for the Republican nomination for president, but this time he refused the nomination of the Progressive party.

When the United States entered the war in April 1917, Roosevelt offered to raise a division of westerners and other "outdoor men" who would be shipped overseas immediately.

Bat, now graying and paunchy, had seen his share of wounded and dying men and had no desire to become a member of Roosevelt's army of "outdoor men" to fight tanks, flamethrowers, and howitzers. But he was still ready with advice.

In May 1917, with more than 250,000 volunteers answering the colonel's call, Masterson wrote an astonishing letter to Roosevelt. He suggested that Roosevelt, the most popular man in the nation, and undoubtedly his party's next presidential candidate, sit down with him and Tex Rickard, a western fight promoter, so they could advise him "how to organize your European Expedition and how to win the battles when you get over there. You know Tex and I are wonders in matters of this kind."[57]

Just as astonishing was Roosevelt's reply the next day inviting Bat and Rickard to meet him at the office of the *Metropolitan* in midtown Manhattan.[58]

What a superb photograph it would have made: the former president of the United States—and possibly the next one—preparing to lead a huge army of volunteers in the most horrible war that the world had ever seen, conferring with a onetime Wild West gunslinger and the colorful, conniving promoter of Jack Dempsey. Apparently no photographer was at hand.

One can only guess at the suggestions Bat gave to Roosevelt. The battle tactics of the buffalo hunters at Adobe Walls? The logistics of waging a war against an Indian army armed with bows, arrows, and Winchesters?

Whatever their advice to Roosevelt, it was unnecessary. Although Congress passed a bill authorizing the creation of two divisions under Roosevelt, the president refused to give his consent.

"This is an exclusive war," Roosevelt said bitterly, "and I have been black-balled by the committee on admissions."

Roosevelt continued to press for speed in military preparations, especially in his *Kansas City Star* and *Metropolitan* magazine articles. But then the fever he had contracted in the Brazilian jungles returned, and in February he was dangerously ill. When he recovered, he returned to his writing and speech-making tours. In their hour of grief, bewilderment, fear, and dread of the future, his countrymen turned to him with deeper affection than at any other time in his long public career.[59]

And always in the shadows was his friend, the aging, flinty-eyed man who represented the mythical frontier West Roosevelt loved so dearly.

Roosevelt died on January 6, 1919, when he could have again won the presidency. No one wept more than his friend Bat Masterson.

The Last Years

Bat spent his declining years in New York City. His routine seldom varied: he had breakfast with Emma, walked down Eighth Avenue to the *Telegraph* office, wrote his column, and spent the afternoon at the various midtown gyms talking to promoters, managers, looking over the latest contenders, interviewing a sports figure or making his selections at the Belmont track. He never failed to have lunch with Emma.

In 1921 Bat was a sixty-seven-year-old gray-haired man, a celebrity on

Your Uncle Bat never believed in life insurance he was very peculiar in some ways so he never was insured he has had Diabetes for over three years had to diet couldent eat any vegitables that grew under the ground had to eat a bread called gluten bread we bought at a bakery and no sweets at all and his feet were so cold every winter since he has had it he wore wollen stockings in bed at nights; He was sick two weeks before he died in bed with cold on his lungs but got better but couldent seem to get his strength back but no one could keep him from going out over to his office to write and told them all over to the office just 15 minutes before he died he felt lots better they were all so shocked over it they immediatelt come and tell me they sent around side soon to me I was waiting lunch for him 12 oclock he was just one block away from where we lived, I dont know what I will do yet when I get straightened out for I am quite an invalid I have Asthma all the time but not bad and have spells ever since I have had the change of life I am 66 years old and hope I will die soon to be with him if I am left—

Emma Masterson's letter to her niece written a month after Bat's death. In it she told how Bat, "peculiar in some ways," had refused to become insured. She also told how Bat suffered with diabetes in his last years and wore woolen stockings to bed. She ended with the hope that she would "soon die and be with him." Emma, who lived alone in New York City, was found dead in her Hotel Stratford room, July 12, 1932. *Courtesy Kansas State Historical Society*

Pictures of Bat Masterson and his wife Emma, taken shortly before Bat's death, October 25, 1921. *Courtesy Fred M. Mazzulla*

Broadway and in the sporting world. On October 21 he had breakfast with Emma as usual, walked down Eighth Avenue, hung up his coat, and began writing his daily column.

Suddenly he slumped over his typewriter. A few minutes later Sam Taub, his assistant and later a sports announcer, found him dead of a heart attack.[60]

The evening newspapers had his death on page one and the *New York Times* published a long obituary recalling Bat's famous days on the frontier. His close friend Damon Runyan described him as a "100 percent, 22 karat real man . . . one of the most entertaining companions we have ever known. . . . There are only a few men in the world like Bat Masterson and his death is a genuine loss."

As Bat Masterson had always predicted, he died with his boots on.

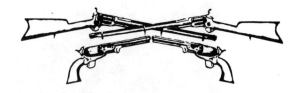

WILLIAM WALLACE

THE COUNTY HALL WAS PACKED WITH ARMED MEN, SOME standing on chairs. For a time there had been chaos, almost a riot, but now in the sudden silence a man shouted a suggestion that the speaker be thrown out. The speaker, a slender, handsome young man grimly eyed the mob from his platform.

"Why don't you come up and try it, sir?" he asked quietly.

When no one accepted his challenge he continued with his speech.

Not many men cared to stand up against William H. Wallace, the courageous, humorless, often prissy prosecutor of Jackson County, Missouri, when it was the nation's "Outlaw State." He was a bantam fighting cock of a man whose whole life was fiercely dedicated to a simple code: "The battle for right is eternal, truth cannot be put to death."[1]

Wallace was the nemesis of Jesse James. Theodore Roosevelt could write that Jesse would always be America's Robin Hood, but to Wallace the man from the dark and lonely ground of Clay County was a common thief and conscienceless killer for all his boasts of carrying a well-read Bible. This was heresy in 1881, when most midwestern frontier lawmen were convinced that no Missouri jury would ever convict Jesse or one of his riders. Wallace proved they were wrong in their estimation of their fellow citizens. With a handful of faithful deputies he broke up the James-Younger gang despite threats, political pressure, official

Counsel for the State.

William Wallace, prosecutor of Jackson County, Missouri, who broke up the James-Younger gang. *The James D. Horan Collection*

corruption, cowardice, incompetence, and perjured witnesses. William Wallace is the unsung hero of the saga of Jesse James.

He brought the fight to the Jameses and Youngers at a time when the outlaw issue had divided the Missouri Democratic party into two factions, one pro-Confederate, the other pro-Union.[2] His party never forgave Wallace for putting Frank James on trial for murder, and denied Wallace a congressional seat and the governor's office.

Many years later he wrote a bitter epitaph to his political career:

"It is a known fact in the history of republics, that he who chooses to espouse the cause of good government received, when attacked, but a scanty defense at the hands of its best citizens.[3]

Wallace was born in Clark County, Kentucky, October 11, 1848, into a family of ministers, scholars, and soldiers. The Scotch-Irish family originally came from Virginia with one of Wallace's ancestors carried in a packsaddle over the Cumberland Mountains into Kentucky. His father, Joseph William Wallace, a graduate of Princeton's Theological College, was the first minister in a long line of frontiersmen and soldiers.

Wallace's great-grandfather, John, was a captain on Washington's staff at Valley Forge, and his grandfather was an Indian fighter along the Kentucky border. His mother, Ann Elizabeth Hockaday of Clark County, was a linguist and Latin scholar. She died when Wallace was a small child. Five years later his father married Jessamine Ryley, a physician's widow, also an educated woman.[4]

When Wallace was eight his family moved to Jackson County, Missouri, not far from Lee's Summit, home of the Youngers, where his father took over a large parish. In 1857 the rolling Missouri prairie was alive with wild geese, prairie chickens, and partridges and, as Wallace recalled, a man could travel from his father's farmhouse to Denver "without passing through a lane."

Wallace's early years were spent working the farm, which boasted cattle, hogs, sheep, and a herd of twenty-three horses. The family strongly supported the Confederacy but remained untouched in the first years of the war. Troops of both sides stopped at the farmhouse, with Wallace feeding the horses of Quantrill's guerillas in the morning and the mounts of the federal patrols in the afternoon.

The war gradually moved closer to the quiet farmhouse on the lonely prairie. One day a troop of Jennison's force sacked the house, stealing blankets, clothing, silverware, saddles, and horses. The bloody battle of Lone Jack, August 1862, was fought nearby with the young farm boy straddling a fence rail listening to the echoes of gunfire as Quantrill's men defeated Federal troops under the command of Major Emory Foster. That night from his bedroom Wallace counted twenty-five farmhouses burning on the open prairie.[5]

On August 21, 1863, Quantrill sacked the city of Lawrence, one of the bloodiest chapters in the terrifying guerilla war. It seemed nothing could stop him. Homes of Union sympathizers were burned, bridges destroyed, communications wrecked. The area was terrorized.

Reverberations finally reached Washington and Brigadier General Thomas C. Ewing in Kansas City was ordered to wipe out Quantrill's guerilla force. Ewing decided that the pro-Southern population of Jackson, Cass, Bates, and half of Vernon counties had to be banished. Four days after the Lawrence raid he issued his famous order number eleven, ordering all residents of those areas to leave their homes within fifteen days. Hay and grain had to be turned over to the quartermasters.

Looting, arson, and violence followed Ewing's order as Federal patrols drove the bewildered farming families from the counties that would soon be known as "the Burnt District."

The Wallaces still had a horse, wagon, and a yoke of oxen. On his father's orders young Wallace drove their neighbors and their few belongings to Independence, the nearest military post. Later he and his father and brothers packed their wagon and left at dawn to the howling and yapping of packs of deserted dogs.

They finally settled in Fulton, where Reverend Wallace obtained a professorship at Westminster College, a small institution barely able to keep its doors open.

The winter of '63 was one of the coldest in Missouri's history. Reverend Wallace sold their horse, wagon, and oxen and the family existed on the few dollars. But when a St. Louis church sent refugees in the area boxes of secondhand clothes, Reverend Wallace politely returned their box with Wallace's mother telling her son, "We still had our pride and would have to shiver in the winter's blast rather than wear them."[6]

The war and banishment gave the farm boy one advantage: as part of his father's small salary he was allowed to attend Latin and Greek classes. After Appomattox, when Reverend Wallace prepared to bring his family back to Jackson County, the local judge who owned the farm they had rented suggested that William remain behind and continue his education at Westminster.

After he graduated, Wallace returned home. The scorched earth of Jackson County was now green again. Farmers were pouring in from other states, the ravished Wallace farm had been rebuilt, and at eighteen William became a teacher in a one-room schoolhouse.

He taught school for a year, then read law at a relative's office in Fulton. He was admitted to the bar and opened a small law office in Kansas City.

One of the biggest attractions on the frontier was a murder trial—especially if it involved a killing over a woman. Farming families for miles around would ride into the county seats, sometimes sleeping in their wagons to be on line early to get seats in the courtroom. The evidence and the rules of law were ignored; they came to hear the prosecutor and defense counsel. Their favorites were those who owned the deep rolling voices of orators and the gestures and dramatic style of actors who could make tears flow or cause the crowded courtroom to rise as one man to cheer a brilliant sally.

In his first murder trial, defending a farmer who had killed his wife's lover, Wallace proved he was a crowd pleaser. Several times during his summation to the jury spectators ignored the furious judge pounding his gavel to cheer the young attorney. Wallace easily won an acquittal and his reputation as a brilliant courtroom performer was established.

During the 1870s when Wallace was engaged as defense counsel in a number of major criminal cases, Missouri was being terrorized by the James-Younger gang. Riders on the Chicago & Alton Railroad refused to pass the Glendale station where the gang had robbed the express car. Bankers insisted capital had stopped coming into the state. Immigration had halted.

For fifteen years the outlaw band had robbed banks, trains, and stagecoaches, but not one of Jesse's riders had ever been arrested, indicted, or jailed. Jesse, his brother Frank, and the Youngers had become a popular symbol of the Lost Cause, the Bonnie Blue Flag, and the South Shall Rise Again. John Newman Edwards, the Missouri newspaper owner, publisher, and writer, the perennial

Left to right: Guerrilla fighters Fletcher Taylor, Frank James, and Jesse James about 1864. *The James D. Horan Collection*

apologist for the gang, had successfully created the image of Jesse and his men as victims of a relentless North that had vowed to kill them all because of their gallant service to the Confederacy.

It was a ridiculous theory. Nearly all the former guerillas had become successful businessmen, politicians, or even lawmen. But a large segment of Missouri's citizens continued to view Jesse as their hero.

Despite the streak of violence that ran deep in Jesse's makeup, he was a charismatic leader and men gladly followed him to the dark depots where their red lantern stopped the trains to be robbed, or swept after him on their horses across the squares of small towns to rob banks and their neighbors' money.

Only a few lawmen had the courage to fight the gang. Informers were quickly murdered. Two Pinkerton detectives, posing as farmhands, who foolishly tried to penetrate Jesse's Clay County, were killed. Another Pinkerton operative was killed in a gun battle with the Youngers. Intimidated businessmen alerted the gang when strangers appeared. A local sheriff tried to arrest Jesse and Frank but the pair shot his mount during the chase.

A paper in Iowa suggested that Missouri be called the "Robber State." The *St. Louis Globe–Democrat* cried editorially, "Poor Old Missouri," and New York's newspapers continuously referred to Missouri as "the Outlaw State."[7]

In 1880 Wallace decided to run for prosecuting attorney of his native Jackson County on a campaign promise to break up the James-Younger gang and put its leader and riders in jail. It was a shocking proposal. No politician had ever spoken out against the gang, except to apologize for them or to try to push amnesty bills through the state legislature.

Wallace's friends warned him he would be ruined politically and financially before he was killed. They pointed out that no informer had appeared in fifteen years to lead lawmen to the hideout of the gang. The outlaws had powerful protectors in Wallace's own party, the Democrats, and no citizen of Missouri would ever be persuaded to testify against Jesse or his men.

The young lawyer was told of the man forced by a grand jury to tell all he knew of a bank robbery committed by the gang. After he had testified he took out a six-shooter, pointed to the notches, and said: "Gentlemen, the notches on this pistol give the number of men I have killed. My life is now in danger and I now desire to say that if anyone is indicted each man on this grand jury can dig his grave."

No one was indicted. The story was probably local folklore but there were still a number of others, all true, attesting to the fear inspired by the gang.

Wallace shrugged off the pleas and fears of his friends. With a gun on his hip he campaigned alone on horseback through the "country sections" of Jackson County, speaking in one-room schoolhouses, halls, saloons, and churches. To the horror of his supporters, he named each member of the gang: its leader, Jesse Woodson James, his brother Frank, and their principal riders, Dick Liddil, Ed Miller, and Bill Ryan. He also listed the banks and trains they had robbed from the gang's first strike at the Liberty, Missouri, bank in 1866 to the Winston, Missouri, train robbery in 1881, during which an unarmed conductor and a passenger were ruthlessly killed.

Wallace ignored the numerous threats that he would be shot down on the speaker's platform; he never failed to appear at a rally. Once he was stopped on a street in Independence by a notorious killer who swore he would kill him if he ever again named his nephew as one of Jesse's men. Wallace not only repeated the charge but also defied the gunman to stop him. Later as prosecutor he accepted the nephew's guilty plea.

Politicians were stunned when the final votes revealed Wallace had been elected. In January 1881 he took office and immediately announced he intended to keep his campaign promise and break up the James gang.

Wallace's simple and effective strategy had been used by prosecutors from the colonial days to Thomas E. Dewey's twentieth-century war against organized crime. Find the weakest link in the chain. That link was Jesse's ruddy-faced rider, Bill Ryan. For years Ryan had used the alias of Tom Hill and under that name had been jailed for minor crimes in between riding with Jesse James. He had served short sentences or won parole, but in those days of no fingerprints, state police communications systems, or computerized rogues' galleries, he had never been identified as Bill Ryan. After the Youngers had been sentenced to life imprisonment in the Minnesota penitentiary for the Northfield raid, Ryan, as Tom Hill, was sent to the same prison. The Youngers stolidly ignored him and a short time later Ryan was paroled and rejoined Jesse's reorganized band.

Ryan's weaknesses were the indiscriminate spending of his stolen gold, whiskey, women, and his firm belief in the newspaper accounts which described him as a notorious badman. One day in 1881 he got drunk in a Tennessee village, drew his guns, and bragged to the crowded saloon he was a well-known desperado. One spectator wasn't impressed and held Ryan in a bear hug until the police relieved Ryan of his guns. A short time later he was extradited to Jackson County, where Wallace shook the state by not only indicting Ryan for taking part in the Glendale robbery of October 7, 1879, but by gathering a group of witnesses, both from Tennessee and Jackson County, who impressed the jury so effectively that they convicted Ryan. The judge accepted Wallace's recommendation and the train robber was sentenced to the state penitentiary for twenty-five years.[8]

Ryan's indictment, trial, conviction, and sentence—Wallace won the appeal too—broke the power of the James gang, and showed that they were vulnerable when an honest, courageous prosecutor was in office.

Wallace's next coup came a short time later when Dick Liddil, Jesse's favorite rider, surrendered to him. Liddil, who knew all the secrets of the gang, talked for endless hours to Wallace.

Wallace organized small posses of expert man hunters and ordered them to bring in Jesse James. There is little doubt that if Bob Ford, that "dirty little coward" of the famous ballad, had not killed his leader a short time later in St. Joseph, Jesse would have eventually been captured and faced Wallace, who had sworn to send him to prison or to the gallows.

In the fall of 1882 Frank James, who was always his own best press agent, dramatically surrendered to Governor Thomas Crittenden in the state house, Jefferson City. The governor ordered the prisoner, who was treated as a celebrity if not a hero by newspapermen and politicians, turned over to Wallace.

A year later James was tried in Gallatin for the murder of Frank McMillan, a young stonemason, during the Winston train robbery in the summer of 1881.

Wallace and Daviess County prosecutor William D. Hamilton worked for a year, carefully putting together the case against James. It was one of the most sensational trials in the history of the western frontier. In return for killing the indictment, powerful politicians offered to support Wallace in a congressional bid. John Newman Edwards, perennial defender of the gang, bluntly told Wallace he would be a congressman if he refused to prosecute the outlaw. Wallace refused the offers and ignored the many threats.

The state's case was strong but circumstantial. None of the passengers could positively identify James as one of the train robbers. However, a string of witnesses, including a blacksmith who had shod the outlaw's mare and a minister who recalled how James had admired his library then "got the best of him" in a discussion of Robert Ingersoll's philosophy and Shakespeare's plays, placed James and another member of the band in the Winston area at the time of the robbery.

In his summation Wallace superbly put together the pieces of the state's case. He thrilled the crowd in the packed Gallatin Opera House, where the trial was held, with his old-fashioned, emotionally filled description of how Jesse James had killed Westfall, the helpless conductor, and then the stonemason.[9]

The press of the day hailed Wallace's closing speech, with the *Kansas City Journal* describing it as "one of remarkable force and power," while the *St. Louis Globe Democrat* called it "the feature of the trial . . . trial judges declare they have never heard its like before for vigor, evenness, power and eloquence."

THE KANSAS CITY STAR. TUESDAY, FEBRUARY 7 1899

RYAN AT STILLWATER.

URE OF THE BANDIT TAKEN
HE WAS IMPRISONED THERE.

Pitcher, Who Knew Him Well,
Identifies It—The Wily Old Han-
Many Aliases—In Jail Here,
Yet None Knew Him.

BILL RYAN, ALIAS HARRY GLENN, ALIAS JOHN MURPHY, ALIAS BILL EVANS, ALIAS BILL JENNINGS.
[From a photograph taken in the Stillwater, Minn., prison in 1896.]

The defense and prosecution staffs in the Frank James murder trial, Gallatin, Missouri, July 1883. *The James D. Horan Collection*

Bill Ryan, "the outlaw with a hundred names." Ryan, one of Jesse's trusted riders, was finally convicted of train robbery by William Wallace and sentenced to a long term in the penitentiary. *The James D. Horan Collection*

But it was wasted effort. As Morrison Munford, owner of the *Kansas City Times* wrote after the jury had been selected: "The composition of the jury is believed to be in favor of acquittal or disagreement and the cuts are in favor of an acquittal." [10]

The jury deliberated only a short time to fulfill Colonel Munford's analysis and acquit Frank James.

The outlaw was then taken into custody by Wallace to be tried for the Blue Cut train robbery. But the state's high court ruled that the testimony of Dick Liddil, a felon, was not permissible in a criminal trial unless he was pardoned. Wallace immediately petitioned Governor Crittenden to pardon Liddil.

Crittenden did not have the inner strength of Wallace. The murder of Jesse James had painted him a villain, even blacker than Wallace, and he realized the powerful pro-Confederate faction of the state's party would probably fight against his nomination for reelection. He refused Wallace's petition.

The Jackson County prosecutor was stunned. Without Liddil he had no case. He bitterly dismissed the Blue Cut robbery indictment against Frank but turned him over to the Alabama prosecutor who wanted James to stand trial for the robbery of the government paymaster at Muscle Shoals. The Alabama trial was only a repeat of Gallatin; the outlaw's one-armed mother was in the courtroom every day and on the streets telling anyone who would listen how her "boys were driven to it." Once again Frank James was romantically pictured as the last remaining Rebel. The jury quickly acquitted him.

When Minnesota requested that James be extradited to be tried for the bloody Northfield raid, a Democratic prosecutor in Missouri quickly announced that he had to try James for the Otterville train robbery. The Republicans scoffed at the idea of trying to find witnesses to the eight-year-old crime. It was, they claimed, a plot by the Democrats to keep their "pet" from being mauled by the Minnesota authorities who claimed they had a good case.

For years, while he was still in office and after he retired to private practice, newspapers and magazines pressed Wallace to write his own account of those tumultuous days. He always refused, until the fall of 1898 when he agreed to tell the whole story to a writer for the *Kansas City World*, probably in appreciation for the paper's support in his congressional race.

The extraordinary account fills thirteen columns. The detailed first person historic story of more than twenty thousand words covers Wallace's fight against the Jameses-Youngers from the period he campaigned for office in the hostile "Cracker Neck" section of Jackson County to the bitter days when he fought political pressure from his own party to finally put James on trial for murder—a trial where guns were checked at the door and Wallace was warned he would never live to hear the verdict.

This is the first time in eighty-two years that Wallace's story has been republished. To retain the flavor of the period, the original grammar, spelling of names, and syntax have been kept. [11]

CHAPTER I
ORIGIN OF THE YOUNGER-JAMES BAND OF OUTLAWS

Immediately preceding the Civil War there existed in the wilds of Kansas a band of cut-throats and plunderers known as the Kansas Jay Hawkers. There was no

HOW THE JESSE JAMES GANG

"There was no chivalry in their conduct as there never has been any in the conduct of any band of outlaws in Kansas or any other country."

WAS WIPED OFF THE EARTH

An Authentic Narrative From the Liberty, Mo., Bank Robbery, Feb. 4, 1866, to the Surrender of Frank James, Oct. 5, 1882.

— BY —

WILLIAM H. WALLACE,

EX-PROSECUTING ATTORNEY.

"With the Exception of a Few Isolated Facts I Have Now and Then Given to a Reporter, Here Is My First Statement From the Time I Was Elected Prosecuting Attorney 18 Years Ago to the Present Time."

WILLIAM H. WALLACE.

The headlines for Wallace's story in the *Missouri World* of how he planned and executed the destruction of the James-Younger gang. *Courtesy State Historical Society of Missouri* chivalry in their conduct as there never has been any in the conduct of any band of outlaws in Kansas or in any other country. There is nothing in the conduct of this or any other band of plunderers to be emulated by the youth of the country, or to excite the admiration of anybody.

It was the custom in those days for freighters to haul goods from Independence, Westport, and other western Missouri towns by ox wagon to Fort Kearney, Denver, Santa Fe and other points in the west. A man named George Quantrell and his brother were engaged as freighters across the plains. They were attacked by this Kansas band of free-booters. George Quantrell's brother was killed and he himself left for dead.

For the purpose of revenge Quantrell, after recovering, joined this band of Kansas Jay Hawkers. He induced three of their number to come with him to Jackson County Missouri to the farm of a rich old man named Morgan Walker, a few miles from where my father's farm was located, for the purpose of stealing money from old man Walker, taking his mules and also taking his negroes to Kansas. This was about the beginning of the war.

Quantrell betrayed these men who were said to be the very men who murdered his brother. When the three went to the house of old man Walker, having been previously apprised of their coming, Walker and his neighbors fired upon them, killing one of them dead in the yard, two of them escaping, one being badly wounded. All search for them was unavailing for several days when, as a negro drove down into the woods with an ox team, he saw one of the Jay Hawkers watching his wounded companion. He immediately raised the alarm. Quantrell, old man Walker and others went at once to the spot. Old man Walker was a splendid shot with a squirrel rifle and could knock a squirrel's head off every time it was set. As the old man approached with his glasses on and his rifle in his hand, the well Jay Hawker ran through the woods and looking back the old man shot him in the forehead killing him dead. Quantrell went up and killed the wounded man. This occurrence actually took place and I have given the details just as I heard them when I was a boy.[12]

The war was now on and Quantrell remained in Jackson County espousing the southern cause. He raised a company of guerrillas in Jackson, Clay, Lafayette and Cass counties, and became thereafter one of the most famous guerrillas in the world's history. I remember his appearance and style of conversation very distinctly. He was said to be a Marylander and was a polished and educated man.

I was too young during these times to be in the army, and was yet old enough to know the country, and on account of my age was in little danger of being molested by the troops on either side. There were several Union men in my father's neighborhood who were very kind to the southern people in the matter of trying to get back property taken by troops from Kansas, and I was sometimes called on for the purpose of identifying property. As the men were often afraid to go into the military posts I frequently accompanied my mother and other ladies to town for the purpose of purchasing goods and groceries. In this way I became a sort of errand boy and saw a great deal of border warfare. I knew many of Quantrell's men and I have a distinct recollection of the appearance and demeanor of old Jennison, Jim Lane, Colonel Pennock, Captain Pardee, Captain Davy and others.[13] I could recall the neighborhood accounts of many fights, assassinations and the like and I distinctly recollect the scenes of burning homes and all that sort of thing out of those terrible days but this would simply burden your column.

Among those in Quantrell's band were Cole Younger and Jesse and Frank James. I recall Cole Younger distinctly. He was a broad shouldered splendid looking fellow and while he became an outlaw and of course a bad man, he was in my opinion the best one of all the Jameses and Youngers. I remember Bob Younger distinctly. He worked after the war in a blacksmith shop of his brother-in-law, Richard Hall, at Lee's Summit where my father had his blacksmithing done. He was too young to be engaged in the war. The James boys were raised in Clay County and while of course I must have seen them with Quantrell's men I do not recall them.

George Quantrell was killed, it is said, in Kentucky toward the close of the war.

After the war was over the Youngers and Jameses organized a notorious band of bank and train robbers. I do not believe that the point so often made by the defenders of the Youngers and Jameses to the effect that it was impossible for them to return to work, and lead peaceful lives after the war, is well taken.

I remember distinctly of seeing Cole Younger in our neighborhood immediately after the war, and at a time when he was not in hiding and when he was not being molested—at least in no greater degree than others who had belonged to Quantrell's band. The people had a great deal of confidence in him and I believe that if he had stayed at home he could have been elected to almost any office in Jackson County.

Of course when I saw him he wore two large pistols, as did scores of other southern men immediately after the war, and this was doubtlessly necessary, but I have never known any man who presented any evidence that there was any greater danger for the Youngers and Jameses immediately after the war than for the balance of Quantrell's men, many of whom I could now name who settled down in Jackson County and went to work and have since led most honorable lives. One of these has held various positions of public trust in this county.

I am not making these statements out of any sort of prejudice against either the Jameses or the Youngers but have never recognized anything as heroic in their exploits and have never hesitated to say so.

About a year ago when an effort was being made to obtain a pardon for the Younger boys I wrote, without solicitation from any person whatever, a long letter to the Governor of Minnesota urging their pardon. I had been frequently urged in years gone by to write such a letter or sign a petition for their pardon but had always refused. I remember when I was a candidate for Congress in 1881 a gentleman who had charge of obtaining petitions and letters for them told me that at a meeting of the friends of the Youngers and Jameses it was decided that if I should write such a letter all opposition to me on their part would be withdrawn but I refused. I did not believe the time had come when they ought to be pardoned but after they had been in the Minnesota penitentiary for over twenty-one years and had never received a black mark for any misconduct it did seem to me that ordinary humanity ask for their release and I wrote the letter on this account.

For a number of years the Youngers and Jameses devoted their attention to robbing banks and killing cashiers or whoever else opposed their plans. The band was finally overthrown at Northfield, Minnesota. This was on Sept. 7, 1876.

The story of their terrible disaster at Northfield was a number of times related to me by Dick Liddell who said he obtained it from frequent conversations with Jesse James.[14] It was as follows:

A fellow named Bill Chadwell who had recently joined the band claimed that he knew of a town named Northfield in Minnesota in which a large amount of cash was always kept. With Chadwell as their guide the band went to Northfield on horseback, starting from Fort Osage Township in Jackson County, Missouri. There were eight members of this band—the three Youngers, Cole, Jim and Bob; the two Jameses, Jesse and Frank and Clell Miller, Bill Chadwell and Charlie Pitts. The true name of the latter was Sam Wells. I knew him well and was raised in the same neighborhood with him.

The tragedy at Northfield was a terrible one. The cashier of the bank, refusing to give up his money was shot. The alarm was given and the citizens of the town seizing their guns fired upon the robbers. Bill Chadwell and Clell Miller were shot dead upon the spot. Dick Liddell says that Jesse James claimed that one of their number shot Chadwell believing that he had betrayed them but the citizens seemed to think they killed him. Every one of the robbers except possibly one of the Jameses was wounded, those being the least wounded taking their other comrades behind them on horseback and fleeing from the town. In their flight a Swede named Gustavason was killed. The people about Northfield for miles around congregated and joined in the chase. The James boys wanted to kill Bob Younger who was too badly wounded to travel but upon Cole's refusing to permit this the Jameses and Youngers parted.[15] The wounded one of the James boys being hauled by his brother to the state of Iowa, Western Nebraska, down to Missouri in a two horse wagon. The wounded man stopped at a house between here and Independence. I do not care to give the name of the owner of this house although I have heard him say myself that he afterwards hauled the wounded bandit from Jackson County, Missouri to Tennessee in a wagon.

The three Youngers and Charlie Pitts [Sam Wells] were surrounded by citizens in Minnesota when a terrific fight ensued. All of the Youngers being further wounded and Sam Wells being shot dead. The Youngers were placed in the Minnesota penitentiary for life. Jesse and Frank James remained at Nashville, Tennessee for a number of years after this, leading for some time, so I was told by a number of the leading citizens of Nashville, peaceable lives. Frank was known in Nashville as Mr. Woodson and Jesse as Mr. Howard. Of course no one in Nashville ever supposed that they were the James boys. After Jesse James reorganized the band, Bill Ryan passed at Nashville as Tom Hill and Dick Liddell generally as Charles Underwood.

CHAPTER II

THE PERSONNEL OF THE BAND AND ITS PRINCIPAL ROBBERIES

While Prosecuting Attorney of Jackson County I spent a great deal of time obtaining a correct list of all the names of those who had belonged to the Younger-James band and the names and places of their principal robberies. I have never seen a published list of the names of the band or their robberies, which was at all correct. I believe mine is. It has never been published by any newspaper. I obtained my information from conversation with Dick Liddell, Clarence Hite, cousin of the James boys, Charley Ford and Tucker Basham, all of whom had been members of the band. I also received much information from Mattie Collins of Jackson County and Mrs. Mattie Bolton, of Ray County, whose names have been so often mentioned in connection with the James boys. I talked also with and examined before Grand juries a great many others whose names would not be fair to divulge.

The band, taken as a whole, existed from the time of the Liberty, Missouri bank robbery, February 14, 1866,[16] to the surrender of Frank James, October 5, 1882, about sixteen years. As a man would be killed it was recruited from time to time and all told twenty-one men belonged to it. Of these twenty-one all are now dead except Cole and Jim Younger, Frank James, Bill Ryan, Dick Liddell and Tucker Basham. All died violent deaths except Clarence Hite, who was pardoned out of Missouri penitentiary and died with consumption. Most of them were killed by someone or their own comrades immediately after some robbery and for the money they had upon their persons.

The following are some of the robberies attributed to this band with the tragic results attendant upon their perpetration. The amounts of money obtained on each occasion are variously estimated and cannot here be definitely stated. It may be said however, that in all the published accounts in the last ten or fifteen years the amounts of money obtained by them have been greatly exaggerated. The following is a list of their principal robberies:

Liberty, Mo. bank robbery. February 14, 1866: Young Wymore, about sixteen years of age killed.

Lexington, Mo. bank robbery. October 30, 1866.

Savannah, Mo. bank robbery, attempted and Judge McLain, cashier wounded, March 2, 1867.

Richmond, Mo. bank robbery, May 23, 1867: Mayor Shaw, B. G. Griffin and son, citizens of Richmond, killed.

Russelville, Ky. bank robbery, March 1868: Mr. Long, cashier, and Mr. Owens, citizen, wounded.

Gallatin, Mo. bank robbery, December 7, 1869: John W. Sheets, cashier, killed.

Corydon, Ia. bank robbery, June 3, 1871.

Columbus, Ky. bank robbery, April 29, 1872: cashier killed.

St. Genevieve, Mo. bank robbery, May 1872.

Kansas City fair robbery, September 26, 1872.

Robbery of Chicago, Rock Island and Pacific train in Adair County, Iowa, July 21, 1873, train derailed and engineer killed.

Gad's Hill, Mo. train robbery, February 1874, express car and passengers robbed.

Muncie, Kansas, train robbery, December 13, 1874.

Huntington, West Virginia. Bank robbery, September 1, 1875.

Missouri Pacific train robbery at Otterville, Mo., July 7, 1876.

Northfield, Minnesota bank robbery, September 7, 1876.

The following are some of the principal robberies by the band as reorganized by Jesse James after the attempted Northfield robbery:

Glendale train robbery in Jackson County, Missouri, on Chicago and Alton Railroad, October 7, 1879.

Dick Liddell and Tucker Basham, both of whom were in the robbery, told me that it was committed by Jesse James, Ed Miller, Wood Hite, Bill Ryan, Dick Liddell and Tucker Basham. Frank James was not in this robbery.

Winston train robbery, on Chicago, Rock Island & Pacific Railroad, July 5, 1881. Conductor Westfall and Frank McMillan, railroad laborer, killed. Dick Liddell and Clarence Hite, neither knowing that I had interviewed the other, agreed that this robbery was committed by Jesse and Frank James, Wood and Clarence Hite and Dick Liddell.

Blue Cut robbery in Jackson County, Missouri on Chicago and Alton railroad, September 7, 1881. Dick Liddell, Clarence Hite and Charlie Ford agreed in separate interviews I had with them as to all the details of this robbery and stated that it was committed by Frank and Jesse James, Wood and Clarence Hite, Dick Liddell and Charlie Ford.

Muscle Shoals, Alabama robbery, March 1881.

Many of the friends of the Jameses and Youngers have claimed that their depredations after the war were committed in pursuance of a kind of just revenge, and that Union men and United States government property were the objects of this revenge. The records show this claim to be absolutely without any foundation.

It is true that Harry Younger, the father of the Younger boys was a Union man and he was doubtless followed out of Kansas City by Federal soldiers and killed for his money. It is also true that the arm of old lady Samuels was blown off and her child killed by a bomb thrown into her house by Pinkertons' detectives.[17] This and the murder of old man Younger were heinous deeds without any excuse or palliation whatever but the records show that these did not contribute the controlling motives in the robberies of this band. The records show that with the exception of the attempted robbery of the bank of Northfield, Minnesota about every bank ever robbed by them was in a southern state, the stock and deposits of which constituted the property of southern people in their different raids; they took a good horse from a southern man as readily as from a northern man.

Probably five-sixths of all the money they obtained was from banks. In several of the bank robberies above mentioned more money was obtained than in the Blue Cut, Glendale and Winston train robberies combined. These train robberies cannot be said to have been committed from any motive of just revenge as they cannot be taken to be the property of any southern or northern man.

It will thus be seen that the second charge that has been disseminated throughout the length and breadth of the United States to the effect that the Jameses and Youngers confined their depredations to northern men is also totally without foundation.

The truth is that their depredations sprung from no motive of revenge or outrages upon their families nor from any political or sectional cause whatever. So that both the charges of their enemies and their friends in this behalf are alike without foundation.

I first found myself arrayed in opposition to the James band during my candidacy for prosecuting attorney of Jackson County in 1880. I have practiced law previous to this time for a number of years at Independence and had built up quite a clientage among the friends and admirers of this band and in this way, as well as from my general acquaintance, having been raised in eastern Jackson County, I was thoroughly convinced in my own mind as to who the leader of this train robbers band were. I made my canvass throughout eastern Jackson County on horseback speaking usually at night.

Before I got through it became about as warm an affair as I have ever engaged in. I stated in express terms on the stump that I believed Jesse and Frank James, Dick Liddell and Bill Ryan were train robbers, and if I was elected I intended to do all I could to bring them to justice. It so happened that my opponent, a very bright man, Mr. John C. Tarsney, was upon the regular Democratic ticket, and while I claimed that he had my place, I was in fact upon no ticket whatever. He had been a Federal soldier and had been in prison, as was then publicly claimed and I have no doubt true, in Libby Prison. His being upon the regular Democratic ticket gave him a great advantage over me from that party and his record as a Federal soldier gave him a decided advantage over me from the rank and file of the Republicans. I beat him I believe by something over 700 votes.

If it had not been for the stand I took in reference to the prosecution of train robbers he would have beaten me out of my boots. Of course, Mr. Tarsney was not a sympathizer with train robbers, but he was shrewd enough to say nothing about it. Let no man say after this race that the people or the Democrats of Jackson County are in sympathy with train robbers. In my second race for prosecuting attorney I was placed on the regular ticket without having electioneered a moment. Train robbery was again the issue and, while they ran me somewhat behind my ticket, I was elected by over 1700.

After being first elected in 1880 I made an earnest effort to redeem my pledge. I summoned every man before the grand jury whom I had any reason to believe was in sympathy with or knew anything about the James boys in Jackson, Clay and Lafayette Counties. I went before the grand jury and examined these witnesses in person.

Of course the implied imputation that they knew anything about train robbery made many of them absolutely furious but to use a somewhat inelegant expression, "I stayed with them" and I obtained a great deal of valuable information which I handed from time to time to the officers who were out in the field in pursuit.

CHAPTER III

THE ARREST, TRIAL AND CONVICTION OF BILL RYAN

In two or three months after I resolved my first commission as prosecuting attorney, January 1, 1881, a telegram and letter of description came from the Chief of Police of Nashville, Tennessee to the chiefs of all the large cities throughout the Union, stating that a man undoubtedly of a desperate character had been arrested for assault near Nashville, Tennessee and asking if he was wanted. The facts attending this arrest, stated in brief are as follows:

A man neatly dressed, riding a splendid horse and carrying two revolvers, had become engaged in a controversy and assaulted a man near Nashville, Tennessee. A man named Earthman came up behind this man, threw his arms around him to prevent his shooting and he was thus taken in charge.[18] He was somewhat intoxicated and declared that he was a desperado and an outlaw and that his name was Tom Hill. Upon being searched it was found that he had two revolvers and wore a buckskin waistcoat next to his person, in which was contained something like one thousand dollars in gold coins.

When Chief Speers of this city received the description above referred to, he telegraphed the chief of police of Nashville that the man was not wanted here. It was the first time I ever knew Chief Speers to make a mistake in this regard. Whig Keshlear, then Deputy marshal of Jackson County, happened to hear the description and stated that he believed Bill Ryan was the man. I went with him and Cornelius Murphy to Chief Speers and as soon as I read the description I told Speers that I was thoroughly acquainted with Bill Ryan and I believed he was the man. A photograph of Ryan was obtained and sent to Tennessee. A telegram immediately followed stating that the man was Ryan. I obtained requisition papers, sent Keshlear to Tennessee and he brought Ryan back to Jackson County and placed him in jail.

The next thing was to convict the prisoner. No train robber had ever been tried by a jury in Missouri and it was generally believed that no jury in Missouri would dare to convict one of the James boys. I informed the officials of the Chicago & Alton Railroad company that Ryan was now in custody charged with robbing one of their trains at Glendale, October 7, 1879, and I wished them to send all the train men to the trial at Independence.

One of their agents told me that after full consultation about the matter the railroad officials requested that I should not insist upon the railroad or the train men having anything to do with the trial: that it would simply anger the James boys against the railroad and cause them to single their road out for other robberies.

I insisted upon their sending the train men which they did but when they reached the trial at Independence and saw the complexion of the crowd formed in the courthouse, they said they would swear nothing and importuned me to release them from testifying which I did.

I proved the fact that there was a robbery by Mr. Grimes, the express manager who was knocked senseless by one of the robbers and of course knew nothing except that about $9000 was taken from the safe.

In anticipation of the fact that the state would need evidence I had suggested to Governor Crittenden that it would be wise to pardon a green fellow named Tucker

Basham, then in the penitentiary, and let him testify against Ryan who was a shrewd and bold member of the gang. This the governor consented to do. Whig Keshlear and Captain Maurice Langhorne, then deputy marshals, had arrested Basham because of the sudden and lavish expenditure of money he was making and on account of certain admissions which had fallen from his lips.

Mr. Peak, then prosecuting attorney, had had an indictment prepared against him and Langhorne and Keshlear obtained a full confession from him and he pleaded guilty. A brother of Up Hayes, a Confederate colonel, brought Basham from the penitentiary in Jefferson City and kept him constantly under guard during the whole trial to prevent his assassination, I myself holding his pardon in my pocket until just in the net of placing him on the witness stand when I handed it to him in full view of the jury, stating to the court that this meant the full release of Basham and that I had promised him the pardon through the governor in the event of his willingness to testify in the case.[19]

The friends of Bill Ryan were so incensed at the appearance of Basham at Independence that they set fire to his house, an old log cabin in the Cracker Neck country and when the oak house refused to burn they took the family effects out into the yard, placed them in a pile and burned them up. Basham fled a short time after the trial imploring me to go with him, stating that there was no question that both he and I were to be killed. I took the precaution of taking him to a photographer and having his photograph taken, telling him that I intended to bring him back as a witness in case another of the James boys was ever on trial. I never saw him afterwards.

I shall never forget the Bill Ryan trial. It was by all odds the most exciting trial I have ever witnessed and I believe, the most exciting ever held in the west.

The excitement attending it was ten-fold greater than the excitement at the Frank James trial in Gallatin, Missouri. The Frank James trial was a set and thoroughly arranged proceeding for which both sides had been preparing for more than a year. James had the most eminent lawyers in the west present with thoroughly prepared and magnificent speeches to deliver in his behalf. The Bill Ryan trial was a pell mell encounter between the poorly organized forces of the law and the thoroughly organized and defined forces of outlawry. Magnificent counsel represented Ryan. Captain Franklin, for many years a Congressman from this district, Hon. R. L. Yeager and Major B. L. Woodson. It was a test case. The law was pitted for the first time against the mask and the black flag of the bandit. The friends of the outlaw, backed by two or three daily newspapers, were certain that these men were being mistreated and had a right to do whatever they had done and that none of them ought to be and could not be convicted by a Missouri jury.

I had been in Nashville, Tennessee and brought a large number of witnesses from there, and of course they knew nothing of Ryan's connection with the robbery, and aside from the testimony of a young man named Miller who testified that on the night of the robbery several men passed by his house on horseback and that he recognized the voice of one of them as the voice of Ryan, I practically had no testimony except that of Tucker Basham, who was about as good material as an expert cross examiner would wish to get a hold of.

The courtroom was packed from sunrise to sundown with the friends of the outlaw armed to the teeth. Many of them staying at night in the courthouse and in the courthouse yard so they could get seats when the trial commenced.

It is safe to say that the crowd in the courthouse stood twenty-five for the defendant to one for the state. The balance of the James gang were then in close proximity to Independence and I knew it. Dick Liddell afterwards told me that the rescue of the prisoners by the assassination of the officers was seriously contemplated.

During the Frank James trial at Gallatin one or more of his friends who had a wide reputation as fighters, openly stated in the streets in the presence of many of the most reputable citizens of the town, that they intended to kill me before the trial was over but I regarded this as simply bluff and it gave me no uneasiness whatever. But during the Ryan trial my assistant, Colonel Southern, a courageous man and myself received a letter which I knew through a detective then in the cell with Ryan, was sent with his approval and threatening that if we did not desist our lives were in danger. I confessed I was uneasy.

It is the secret threat that counts. When other threats than this came to our ears, and officers of the court who had been in the Confederate army said to me frankly that they thought the probabilities were that I would be shot, I confess that I was anxious. But I was into it and as I regarded it, to show the white feather meant disgrace for life and I resolved that safety was to be found in the very boldest fight I could wage. I have been asked a great many times to give at least a synopsis of my speech in the Bill Ryan trial.

I am satisfied that of all my speeches which have been poor at all times this was thirty times the best of them and was the only time in my life when it was no effort whatever for me. I am satisfied the speech would read poorly in print. In fact a man who heard it complimented it as possessing anything of literary merit.

A polished Presbyterian minister who heard the speech used to laugh at some of my illustrations. The only one compliment I believe I ever received was from Bill Ryan himself who said the officer who had him in charge was lifted out of his chair a number of times during its delivery. All I was trying to do was to inspire by my own words and conduct sufficient courage in the breast of the jury to cause them to convict. Whether my effort aided any or not they did it.

Bill Ryan was convicted and his punishment assessed as twenty-five years in the penitentiary. No jury ever sat who were more justly entitled to the thanks of the commonwealth than the jury in that case. Many of them were thoroughly acquainted in eastern Jackson County and they sat facing the friends of the accused, who thronged into the courthouse until the most prominent among them occupied nearly every seat inside of the bar and were actually in touching distance when I spoke.

Many of the jurors had to go to their homes in the very midst of the friends of the defendant. One of them I remember, a brother of ex-sheriff Hickman, lived in the edge of the woods within a few miles of the farm upon which Bill Ryan was raised. Nor can too much praise be given to Cornelius Murphy, the marshal who summoned this jury in person.

In their motion for a new trial the counsel for the defendant laid much stress upon the fact that the government of the state hearing of the great excitement existing at the trial, had sent a box of guns to Independence, and that the jury was thus overawed by the state. I believe the guns came but the box was never opened. In fact I never saw one of the guns in the hands of anyone and I am satisfied no one else did. I obtained an affidavit from each of the jury to the effect that during the whole trial they were kept together in charge of the marshal, and they had never never heard about the guns being shipped to Independence until their verdict had been returned and that they were governed only by the law and the evidence in the case.

CHAPTER IV
THE BACKBONE OF OUTLAWRY BROKEN AT LAST

The jury which convicted Bill Ryan broke the back of outlawry in the state of Missouri. Thousands of mouths in Jackson and adjoining counties which had been locked by fear were opened, and the denunciation of train robbery was open and unstinted. The desire to rid Missouri of the stain of outlawry reached fever heat and the officers of the law were greatly encouraged and posses of men began to search in every direction for the bandits.

It was but a few weeks until Mattie Collins, whom I had assisted in defending for the murder of her brother-in-law, Jonathan Dark, came to Whig Keshlear and told him that she desired an interview with me with reference to the surrender of Dick Liddell.[20] She said the James boys were greatly discouraged: that they were very suspicious of each other, that Jesse James and Dick Liddell had parted company, Jesse threatening to kill the latter on sight, and that the officers were pursuing Dick in the Six-Mile country and on several occasions had barely missed capturing him.

With Jesse James on one side and the officers on the other Dick Liddell was between the devil and the deep sea and he wanted to give up and tell everything he knew if I would promise him protection.

Of course I jumped at the offer saying that if Dick would come in and assist the officers in completing the overthrow of the band I would promise him perfect immunity for all crimes in which he had participated in Jackson County, but that I could not promise him immunity for any other county, and that she had better go back and tell him we must arrange to see the governor as to be promised immunity for the whole state.

Captain Craig who was ignorant of Mattie Collins' visit to me was in pursuit of Dick Liddell in the Six-Mile country and Dick was immediately compelled to leave going over into Ray County where he told Mattie Bolton what had been suggested as to going to the governor, and getting his promise of protection in case he would surrender.

Mrs. Bolton at once went to see the governor. The governor at once acceded to the request and instructed Mrs. Bolton to have Dick Liddell surrender to Sheriff James R. Timberlake of Clay County, and the governor could certainly have selected no better man.

I was ignorant of the visit of Mrs. Bolton to the governor, and never saw Dick Liddell or either of the Ford boys or Mrs. Bolton herself for that matter until after Jesse James was killed. Dick Liddell immediately surrendered to Timberlake and gave full information as to the names and whereabouts of the different members of the band.[21]

It was doubtless he who told the officers of Bob and Charlie Ford, although I knew nothing about this at the time. Upon Liddell's information Henry Craig went to Kentucky and arrested Clarence Hite, a companion of the James boys, brought him to Missouri and he plead guilty and was placed in the Missouri penitentiary for twenty-five years. After staying there some time and being in a dying condition, he was pardoned and shortly after died with consumption. I neglected to state that Bill Ryan was sent to the penitentiary and after serving about seven years was pardoned by Governor Morehouse, it being represented to him that Ryan was in failing health.

Just before the surrender of Dick Liddell, upon going to the home of Mrs. Mattie Bolton, and after staying there all night, to his surprise the next morning Wood Hite came down the stairway lead—into a room where Liddell was seated. Hite was a cousin of Jesse James and sided with Jesse in a feud between Liddell and Jessie.

The shooting at once commenced, Liddell being shot in the arm by Hite. The room was so filled with smoke that neither man could well take aim, and Bob Ford who stood a little to one side of Wood Hite, drew his pistol and killed him. Bob Ford was tried for the killing of Wood Hite, upon change of venue from Ray County to Clinton County, and most ably prosecuted by Mr. Joseph M. Lowe, now a prominent citizen of Kansas City with offices in the Massachusetts building. Bob Ford was acquitted upon evidence to the fact that Liddell killed Hite but the truth is both Liddell and Ford engaged in the shooting and both were guilty unless done in self defense which Liddell always claimed was his attitude in the shooting. Wood Hite's body was thrown into an old well on the Ford farm near Richmond, Missouri where it was afterwards discovered by neighbors.

Mattie Collins told me that she saw Bob Ford in Kansas City a few days after the killing of Hite, with Hite's coat on with the blood stains not even wiped off.

In a short time after Dick Liddell surrendered to James R. Timberlake Jesse James was killed by Bob Ford at St. Joseph, Missouri. I had nothing to do with this directly or indirectly and I am glad of it although I shed no tears on account of his taking off. His death was a blessing to the state, but I certainly would not have employed a man to kill him and I do not know that anyone else did this. Bob Ford spoke to me in my office and stated he wanted me to bring suit against the officers who had not fairly divided the reward money with him. I refused to hear his story and would not have believed it in all probability if he had told it. I refused to allow him to give any names.

Bob Ford was killed a few years ago while engaged in a row in a saloon at Crede, Colorado. Charlie Ford in bad health and filled with remorse, I suppose, died by his own hand within a year or two after the death of Jesse James.

I find here among my old papers with reference to the James boys quite a lengthy paper in my own handwriting headed, "Voluntary Statement of Mattie Liddell made to William H. Wallace and W. G. Keshlear, April 25, 1882." This paper is signed by Mattie Liddell herself and it is too lengthy for publication and besides it gives the names of citizens who have never appeared in the public press as friends of the James boys and I believe for this reason that I ought not to publish it.

Suffice it to say this paper after giving in detail her acquaintance with Jesse James, Bill Ryan, Jim Cummins and a number of robberies that some of them had told her about. She then goes into some detail with reference to her coming to Whig Keshlear for the purpose of consulting him and myself with reference to the surrender of Dick Liddell and dwells at some length upon her efforts in persuading Dick to surrender; that she had told him that I had said that application must be made to the governor; that she pawned her watch and gave him fifty dollars, also gave him ten dollars more making sixty; that Liddell immediately afterwards was driven by the officers over to Ray County and got Mrs. Bolton to go and see Governor Crittenden and that Liddell told her that money she had given him was used for traveling expenses in going to see the governor. I mention this paper because I have recently seen a published statement in which it was asserted that Timberlake and Mattie Collins planned the surrender of Dick Liddell. It was W. G. Keshlear and not Sheriff Timberlake who consulted me as to the proposal of Mattie Collins that Dick Liddell should surrender. I do not believe Sheriff Timberlake ever saw Mattie Collins, who lived in Jackson County, until I introduced him to her at St. Joseph after the killing of Jesse James.

I had gone to St. Joseph upon hearing of the death of Jesse James and a man named Clay and Mattie Collins for the purpose of having them identify Jesse James as it was then claimed by Jesse's friends that Bob Ford and Charlie were simply trying to play the same game attempted by George Shepherd near Joplin some years before and it was not Jesse James who was killed. The three witnesses went to St. Joseph with a firm belief that Jesse James was not the man, but as soon as they saw him they said there was no question that it was Jesse James. I am sure this is the first time Sheriff Timberlake ever saw Mattie Collins or Mattie Liddell as she signed the paper to which I refer.

I also find here among my papers the statement of Mrs. Mattie Bolton in my handwriting going into details as to her knowledge of the Jameses, her visit to the governor in behalf of Dick Liddell and so forth, but it is very lengthy and simply corroborative of confessions of the gang often published in the papers.[22] I also find a confession in my handwriting made by Clarence Hite in the penitentiary at Jefferson City, which is corroborative in the minutest detail of the statements of Dick Liddell and Charlie Ford as to the Winston and Blue Cut robberies. None of these three papers have ever been published and they are only valuable as corroborative of the details I have been given, and as they would burden your columns as well as for the reason that they name persons whose names I believe it would be wrong for me to permit to be published I shall withhold them from publication.

CHAPTER V
FRANK JAMES GIVES HIMSELF UP—LAST OF THE GANG

With Jesse James killed by Bob Ford at St. Joseph, Wood Hite shot by Liddell and Ford in Ray County, Ed Miller killed by Jesse James in Saline County, Bill Ryan and Clarence Hite in the Missouri penitentiary, the only remaining member of the band at large was Frank James. And with Liddell and Ford to assist the officers and a $10,000 reward hanging over his head, Frank James was being hunted down throughout the length and breadth of the land.

Just at this juncture two ladies drove up in a hack and came to my office one day in Kansas City. One of them was old Mrs. Samuels whom I had never seen before and the other was Frank James's wife, whom I had known as Miss Anna Ralston before she was married to Frank.[23] Mrs. James said that her husband's life was more horrible than death; that he was in constant apprehension least someone would assassinate him and as she expressed it, could not cut a stick of wood without looking behind him to see if someone was coming up to shoot him.

She and Mrs. Samuels said that they were afraid of the other officers, and that they wanted to effect Frank James's surrender through me; that they did not believe that I had anything whatever to do with the assassination of Jesse James. I told them that I certainly had not but that I thought that they were unnecessarily apprehensive about the other officers. I told them that I would inform the governor and do everything that I could to see that Frank James was protected in his surrender.

I wrote or telegraphed to the governor and he answered by saying that he would leave the makings of the terms of surrender entirely to me. That was the nearest I ever came to being governor. I wrote out the terms of Frank James's surrender, a copy of which I seem to have misplaced but the substance of the paper was that Frank James should give himself up, go to the penitentiary for a short term, and upon his release from the penitentiary he and the whole James fraternity should leave the state of Missouri and never come back again. I immediately received word back that the terms were too harsh and that they would not be accepted.

I heard nothing more of the matter for some weeks. When I received a telegram from Governor Crittenden stating that Frank James had surrendered to him at Jefferson City and requested that I should be present at Independence the next morning to take charge of him at the train.

WILLIAM WALLACE

I went to Independence requesting the marshal and one of his deputies to accompany me and received Mr. James and had him locked up in jail.

I found upon reaching Independence that James's friends were aware of his coming and that men worth full half a million dollars were present ready to go on his bond. The controversy immediately arose as to him being bailed.[24]

He was indicted in Jackson County, Missouri for murder and I refused to permit him to give bond without the usual showing in such cases. Of course he could not do this and his friends became very indignant and stated their great astonishment at my conduct. Judge H. P. White was consulted and he said he would agree to giving bail if I would. They then said that a judge from New York was willing that the defendant should give bail when a young man of southern parentage and raised in Missouri was unwilling.

Major Edwards, one of James's most ardent friends, called me to one side at the Merchants Hotel in Independence and stated that Frank was the last remaining member of a band that had been butchered and assassinated with relentless cruelty, and made a most eloquent appeal to me to agree that Frank should be bailed.

He said it would be the most popular act of my life and would make me governor, and if I would do it he would most gladly assist in bringing about this result. I told him the offer was a tempting one but that it came too high. This ended the controversy and Frank James was placed in jail where he remained for over a year.[25]

Shortly after Frank James was placed in jail, W. D. Hamilton then Prosecuting Attorney of Daviss County and one of the truest and most courageous men I have ever known, accompanied by one of the attorneys of the Chicago, Rock Island & Pacific, came to see me in Kansas City. They stated that Frank James doubtless had many friends in Jackson County and that they did not believe I could convict him here. I told them that he had many friends but none of the officers here were in sympathy with him and I believe that he would unquestionably be convicted here for the Blue Cut robbery.

They insisted that Daviess County was the place to try him and when I remembered the difficulty which I had experienced in getting transportation for my witnesses in the Bill Ryan trial and the numerous favors it would be necessary to ask from the railroads in the matter of the transportation of witnesses and the prosecution of James, I acceded to their request, in which I am satisfied they were perfectly honest and conscientious.

Frank James was thereupon by my consent removed to Daviess County and placed in the jail at Gallatin with a distinct understanding that I should come to Gallatin and assist in the prosecution. I have been censured for going to Gallatin. I received no fee whatever and went voluntarily and of my own accord. The Chicago, Rock Island & Pacific railroad and the Chicago & Alton railroad, paid me back part of the money which I had expended, in fact all I ever asked them for, but I am out still quite a large sum of money which I do not begrudge. I never at any time received any fee except $12.50 allowed me for the prosecution of Bill Ryan. I state this because some years ago the friends of the band did a good deal of talking about my being well paid. The truth is I never received a cent beyond what I have stated above.

Before proceeding with a short account of the Frank James trial I want to pay a tribute to some of the officers who assisted in the overthrow of this band of outlaws. Their magnificent services have never been properly appreciated by the people.

In chapter six Wallace paid tribute to the men who had fought with him to break up the James-Younger gang. Among those he mentioned were James R. Timberlake, Sheriff of Clay County, "an honest, open, faithful servant" who joined Wallace "after he read in the papers I was fighting the whole James gang and the entire state administration combined"; Maurice M. Langhorne, a Jackson County deputy sheriff, "a quiet, unassuming man with nothing of the daredevil about him but his courage was as superb as that of Timberlake. . . . Langhorne, an old ex-Confederate was a captain in Shelby's brigade . . ."

Wallace revealed that at one time, Langhorne, who had Liddil in custody, was warned "by a committee of Frank James' friends" to turn over his prisoner but Langhorne quietly warned the "head of the posse he would certainly be killed" if any attempt was made to take Dick Liddil.

Wallace, in this chapter, also mentioned General J. O. Shelby, the close friend of Frank James. As Wallace wrote, "I made no apology to him during his life and do not now to his friends, yet I wish to stand for a moment at his grave with bowed head and due him that justice which is his due. . . ."

Wallace wrote:

"I remember that in the presence of a large number of gentlemen at the St. James hotel, while talking to me he [Shelby] paid me quite a compliment, although fighting men would not regard it as such. He said that he had seen a great many men who would make charges in battle but that I possessed the queer gift of being the first durned fellow he had ever known who stood up for three years in front of the abuse and fire of men who had been regarded as killers without ever showing any disposition to run. I do not know whether I ought to have said this or not, but whether indeed it was a compliment, but I do regard it.

General Shelby died one of my warmest friends and while he had some glaring faults yet they were such that we were bound to admire them after all and taken all together he was a noble and chivalrous man.[26]

CHAPTER VII

FRANK JAMES ACQUITTED, BUT BECOMES A LAW-ABIDING CITIZEN

While I have nothing but condemnation for the bandit life of Frank James I entertain for the fellow not a particle of resentment. I had begrudged him his liberty for a number of years, but after watching his law-abiding life for a long while I got over all this. I candidly admit that upon the brow where I once thought the curse of Cain ought to have been branded, I am now willing to write the word FORGIVEN, in the sincere hope that Frank James will continue to lead a law-abiding and a happy life. I feel personally the same way towards Bill Ryan.

I am told that Frank James's son is now in the Federal army, and I trust his boy's career will be an honorable and a brilliant one. It does remind us of the tremendous changes a few years will bring about and of the fact there is now no north and no south, when we reflect that the same blue uniform at which the pistols of Quantrell's guerrillas were once directed with such deadly aim is now worn by the son of Frank James.

I want to say a word about Frank James's wife, I have not a word of condemnation for any portion of her life. The truth is, she receives my unstinted admiration. Her devotion to her husband, even during his bandit days, should act as a constant rebuke to the hundreds of persons who are disgracing our courts by asking divorces on trivial grounds.

I will conclude this ad captandum talk by a brief allusion to the trial of Frank James at Gallatin, Missouri during the latter part of August and first of September,

1883. This trial was probably not even excepting the trial of Guiteau, the most widely read trial that ever occurred in America.

I spent a good portion of my time for about a year preparing the state's case for this trial, and traveled thousands of miles in collecting evidence. My recollection is that we corroborated Dick Liddell in Sixty-Six Particulars. I had ten times the case that I had against Bill Ryan, but I will not go into the evidence.

For fifteen years the friends of Frank James, about every one of whom has become friendly to me, sometimes triumphantly, oftener jokingly, have been accustomed to reminding me of my great discomfiture in the trial of Frank James at Gallatin. I have known all along how people are wont to regard a lawyer who after he is beaten, whines about an unfair trial, but now, when by the lapse of all these years, every feeling of resentment must have been obliterated, even at the risk of being adjudged a whiner I am going to state for the first time some facts which came under my observation as to the selection of the jury in the Frank James case.

The jury in this case was PACKED, and yet no member of it was corrupt. They were so intensely in sympathy with the defendant and so indignant at the state for prosecuting a man whom they honestly regarded as the last returning soldier of the Confederate cause that no amount of evidence ever could have compelled them to convict the defendant.

The jury was deliberately and advisedly selected by the then sheriff of Daviess County. Yet I do not believe that the sheriff acted corruptly in the selection of the jury.

In my opinion, Frank James's friends, by making against him a few threats such as they were accustomed to send myself and other officers, caused him to do their bidding from sheer fear.

After we had announced that we were ready for trial, and while sitting on the veranda in front of Mr. Hamilton's office at Gallatin, I saw the sheriff standing in the courthouse yard and every now and then taking a paper from his inside pocket and after looking at it, go across the street to the crowd and accost a man and then go back to the same place in the courthouse yard and repeat the same thing.

I went over to where he was and told him that he had promised me the day before that he would go out into the country and get this jury; that, as I then said to him, the friends of the defendant would bring every admirer he had in the county to town so that however honest he might be, he would be almost sure to select a large number of them as jurors. He replied there were so many men in town that he was getting a splendid jury anyway and that he had his list about complete.

I went back to Mr. Hamilton's office and informed him of what I had seen. Hamilton was a truly courageous fellow and he had already suspected what I had seen. He and I at once agreed that we would prepare an affidavit and swear to it jointly, setting out the facts and charging the sheriff with incompetency and asking that he be removed from office for this particular case, and the coroner placed in his stead as provided by the law.

What I saw was a small part of what we afterwards learned as to the selection of the jury. For instance, a man came into Hamilton's office during the trial, and said that in his township there were only two men in favor of James and both were on the jury.

Upon informing our associate counsel, all of whom were older than either of us, of our intention they strenuously objected. The gist of their objection seemed to be that the sheriff had been a Union man and I believe a Federal soldier while the coroner, a Mr. Clagett was an ex-Confederate. I asked them if Mr. Clagett was a conscientious and courageous man. It was agreed on all sides that he undoubtedly was. I then said: "Gentlemen, let's have the ex-Confederate get this jury. Every blow that has been given to the James band had been struck by a Democrat and the severest of them by ex-Confederate soldiers." But my argument did not win. After considering the matter for two or three hours I was told that the judge, whom I knew to be a thoroughly honest man, had been informed of our intention; that the judge had confidence in the sheriff and thought our move not only unwise but as he expressed it, revolutionary. Hamilton and I persisted, and we were finally given to understand that there was no question but that our application for the substitution of the coroner for the sheriff would be overruled.

I went down to the hotel, packed my grip, brought it up to Hamilton's office on the square, and told them that I was going home. My associates all besought me to stay, saying that they only understood the Daviess County evidence in the case, and that now for me to go away would leave them in a terrible predicament; in fact that it would be a desertion on my part.

I consented to stay but I remember to this day my exact words when I did so. Said I: "Gentlemen, we will try Frank James before the world but not before the jury which is now being selected. The verdict is already written."

After the acquittal of Frank James, Wallace did not slip into oblivion. His record as a prosecutor remained impressive; he estimated that he sent more criminals to the state penitentiary than were sent from St. Louis, five times as large as Kansas City. Dedication to the law and the prosecutor's office remained his whole life. He once created a sensation by dismissing an indictment for murder after he had conducted his own investigation and found the defendant had killed in self-defense. He wrote: "I would have been a coward to put that responsibility upon a jury. I represented not only the state but the defendant who was practically friendless, and it was my duty to protect him." [27]

Wallace's determination to enforce the law forbidding the sale of liquor on Sunday made him an enemy of the powerful distillers, but despite political pressure from his own party he continued closing the Kansas City saloons and arresting and indicting the owners of "blind tigers" (speakeasies). At one time sixty-five grocers selling liquor without a license were indicted. The grocers warned Wallace that they would wear him out by forcing him to try each case separately. Wallace ignored their threats, tried every case himself and with only one exception, won guilty verdicts.

Wallace also fought the state's largest department store owners when he enforced the law against Sunday store openings. This time the Kansas City police chief demanded approval from the Jackson County police commissioners before he would make an arrest. Wallace went to H. H. Craig, his old partner in the pursuit of the Jameses-Youngers, and asked him to introduce a resolution at the next meeting of the commissioners, demanding that the law forbidding the opening of department stores on Sunday be enforced, and then to alert the reporters that an important decision would be made at the meeting.

Craig, a firm supporter of Wallace, followed the prosecutor's suggestion. While the delighted reporters looked on, the infuriated police commissioners were forced to approve Craig's resolution. Bribery, intimidation, and threats failed to stop Wallace when the so-called Johnson law, designating gambling a felony, was passed by the legislature. Wallace raided so many gambling halls and arrested so many owners and dealers that a delegation of gamblers visited his office to ask if he intended to keep up this drive or was it a mere political pose? Wallace tersely informed them that in a short time there wouldn't be a gambling hall left in Kansas City, Missouri. The gamblers promptly went to Kansas City, Kansas.

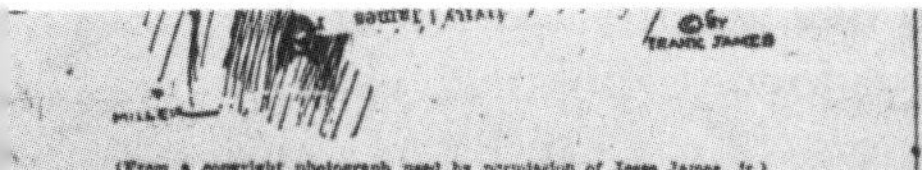

(From a copyright photograph used by permission of Jesse James, Jr.)
NK JAMES, THE FORMER BANDIT, WHO DIED YESTERDAY AT HIS HOME NEAR KEARNEY, MO.

waving across the track, the train wly grinding to full stop, then the d, demoniacal screaming of masked in the darkness, and the fusillade revolver shots while one man guards engineer and two overawe the express messenger, rob his safe and away in, to melt into the blackness of the ht.

heir training in night riding and nt hiding, in sleeping anywhere, in wing how to make cover through a ole day for men and horses in a ch of hazel brush, learned in the rrilla days, made escape easy for m.

or seventeen years they rode and bed, and sometimes killed. How ny hundreds of thousands of dollars r loot amounted to no one will ever w.

HEN FRANK JAMES GAVE UP.

Walked Up to Governor Crittenden and Gave Him His Pistol.

he James boys robbed from the Missippi to the Rio Grande, and no one ld catch them.

ut in the late seventies the lines re tightening about them all the time. country was filling up. It became re difficult to escape, to hide. Big vards offered by states and corporans bred treachery in their camps.

t was this that brought the death of se James, shot down from behind by Ford boys, in his own home in St. eph, in sight of his wife and two dren, for a reward of $50,000 offered the state of Missouri. So many robies within the state by a band of her n, had made Missouri infamous. It ured business. Travelers were afraid pass this way. Hence the big reward; treachery, the death of Jesse James. rank James told the writer of this long before the death of his brother, se, he, Frank, had given up outry, foreseeing the end that was sure e, and that then he was living peacey in a Southern state, with his wife family, under an assumed name.

rank denied that he was at the roby of the train at Winston, Mo., one ht in July, 1879, when the conductor, liam Westfall, and John McMillen re killed by the bandits.

ut Frank was under suspicion of ving been there and a grand jury had ned him in an indictment for the rder. He was a fugitive from justice. he system of train robbery invented him was yet being practiced and for h one Frank was blamed. He ded to surrender and take his chances. T. Crittenden was governor of Misri. October 6, 1882, Frank James, ompanied by a few faithful friends, t to the office of the governor in ferson City. What occurred is debed as follows in Leonard's History Missouri:

aj. John N. Edwards advanced to governor, shook hands with him and an easy, matter-of-fact way introduced friend, Mr. Frank James." They took another by the hand, the chief magiste and the brigand, and then the uned-for visitor unbuttoned his coat and, uckling his belt, handed it, with the ol in it, to the governor as a token of render and delivery.

Governor Crittenden," he said, as he ffered the butt of the revolver—a .44 ber Remington—which had been preted, muzzle foremost, on many a crit- occasion, and made to do its part many a fierce combat. "I want to hand to you that which no man living, ext myself, has ever been permitted to h since 1861, and to say that I am r prisoner. I have taken all the cartes out of the weapon and you can dle it with safety."

overnor Crittenden took the revolver by butt and, turning to the company in room, who had not understood what going on, said: "Gentlemen, this is nk James, and I take pleasure in introng him to you."

here was a look of surprise at the an-

It was a famous trial. John F. Philips, afterward United States judge, now a practicing lawyer in this city, defended James. William Wallace, now a lawyer in this city and widely known as prohibition candidate for governor in several elections, prosecuted James.

"LIVING IT DOWN."

How Frank James Kept His Promise to Governor Crittenden.

After his acquittal Frank James went to St. Louis to live and for several years was doorkeeper of the Standard Theater there. He was acting in that capacity some ten years ago, when the writer of this, accompanied by a publisher of books, went to see him to try and induce him to agree to the publication of a book about his life and adventures.

"I promised the governor of Missouri when I surrendered that I would never write a book about myself or permit it to be done if I could prevent it. I am going to keep that promise," said Frank.

The publisher tried to get his consent, offered to pay him an enormous sum in cash outright, but Frank said:

"Gentlemen, if you should give me a million dollars in gold, I would not do it. I have got a lot to live down, and I can't help do that by writing books about myself." And that was the end of it.

Frank James never wrote a word of his adventures and would not be interviewed about them.

He was living in rather poor circumstances at the time the publisher made that offer to him, and $10,000 would have been a fortune to him, but it did not even tempt him to break his promise.

He did add to his income by acting as starter at horse races in county fairs in many places in the Southwest, and for a brief period he appeared with Cole Younger in a tent show, but he gave that up when he found that he was expected to pose as an actor in a border drama.

After the death of his mother, Mrs. Samuels, a few years ago, Frank James inherited the farm near Kearney, and he went there to live quietly.

He was a quiet, unassuming man, of irreproachable habits and character in his later years. He was devoted to his family, never drank, talked little, and kept in the background. There was much that was pathetic and impelling of sympathy in him as he went quietly about his way, with one deep aim always uppermost—the yearning, as he expressed it to the governor when he surrendered, "to regain the citizenship which I lost in the dark days, to prove that I am not unworthy of it."

Surely he did prove that, and no matter what he may have been and what he may have done in what he called the "dark days," no one will deny him the honor that is due him for his striving to make amends.

JAMES BOYS CHRONOLOGY.

Their Career Began in 1862, When They Joined Quantrell.

1862—Frank James joins Quantrell's band of guerrillas. Jesse James joins the band several months later.

July, 1862—Frank and Jesse James, with Capt. George Todd's company of Quantrell's guerrillas, meet Major Ransom's Federal cavalry on the Pleasant Hill and Blue Springs road and several Federals are killed.

July, 1863—Frank James and other guerrillas surround a house four miles east of Wellington, Lafayette County, and kill ten Federals.

August 21, 1863—Frank and Jesse James in the sack of Lawrence, Kas.

July, 1864—Jesse James and Arch Clements shoot four Federals in an apple orchard.

August 13, 1864—Frank and Jesse James kill seven Federals in Ray County.

September 27, 1864—Frank and Jesse

of a large sum.

1873—The box office at the fair grounds in Kansas City robbed of about $9,000 in broad daylight.

January, 1874—The Malvern and Hot Springs, Ark., stage held up and passengers robbed of $3,000.

January 31, 1874—The James gang commits its second train robbery on more improved methods than it followed in the first. This time the train is not wrecked but is flagged to a standstill. A train of the Iron Mountain Road at Gadshill, Mo., held up and robbed of $10,000.

February 11, 1874—The store of Craig & Son at Bentonville, Ark., robbed in broad daylight.

March 10, 1874—J. W. Whicher, a Pinkerton detective, killed by Jesse James at Rocky Ford, near the James home, in Clay County.

January 25, 1875—Detectives surround the James home, near Kearney, and throw an ignited bomb into the house. It explodes and tears off the arm of Mrs. Samuels, mother of Frank and Jesse James, and kills her son, Archie.

March 1, 1875—Introduction into the Missouri Legislature of a bill granting amnesty to the James and Younger outlaws. The bill is defeated.

April 12, 1875—Daniel Askew, a neighbor of the James's, who had harbored detectives, is murdered on his doorstep by the James gang.

December, 1875—Robbery of a Union Pacific train at Muncie, Kas., ten miles from Kansas City; $55,000 stolen.

Winter of 1876—Robbery of the Bank of Corinth, Miss.

April 1876—Robbery of the bank at Huntington, W. Va. Jack Kean captured, Thomp McDaniels, brother of Bud, killed in the fight. Frank and Jesse James have an exciting run to Missouri.

July 8, 1876—Robbery of a Missouri Pacific train at Otterville, Mo., and $17,000 taken. In this robbery were the two James brothers, the three Younger brothers, Hobbs Kerry, Bill Chadwell, Clell Miller and Charlie Pitts.

September 7, 1876—Attempted robbery of the bank at Northfield, Minn. J. L. Haywood, the cashier, murdered. The citizens of the town opened fight. Bill Chadwell and Clell Miller were shot down in the street. Bob Younger was shot in the arm and jaws. Cole Younger picked him up and threw him across his horse. Cole, Jim and Bob Younger were captured and sentenced to the penitentiary in Stillwater for life. Jesse and Frank James escaped through great dangers and fled to Mexico, where they stayed a year or two. There they killed the guards of a pack train near Carmen, Chihuahua, and stole 150 pounds of silver. In the spring of 1877 they killed two men in a brawl at Piedras Negras, and later killed seven men in a fight near San Luis Potosi. They returned to Missouri in the summer of 1877.

September 17, 1877—Robbery by reconstructed James gang of a Union Pacific train at Big Springs, Neb., and $62,000 in gold stolen from the safe of the Wells-Fargo Express Company.

October 7, 1879—Robbery of a Chicago & Alton train at Glendale (now Seise), Jackson County, near Independence. This was the first train robbery in the noted Crackerneck district. The bandits stole $40,000. Jesse and Frank James, Dave Poole, Charley Ford, Wood Hite and Clarence Hite supposed to be the robbers.

July 11, 1881—Robbery of Davis & Sexton's Bank at Riverton, Ia., and $5,000 taken.

July 15, 1881—Robbery of a Chicago, Rock Island & Pacific train at Winston, Mo. W. H. Westfall, conductor, and a stonemason named McCulloch killed. The robbers got $15,000.

September 7, 1881—Second robbery of a Chicago & Alton train at Glendale (now Seise), Jackson County.

April 3, 1882—Jesse James shot and killed in his home at St. Joseph, Mo., by Charley Ford for a reward of $50,000, offered by Thomas T. Crittenden, governor.

October 5, 1882—Frank James surrenders to Governor Crittenden in Jefferson City.

Mrs. A. L. Mason's Funeral Today.

The funeral services for Mrs. A. L. Mason, who died Wednesday, will be held at the residence, 636 East Armour Boulevard, at 2:30 o'clock this afternoon. Burial will be in Elmwood Cemetery. The honorary pallbearers will be: Dr. James E. Logan, E. P. Pratt, Dr. J. H. Thompson, E. W. Smith, J. F. Richards, Alexander Massey, Judge Stuart Carkener, M. W. Foster and Richard Patterson. The active pallbearers will be: Frank Askew, Kirk Askew, Fred Askew, Harry Askew, H. C. Whitehead, St. Clair Alexander, John H. Thompson, jr., and George Mersereau.

The story of how Frank James turned down a publisher's "enormous sum" for his memoirs. *The James D. Horan Collection*

WAS NOT WITH FRANK JAMES.

MR. WALLACE DECLARES THAT HE STANDS BY HIS SPEECH FOR THE PROSECUTION IN THE CELEBRATED TRIAL AT GALLATIN, MO.

[From the Kansas City Star, November 13, 1901.]

To the Star: In your issue of November 11, appears a statement which I am assured has gone broadcast through the state and which does me a great injustice. In an editorial in reference to the appearance of Frank James as an actor, you state that Mr. James should make his debut in Kansas City. This language is then used: "No doubt the boxes will be filled with former Missouri officials, with some present office holders and a number of distinguished laymen in the theater parties. Mr. William H. Wallace, candidate for United States Senate, who is now on a hunting trip with Mr. James in the Indian territory, would surely do his utmost to live down his record as the prosecuting attorney of Jackson county during the James regime."

I do not censure the Star for the statement that I was hunting with Frank James in the Indian territory, because I am assured by friends that it had been previously published—they do not recall in what paper—that such was a fact. Nor considering the lights before you can I object to the inference you draw, namely, that being a candidate for United Sttates senator I was endeavoring in this way to obtain the favor and support of Frank James and his friends. But the fact is that your information was absolutely false. I have not been hunting with anyone for years, and never hunted in the Indian territory in my life. I have not seen Frank James, nor have I communicated with him, nor he with me, directly or indirectly, upon any subject whatever.

I have never gloated over the downfall of the Missouri bandits. This would be cowardly. But while this is true I defy any man to cite a single act or utterance of mine during the whole eighteen years that have elapsed since the destruction of the James gang, which could be tortured into the slightest apology for my official conduct. I spoke to a packed house at Liberty, in Clay county, the former home of the James boys, on the 4th of this month. I was told that there was in the audience a large number of men from the vicinity of Kearney, where Frank and Jesse James were raised. Before beginning my speech, word came twice from persons I knew were my friends, advising me to make no reference in my address to the Missouri bandits. These warnings assured me that it was thought there were some persons present who were opposed to me because of my prosecutions of train robbers. I stated to the audience that I devoted three years of my life to the work of assisting in the overthrow of one of the shrewdest and most desperate bands of outlaws known to modern times; that I had no apologies to make, and that if I had my official life to live over, my conduct would be precisely the same.

Extremely rare "card" published by William Wallace to deny the *Kansas City Star*'s story he had been on a "hunting trip to the Indian Territory with Frank James." The *Star*'s story hurt Wallace's campaign for the senate. *The James D. Horan Collection*

FRANK JAMES WAS HAUNTED BY FEAR OF BRAIN AUTOPSY

Requested Cremation of Body to Ihsure Scientists Would Not Get It.

RELATIVES ON GUARD

Former Bandit Believed Brother Jesse's Body Was Mutilated by Doctors.

Newspaper story describing the fear Frank James had of an autopsy. *The James D. Horan Collection*

There is little doubt that Wallace's vigorous and courageous prosecution of the Jameses-Youngers ruined what could have been a glowing political career. During his last year as prosecutor he became a congressional candidate. His district was composed of Jackson, Johnson, and Lafayette counties, with Jackson controlling the nomination by a majority. Wallace carried every ward and precinct in the city, but at the convention the chairman of the congressional delegation, a distiller, refused to accept the credentials of the delegates voting for Wallace. After a bitter floor fight, half the convention voted for Wallace, half for a Lexington candidate. Rather than split the party, Wallace withdrew. The distillers now had their revenge.

Friends of Wallace tried to get him the Democratic party's nomination for governor but were bluntly told by the leaders meeting in caucus to select the nominees: "We could not handle Wallace."

Wallace was then a criminal court judge in Kansas City, still battling the distillers and major department store owners. Almost perversely he had started a grand jury investigation of speakeasy owners and drugstores illegally selling liquor on Sunday, and the flood of indictments and convictions had outraged many. Threats were made to bomb his house, and to shoot his wife and two small children. A mob tried to storm his office and he was denounced editorially across the state. But many citizens' groups publicly applauded his courage in enforcing a very unpopular law.

Two weeks before the primary his supporters started an independent campaign to get him the gubernatorial nomination. Wallace refused to abandon the court, which lacked judges, to go on a speaking tour. He was only narrowly defeated. He wrote later: "Politicians said that if I had two more weeks I would have been nominated. But there is no use making excuses. The fact is I was defeated." [28]

While he was on the bench Wallace also created a furor by announcing he intended to enforce the law, ignored for years, forbidding the carrying of sidearms. The frontier had been officially dead only a few years. The Civil War was still vividly recalled, and in the deep West lawmen were hunting for riders of the Wild Bunch. Carrying a gun was commonplace, even in Kansas City.

Wallace was ridiculed and his supporters warned him he was attempting to enforce an unenforceable law. But Wallace grimly launched his campaign, instructing a grand jury to indict those arrested. To underscore his determination that the firearms law had to be obeyed, he handed out jail sentences instead of fines.

"The decrease in the habit [of wearing guns] astonished me, and doubtless many lives have been spared," he observed in his autobiography. "As I remember it has been several months now since a defendant has been arraigned in my court charged with carrying concealed deadly weapons." [29]

Wallace also pioneered in establishing a parole system, ordering parolees to file a report of their activities and to regularly visit a parole officer. He was far beyond his times when he attempted to stamp out organized prostitution. Not only did his grand jury indict 175 brothel owners, but also 85 Kansas City real estate owners who allowed their property to be used for the purpose of prostitution. Most of those indicted were given stiff fines and jail sentences. [30]

During the years he was on the bench, Wallace was relentless in his determination that the law had to be served. Democrats and Republicans felt his wrath from the bench. He was called a "radical," "fanatic," a "menace to the good name of the Democratic party," but he also had his supporters, people who knew Wallace could not be bought.

After years on the bench Wallace returned to private practice. He was persuaded by a state temperance group to campaign across the state at an annual salary of $3,000 against the increase in the number of saloons. Wallace never touched his salary. After four years he turned the accumulated $12,000 to the temperance cause.

Wallace also founded the *Citizen*, devoted to good government. To keep the paper from folding he went into debt, "far more deeply than I ever imagined I would be," he wrote in 1914. "Honest men tell me I have done good but I sincerely regret I have not done more."

Wallace continued to be one of the most controversial figures in midwestern politics. He never stopped fighting the distillers (who were major contributors to his party), prostitution, store merchants who wanted to open on Sunday, and the carrying of concealed firearms. He lived to write one of the first letters to the Minnesota Parole Board pleading for the release of Cole Younger and his brother Jim who had served twenty-five years of their life sentences.

When he was criticized, he replied firmly, "Humanity dictates that I do this."

Examples of the Bertillon method used in the 1880s by private detective agencies, stockmen's detectives, and large city police departments to identify criminals. The Wild Bunch's Ben (The Tall Texan) Kilpatrick was identified by this method after he had been captured in St. Louis in 1901, trying to cash forged bank notes stolen in a train robbery. *The James D. Horan Collection*

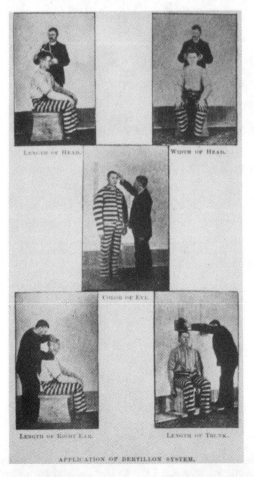
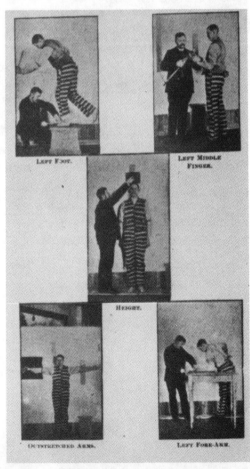

THEODORE ROOSEVELT: FRONTIER PHOTOGRAPHER

Theodore Roosevelt was truly a man for all seasons: politician, leader of his party, author, critic, historian, western rancher, horseman, marksman, New York City Police Department commissioner, governor, vice-president and president of the United States. And cameraman.

When he went west for long vacations on his ranch, TR never failed to bring his camera. Perhaps he was conscious his western adventure would some day be part of history and he was determined to leave behind a heritage of glass plates.

Almost immediately after the main house had been finished and his herd collected, Roosevelt began making a pictorial record of his Elkhorn ranch. He used some of the photographs to illustrate his articles in *Century* Magazine and his books on the West.

In his typical intent fashion Roosevelt wanted to know everything about photography. He counted among his friends L. A. Huffman, who photographed the Montana and Dakota frontiers and D. F. Barry, the Indian photographer. Huffman visited the Elkhorn and undoubtedly gave Roosevelt advice on his picture taking.

Fortunately for the researcher, TR captioned in his own handwriting every photograph he took, in addition to the mounted prints presented to him by Huffman.

What appear to be three expensively bound red leather books are actually containers for Theodore Roosevelt's photographs of his Elkhorn ranch and the pictorial record he made of his chase after the outlaw trio down the Little Missouri in March 1886. They were discovered twenty-five years ago and are now in the James D. Horan Civil War and Western Americana Collection. *Photo by Victor Veygel, Little Falls, New Jersey Photography*

Examining a dim brand during the roundup. *The James D. Horan Collection*

Branding calves on the Elkhorn during the 1884 roundup. *The James D. Horan Collection*

The midday meal at the chuck wagon. *The James D. Horan Collection*

The horses and the horseman. *The James D. Horan Collection*

The saddle band in the rope corral. *The James D. Horan Collection*

A roped bronc in the corral. *The James D. Horan Collection*

The front view of the Elkhorn ranch. *The James D. Horan Collection*

Roped. Taken by Huffman for TR's article, "The Roundup." All appeared in *Century* magazine in the 1880s. *The James D. Horan Collection*

The Elkhorn ranch house in the summer. In 1886 the row of trees stopped huge ice crags from the nearby Little Missouri from crushing the house. *The James D. Horan Collection*

THEY ALL PLAYED A ROLE IN THEODORE ROOSEVELT'S STORY OF THE WILD WEST

Sylvane Ferris, Dakota Territory cattle rancher. When Roosevelt was looking for a ranch to buy he stayed overnight in the Ferris log cabin of the Maltese Cross Ranch. Wrapped in a blanket, he slept on the dirt floor. *Courtesy State Historical Society of North Dakota*

William Merrifield, part owner of the Maltese Cross. Merrifield and the Ferris brothers later joined Roosevelt in the cattle business. *Courtesy State Historical Society of North Dakota*

The marquis de Mores, 1886. The French nobleman's North Pacific Refrigerator Car Company shipped daily loads of dressed beef to the East while he was planning to build a chain of icehouses as far west as Oregon so that fresh Columbia River salmon could be sent to New York in a week. The marquis wore a large white sombrero and an expensive silk shirt braided with yellow cord when he rode up and down the main street of Medora. He served his guests the best of French champagne and once invited Roosevelt to fight a duel. *Courtesy State Historical Society of North Dakota*

Medora, 1886, named by the marquis after his wife, Medora von Hoffman, a wealthy New York banker's daughter. *Courtesy State Historical Society of North Dakota*

Theodore Roosevelt, rancher and Billings County Deputy Sheriff. *The James D. Horan Collection*

Arthur Packard, Roosevelt's friend and editor of the Medora's weekly, *Bad Lands Cowboy*. Packard introduced Teddy to the *Cowboy*'s readers as "a young New York reformer . . . in full cowboy regalia." *Courtesy State Historical Society of North Dakota*

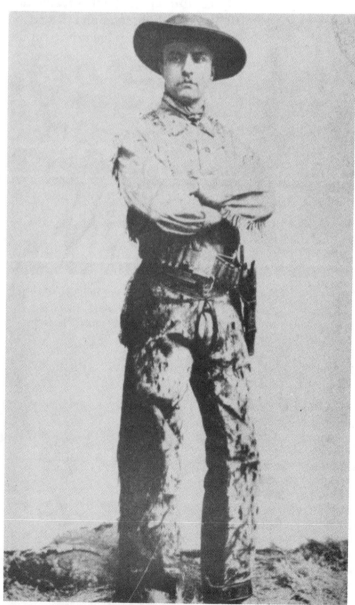

Among the many ideas of the marquis was a stagecoach line. Here is a poster for his Medora & Black Hills Forwarding Company. *Courtesy State Historical Society of North Dakota*

THEODORE ROOSEVELT:
DEPUTY SHERIFF

When a band of horse thieves, led by "Red" Finnegan, "a hard character," stole Deputy Sheriff Theodore Roosevelt's boat in the early hours of March 20, 1886, an outraged Teddy decided to pursue the outlaws and return them to face justice. A freakish March thaw had filled the Little Missouri with ice, leaving only a narrow millrace. The weather had turned the ground into a thick muddy glue, so horses were useless; the Missouri was the only remaining highway to get downriver. Roosevelt's two ranch foremen, William Sewall and Wilmot Dow, both Maine rivermen, built another boat. After a blizzard had blown itself out, the trio started down the Little Missouri on the morning of March 30. Roosevelt, in fringed buckskins and bundled in a buffalo robe, spent most of the journey writing the first chapter of his biography of Thomas Hart Benton and reading Tolstoy's *Anna Karenina*. He photographed the passage downriver and the final capture at gunpoint of the three outlaws. Roosevelt not only captioned each mounted photograph but also made crop marks for Frederic Remington, who did the sketches for his article on the manhunt published in *Century* Magazine.

Ready to start. Wilmot Dow and Bill Sewall in the riverboat they built in three days to chase the outlaw band down the Little Missouri. *The James D. Horan Collection*

A butte on the river bank. Sewall and Dow never forgot the freezing wind that roared across the Badlands: "the crookedest wind in Dakota," Sewall called it. The more romantic Roosevelt remembered the buttes as "crouching figures of great goblin beasts." *The James D. Horan Collection*

Billings County Deputy Sheriff Theodore Roosevelt, future president of the United States, guarding the half-breed, Burnsted; the German, Pfaffenbach; and their leader, "Red" Finnegan, who later told Teddy, "If I'd had any show at all, you'd have sure had to fight, Mr. Roosevelt." *The James D. Horan Collection*

Another view of TR guarding his prisoners. He made crop marks and added this notation for Remington: "Put figure of rifleman in place of smaller figure in picture 4." *The James D. Horan Collection*

This is Remington's sketch in *Century* magazine based on TR's photographs and instructions Roosevelt gave him. *The James D. Horan Collection*

The following are sketches made by Remington for Theodore Roosevelt's article, "Down the Little Missouri" and for his book, *Ranch Life and the Hunting Trail*, published in 1897. The first is "The capture of the German [Pfaffenbach]." *The James D. Horan Collection*

"Take off your shoes." To make sure his prisoners did not escape during the night, Roosevelt ordered the outlaws to take off their shoes. Mandan was more than 150 miles downriver and their provisions were running out. But TR was determined to bring the trio of bad men to justice. *The James D. Horan Collection*

"The capture of Finnegan." *The James D. Horan Collection*

"On the road to Dickinson." Roosevelt trudged in the bitter cold behind the wagon in the ankle-deep, gluelike mud. He later wrote he remained on guard for thirty-six straight hours until he reached Dickinson, where he turned over his prisoners to the sheriff. As a deputy sheriff he received a fee of $50 for "making the arrests and mileage." *The James D. Horan Collection*

"Down stream." Roosevelt, Sewall, and Dow, using the two small boats, poled their way down the ice-clogged river for eight days. Their provisions gave out and the six men were reduced to eating flour mixed with river water and rolled into balls. On April 7 they reached a cow camp where Roosevelt borrowed a pony and rode fifteen miles to a ranch; its owner agreed to drive TR and his prisoners to Dickinson, forty-five miles to the south, while Sewall and Dow moved downriver to Mandan in the two boats. *The James D. Horan Collection*

THE DAKOTA TERRITORY: TEDDY ROOSEVELT'S COUNTRY

Theodore Roosevelt deeply loved the Dakota Territory with its endless prairies dotted with wild flowers bending to the high keening winds, sparkling twisting rivers, tortured buttes, and fantastic Badlands—"Hell with the fires out." Another man loved the same land. His name was John Talbot Pitman, a professional soldier from Rhode Island who had enlisted as a private in the Civil War. By Appomattox he was a battle-hard colonel of the Ninth Regiment, Rhode Island Volunteers. At some time during the war he had met a combat photographer, perhaps one of Brady's corps of cameramen—Tim O'Sullivan, Alexander or Jim Gardner—and had become an enthusiastic amateur photographer.

After Congress had cut Grant's army to 25,000, Pitman remained with the Indian Fighting Army. He was first assigned to Fort Snelling, Minnesota, once the army's furthest northwest post, the headquarters for explorers, fur traders, and a scene of many historic Indian councils.

He was then transferred to Fort Abraham Lincoln in the Dakota Territory as chief ordinance officer, Department of the Dakotas.

Apparently a camera accompanied Pitman wherever he went. He made hundreds of glass plates of Indians, posts, forts, Missouri steamboats, the endless prairies, homesteaders, officers and their ladies on "Custer's porch," General Crook, and many others. At intervals he would have the fort's carpenter make him a sturdy wooden box which he used to ship the plates to his sisters living in a beautiful Victorian mansion in Orange, New Jersey.

Over twenty-five years ago this writer discovered the collection of Pitman's glass plates and mounted prints.

On the following pages are scenes of the Dakota Territory, the land both Theodore Roosevelt and John Pitman loved so deeply. The unpublished prints have been developed from the original plates, all part of the James D. Horan Collection.

FORTS, TROOPERS, FRONTIER TOWNS AND HOMESTEADERS

Extremely rare view of troopers at Fort Abraham Lincoln on the firing line during maneuvers. Note the heavy powder smoke. *The James D. Horan Collection*

An army carriage. *The James D. Horan Collection*

Officers and their ladies on a Sunday afternoon, sitting on the steps of "Custer's porch." Custer rode out of Fort Abraham Lincoln to Little Big Horn. Legend has Elizabeth waving goodbye to her husband from this porch. Also in these quarters she was told of his death. *The James D. Horan Collection*

A blockhouse, probably Fort Rice. *The James D. Horan Collection*

A lone trooper hunting on the prairie. *The James D. Horan Collection*

Winter scene, looking beyond Fort Scully, where in the winter of 1864 Sitting Bull turned over Fanny Kelly, a celebrated white captive called "Real Woman," to the army. *The James D. Horan Collection*

Fort Abraham Lincoln, looking southeast toward the river. *The James D. Horan Collection*

Camp in the lowlands below Fort Scully. *The James D. Horan Collection*

Lincoln's guns and one-room schoolhouse. *The James D. Horan Collection*

An early picture of Huron, Dakota Territory, looking south. *The James D. Horan Collection*

The open prairie, looking southeast to the Missouri River beyond Fort Abraham Lincoln. *The James D. Horan Collection*

The parade of Fort Abraham Lincoln. *The James D. Horan Collection*

A horse with a cross hobble. To hobble one front foot to the hind one on the opposite side was a dangerous practice. It could throw a nervous horse into a panic. Fighting the hobble, the animal could throw itself and be injured. *The James D. Horan Collection*

A regimental band from Fort Yates playing at what may be the Parkin ranch, a short distance from Standing Rock Agency. Here Mrs. Catherine S. Weldon, the Brooklyn artist who lived with Sitting Bull and his wives in their Grand River camp, stayed after she left the chief when he refused to stop the Ghost Dancers. The flamboyant artist, called "Woman Walking Ahead," was a bitter enemy of James (White Hair) McLaughlin, the Indian agent at Standing Rock. Mrs. Weldon's prediction to Sitting Bull that the Ghost Dance would only end in his death came true on December 15, 1890, when McLaughlin's Indian police killed the famous chief. The Massacre of Wounded Knee soon followed. Note the non-commissioned officer at the far right wearing a pith helmet, standard equipment for the Indian Fighting Army. *The James D. Horan Collection*

Officers of the Eighth Cavalry who took over Fort Abraham Lincoln after the death of Custer and his troopers. They are sitting on "Custer's porch." *The James D. Horan Collection*

An officer's wife, sweeping her front porch, paused momentarily to pose for Pitman's camera. Note the two bicycles; one has the big front wheel of the 1870s. *The James D. Horan Collection*

An officer and his wife bundled up in buffalo coats. *The James D. Horan Collection*

Troopers with snowshoes and a toboggan. *The James D. Horan Collection*

After a blizzard. The depth of the snow at Fort Abraham Lincoln can be measured by the lamp post. *The James D. Horan Collection*

Cavalry encampment near Bismarck. *The James D. Horan Collection*

A damaged plate showing troopers sawing wood. The belt was made of buffalo hide. *The James D. Horan Collection*

A general view of Fort Abraham Lincoln, looking southeast to the Missouri River. *The James D. Horan Collection*

Tenting on the plains. An officer's family picnicking. *The James D. Horan Collection*

An officer's quarters, similar to Custer's, at Fort Lincoln. *The James D. Horan Collection*

To put the immensity of the land into perspective, Pitman had two of his companions climb to the top of this hill and pose. *The James D. Horan Collection*

Cannon Rock, a formation in the Badlands. *The James D. Horan Collection*

The main street of Bismarck, the terminus of the Northern Pacific Railroad. Here army wives stayed overnight at the old Sheridan Hotel to take a stern-wheeler up the Missouri to Ford Buford or be picked up by an army wagon and driven to Fort Abraham Lincoln several miles down the river. An early visitor recalled Bismarck as a roaring river town offering saloons, gambling halls, and bawdy ladies. *The James D. Horan Collection*

Bismarck, Dakota Territory, in the distance. *The James D. Horan Collection*

Walls of ice, the kind Roosevelt encountered on his downriver journey, pushed up on the bank of the Missouri, almost crushing the small log house. *The James D. Horan Collection*

A homesteader and his cabin. Note the grass growing on the sod roof. The carriage, driven by a trooper and two boys dressed in their Sunday best, came from Fort Lincoln. *The James D. Horan Collection*

The main street of Huron, Dakota Territory. *The James D. Horan Collection*

Among Pitman's plates was this rare mounted, gold-edged photograph taken on August 7, 1889, by the famous Indian photographer D. F. Barry, of a singular group of people who had made frontier history. Seated *(left to right)* are: Mrs. L. Powell, General Crook, Major General Powell, Governor Fasler, Major Powell, Major Warner, and Major Randall. Barry began his career in Bismarck in 1875 as an assistant to pioneer photographer Orlando Scott Goff. He persuaded Gall, famous chief of the Hunkpapa Teton Sioux who showed his military genius at Little Big Horn, to pose in his Bismarck gallery. Gall later returned threatening to kill Barry if he didn't destroy the glass plate which had "stolen his shadow." Barry hid it, although Gall, armed with a knife, went on a rampage in the gallery. Barry was a friend of Pitman's and visited the officer many times at Fort Lincoln, where this historic photograph was taken. *The James D. Horan Collection*

INDIANS

An extremely rare glass plate of the sacred "Legend Stone" or "Standing Rock" of the Sioux Nation. This photograph was taken during the reign of Major James McLaughlin, Indian agent at Standing Rock Agency. McLaughlin, called "White Hair" or "White Haired Father" by the Sioux, erected this stone pedestal, the stone's first foundation. The Stone is one of the earliest religious symbols of the Plains Nation. Myth claims it to be of a woman and child turned to stone after they had been abandoned by their warrior husband and father. This plate is believed to be the only existing one of the Legend Stone on its original foundation. McLaughlin, the agency's agent for many years, was a bitter enemy of Sitting Bull. In December 1890 he ordered the arrest of the famous chief. During a struggle in the early morning darkness, Lieutenant Bullhead, head of the Indian police, killed Sitting Bull. Years ago the late J. L. Jennewein, the well-known western historian, examined and helped to identify some of the Pitman glass plates. He described this plate as: "An important part of North Dakota's history and the Sioux."

Indian burial platform. The corpse was strapped to a platform of boughs and left to the elements. *The James D. Horan Collection*

A proud Sioux warrior standing on the steps of the trader's post, Standing Rock Agency. Legend has it that the row of sleigh bells he is wearing identify him as a member of Sitting Bull's bodyguard, who had sworn to die if necessary to protect their chief. *The James D. Horan Collection*

Sioux warriors and their interpreter in 1889, Standing Rock Agency, before the Ghost Dance swept through the Indian nations of the West. The dance taught that the Messiah had returned, this time as an Indian, since the whites had denied and crucified him. He would resurrect the dead, remove the white men from the land, and bring back herds of buffalo. The Ghost Dance religion led to the death of Sitting Bull and finally the massacre at Wounded Knee. It is not improbable that some of these warriors died at Wounded Knee or in the bitter struggle of that dark December morning when Sitting Bull was killed and Indian fought Indian. Note the amused trooper, his cape flapping in the wind *The James D. Horan Collection*

Mounted Sioux warriors. By the time Pitman took this picture the Plains Indians were mixing the white man's clothes with their native dress. Note the rider wearing what appears to be a battered derby. *The James D. Horan Collection*

On the road to Standing Rock Agency. The dog travois was a favorite method of Indian mothers to transport their small children. Its springiness soon lulled the child to sleep. A dome-shaped case made of willow rods, used to keep off the summer sun or rain, was securely closed after the children had been put inside. This type of dog travois was first mentioned in the journals of Coronado's expedition, 1540-42. *The James D. Horan Collection*

Horse travois, the litter type of transportation commonly used among the Plains Indian nations. When a family or a tribe decided to move and the tepee had been taken down, the poles of each tepee were tied in two bunches of about twelve poles each by means of rawhide ropes passed through holes already bored for that purpose. They were then tied on each side of the horse with a rope, passing in front of the saddle so that the ends of the poles rested on the animal's upper shoulders while the lower ends trailed behind on the ground. The buffalo-hide tepee covered the poles to form a litter for household goods, including, sometimes, old people. When a new campsite was selected, the load was unpacked and tepee erected by the women, usually within minutes. *The James D. Horan Collection*

A remarkable plate of a council of Indian women, Standing Rock Agency, 1889. Note the wash line, the woman seated who quickly covered her head when she saw the "shadow catcher" with his camera, and the mother with her papoose in a carrying cradle—the type adopted by modern mothers and commonly seen in today's supermarkets. *The James D. Horan Collection*

Indian tepees on the plains near Fort Yates, Dakota Territory. *The James D. Horan Collection*

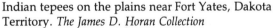

Indian women in the white man's world were dignified, impassive. Here is an unusually smiling Sioux woman turning to greet Pitman as he clicks the shutter of his camera. *The James D. Horan Collection*

STEAMBOATS ON THE MISSOURI

Like all the officers, enlisted men, and their families, General John T. Pitman used the riverboats to travel up and down the Missouri. He never forgot to take his camera. This extremely rare and slightly damaged glass plate shows troopers transferring from one sternwheeler to another while women and children promenade on the upper deck. *The James D. Horan Collection*

Loading a Missouri riverboat, with officers on the top deck. Note the roustabouts at the woodpile on the lower deck. *The James D. Horan Collection*

Coming downriver. The Missouri was a treacherous river, constantly changing its tortuous course, filled with invisible snags, sandbars, and drowned buffalo ready to splinter a stern wheel. Mark Twain wrote that in order to be a Missouri River pilot, "a man had to learn more than any other man ought to be allowed to know; he was to learn it all over again in a different way every twenty-four hours." *The James D. Horan Collection*

The *Helena*, pride of T. C. Powers's Benton Transportation Company and queen of the Missouri's riverboats. Powers, a frontier store owner, founded the famous western steamboat and mercantile empire to challenge the Northern Pacific Railroad. By 1885 his stern-wheelers ruled the upper river. Powers's company had government contracts to transport troops and cargo to the forts along the river. Note the "P" between the smokestacks, Powers's trademark. *The James D. Horan Collection*

Riverboat taking on troopers from Fort Abraham Lincoln. *The James D. Horan Collection*

The *Helena*, steaming upriver. *The James D. Horan Collection*

The *Rosebud*, well known to the officers and troopers at Fort Abraham Lincoln, drawn up on the Missouri bank. Before the winter set in, steam rigs pulled the boats up log ways so the stern-wheelers could be repaired and be safe from the walls of ice moving downriver in the spring thaw. Shortly after the Civil War, twenty-six stern-wheelers were crushed against the St. Louis levee by crags of ice moving downriver. *The James D. Horan Collection*

THEODORE ROOSEVELT, DEPUTY SHERIFF

THEODORE ROOSEVELT FIRST CAME TO THE DAKOTA Territory in September 1883 on a vacation to shoot buffalo. During the past year he had "soared like a rocket" and then become an "awful cropper" as a New York State assemblyman and Republican minority speaker.

His triumphs included guiding the Civil Service Reform Bill through the Tammany-dominated assembly to Governor Cleveland's desk and pen. Politicians were talking about Teddy, the youngest man in the state legislature, and experts were predicting the country would some day hear about him. A few even hinted he could be on the road to the White House.

There were others, even fellow Republicans, who disliked his arrogance, confidence and impulsive remarks. Some thought he was an insufferable prig, others considered him a leader who was determined at any expense to keep his name on page one of the New York City newspapers. But both Republicans and Democrats knew Roosevelt was not a man who could be ignored.

Before the session had ended he had been politically humbled in the losing fight over the "Five Cents Bill" which would have reduced the fare of Jay Gould's Manhattan elevated train from ten to five cents. However, his Civil Service Reform Bill victory restored his prestige.

After the exhausting legislative session Roosevelt, at the invitation of a friend, went to the Dakota Territory for a buffalo hunt.

Roosevelt's arrival on the dying frontier was slightly less than a decade after Custer and his men had been wiped out at Little Big Horn. The cattle market was

130

booming, free range was for the asking, the tribes had been broken and forced into reservations, and the Northern Pacific extended from St. Paul to the West Coast running through the Dakota Territory. The Little Missouri Valley was open range occupied only by cattle.[1]

One rancher was the eccentric Marquis de Mores, a wealthy Frenchman who had come to the territory the year before to invest in the beef market. His grandiose schemes had stunned the settlers. He intended to buy every available herd, build a gigantic slaughterhouse, and ship the beef east in refrigerated cars. In April "that crazy Frenchman" had fenced large sections of the range, started his slaughterhouse, and founded a town he named Medora after his wife. His hilltop ranch house overlooking the Little Missouri Valley was called "Chateau de Mores."

Some of the settlers were enraged by the Frenchman's fences, but as many times as they tore them down they were rebuilt. When he heard three ranchers were in Medora threatening to kill him, de Mores telegraphed the sheriff at Mandan, then ambushed the trio, killing one and wounding the others. Murder charges were later dismissed and the Frenchman continued to turn his strange dream into reality.[2]

Roosevelt's guide, Joe Ferris, undoubtedly told him the story as they moved deeper into the Badlands searching for the last herds, now almost extinct. They sighted two cows, wounded one, and finally feasted on buffalo steaks. But buffalo was not all that important to Roosevelt; he had fallen in love with that beautiful savage country and was determined to own part of it. Before he left for New York he had given his rancher hosts, Sylvane Ferris, Joe's brother, and Bill Merrifield, a check for $14,000 as a down payment for a thousand head of cattle costing $24,000.

During the following year Roosevelt rushed down from Albany to be with his wife, Alice, who had recently given birth to a daughter, but was in poor health. Her life ebbed away, and then Roosevelt had to tend to his dying mother.

"The light has gone out of my life," he wrote in his diary after he had buried both on the same day.[3]

Roosevelt's singular toughness and decisiveness helped him survive the double tragedy. In February he was back in Albany plunging into work, a man in almost constant motion. He made speeches, fought for his party's bills, and guided them through the complex political machine of the Albany legislature. He wrote reports and led the Independents at the New York State Republican Convention in Utica, almost single-handedly making Vermont senator George F. Edmunds a serious White House contender.

Yet for all his triumphs close friends knew that his grief was increasing instead of fading away. He refused renomination as assemblyman and in a letter to an upstate newspaper confessed he "felt tired and restless" and was yearning for the frontier.[4]

In May he was at the Republican National Convention held in Chicago. President Arthur and James G. Blaine were favorites, with the dull Senator Edmunds only another hopeful among the dark horses. Roosevelt fought hard for Edmunds but Blaine, the Plumed Knight, won the nomination.

A few days after the last notes of the noisy convention had died away, Roosevelt was on his way to the Dakota Territory.

Roosevelt lost himself for days in the emptiness of what he called "the never ending plains." He would sleep under the cottonwoods, his horse, Manitou, grazing nearby. In Medora he met Arthur Packard, editor of the *Bad Lands Cowboy*, who told him dispatches reported that the reform press was denouncing him for his statement that he would support Blaine. Roosevelt shrugged off the political news and rode back to the Little Missouri country.

Sometime in June of that year Roosevelt found a spot on the river north of Medora, where he decided to build his log ranch house. Earlier that year he had asked Bill Sewall and Will Dow, two former Maine backwoodsmen who had often acted as Roosevelt's guides, to run his ranch. They were persuaded to come west by a share of the profits and a guarantee that their salaries would be paid, success or failure. The wives of both would join them after the ranch house was built.[5]

When Sewall and Dow arrived in August, Roosevelt gave them a tour of the property. In the woods bordering the river they found two elk skulls with locked horns. Roosevelt promptly called his new ranch Elkhorn.

While the Maine backwoodsmen built the ranch house, Roosevelt continued to explore the Badlands, riding as many as seventy miles a day. His body toughened, his face tanned, and he confessed in a letter to his sister that he was in prime physical condition and looked like a "cowboy dandy."

During this period Roosevelt had his famous encounter with a frontier bully in Mingusville, west of Medora. Roosevelt had been out on the plains searching for lost horses when he came up to Nolan's Hotel. As he entered, two shots were fired. He found himself in the saloon with a frightened bartender and several customers staring at a "shabby individual" waving a cocked six-shooter and taking shots at the clock.

The gunman greeted Roosevelt as "Four Eyes" and demanded that he treat the house. Roosevelt ignored him and sat down but the gunman followed, poking the cocked gun in Roosevelt's face and demanding that "Four Eyes" set up the drinks.

Roosevelt laughed, stood up, then suddenly swung around "with a right to the point of his jaw, hitting with my left as I straightened out and then again with my right. He fired the gun but I do not know whether this was a convulsive action of his hand or whether he was trying to shoot me. When he went down he struck the corner of the bar with his head."

The now very brave customers and bartender dragged the unconscious gunman to a shed and locked him in. He left by the time Roosevelt appeared the following morning.[6]

Roosevelt had another confrontation that fall. When he heard that one of de Mores's supporters had threatened to kill "Four Eyes" unless he paid him for the Elkhorn property, Roosevelt rode over to the man's ranch.

"I understand that you have threatened to kill me," he snapped. "I have come over to see when you want to begin the killing." The de Mores supporter quickly wilted under Roosevelt's cold glare and protested someone had been putting words in his mouth.[7]

Roosevelt returned to New York to write his *Hunting Trips of a Ranchman*, which was published in July 1885 to glowing reviews. He was soon back at the Elkhorn supervising the arrival of a new herd.

Saddling the wild horse, 1894. Layton A. Huffman, the frontier photographer who took this photograph of Andy Speelman, a Montana cowboy and professional bronc-buster, recalled that Speelman "proceeded to rope, blindfold and bridle the grey horse, then took him outside at my request and flung on the saddle, holding the horse by the bridle and hackmore. The picture was made just at the instant when he gave the first pull at the latigo, cinching the saddle." *The James D. Horan Collection*

A few weeks after the arrival of his cattle Roosevelt joined the Badlands roundup. He generally took the "Four Eyes" jibes with good humor but once had to warn a Texas cowboy that "Storm Windows" was too much. He was constantly in the saddle, roping steers until his hands were raw, and riding wild broncs to the admiration of the cowhands.

The Little Missouri Valley roundup covered more than three hundred miles with clouds of bitter-tasting alkali dust rising like dirty walls in the midday heat as the hands separated the protesting cattle into the herds of their owners. Roosevelt worked without complaining, branding the bellowing steers from dawn to dusk.

In the fall of 1885 the eight-room ranch house was completed with a row of cottonwoods between the river and the veranda, or piazza, as they called it. A young bronc buster named Rowe was hired to help Sewall and Dow with the cattle and horse herds. Roosevelt returned from a visit to the East to find that the wives of Sewall and Dow had joined their husbands and both were pregnant.

There was also a grim surprise—a letter from de Mores charging that Roosevelt was his "enemy" and hinting that as gentlemen a duel might settle their affair of honor.

Roosevelt, who refused "to be bullied by a Frenchman," immediately informed the marquis he was not his enemy but also pointed out he did not like threats and would be on hand any time the nobleman called.

De Mores quickly sent back a conciliatory note insisting he did not intend to make any threats and the confrontation the local cowboys were hoping for never took place.[8]

In the fall of 1885 Roosevelt returned east to attend the Republican State Convention, finish the big house at Sagamore Hill, go fox hunting, and fall in love with Edith Carow, friend of his sister Corinne. After they became secretly engaged she went to Europe with her mother and sister. The engagement had to be kept secret. It was only twenty-two months since Alice had died in his arms, and the Victorian society would have been shocked to discover Roosevelt was about to take a new wife.

He was bored by a winter of socializing and in March 1886 returned to the frontier to find his friend Joe Ferris married and an immense wall of ice inching down the Little Missouri from a bend in the river called Ox-bow. At night when the ice neared the Elkhorn, Roosevelt and the others in the ranch house listened to the floes grinding, crunching, and roaring like a pinioned giant writhing in pain.

The jam finally overflowed the banks to pile up against the row of cottonwood trees. For a time it appeared the pressure would uproot the trees and advance on the sturdy log house. In the moonlight the weird shapes of the floes appeared like wondrous fairyland castles bordering both sides of the Little Missouri.

One morning they came out on the veranda to find a narrow channel, like a millrace, flowing between sheer walls of glittering ice. Roosevelt wrote to his sister Bamie, describing how difficult it was to travel: "No horse could by any chance get across the river. We men have a boat, and even thus is laborious carrying it out to the work. We work like Arctic explorers."[9]

Before the ice jams appeared Sewall and Dow had crossed the river and killed four deer, which they hung in a tree to keep the meat from coyotes. One day Roosevelt, Sewall, and Dow set out to bring back the deer. This time they used the ranch's boat to cross the river. It was small but trim and the former river men kept it caulked, painted, and watertight. After a laborious journey of slipping, sliding, and wallowing in the gluelike mud, they finally reached the thicket of dwarf cedars where the deer had been hung. All they found were scattered bones and bits of hide.

Tracks disclosed that a pair of cougars had eaten the deer. Roosevelt and his men followed the tracks until dark, then returned to Elkhorn with Roosevelt determined to pick up the trail the following day and kill the cougars. At the bank Sewall tied the boat to a tree so it wouldn't be swept downriver by the moving ice.

In the morning Sewall found the boat gone, the rope had been cut; the thieves had left a red mitten with a leather palm. The laconic lumberjack served and ate breakfast with Dow; Roosevelt, who quickly finished, observed it was a fine day for cougar hunting.

"I guess we won't go today," Sewall said.

"Why not?" Roosevelt demanded.

Sewall showed him the red mitten and the rope with one end cut by a sharp knife.

"Someone has gone off with the boat," he said. [10]

The three men agreed that the thieves had to be the "three hard characters" who lived in a shack twenty miles upriver from Elkhorn. The leader was a tall, slender, hard-eyed man whose shoulder-length curly red hair had earned him the nickname of "Redhead" Finnegan. The second member of the band was a German named "Dutch Chris" Pfaffenbach. Sewall later described Pfaffenbach as "an oldish man who drank so much poor whiskey that he lost most of his manhood he never possessed." The third was Burnsted, known as the "half-breed."

Pfaffenbach and the "half-breed" were not considered dangerous but Finnegan was "a hard ticket." A suspected horse thief, he was surly, uncommunicative, and had a violent temper. In Bill Williams's Medora saloon he had boasted that he came from "Bitter Creek, where the further you went up the worse people got."[11]

One night Finnegan drank enough of Williams's "conversation juice to be laid out all right." A practical joker borrowed the town barber's hair clipper and clipped off one side of Finnegan's beard and moustache and the fringe on one side of his buckskin jacket. Then he was placed on the saloon's billiard table to sleep off his drunk. The following morning when he saw himself in the mirror behind the bar, Finnegan went berserk. He rode back to his cabin, got a rifle, and besieged the town, "pumping lead into everything in sight."

A shot whistled past the head of John Fisher, one of Roosevelt's friends, who was shaving in the office of Arthur Packard, the *Bad Lands Cowboy* editor. Packard, on horseback, was descending a bluff behind Medora and had a bird's-eye view of the action that followed Finnegan's shots.

Fisher, half his face covered with soap, rushed out of the *Bad Lands* office, unhitched his horse, swung up, and charged directly at Finnegan sprawled in the brush near the store owned by the Marquis de Mores. Before the redheaded sniper could get to his feet, Fisher's horse bowled him over and he was knocked out. Finnegan woke up with a headache in a darkened, sealed boxcar that the town used as a jail.

Following the Medora incident stockmen who had experienced horse thefts began to talk of vigilante action to force the trio to leave the area. It was then that the redheaded leader told his shabby hands they were leaving. Travel by foot or on horseback was impossible. They also had a small boat, but it leaked so badly Finnegan decided to steal Roosevelt's.

When he found his boat stolen, Roosevelt was so outraged that Sewall and Dow had to stop him from saddling Manitou and taking off after the outlaws. Sewall pointed out that he and Dow could put together a flatboat within three days and catch up with the trio. Roosevelt agreed. With his herd of forty to fifty cow ponies on the other side of the river, the boat was important. But the loss of the small boat was not the primary reason for Roosevelt's anger. On a frontier where justice was the six-shooter on a man's hip, Roosevelt knew that if he let Finnegan's band go unpunished it would be a signal for other thieves to plunder his beloved Elkhorn ranch. The outlaw trio had to be pursued, captured, and turned over to the law and the boat had to be recovered.

On his last trip east Roosevelt had agreed to write a biography of Thomas Hart Benton for the American Statesman Series. He had done some preliminary research in the eastern libraries and by March 27, 1886, the day Sewall and Dow finished building their scow, he had completed his opening chapter.

A blizzard delayed their departure for three more days. Roosevelt returned to his biography and wrote a letter to his friend Henry Cabot Lodge, complaining how difficult writing could be.

> It is terribly hard work and I make slow progress. I have some good ideas in the first chapter but I am not sure they are worked up rightly; my style is very rough and I do not like a certain amount of *sequitur* that I do not seem able to get rid of . . . as soon as it lightens up I shall start downriver with two of my men in a boat we have built while indoors, after some horse thieves took our boat the other night to get out of the country with; but they have such a start we have very little chance of catching them. I shall take Matthew Arnold along; I have had no chance at all to read it as yet.[12]

The following day he wrote to his sister describing life at Elkhorn:

> I have clean sheets, the cooking is pretty good, and above all I have a sitting room with a great fireplace and a rocking chair which I use as my study.
>   The walking is horrible; all slippery ice or else deep, sticky mud . . . in a day or two I shall start down the river to go to Mandan; the trip should ought to take ten days more or less. It will be fun.[13]

Roosevelt obviously emphasized the monotonous frontier life so as not to alarm his sister.

On the morning of March 30 the storm subsided. Sewall and Dow filled the provision box with bacon, flour, and coffee, enough for three weeks. Roosevelt also insisted they pack his camera, along with Tolstoy's *Anna Karenina* and a book by Matthew Arnold.

Finally they pushed off, the clumsy boat catching the water of the swift narrow channel. On the bank, Rowe, the young bronc buster, and the two worried and pregnant wives, shouted their good-byes until the small boat vanished beyond the walls of ice.

Sewall and Dow, both river men, were at home in the flatboat. While Sewall steered, Dow crouched in the bow watching for debris or ice. Roosevelt, wrapped in a buffalo robe, read Tolstoy and worked on his Thomas Hart Benton biography.

The ice thinned out, but the country they were traveling through was bleak, somber, and awesome. Beyond the riverbanks loomed the rugged, brooding buttes, twisted by time and weather into fantastic shapes and colors. At night veins of coal running through the formations glowed eerily in the darkness. Coyotes barked and occasionally a wolf leader summoned his pack with a long, drawn-out wavering howl. Back on the river the weather turned; the temperature dropped to below zero and the wind rose, a cold blade in their faces as it swept across the twisting river.

"We're like to have it in our faces all day," Dow called back from the bow.

"We can't unless it's the crookedest wind in Dakota," Sewall replied.

As they followed the river's erratic course, the wind continued to buffet them.

"It *is* the crookedest wind in Dakota," Sewall agreed.

Wrapped in his buffalo robe Roosevelt memorized the conversations of his men, the feel of the wind, and the impressive scenery as he thoughtfully felt the shape of the camera. The expedition might make an article—perhaps for *Century* Magazine.

Two years later Roosevelt's account of the manhunt, with sketches by Frederic Remington, based on photographs Teddy had taken, appeared in *Century*. Later this account became a chapter in his book, *Ranch Life and the Hunting Trail*, also published by Century.

Here is the future president of the United States trailing and capturing a band of outlaws in the Badlands of Dakota Territory in March 1886.[14]

Sheriff's Work on a Ranch

There could have been no better men for a trip of this kind than my two companions, Seawall and Dow.* They were tough, hardy, resolute fellows, quick as cats, strong as bears, and able to travel like bull moose. We felt very little uneasiness as to the result of a fight with the men we were after, provided we had anything like a fair show; moreover, we intended, if possible, to get them at such a disadvantage that there would not be any fight at all. The only risk of any consequence that we ran was that of being ambushed; for the extraordinary formation of the Bad Lands, with the ground cut up into gullies, serried walls, and battlemented hilltops, makes it the country of all others for hiding-places and ambuscades.

For several days before we started the weather had been bitterly cold, as a furious blizzard was blowing; but on the day we left there was a lull, and we hoped a thaw had set in. We all were most warmly and thickly dressed, with woolen socks and underclothes, heavy jackets and trousers, and great fur coats, so that we felt we could bid defiance to the weather. Each carried his rifle, and we had in addition a double-barreled duck gun, for water-fowl and beaver. To manage the boat, we had paddles, heavy oars, and long iron-shod poles, Seawall steering while Dow sat in the bow. Altogether we felt as if we were off on a holiday trip, and set to work to have as good a time as possible.

The river twisted in every direction, winding to and fro across the alluvial valley bottom, only to be brought up by the rows of great barren buttes that bounded it on each edge. It had worn away the sides of these till they towered up as cliffs of clay, marl, or sandstone. Across their white faces the seams of coal drew sharp black bands, and they were elsewhere blotched and varied with brown, yellow, purple, and red. This fantastic coloring, together with the jagged irregularity of their crests, channeled by the weather into spires, buttresses, and battlements, as well as their barrenness and the distinctness with which they loomed up through the high, dry air, gave them a look that was a singular mixture of the terrible and the grotesque. The bottoms were covered thickly with leafless cottonwood trees, or else with withered brown grass and stunted, sprawling sage bushes. At times the cliffs rose close to us on either hand, and again the valley would widen into a sinuous oval a mile or two long, bounded on every side, as far as our eyes could see, by a bluff line without a break, until, as we floated down close to its other end, there would suddenly appear in one corner a cleft through which the stream rushed out. As it grew dusk the shadowy outlines of the buttes lost nothing of their weirdness; the twilight only made their uncouth shapelessness more grim and forbidding. They looked like the crouching figures of great goblin beasts.

---

*Curiously, Roosevelt misspelled the names of Sewall and Finnegan.

> Those two hills on the right
> Crouched like two bulls locked horn in horn in fight—
> While to the left a tall scalped mountain. . . .
> The dying sunset kindled through a cleft:
> The hills, like giants at a hunting, lay
> Chin upon hand, to see the game at bay—

might well have been written after seeing the strange, desolate lands lying in western Dakota.

All through the early part of the day we drifted swiftly down between the heaped-up piles of ice, the cakes and slabs now dirty and unattractive looking. Towards evening, however, there came long reaches where the banks on either side were bare, though even here there would every now and then be necks where the jam had been crowded into too narrow a spot and had risen over the side as it had done up-stream, grinding the bark from the big cottonwoods and snapping the smaller ones short off. In such places the ice-walls were sometimes eight or ten feet high, continually undermined by the restless current; and every now and then overhanging pieces would break off and slide into the stream with a loud sullen splash, like the plunge of some great water beast. Nor did we dare to go in too close to the high cliffs, as bowlders and earth masses, freed by the thaw from the grip of the frost, kept rolling and leaping down their faces and forced us to keep a sharp lookout lest our boat should be swamped.

In the morning it was evident that instead of thawing it had grown decidedly colder. The anchor ice was running thick in the river, and we spent the first hour or two after sunrise in hunting over the frozen swamp bottom for white-tail deer, of which there were many tracks; but we saw nothing. Then we broke camp and again started down-stream—a simple operation, as we had no tent, and all we had to do was to cord up our bedding and gather the mess kit. It was colder than before, and for some time we went along in chilly silence, nor was it until midday that the sun warmed our blood in the least. Long before the sun went down the ice had begun to freeze on the handles of the poles, and we were not sorry to haul on shore for the night. For supper we again had prairie fowl, having shot four from a great patch of mulberry bushes late in the afternoon. A man doing hard open-air work in cold weather is always hungry for meat.

During the night the thermometer went down to zero, and in the morning the anchor ice was running so thickly that we did not care to start at once, for it is most difficult to handle a boat in the deep frozen slush. Accordingly we took a couple of hours for a deer hunt, as there were evidently many white-tail on the bottom. After a short consultation, one of our number crept round to the head of the gorge, making a wide detour, and the other two advanced up it on each side, thus completely surrounding the doomed deer. They attempted to break out past the man at the head of the glen, who shot down a couple, a buck and a yearling doe.

This success gladdened our souls, insuring us plenty of fresh meat. We carried pretty much all of both deer back to camp, and, after a hearty breakfast, loaded our scow and started merrily off once more. The cold still continued intense, and as the day wore away we became numbed by it, until at last an incident occurred that set our blood running freely again.

We were, of course, always on the alert, keeping a sharp lookout ahead and around us, and making as little noise as possible. Finally our watchfulness was rewarded, for in the middle of the afternoon of this, the third day we had been gone, as we came around a bend, we saw in front of us the lost boat, together with a scow, moored against the bank, while from among the bushes some little way back the smoke of a camp-fire curled up through the frosty air. We had come on the camp of the thieves. As I glanced at the faces of my two followers I was struck by the grim, eager look in their eyes. Our overcoats were off in a second, and after exchanging a few muttered words, the boat was hastily and silently shoved towards the bank. As soon as it touched the shore ice I leaped out and ran up behind a clump of bushes, so as to cover the landing of the others, who had to make the boat fast. For a moment we felt a thrill of keen excitement, and our veins tingled as we crept cautiously towards the fire, for it seemed likely that there would be a brush; but, as it turned out, this was almost the only moment of much interest, for the capture itself was as tame as possible.

The men we were after knew they had taken with them the only craft there was on the river, and so felt perfectly secure; accordingly, we took them absolutely by surprise. The only one in camp was the German, whose weapons were on the ground, and who, of course, gave up at once, his two companions being off hunting. We made him safe, delegating one of our number to look after him particularly and see that he made no noise, and then sat down and waited for the others. The camp was under the lee of a cut bank, behind which we crouched, and, after waiting an hour or over, the men we were after came in. We heard them a long way off and made ready, watching them for some minutes as they walked towards us, their rifles on their shoulders and the sunlight glinting on the steel barrels. When they were within twenty yards or so we straightened up from behind the bank, covering them with our cocked rifles, while I shouted to them to hold up their hands—an order that in such a case, in the West, a man is not apt to disregard if he thinks the giver is in earnest. The half-breed obeyed at once, his knees trembling as if they had been made of whalebone. Finnigan hesitated for a second, his eyes fairly wolfish; then, as I walked up within a few paces, covering the center of his chest so as to avoid overshooting, and repeating the command, he saw that he had no show, and, with an oath, let his rifle drop and held his hands up beside his head.

It was nearly dusk, so we camped where we were. The first thing to be done was to collect enough wood to enable us to keep a blazing fire all night long. While Seawall and Dow, thoroughly at home in the use of the ax, chopped down dead cottonwood trees and dragged the logs up into a huge pile, I kept guard over the three prisoners, who were huddled into a sullen group some twenty yards off, just the right distance for the buckshot in the double-barrel. Having captured our men, we were in a quandary how to keep them. The cold was so intense that to tie them tightly hand and foot meant, in all likelihood, freezing both hands and feet off during the night; and it was no use tying them at all unless we tied them tightly enough to stop in part the circulation. So nothing was left for us to do but to keep perpetual guard over them. Of course we had carefully searched them, and taken away not only their firearms and knives, but everything else that could possibly be used as a weapon. By this time they were pretty well cowed, as they found out very quickly that they would be well treated so long as they remained quiet, but would receive some rough handling if they attempted any disturbance.

Our next step was to cord their weapons up in some bedding, which we sat on while we took supper. Immediately afterward we made the men take off their boots—an additional safeguard, as it was a cactus country, in which a man could travel barefoot only at the risk of almost certainly laming himself for life—and go to bed, all three lying on one buffalo robe and being covered by another, in the full light of the blazing fire. We determined to watch in succession a half-night apiece, thus each getting a full rest every third night. I took first watch, my two companions, revolver under head, rolling up in their blankets on the side of the fire opposite that on which the three captives lay; while I, in fur cap, gantlets, and overcoat, took my station a little way back in the circle of firelight, in a position in which I could watch my men with the absolute certainty of being able to stop any movement, no matter how sudden. For this nightwatching we always used the double-barrel with buckshot, as a rifle is uncertain in the dark; while with a shot-gun at such a distance, and with men lying down, a person who is watchful may be sure that they cannot get up, no matter how quick they are, without being riddled. The only danger lies in the extreme monotony of sitting still in the dark guarding men who make no motion, and the consequent tendency to go to sleep, especially when one has had a hard day's work and is feeling really tired. But neither on the first night nor on any subsequent one did we ever abate a jot of our watchfulness.

Next morning we started down-stream, having a well-laden flotilla, for the men we had caught had a good deal of plunder in their boats, including some saddles, as they evidently intended to get horses as soon as they reached a part of the country where there were any, and where it was possible to travel. Finnigan, who was the ringleader, and the man I was especially after, I kept by my side in our boat, the other two being put in their own scow, heavily laden and rather leaky, and with only one paddle. We kept them just in front of us, a few yards distant, the river being so broad that we knew, and they knew also, any attempt at escape to be perfectly hopeless.

For some miles we went swiftly down-stream, the cold being bitter and the slushy anchor ice choking the space between the boats; then the current grew sluggish, eddies forming along the sides. We paddled on until, coming into a long reach where the water was almost backed up, we saw there was a stoppage at the other end. Working up to this, it proved to be a small ice jam, through which we broke our way only to find ourselves, after a few hundred yards, stopped by another. We had hoped that the first was merely a jam of anchor ice, caused by the cold of the last few days; but the jam we had now come to was black and solid, and, running the boats ashore, one of us went off down the bank to find out what the matter was. On climbing a hill that commanded a view of the valley for several miles, the explanation became only too evident—as far as we could see, the river was choked with black ice. The great Ox-bow jam had stopped, and we had come down to its tail.

We had nothing to do but to pitch camp, after which we held a consultation. The Little Missouri has much too swift a current,—when it has any current at all,—with too bad a bottom, for it to be possible to take a boat up-stream; and to walk meant, of course, abandoning almost all we had. Moreover we knew that a thaw would very soon start the jam, and so made up our minds that we had best simply stay where we were, and work down-stream as fast as we could, trusting that the spell of bitter weather would pass before our food gave out.

The next eight days were as irksome and monotonous as any I ever spent: there is very little amusement in combining the functions of a sheriff with those of an arctic explorer. The weather kept as cold as ever. During the night the water in the pail would freeze solid. Ice formed all over the river, thickly along the banks; and the clear, frosty sun gave us so little warmth that the melting hardly began before noon. Each day the great jam would settle down-stream a few miles, only to wedge again, leaving behind it several smaller jams, through which we would work our way until we were as close to the tail of the large one as we dared to go. Once we came round a bend and got so near that we were in a good deal of danger of being sucked under. The current ran too fast to let us work back against it, and we could not pull the boat up over the steep banks of rotten ice, which were breaking off and falling in all the time. We could only land and snub the boats up with ropes, holding them there for two or three hours until the jam worked down once more—all the time, of course, having to keep guard over the captives, who had caused us so much trouble that we were bound to bring them in, no matter what else we lost.

We had to be additionally cautious on account of being in the Indian country, having worked down past Killdeer Mountains, where some of my cowboys had run across a band of Sioux—said to be Tetons—the year before. Very probably the Indians would not have harmed us anyhow, but as we were hampered by the prisoners, we preferred not meeting them; nor did we, though we saw plenty of fresh signs, and found, to our sorrow, that they had just made a grand hunt all down the river, and had killed or driven off almost every head of game in the country through which we were passing.

As our stock of provisions grew scantier and scantier, we tried in vain to eke it out by the chase; for we saw no game. Two of us would go out hunting at a time, while the third kept guard over the prisoners. The latter would be made to sit down together on a blanket at one side of the fire, while the guard for the time being stood or sat some fifteen or twenty yards off. The prisoners being unarmed, and kept close together, there was no possibility of their escaping, and the guard kept at such a distance that they could not overpower him by springing on him, he having a Winchester or the double-barreled shot-gun always in his hands cocked and at the ready. So long as we kept wide-awake and watchful, there was not the least danger, as our three men knew us, and understood perfectly that the slightest attempt at a break would result in their being shot down; but, although there was thus no risk, it was harassing, tedious work, and the strain, day in and day out, without any rest or let up, became very tiresome.

The days were monotonous to a degree. The endless rows of hills bounding the valley, barren and naked, stretched along without a break.

Finding that they were well treated and were also watched with the closest vigilance, our prisoners behaved themselves excellently and gave no trouble, though afterward, when out of our hands and shut up in jail, the half-breed got into a stabbing affray. They conversed freely with my two men on a number of indifferent subjects, and after the first evening no allusion was made to the theft, or anything connected with it; so that an outsider overhearing the conversation would never have guessed what our relations to each other really were. Once, and once only, did Finnigan broach the subject. Somebody had been speaking of a man whom we all knew, called "Calamity," who had been recently taken by the sheriff on a charge of horse-stealing. Calamity had escaped once, but was caught at a disadvantage the next time; nevertheless, when summoned to hold his hands up, he refused, and attempted to draw his own revolver, with the result of having two bullets put through him. Finnigan commented on Calamity as a fool for "not knowing when a man had the drop on him"; and then, suddenly turning to me, said, his weather-beaten face flushing darkly: "If I'd had any show at all, you'd have sure had to fight, Mr. Roosevelt; but there wasn't any use making a break when I'd only have got shot myself, with no chance of harming any one else." I laughed and nodded, and the subject was dropped.

Indeed, if the time was tedious to us, it must have seemed never-ending to our prisoners, who had nothing to do but to lie still and read, or chew the bitter cud of their reflections, always conscious that some pair of eyes was watching them every moment, and that at least one loaded rifle was ever ready to be used against them. They had quite a stock of books, some of a rather unexpected kind. Dime novels and the inevitable "History of the James Brothers"—a book that, together with the "Police Gazette," is to be found in the hands of every professed or putative ruffian in the West—seemed perfectly in place; but it was somewhat surprising to find that a large number of more or less drearily silly "society" novels, ranging from Ouida's to those of The Duchess and Augusta J. Evans, were most greedily devoured. As for me, I had brought with me "Anna Karenina," and my surroundings were quite gray enough to harmonize well with Tolstoï.

Our commons grew shorter and shorter; and finally even the flour was nearly gone, and we were again forced to think seriously of abandoning the boats. The Indians had driven all the deer out of the country; occasionally we shot prairie fowl, but they were not plentiful. A flock of geese passed us one morning, and afterward an old gander settled down on the river near our camp; but he was over two hundred yards off, and a rifle-shot missed him. Where he settled down, by the way, the river was covered with thick glare ice that would just bear his weight; and it was curious to see him stretch his legs out in front and slide forty or fifty feet when he struck, balancing himself with his outspread wings.

But when the day was darkest the dawn appeared. At last, having worked down some thirty miles at the tail of the ice jam, we struck an outlying cow-camp of the C Diamond (C   ) ranch, and knew that our troubles were almost over. There was but one cowboy in it, but we were certain of his cordial help, for in a stock country all make common cause against either horse-thieves or cattle-thieves. He had no wagon, but told us we could get one up at a ranch near Killdeer Mountains, some fifteen miles off, and lent me a pony to go up there and see about it—which I accordingly did, after a sharp preliminary tussle when I came to mount the wiry bronco (one of my men remarking in a loud aside to our cowboy host, "the boss ain't no bronco-buster"). When I reached the solitary ranch spoken of, I was able to hire a large prairie schooner and two tough little bronco mares, driven by the settler himself, a rugged old plainsman, who evidently could hardly understand why I took so much bother with the thieves instead of hanging them off-hand. Returning to the river the next day, we walked our men up to the Killdeer Mountains. Seawall and Dow left me the following morning and went back to the boats, and had no further difficulty, for the weather set in very warm, the ice went through with a rush, and they reached Mandan in about ten days, killing four beaver and five geese on the way, but lacking time to stop to do any regular hunting.

Meanwhile I took the three thieves into Dickinson, the nearest town. The going was bad, and the little mares could only drag the wagon at a walk; so, though we drove during the daylight, it took us two days and a night to make the journey. It was a most desolate drive. The prairie had been burned the fall before, and was a mere bleak waste of blackened earth, and a cold, rainy mist lasted throughout the two days. The only variety was where the road crossed the shallow headwaters of Knife and Green rivers. Here the ice was high along the banks, and the wagon had to be taken to pieces to get it over. My three captives were unarmed, but as I was alone with them, except for the driver, of whom I knew nothing, I had to be doubly on my guard, and never let them come close to me. The little mares went so slowly, and the heavy road rendered any hope of escape by flogging up the horses so entirely out of the question, that I soon found the safest plan was to put the prisoners in the wagon and myself walk behind with the inevitable Winchester. Accordingly I trudged steadily the whole time behind the wagon through the ankle-deep mud. It was a gloomy walk. Hour after hour went by always the same, while I plodded along through the dreary landscape—hunger, cold, and fatigue struggling with a sense of dogged, weary resolution. At night, when we put up at the squalid hut of a frontier granger, the only habitation on our road, it was even worse. I did not dare to go to sleep, but making my three men get into the upper bunk, from which they could get out only with difficulty, I sat up with my back against the cabin-door and kept watch over them all night long. So, after thirty-six hours' sleeplessness, I was most heartily glad when we at last jolted into the long, straggling main street of Dickinson, and I was able to give my unwilling companions into the hands of the sheriff.

Under the laws of Dakota I received my fees as a deputy sheriff for making the three arrests, and also mileage for the three hundred odd miles gone over—a total of some fifty dollars.

In Medora, Roosevelt's friend John Simpson, owner of the Hash-knife brand and a well-known rancher in the Badlands, slowly shook his head when he met Roosevelt.

"Roosevelt," he said, "no one but you would have followed those men with just a couple of cowhands. You are the only real damn fool in this country." [15]

Other ranchers, with puzzled looks on their faces, asked Roosevelt why he didn't shoot the trio. They pointed out, "They would have shot you!"

Roosevelt replied, "I didn't come out here to kill anyone. All I wanted to do was to defend myself and my property. There wasn't anyone around to defend them for me so I had to do it myself." [16]

The three horse thieves were indicted and Roosevelt later returned to Dickinson to testify at their trial. He withdrew charges against the dim-witted Pfaffenbach, commenting that the old man "didn't have the sense to do anything good or bad," but Finnegan and the half-breed Burnsted were found guilty and sentenced to three years in the territorial prison at Bismarck.

Sometime later the redheaded horse thief wrote Teddy a letter from prison.

Roosevelt used the letter in his *Ranch Life and Hunting Trail*, commenting that Finnegan's letter "is worth giving out, not only because it's his own story, but also for the sake of the delicious sense of equality shown in the last few sentences." [17]

Theodore Roosevelt Gets a Letter From a Horse Thief

In the first place I did not take your boat, Mr. Roosevelt, because I wanted to steal something, no indeed, when I took that vessel I was labouring under the impression, die dog or eat the hatchette . . . when I was a couple of miles above your rance the boat I had sprung a leak and I saw I could not make the Big Missouri in the shape that it was in. I thought of asking assistance of you but I suppose you had lost some saddles and blamed me for taking them.

Now there I was with a leaky boat and under the circumstances, what was I two do, two ask for your help, the answer I expected two get was two look down the mouth of a Winchester. I saw your boat and made up my mind to get possession of it. I was bound to get out of that country, cost what it might, when people talk lynch law and threaton a persons life. I think that is about time two leave. I did not want to go back up river on the account that I feared a mob. . . . I have read a good many of your sketches of ranch life in the papers since I have been here, and they interested me deeply.

Yours sincerely

& c/

P.S. Should you stop over at Bismarck this fall make a call to the prison. I should be glad to meet you.

Roosevelt finished his biography of Thomas Hart Benton at the Elkhorn ranch in midsummer 1886. He also presided over the semiannual meeting of the Little Missouri Stock Association held in Miles City. The small cow town was filled with wild-eyed cowhands and the scenes were reminiscent of Abilene or Dodge City when the herds arrived. The Fifth Infantry Band from Fort Keogh headed a parade of carriages, wagons, and cowboys, but the horses of the lead carriage, driven by the president of the association with the vice-president and secretary as his passengers, became frightened at the noise, bolted into the band, scattering the bandsmen and sending bugles, tubas, and drums flying in all directions. This prompted the cowboys to charge down the main dirt street, whooping, yelling, and firing their six-shooters "to strike terror in the heart of the tenderfoot."

A few years later Roosevelt described that summer of 1886 as "very pleasant." He wrote:

> I was much at the ranch where I had a great deal of writing to do; but every week or two I left to ride among the line camps, or spend a few days at any roundup which happened to be in the neighborhood.
>
> At dawn we were in the saddle, the morning air cool in our faces, the red sunrise saw us loping across the grassy reaches of prairie land, or climbing in single file the rugged buttes. All forenoon we spent riding the long circle with the cowpunchers of the roundup; in the afternoon we worked the herd, cutting the cattle, with much break neck galloping, halting and wheeling.[18]

Roosevelt also wrote to Lodge that he was "in the saddle at 2 A.M. and except for two very hearty meals, after each of which I took a fresh horse, did not stop working until 8:15 P.M. and was up at half past three this morning."

Roosevelt continued this schedule until the roundup ended in Medora where it had begun. On July 4 he was in Dickinson to give an Independence Day speech. On the platform Doctor Stickney was impressed by Roosevelt's simple, direct talk on the duties of every American citizen.

Roosevelt told the small crowd, "It is not what we have that will make us a great nation; it is the way in which we use it."

The train back to Medora was packed with drunken singing cowboys. Roosevelt sat with Packard, the *Bad Lands Cowboy* editor, and they discussed the speech. Packard said later: "It was only then that I first realized the potential bigness of the man. One could not help believing he was in deadly earnest in his consecration to the highest ideas of citizenship. I learned on the return journey to the Bad Lands that day, that he believed he could do better work in a public and political way than in any other.

"My conclusion was immediate, and I said, 'Then you will become President of the United States.'

"I remember distinctly that he was not in the least surprised by my statement. He gave me the impression of having thoroughly considered the matter and to have arrived at the same conclusion that I had arrived at. I remember only this of what he said.

"'If your prophecy comes true, I will do my part to make a good one.'"[19]

A short time after the Dickinson celebration Roosevelt went east to sniff the political wind. He turned down an offer to become New York City's health commissioner and left Manhattan trailing streamers of rumors; the strongest was that he could have the city's mayoralty nomination for the asking.

When he returned to Elkhorn, Roosevelt was restless. The visit to New York, the conferences he'd had with old associates and advisers, had stirred his political juices. Now the Badlands were beginning to lose their mysterious lure. New York, for all its dirt, noise, hack politicians, and corruption, presented a new and exciting challenge. The frontier had given him peace in a time when he had reached the ebb of his life. It had toughened him physically, tested him, brought out the best that was in him. But now that part of his life was finished. He wanted to go back east.

His last adventure in the West was hunting for a white mountain goat in the Coeur d'Alenes, in northern Idaho. He narrowly escaped death when a ledge crumbled and he slipped off a precipice. But Roosevelt's luck held and after falling forty or fifty feet he landed in the top of a thick balsam. He promptly climbed back up to join his guide and finally got his "goat."

In the middle of September 1886 Roosevelt returned to the Elkhorn to find Sewall and Dow asking to cancel their contract. Sewall explained that in his absence he had taken a herd to Chicago only to discover the best price he could get was $10 a head less than what it had cost to raise and transport them.

Sewall and Dow had "figured things out" and come to the conclusion that the combination of the severe summer drought and the falling beef market would leave no profits to share. Roosevelt could suffer a staggering loss if they continued the Elkhorn operation.

In a way, the decision of Sewall and Dow was a relief to Roosevelt. It had become apparent at the roundup and from meetings he had had with other ranchers, that cattle-raising was now a financially precarious business. The $85,000 investment in Elkhorn was gradually slipping away. If he didn't sell out soon he would encounter severe losses.

He called the two men into his room and told them he would stand by his agreement with them if they wished to remain. But if they were willing, he suggested it was time to quit the ranching business "and go back."

In addition to their concern over their friend's possible financial disaster, Sewall and Dow had an added incentive to leave the Badlands. Both their wives had given birth to sons without the help of Doctor Stickney, who was so many miles away. The women had recovered but their husbands had agreed it was best they return to the Maine woods and towns where physicians were available to care for their offspring.

Sewall and Dow didn't hesitate in answering Roosevelt; they wanted to return to Maine.

"How soon can you leave?" Roosevelt asked.

After a conference with "the womenfolk" Sewall returned to inform Roosevelt they could leave within three weeks.

Roosevelt nodded. "Three weeks from today we go." At that moment he may have recalled Bill Sewall's wise prediction when they had first come to Elkhorn and Roosevelt had been sad and depressed.

"You'll come to feel different," the guide had told him, "and then you won't want to stay here."

Life had brightened considerably for Roosevelt that late summer. His engagement to Edith Carow had been made public and he was impatient to greet her when she returned from London.

On one of their last rides across the empty prairie Bill Sewall suggested to Roosevelt that he return to politics. "If you do and if you live," he said, "I think you'll be President."

"That's looking a long way ahead," Roosevelt said, laughing.

"It may be a long way ahead to you," Sewall told him, "but it isn't as far ahead as it's been for some of the men who got there."[20]

On September 25, 1886, Bill Sewall wrote in his account book: "Squared accounts with Theodore Roosevelt."

On the same day Roosevelt signed a contract with Sylvane Ferris and Bill Merrifield to take over his herds. The cattle, valued at $60,000, would be sold over a four-year period with Ferris and Merrifield sharing the money.

One morning Roosevelt shook hands with Sewall and Dow, kissed their wives and babies and waved good-bye.

In early October the two families closed the door of the sturdy ranch house. Back in Maine they would read Roosevelt had accepted the Republican nomination for mayor of New York City.

As Packard, the frontier editor, and Sewall, the Maine guide, had predicted, the Badlands cowboy, "brown as a berry and tough as a pine knot," who had chased a band of horse thieves for more than three hundred miles, was on his way to the White House.

BILL TILGHMAN

WE MUST START WITH A MILD-MANNERED, GRAYING LAW officer standing on the wooden main street of Cromwell, Oklahoma, a boom oil town. He had just disarmed a wild-eyed drunk when the man suddenly produced a hidden revolver and killed him. It was August 1924, and it is hard to believe that this senseless act in the first quarter of the twentieth century ended the life of Bill Tilghman, one of the greatest law enforcement officers in the history of the American West.

It was an act of supreme irony. In another century Tilghman had survived prairie fires, Indian attacks, buffalo stampedes, homicidal gunmen, bush-whackers, and savage blizzards on the plains to enter the new, so-called civilized age only to be gunned down by a fellow officer—a Prohibition agent.

He died in an alien time of Model T Fords, bootleg whiskey, and narcotics. The man who had arrested and killed some of the deadliest gunfighters in the West had been investigating a cocaine smuggling ring.

Tilghman's murder stunned Oklahoma. There were few who didn't know or had not heard of "Uncle Bill," the smiling, courteous, dedicated officer who had tamed America's last frontier.

The Tilghman family had long been rooted in the land and history of America. The first one arrived in Maryland to claim a land grant from his friend, Lord

Extremely rare letter signed October 27, 1777, by the first William Tilghman, the ancestor of the famous frontier law officer, stating he had been given permission by George Read, a signer of the Declaration of Independence, to search for his seventeen-year-old brother on the British prison ships in the Delaware River. Bill Tilghman was a member of a distinguished Maryland family founded by Richard Tilghman, a leading London surgeon. *The James D. Horan Collection*

Baltimore. His grandson, Matthew Tilghman, was a member of the convention that framed the Declaration of Independence. Matthew's son, Richard, was a major in the Continental army. Bill Tilghman's father, William Matthew, fought in the Seminole and Mexican wars and then became a sutler at Fort Dodge, Iowa. Bill was born at the fort on July 4, 1854. Curiously, the national holiday was also his father's birthday. He later moved his family to Fort Ridgely, Minnesota, simply a small blockhouse and two log cabins.[1]

The future frontier law officer went under fire for the first time when he was only a few weeks old. The Sioux attacked, their warriors sweeping up to the blockhouse before they were driven off. His mother, Amanda, was holding him in her arms when an arrow tore through her sleeve missing her son by inches. The following year the family settled on a farm near Atchison, Kansas. The Civil War came, and his father marched off at the head of a company. Eight-year-old

Bill became the head of the family, working the farm with his mother and attending a one-room schoolhouse.

Trapping gophers for nearby farmers earned him enough money to buy a cap and ball pistol. By the time his father returned from the war, Bill was a sturdy twelve-year-old who not only knew how to run a farm but had also developed a startling skill with a pistol and rifle.

In the spring of 1871 Bill and two other Atchison County teen-agers became buffalo hunters, bringing their meat to Hays and Ellsworth, the two principle shipping points on the Kansas Pacific. They stayed out all that summer into the fall, narrowly escaping Indian war parties and finally a blizzard that caught them out on the plains. They abandoned their wagon and made their way on foot to a small ranch, its one-room dugout jammed with hunters fleeing the storm.

Later Bill and his partners wrapped themselves in blankets and walked through the drifts until they located the wagon and its mounds of frozen meat. With a borrowed mule they dragged the wagon to Ellsworth, where they sold it.

The narrow escape from the savage storm sent Bill's two companions back to the farm, but for young Tilghman the months on the prairie had been an exhilarating adventure. He wrote to his mother and father saying that he intended to spend the winter with a friend who had a claim near Ellsworth.

The storm had wiped out large herds of cattle and Tilghman and his companion spent the winter skinning the hides and hunting wolves and coyotes for bounty money. Bill, now an expert with a six-shooter and rifle, also brought in wild turkeys which sold in Ellsworth for seventy-five cents.

For the next few years Bill, with his brothers and friends from Atchison County, formed partnerships, shooting, skinning, and selling buffalo robes and meat. He became known to the Cheyennes and Osages and spent many days in their camps.

One of his close friends, "Hurricane Bill" Martin, spoke Cheyenne, and boasted so much about Tilghman's marksmanship that Roman Nose, a Cheyenne chief, demanded proof of young Bill's skill with a rifle.

On New Year's Day 1874, Bill brought his Sharps rifle to the Cheyenne camp. Roman Nose—not the famous chief of the same name—carefully examined it, then pointed to two buffalo bulls who were grazing on a small rise far from camp.

Tilghman, using a rifle "rest," took careful aim and fired. Twice his balls were short but at the third shot the Indians grunted when the bull toppled over. Martin insisted the distance be measured; Indians and white men agreed it was one full mile. Bill kept the horns of the bull for many years as a memento of that incredible shot.[2]

Out of a total of eleven thousand buffalo killed that winter, Bill Tilghman's Sharps rifle accounted for seventy-five hundred

A young Bill Tilghman during his buffalo-hunting days. Tilghman met Bat Masterson at Adobe Walls shortly after the Indian attack. *Courtesy Denver Public Library, Western History Department*

But the tribes became hostile as the herds began to diminish; it was hazardous to move about the plains. After Dick Tilghman, Bill's younger brother, was killed by a war party, Tilghman and his fellow buffalo hunters left the Texas Panhandle and headed for Dodge City. He reached Adobe Walls three days after the big attack by Quana Parker's warriors, and there Bill first met Bat Masterson, who would be his lifelong friend.

The following year Masterson, Neil (also spelled Neal) Brown, and Tilghman formed a partnership and the trio hunted the dwindling herds from the Colorado to Texas. Then suddenly, as if it had happened overnight, the buffalo was gone.

Tilghman followed Masterson and Brown to Dodge City, where Bat was elected sheriff of Ford County and took office in January 1878. The following year Bat's brother, Jim, and Brown were sworn in as marshal and assistant marshal to replace Charlie Bassett and Wyatt Earp. The city council reappointed both the following May.

The story of Masterson appointing Tilghman as his deputy is difficult to confirm. Dodge City official records do not support it and in the *Dodge City Times* account of the posse shooting of Jim Kennedy, who had killed Dora Hand, the dancer, in the fall of 1878, Tilghman is simply listed as a rider, without an official title.

However, a long and detailed newspaper account of Tilghman's life has Bat appointing Tilghman as his deputy shortly after Bill had come to his assistance when a group of "high heels" tried to kill Masterson. A herd had just come in and cowboys were shooting up the town. Bat had disarmed several and taken them prisoner "in front of George Cox's old Dodge House," when another group fired at Masterson. Tilghman took on the "star shooters" and was soon joined by Jim Masterson and Ben Daniels. After a brief gunfight they were all disarmed and arrested.[3]

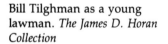

Bill Tilghman as a young lawman. *The James D. Horan Collection*

(4–404.)

THE UNITED STATES OF AMERICA,

To all to whom these presents shall come, Greeting:

Homestead Certificate No. *4359*

APPLICATION *15992*

Whereas There has been deposited in the General Land Office of the United States a Certificate of the Register of the Land Office at *Dodge City, Kansas*, whereby it appears that, pursuant to the Act of Congress approved 20th May, 1862, "To secure Homesteads to actual Settlers on the Public Domain," and the acts supplemental thereto, the claim of *Charles W. Bannister* has been established and duly consummated, in conformity to law, for the *east half of the North West quarter and the West half of the North East quarter of section seven in Township twenty eight South of Range thirty six West of the Sixth Principal Meridian in Kansas, Containing one hundred and sixty acres*

according to the Official Plat of the survey of the said Land, returned to the General Land Office by the Surveyor General:

Now know ye, That there is, therefore, granted by the **United States** unto the said *Charles W. Bannister* the tract of Land above described: TO HAVE AND TO HOLD the said tract of Land, with the appurtenances thereof, unto the said *Charles W. Bannister* and to *his* heirs and assigns forever.

In testimony whereof, I, *Grover Cleveland*, President of the United States of America, have caused these letters to be made Patent, and the Seal of the General Land Office to be hereunto affixed.

Given under my hand, at the City of Washington, the *thirtieth* day of *January*, in the year of our Lord one thousand eight hundred and *ninety five*, and of the Independence of the United States the one hundred and *nineteenth*.

BY THE PRESIDENT: *Grover Cleveland*

By *M. McKean*, Secretary.

L. Q. C. Lamar, Recorder of the General Land Office.

Recorded, Vol. *10*, Page *207*

Original Dodge City homesteader's application. *The James D. Horan Collection*

Rare photograph of Bill Tilghman in the early frontier days. *The James D. Horan Collection*

The official records do show that Tilghman, after serving briefly as deputy under Sheriff Pat Sughrue, finally became marshal of Dodge City in April 1884. Before that he had been the co-owner of a Dodge City dance hall and saloon, a respected business on the frontier.

Tilghman was not a flamboyant man. He was not sought out by correspondents from eastern newspapers, nor did he have a natural flair for publicity and self-glorification like Wyatt Earp. But frontiersmen from the Canadian border to the Texas Panhandle knew and respected Tilghman as a dedicated law officer who would travel miles to capture a dangerous horse thief, return him for trial, and face down a mob determined to take away his prisoner.

Tilghman's fast draw, marksmanship, and unwavering courage could not be matched. Gunfighters and cowboys seeking to make a reputation as a killer always turned over their weapons to the soft-spoken man with the cold gray-blue eyes.

Dodge City's reign as queen of the cow towns ended after the massive blizzard of 1886 destroyed a large part of the herds in western Kansas. Gradually the town settled into a country community, with the ladies' fair as a major excitement. Bill turned in his badge to run his small ranch near Fort Dodge.

In 1887–88 the Kansas County Seat Wars broke out, with riots and gunfights spreading across the state as towns fought for the privilege of being the county seat. Bands of hired gunfighters faced each other over ballot boxes, and county seals and records were stolen in night raids. Eleven men died in the battle between Leoti and Coronado and in Dighton a mob lynched two leaders from an adjacent community.

Bill Tilghman, Jim Masterson, and Pat Sughrue were hired by the townspeople of Leoti when a new election was ordered by the courts. One man was killed when he foolishly tried to outdraw Tilghman after boasting in a saloon he would send the lawman back to Dodge City in a pine box.

In Gray County, adjacent to Ford, the battle between Cimarron and Ingalls simmered for months. The Ingalls group was led by a young surveyor, George Bolds, who had ridden as a Dodge City posseman under both Masterson and Tilghman. In the fall of 1887 Cimarron won the election as county seat but Ingalls insisted it was a fraudulent victory because Cimarron had brought in railroad workers from the Montezuma Railroad. The battle dragged on in the courts for a year until the Kansas Supreme Court finally designated Ingalls as the county seat. After Bolds was driven out of Cimarron at gunpoint the winning town turned to Tilghman to recover the official records held in the Cimarron County Clerk's office. The Cimarron citizens had warned Bolds that he and his followers would be met with gunfire if they attempted to enter Cimarron.

Bill Tilghman accepted Ingalls's offer to bring back the county seal and the records for a $1,000 fee. He selected Jim Masterson, Wyatt Earp, Neil Brown, Fred Singer, Ed Brooks, and young Bolds as his official deputies.[4]

On a bright, cold January morning the hired guns set out for Cimarron in a spring wagon. Tilghman, who had been appointed a temporary sheriff, picked a Sunday morning "because the boys would be sleeping it off."

But the townspeople were not "sleeping it off" as Tilghman believed. When he and Bolds were loading their wagon with county records a posse of outraged

Cimarron citizens surrounded the county clerk's office. Bolds and Tilghman ducked back into the building under rifle and revolver fire.

After fighting from the county clerk's office for hours, Tilghman and his men made a dash for their wagon. Bolds was shot twice. When the townsmen moved in, Tilghman drove them back with his buffalo gun. One of the Ingalls men grabbed the reins and with Tilghman's heavy buffalo rifle booming in the early morning quiet, they made their way out of town. The fight continued across the prairie until riders from Ingalls came out to reinforce them. The combined firepower finally forced the Cimarron possemen to return to their town where J. W. (Will) English had died of his wounds and two other defenders were badly wounded.

Bales of hay were stacked around Ingalls as a firing wall. All day townsmen watched the empty prairie for the returning Cimarron riders. But before hostilities could flare up again, Governor Martin called out the state militia, "as the Ingalls people have threatened to kill the Cimarron people the first time an opportunity presents. . . . Only the presence of a strong force of militia will prevent another conflict." Bolds survived his wounds to become a prominent livestock dealer during World War I.

Mrs. Zoe Tilghman told this writer:

> Bill always remembered that morning, especially young George Bolds who was bleeding so much from his wounds the blood was running from the sides of the wagon. Even the county clerk records they had managed to get before the shooting started were soaked with George's blood. Bill said the boys never thought he would make it, but when they left Ingalls George was back in his office, one leg up on a box, his neck wrapped in bandages with his Winchester by his side, in case the Cimarron posse decided to return and continue the fight. As I recall, Bill said Jim Masterson was treed on the top of a safe in the county clerk's office for a long time and was almost lynched by the Cimarron men.[5]

The County Seat Wars were replaced by a creeping depression. Banks took over farms, and Bill, who had been offered $40,000 for his spread along the Arkansas River, watched a good part of it go for taxes.

The wild cow towns were now memories. Outlaws and gunfighters legends. Kansas was worn out. In 1889 Bill Tilghman and Neil Brown left Dodge for the last time to join the Oklahoma Land Rush.

Tilghman found himself in Guthrie, Oklahoma, a town that had sprung up overnight. When the mayor wanted to establish Oklahoma Avenue he asked Tilghman to find a way to cut a wide swath down the center of the milling crowds. After he had publicly read the mayor's proclamation, Bill selected two logs, which he fastened with chains to a team of mules. Then with Jim Masterson, he slowly drove the mules and the bumping logs through the center of Guthrie. An observer recalled: "For the first time since the occupation of Guthrie you could stand on the hill and look straight down to the Santa Fe station."

Accompanied by Neil Brown, he made the second "run" when the lands of the Iowa, Sac and Fox, and Pottawatomie were opened in September 1891. He staked a claim near the present city of Chandler and later found a farm site for his mother and father, who had received preference because his father was a Civil War veteran.

A year later he again wore a silver star as deputy United States marshal of the new territory.[6]

For years the lands of the Indian Nations had been the traditional hiding place for the worst fugitives in the West, including whiskey peddlers who sold their rotgut to the tribes. Also, as the towns grew rapidly, banks were established and express cars began delivering gold and valuables. Outlawry was inevitable. The Dalton, Doolin, Cook, Jennings, and Starr gangs began riding with Bill Tilghman on their trail.

Bat Masterson was now moving toward the East, finally to settle down in New York City, and Neil Brown announced he had hung up his guns to manage a thoroughbred horse farm. Their places were taken by Chris Madsen, a round little former Danish army officer, veteran of the Foreign Legion and the Franco-Prussian War, Indian scout, cavalryman, and quartermaster for Roosevelt's Rough Riders; and Heck Thomas, Stonewall Jackson's boy courier, express messenger and a deputy for "Hanging Judge" Parker's court. Tilghman, Madsen, and Thomas became known as the "three guardsmen" of Oklahoma.

Their first target was the Doolin gang, the largest on the last frontier. Legend has the leader, Bill Doolin, missing the Coffeyville, Kansas, raid with the Daltons because of a lame horse. He was tall and slender, with a charisma that attracted men and women on both sides of the law. His first in command was Bill Dalton, who had refused to ride into Coffeyville with his notorious brothers; "Little Bill" Raidler; George Weightman, known as "Red Buck," a dangerous killer; George Newcomb, a handsome young cowboy called "Bitter Creek"; Charlie Pierce; "Little Dick" West; Jack "Tulsa Jack" Blake; Dan Cryton, alias "Dynamite Dick"; and Tom Jones, known as "Arkansas Tom."

In September 1893 a party of marshals discovered that the Doolin gang was hiding out in the town of Ingalls. The plan was to surround the tiny frontier community and move in on the O. K. Hotel and Ransom and Murray's saloon used by Doolin and his men.

However, a small boy discovered the lawmen's camp on the outskirts of town

Bill Tilghman during the siege by lawmen of a ranch on Thompson's Creek, southwest of Guthrie, January 1, 1898, when Tilghman and Heck Thomas killed Dick West, also known as Dynamite Dick, the explosives expert of the Doolin gang of outlaws. *The James D. Horan Collection*

and alerted the gang. At first they ignored the excited child who kept tugging at Doolin's sleeve babbling about the "sheriffs are comin' in to arrest you."

Bitter Creek Newcomb finally talked to the youngster and walked outside. A few minutes later the "Battle of Ingalls," one of the bloodiest encounters in the history of the territory, had begun. And from it came the romantic legend of Rose of the Cimarron, the beautiful convent-educated girl who had fallen in love with Bitter Creek Newcomb, the handsome young outlaw.

Mrs. Tilghman described what had happened that morning.[7]

The Bloody Battle of Ingalls

Bill said they had suspected for a long time that the Doolin gang was using Mary Pierce's hotel and Ransom and Murray's saloon in Ingalls. Finally they received information that Doolin and his men had ridden into the town and were at the O. K. Hotel, run by Mrs. Pierce, who knew Doolin. Bill had a broken ankle and couldn't go along, but helped plan the raid with Marshal Evett Nix.

It was decided that the marshals would use covered wagons, a common sight in those days which would not arouse suspicion. On the night of September 8, 1893, two wagonloads of officers stopped outside of Ingalls. However, a small boy playing nearby had not only seen them arrive but had overheard them making plans. He scooted back to town inflated with importance because he knew, as he told the gang who were playing poker in the hotel, "that the marshals are comin'."

At first they didn't pay much attention to the noisy youngster. But Bitter Creek Newcomb believed the boy was telling the truth and insisted they saddle up. He finally convinced Doolin, who ordered his men to follow him to the livery stable. After they had saddled their horses they decided to start a poker game in the Ransom and Murray saloon. This was about nine o'clock. At 10:30 the canvas-covered wagons with about twenty-seven officers hidden inside lumbered into town. Two stopped at Light's smithy and one in front of Doctor R. Pickering's residence.

When Bill and Marshal Nix planned the raid they agreed that the best lawmen in the territory had to be recruited. Among the men I recall Bill mentioning were Frank Canton, Dick Speed, Tom Houston, and Jim Masterson. Johnny Hixton may have been in command.

As the officers took up their positions, Bitter Creek abruptly threw down his poker hand and walked to the saloon's front door.

"Where are you going?" Doolin called out.

"I still think that kid was tellin' us the truth," Newcomb replied. "I'm goin' to look around."

This time Newcomb decided to water his horse and bring the animal around to the town pump. As he reached the pump he saw a man armed with a Winchester talking to a boy. When the man saw Bitter Creek he aimed and fired. The outlaw grabbed his rifle from the boot but couldn't get a shot off in time. Marshal Dick Speed's bullet shattered the stock of his Winchester and a part of it was blown into Newcomb's leg. As he fell he jerked out his six-shooter and fired, hitting Speed in the shoulder.

Arkansas Tom, who was in bed in a room on the second floor of the hotel, heard the shooting and ran to the window. He saw Speed get to his feet after being hit by Newcomb and stagger backward to the door of a store. Arkansas Tom fired, killing the wounded marshal. The Battle of Ingalls had begun.

While the marshals commenced firing from many positions, the gang rushed to the windows and doors of the hotel and saloon trying to help Newcomb with a covering fire as the outlaw, bleeding badly, tried to mount his horse. He clung to the saddle, was hit again, and fell. The frightened horse bolted away.

Jerry Simonds, the boy Bitter Creek had seen talking to Marshal Speed, was hit by a ricocheting bullet as he ran out of the smithy's, and I believe later died of his wound. He was about fourteen.

Bill said the marshals told him they kept up such an intense fire they could see splinters flying from the wooden fronts of the hotel and saloon.

They could see Tulsa Jack appear in the doorway firing, but Doolin, an excellent shot, yanked him back and took his place. A man by the name of Walker, I believe, and both Murray and Ransom, the saloon owners, were badly wounded.

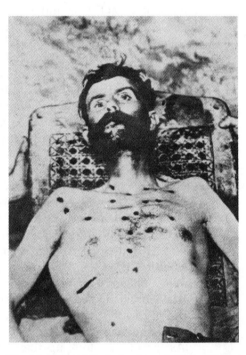

U.S. Marshal Evett Dumas Nix, who became a partner of Tilghman in a pioneering film production company. *The James D. Horan Collection*

The bullet-riddled body of Bill Doolin, leader of the Oklahoma band of outlaws. *The James D. Horan Collection*

Charlie Pierce and George (Bitter Creek) Newcomb, killed in July 1895 by Deputy U.S. Marshals Bill Tilghman and Heck Thomas at Rock Fort ranch, Oklahoma Territory. Newcomb was the sweetheart of the legendary "Rose of the Cimarron." *The James D. Horan Collection*

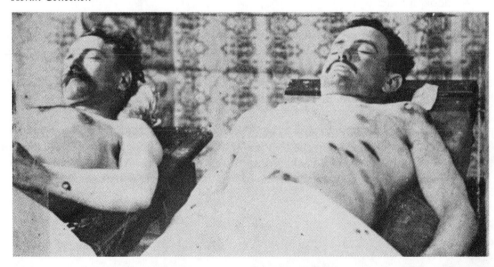

A rare photograph of "Arkansas Tom" Jones, the deadly marksman of the Doolin gang, who finally surrendered after killing three lawmen during the Battle of Ingalls, September 1893. In 1914, when Tom was released from prison, Tilghman persuaded him to join the cast of his pioneering movie company. Jones played himself robbing a frontier bank. *The James D. Horan Collection*

Finally Doolin ordered his men to make a break for their horses in the rear of the saloon. Sheriff Tom Houston, when he saw their move, sprang up and started to fire but Arkansas Tom, from his perch on the upper floor of the hotel, fired and killed him.

Bill Dalton and Tulsa Jack covered Doolin and Dynamite Dick as they went for the horses, going out a rear door of the saloon and down a draw in back of the stable. Dalton and Tulsa Jack followed, scooting out the front door and made for their horses in a weaving run. Doolin was slightly wounded and Dalton's horse was shot in the jaw. As the mount went down, Dalton jumped free and ran to a fence where the others were frantically trying to cut the wire with a wire cutter. They finally succeeded in doing this as the marshals began moving in.

Marshal Shadley, a fine officer, was in the lead, running and firing. From the window on the second floor, Arkansas Tom fired three rapid shots. Shadley spun around and fell, to die later. Bill said Doctor Pickering told him the wounds were so close together he could cover them with one hand.

When Shadley and Speed fell, the marshals' advance slowed down. But they still tried to shoot the gang out of their saddles. The horses of the outlaws, although trained to gunfire, were rearing and bucking from the unusually intense exchange and the outlaw gang had a difficult time getting through the fence, which still had strands of wires dangling from the posts.

The officers continued to move in on the gang and both parties kept up a rapid exchange of both rifle and six-shooter fire. When they reached a small rise, Doolin severely wounded Frank Briggs, who was trying to get between them and the route to the Cimarron River.

Meanwhile a very romantic legend was being born back in Ingalls.[8]

The True Story of Rose of the Cimarron

This is the true story of Rose of the Cimarron and the first time I have told it in detail. As you will recall, I revealed to you her identity for the first time in 1951, for the chapter on Rose which appeared in your book *Desperate Women*. I had kept that secret for more than half a century.

First of all, Rose of the Cimarron was Rose Dunn, a beautiful young girl who lived on the Dunn place about seven miles northeast of Ingalls.

Rose was unusually attractive, one of the most attractive girls in the territory. In fact, the whole family was noted for their good looks. As I recall, one of her cousins won what was probably the first beauty contest in the American West.

Rose grew up in a big family. One of her four brothers, Bee, made the 1889 Oklahoma Run and settled near the Dunn ranch. As I recall the story, Bee was shot and killed in a gunfight with Frank Canton, who had been a member of the cattle barons' army which "invaded" Wyoming in the 1880s.

The Dunns were not poor. When Rose was in her teens her father sent her to a convent school in Wichita. When Rose came back she was not only educated but had a polished air about her.

That's why when she began to associate with Bitter Creek the community was shocked. Now you must remember this was a frontier society and the folks were very straitlaced in those days, and for a very correct young lady to be seen in the company of a rascal like Bitter Creek who everyone predicted would end up to no good—well, you just didn't do things like that half a century ago.

But Rose was not only an educated and poised girl but also a girl with a mind of her own. She fell in love with Bitter Creek and tried her best to get him to leave the Doolin gang. Newcomb, a handsome young man, was like many of the cowboys who had a happy-go-lucky philosophy: take care of today and face tomorrow when it comes.

Rose was in Ingalls talking to Mrs. Pierce when the battle started. When Bitter Creek was hit and lay sprawled helpless in the street, Rose told Mrs. Pierce she was going to help him.

"My God, child," the woman said, "you'll be killed if you go out there!"

Rose ignored her warning and ran to an upstairs room where there were some rifles, six-shooters, and ammunition. She tore some bedsheets into strips and tied them together into a rope. She first lowered the weapons, then followed, herself.

She must have been deeply in love with the boy because Bill said the marshals later told him the firing that day was the most intense they had ever seen. Perhaps

For more than a half century this photograph was accepted as that of "Rose of the Cimarron," sweetheart of Bitter Creek Newcomb, who had risked her life to help him during the bloody battle of Ingalls. However, in 1951 Zoe Tilghman, widow of the lawman, disclosed to this writer that the photograph had been deliberately staged by her husband to protect Rose's real identity. The girl in the photograph is a young juvenile delinquent. Tilghman gave her the six-shooter to pose for the benefit of a persistent photographer who hounded Tilghman to let him into the jail to take pictures of Rose. *The James D. Horan Collection*

she counted on the chivalry of the West and knew that none of them would shoot her. She found one of the saddled horses and led him out into the street to where Newcomb lay. The marshals, who were still firing up at Arkansas Tom on the second floor of the hotel, left her alone and she managed to get Newcomb up into the saddle. Then she led the horse around the hotel and gave it a slap on the rump. Bitter Creek, who was weak from the loss of blood, managed to stay mounted for a short time until the others took care of him and delivered him to a local doctor who treated his wound.

Bill picked up Rose but, as he said, he didn't have any criminal charge against her. She had only helped a badly wounded boy and as he later learned, she had also brought him food and medicine.

After the battle of Ingalls she was quite a celebrity but Bill never gave out her name; he just called her Rose of the Cimarron. The local photographer kept pestering Bill to let him take a picture of the girl. Bill wanted to do everything to protect her because she was going to be released. So finally when the photographer came into his office that afternoon he had a sudden thought.

In the jail at the time was a young girl, very pretty, who had been arrested on a charge of stealing a horse. She was a wild young thing and the judge had ordered her sent to a reformatory. Bill led her into his office and told the photographer this was the famous Rose of the Cimarron. At the photographer's insistence he let her hold one of the deputies' six-shooters. The photographer captioned his print "Rose of the Cimarron" and this innocent playacting to protect a girl's name has appeared numerous times in serious histories of the West. There has never been a published picture of the real Rose.

I heard these details many times from Bill of the Ingalls battle and how he started the Rose of the Cimarron legend. He was never a flamboyant man who spun tall tales of the West, and I know he never talked about this episode.

So now, over a half century later, you know the inside story. Romantic as it sounds, it's the truth of what happened that day so long ago.

After the Battle of Ingalls it became a dangerous game of hounds and hare between Bill Tilghman and his men and the Doolin gang.

The gang boasted of how they had "defeated" the small army of lawmen at Ingalls. Infuriated sheriffs and marshals from all the territory offered to join Tilghman, but he refused. Large parties only impede manhunts, he told them. It is best to go in alone or with one or two completely trustworthy deputies.

All that fall and into the winter Tilghman, Madsen, and Brown moved across the wilderness searching for the hard-riding outlaw band.

Then, on a bitterly cold January day in 1895, Bill Doolin saved the life of the man who was hunting him.

As Mrs. Tilghman told the story to this writer, Tilghman and Brown were on the trail of Bill Dunn, hoping to capture Dunn and from him get information linking the four Dunn brothers to the Doolin gang.[9] They stopped at the Dunn dugout and Tilghman, armed only with a six-shooter, went in alone. Al Dunn, a surly, hard-bitten rogue, was the only one in the room. At the far end were tiers of bunks, enough to sleep about twenty men. Each one had a curtain. Dunn barely acknowledged Tilghman's greeting as the lawman held out his hands to the fire.

After trying to draw Dunn into conversation, Bill casually looked about the room. Suddenly he froze, tips of rifles and six-shooters appeared under the curtains, all aimed at him. After a few minutes Tilghman said good-bye and left.

"Drive ahead and not too fast," he whispered to Brown, "the dugout's full of outlaws." Later, Tilghman discovered, shortly after he left, Doolin and his riders who had been hiding in the bunks, gathered their gear and quickly rode off. Red Buck wanted to kill Tilghman but Doolin refused.

"Bill Tilghman is too good a man to shoot in the back," he told the raging Red Buck.

In the following months, Bill Dalton, Doolin's favorite rider, was killed in a gun battle at his hideout thirty-five miles west of Ardmore. Jack Blake, known as Tulsa Jack, was killed in May 1895, shortly after the gang held up the Rock Island train at Dover. Tilghman and his deputies later trapped and killed Charles Pierce and Bitter Creek at Rock Creek Ranch. Tilghman also found Little Bill in his hideout and after the fast-shooting outlaw refused to surrender, the lawman shot him. When he was brought to Elgin, Kansas, in a wagon, doctors gave the outlaw only a few hours to live. But he survived his wounds, and was tried and convicted at Kingfighter for train robbery. He was later paroled only to die of his wounds.

A year later, in March, the deadly Red Buck was found hiding in a dugout near Arapahoe. Like the others he refused to surrender. After a fierce exchange of gunfire he was killed as he tried to escape.

All this time Tilghman was doggedly following the twisting trail of Bill Doolin. In the spring of 1896 it appeared the outlaw leader was trying to abandon outlawry and become an honest citizen. After a hazardous courtship he finally married Edith Ellsworth, the attractive daughter of a Lawton preacher.

Mrs. Tilghman recalled how her husband finally tracked down Doolin and captured him.

Doolin, either needing money or finding it hard to completely forget the exciting life of an outlaw leader, gathered his gang together for one last strike, the robbery of a train. After the holdup he returned to his father-in-law's place, picked up his bride, and both rode to Arkansas where they hid out.

After their baby was born, Doolin made a final break. He said good-bye to what was left of his gang, packed their household goods on a wagon, and started west.

At Burden, Kansas, Mrs. Doolin sent a letter to Mrs. Pierce, the owner of the hotel in Ingalls where the famous battle had taken place. Bill told me the letter sent by the outlaw's wife had something to do with a ring Doolin had given her during their courtship. She had left it with Mrs. Pierce for safekeeping and asked that it be sent to her.

Bill paid a visit to Ingalls and stayed at the Pierce hotel. Mrs. Pierce was a friendly, energetic woman but she knew Bill was on Doolin's trail and changed the subject every time he started to talk about the outlaw. However, once when he brought up a recent train robbery in Texas and said it had been committed by Doolin and his gang, Mrs. Pierce vigorously defended Doolin, insisting he couldn't rob a train in Texas and be in Eureka Springs taking the baths for his rheumatism at the same time.

This was all Bill needed to know. He told E. D. Nix, the United States marshal, he had a tip where Doolin was hiding and intended to go after him. Nix tried to persuade him to take a few deputies, but Bill insisted that could bring on a shootout; if he went alone there would be "no fuss," as he put it.

The only thing he wanted from Nix was the latter's top hat and Prince Albert. Bill had never worn such an outfit and when he tried it on Nix told him he wouldn't recognize him even if they were alone on a prairie. Bill arrived in Eureka Springs, Arkansas, in January 1896. The community was small and he decided to first look it over. He was walking down the street when he saw a man filling a bottle from one of the springs. He was tall, limping with the aid of a cane, and wore cowboy boots. When he straightened up Bill saw it was Doolin. He also spotted the bulge of the .45 in a shoulder holster. Keeping a careful distance, he followed Doolin to a rooming house.

Bill knew he had to take the outlaw as quickly and inconspicuously as possible. He certainly couldn't be seen walking around with a shotgun, so he broke his gun and hired a carpenter to fashion a small hinged box, something like musicians carry. With his Prince Albert, Bill was sure he could pose as a member of the local band.

It was the old story of man's best laid plans. That afternoon he entered a bathhouse and was walking toward the register when he saw something that made him turn away. In a corner reading a paper was Doolin.

Bill quickly engaged a bath. For a long time he waited for footsteps; he still wasn't sure that Doolin had not seen him. Gradually he inched open the door and through a slit could see the outlaw still buried in his newspaper.

Bill tiptoed across the room using a large stove as a shield. Then he lunged at Doolin with a sharp command for the outlaw to put up his hands.

When Doolin tried to grab his six-shooter, Bill reached for the outlaw's hand but missed, catching his jacket sleeve. What followed then was a grim struggle, with Doolin making every effort to reach the revolver inside his jacket while Bill fought him with one hand, the other holding his gun. He could easily have killed Doolin but that was not Bill's way. By this time he also knew how Doolin had saved his life in the dugout and wanted to repay him.

They fought back and forth across the parlor, overturning chairs and tables. The grip Bill had on Doolin's coat sleeve was precarious—inch by inch the cloth was tearing. If it ripped away Doolin could reach his gun. Instead of coming to Bill's assistance the customers fled, leaving him alone.

"Don't make me kill you, Bill," he kept telling the outlaw. He recalled many times how the sleeve was tearing and how Doolin was desperately trying to reach inside the jacket.

Finally Bill told him for the last time he would shoot unless he stopped. Doolin, I guess, believed what he heard. He dropped his arm and Bill reached in and removed his revolver.

Later after he collected his clothes—and packed away the city dude's outfit—Bill marched Doolin down to the bank and let him withdraw what money he had deposited. When they were packing Doolin's things, Bill found a small silver mug. Doolin said he had bought it as a present for his infant son.

"I'll see that the baby gets it, Bill," he said.[10]

Bill returned Doolin to Guthrie. Before they left Eureka Springs, Bill told Doolin he wouldn't handcuff him if he gave his word he would not try to escape. Doolin gave his word and the entire journey to Guthrie was made with Doolin riding the train as any other passenger. In fact, in Guthrie they walked down the street together to the jail with Doolin uncuffed. Many years later this might sound strange for a lawman to put such trust in the word of an outlaw, but on the frontier a man's word was more valuable than gold. It was a code never to be broken by either the man serving the law or the man outside the law.

In jail Doolin's rheumatism appeared to cripple him and he was given more liberty than any of the other prisoners. While he probably suffered from rheumatism, the freedom he received gave him an opportunity to carefully study the jail. Bill had warned the jailers Doolin would try to escape but the outlaw soon became a celebrity and a showpiece for the jailers, who let down their security.

On the evening of July 5, 1896, Doolin made his escape. He overpowered a guard, took his two revolvers, bound and gagged him and released the other prisoners. A fight broke out among two prisoners and Doolin pointed one of the pistols at the brawlers and warned he would kill both of them if they didn't stop. They stopped at once.

Doolin captured a horse and buggy and after riding some miles, unhitched the horse and made his way into Arkansas where he found friends and shelter.

Mrs. Doolin meanwhile had returned to Lawton, Oklahoma. Doolin ignored the obvious danger to join her. One night they set out for Arkansas in a wagon, with the outlaw walking ahead. It was a full moon and the road was clear as day.

Doolin had supreme self-confidence and foolishly had not tried to hide his appearance. He had loaded their furniture in the daylight and had been seen. Word was immediately sent to the officers who covered both sides of the road. When Heck Thomas called out a command for Doolin to throw up his hands, the outlaw fired, but Thomas was faster and more accurate; his shotgun blast killed Doolin instantly.

I have always wondered at the terror which gripped the woman's heart back there on the driver's seat of the wagon when she heard the roar of the shotgun shattering the quiet night. She must have known the worst had happened as she gathered up her child and ran to where Heck Thomas was standing over the body of her husband.

The possemen tried to shield her from the sight but she broke through them and knelt down to cradle her dead husband and sob with a broken heart. Bill wasn't there that night but Heck later told us it was a sight he would never forget.

Word was soon received in Guthrie that Doolin had been killed. Crowds lined the streets when they returned with the body in a wagon. An endless file of people passed in and out of the morgue the next day when they put Doolin's body on exhibit.

Now "Little Dick" West was the only surviving member of the gang.

After destroying the last of the outlaw gangs, Bill Tilghman returned to the routine duties of the federal marshal's office. In 1900 the nation was shocked at the news stories of how a mob had burned to death two young Indians falsely accused of being suspects in the murder of a white man. After months of investigating the case in the hostile backwoods, Tilghman arrested the leaders of the mob. However, a friendly judge and sheriff soon made it evident there would be no conviction by a local jury. The outraged Tilghman proved to the United States attorney in Oklahoma City that the mob had crossed into Indian lands, thus bringing the case under federal jurisdiction. On the evidence uncovered by Tilghman the leaders were convicted and sent to prison for long terms.

A few years later Tilghman entered politics, winning a state senate seat by a large majority. But the post of United States marshal for the Oklahoma Territory was a cherished dream; he was promised the appointment many times but politicians always passed over his name. Tilghman refused to become embittered. He now had other interests—he was about to become a movie producer and director!

William Tilghman: Director and Producer

A series of unrelated and bizarre incidents, including a wildly hilarious amateur band of outlaws whose loot included a stalk of bananas, a convicted train robber who became a gubernatorial candidate, and a cowboy who caught wolves with his hands, led William Matthew Tilghman, buffalo hunter, gunfighter, and frontier lawman, to become one of the most unusual directors and producers in the history of American film.

It all started with the outlaw band put together by "Little Dick" West after his lost leader, Bill Doolin, had been killed. West was the only experienced outlaw in his new group of riders, which included Al and Frank Jennings, sons of a probate judge in Pottawatomie County. Al had once served as county attorney in El Reno.

After he left El Reno, young Jennings drifted about the Oklahoma frontier. He became friendly with the O'Malley brothers, two former possemen—volunteer man hunters paid by the day or the mile—who had been discharged after the Department of Justice discovered they were padding their expense accounts. The O'Malleys introduced Al and Frank Jennings to Dick West and the new gang was formed.

Their first attempt at train robbery was a fiasco. On August 18, 1897, they stopped a train at Edmond, a short distance from Oklahoma City, but when the conductor demanded to know why the gang was studying the door of the express car, the bandits bolted for their horses and disappeared in a cloud of dust.

Tilghman took up the trail and soon had the gang's horse holder in custody. He quickly turned informer and named the other members of the gang. Federal warrants were issued and Heck Thomas joined Tilghman in the manhunt.

West led his men to Muskogee where they again unsuccessfully tried to rob a train, then later to two small towns where they decided not to hold up the banks because armed guards were seen inside. Their one successful train robbery took place in an unsettled section of the Chickasaw Nation when at noontime they forced a flagman to stop a Rock Island train.

Dick West, known as "Little Dick" or "Dynamite Dick," Doolin's rider and explosives expert. West escaped the Rock Fort shootout in which Charlie Pierce and Bitter Creek Newcomb were killed. He later organized the short-lived "Al Jennings gang," which included among its loot a bunch of bananas. West, disgusted with his amateur followers, abandoned them after an aborted train robbery. West was killed by Bill Tilghman and his deputies Thomas Rhinehart and William B. Fosset on April 7, 1898. The outlaw was trapped in a barn while currying his horse. A skilled shot with either hand, West was killed after he refused to surrender. *The James D. Horan Collection*

"This here is Jesse James," Al Jennings, onetime Oklahoma frontier train robber, cried when he first saw J. Frank Dalton, who passed himself off as the "real" Jesse James. This photograph was taken July 24, 1948, when Jennings and Dalton met at the San Leandro Rodeo. Dalton claimed he was then 101 years old. Jennings had never met the real Jesse James. He was a small boy when Jesse was killed in St. Joseph, Missouri. Jennings starred in Bill Tilghman's early movie about Oklahoma outlaws robbing a bank. *The James D. Horan Collection*

This time they forced open the express car door and in one corner found the large iron safe. Dynamite was placed under the safe, a fuse attached, and the bandits hurriedly retreated. A shattering explosion blew the car apart. West, bewildered at the unexpected force of the blast, led his men back into the remains of the car only to find the safe intact.

When he ordered more dynamite placed around the safe his riders only stared at him. West soon discovered why there had been such a big blast; someone had left the remaining sticks back in the car before the charge had been touched off. Doolin's rider could only close his eyes and shudder. There was one thing left to do, he told his men—rob the passengers.

In the best Jesse James tradition they put on masks, walked down the aisles of the cars flourishing their six-shooters, muttering threats and holding out a grain sack. The passengers contributed $300, a stalk of bananas, and a jug of whiskey. But as the gang ran from the car Jennings's mask slipped down and he was recognized.

Tilghman and Thomas again took up the trail. This time they used the technique of the railroad and private detectives hunting the Wild Bunch in Nevada and Wyoming. They loaded their horses and supplies on a flatcar attached to a Santa Fe passenger train. Tilghman's plan was to head off the bandits he assumed were riding for the Jennings home in Tecumseh.

Instead, the gang made a wide circle and reached a hideout on the Cotton-wood Creek near Guthrie, where they divided their loot. Each received $60. There is no evidence of how the bananas or whiskey were divided.

Dick West, understandably disgusted with his recruits, went on alone while the O'Malley and Jennings brothers hid out at the Spike S ranch near Cushing. A general store owner who had sold the quartet new clothing told the lawmen where the train robbers were hiding. On December 1, 1897, after a brief gun battle in which both Jennings brothers were wounded, Marshal Bud Ledbetter took them all into custody. Al Jennings received fifty years in the Columbus, Ohio, federal penitentiary, while the other three were given short terms of five years.

Tilghman and Heck Thomas continued to hunt for West. They found him currying his horse in a stable on Thompson Creek, southwest of Guthrie. He refused Tilghman's demand that he surrender, fired, turned and ran, but Tilghman's single shot killed him.

After a few years, John Jennings, Al's older brother, campaigned for the release of Al, Frank, and the O'Malleys. Through a judge who lived in

A 1915 ad for Al Jennings's movie, *Beating Back. The James D. Horan Collection*

Kingfisher, an old friend of President McKinley, Al Jennings's sentence was reduced to five years and they were all released.[11]

Several years passed. During this time Tilghman returned to his family's ranch in Chandler to run for sheriff, bucking the Republicans, who controlled Lincoln County. He was the first Democrat ever to be elected. Another winner was J.B.A. Robertson, a young lawyer who took the county prosecutor's office. Tilghman found the physically powerful Robertson to be honest and vigorous and together they vowed to clean up the county.

Wild and sparsely settled Lincoln County, one of the largest in the territory, bordered on the Creek Nation and was a favorite hiding place for horse thieves, rustlers, and fugitives. Shortly after he took office, ranchers complained to Tilghman that their horse herds were dwindling. Tilghman saddled up with Neil Brown, his old friend from the Dodge City days, whom he had appointed as his jailer, and within a few weeks eight horse thieves were scrubbing the jail floor while waiting for Robertson to try them.

Tilghman's record was impressive. He once trailed an escaped prisoner to Nebraska and brought him back. And for more than a year he doggedly investigated the murder of a farming family until he finally found the killer. Robertson convicted the killer, who was sentenced to life.

In 1908 Al Jennings became a national figure after the *Saturday Evening Post* serialized the book, *Beating Back*, written by Will Irwin, a well-known author of the time. The fictitious account of Jennings's career pictured him as a romantic leader of a gallant band of outlaws, a man who was the Robin Hood of America's last frontier.

On Christmas Day, a few years earlier, Colonel Cecil A. Lyon, Republican National Committeeman, and close friend and hunting partner of President Theodore Roosevelt, had witnessed Jack Abernathy, a former Texas cowboy, catch huge Lobo wolves with his bare hands. At a fair held near Denison, Texas, Lyon watched Abernathy capture several big "loafer" wolves by thrusting his hand into the animal's powerful mouth, clutching the lower jaw until he tied the wolf's legs together and wired its jaw. Lyon told Roosevelt about Aberanathy's feat, but the skeptical President, who knew wolves at first hand from his ranching days, asked Abernathy to "stage a wolf hunt for me."

The wolfer agreed. On April 5, 1905, Abernathy, his horse Sam Bass and his pack of wolfhounds, were the feature of a six-day show staged in honor of the President near Big Pasture, Oklahoma. After Abernathy caught two "loafers" with his bare hands, an amazed Roosevelt congratulated him.

"Bully!" Teddy cried, pumping the wolfer's hand. "I haven't been skunked!"

It was an astonishing performance, but when Roosevelt repeated the story in Washington it was greeted with skepticism.

To prove his story, Roosevelt sent a cameraman, J. B. Kent, to photograph Abernathy repeating the show he had put on during the president's visit. Kent, who had a moving picture camera, arrived in Cache, the town nearest to the Wichita National Preserve where the wolf hunt was to be held.

At the time, a bitter gubernatorial primary contest was taking place. Prosecutor Robertson, with Tilghman as an active supporter, was running in a three-man race against a local judge and Al Jennings, the former outlaw who boasted he was the "reformed" candidate. The *Saturday Evening Post* serial had given him a great deal of publicity and large crowds appeared whenever he spoke.

Jennings was in Cache at the time Kent was making arrangements for the wolf hunt with Abernathy. The cameraman met the former outlaw and was captivated by Jennings's fictitious tales of his outlaw days. Kent decided he would make two movies, one of the wolf hunt, the other of Jennings robbing the Cache bank.

Accompanied by a caravan of spring wagons, supplies, and saddle horses, Kent set out for the wild preserve. He picked up Abernathy, who brought along his family "for a vacation." Later, Chris Madsen, the celebrated deputy, joined the ragtag movie company. Two weeks passed but Abernathy couldn't stage the wolf-catching act. Then Madsen told Kent he was going to ask Tilghman to help because the lawman "knew how to get things done."

The primary was over, and Robertson had lost by a slim margin, so Tilghman, believing Madsen's telegram meant a manhunt, rode to the preserve. He was astonished when he found that the movie company wanted his help to prove the president of the United States was not a liar.

"Bill told them he didn't know the first thing about making a movie," Mrs. Tilghman told this writer, "but they insisted he knew how to get things done, so he agreed to help. He had known President Roosevelt for years and they were close friends. He first rode to Quana Parker's home at the foot of the Wichita Mountains and explained the problem. Parker, the Comanche chief who led the raid on Adobe Walls, also was an old friend of Bill's. The chief agreed to help and they rode back to the Abernathy camp.

"Bill and Quana saw it wasn't hard for Abernathy's dogs to scare up a wolf but the problem was this whole business of Abernathy catching the big animal with his hands, which had to be staged in front of a camera. Bill and Quana got the idea of attaching a thin wire, not visible to the camera, to a big lobo wolf, after Kent, the cameraman, got shots of Abernathy and his dogs running the wolf down. Then the cameraman switched to the wolf—one leg attached to the wire— standing on a rock by the bank of a creek. When everything was set, Abernathy and his dogs appeared. The wolf saw the dogs and leaped into the creek. That's when Abernathy went into action.

"Now Kent's camera ground away as Abernathy wrestled and finally subdued the animal. The lobos were big and mean with slashing teeth and it required a great deal of courage and skill on Abernathy's part to control the frenzied animal. Abernathy used a glove to get an iron grip on the wolf's lower jaw, which rendered the wolf helpless. Bill said sometime later they all went to the White House to show the film. President Roosevelt had a hunter's sharp eye and once he asked Bill why the wolf kept lifting the paw attached to the wire. Bill, thinking fast, replied it was probably because the rock was very hot. The president just nodded."[12]

Kent shot his second film, of the Cache bank robbery, also with the help of Tilghman, who had become interested in film making. Tilghman not only served as director and presumably technical adviser but also played the role of the sheriff.

Tilghman may have helped to write the brief script, which had Jennings leading his gang into the frontier town, holding up the bank, and escaping. The posse led by Tilghman finally discovered them in a quiet valley, where there is a shootout, and Tilghman returns Jennings to Cache.

From viewing the film it appeared Kent had recruited another cameraman, probably someone in the town. In the excitement of the filming of the robbery, he went from the fleeing outlaws to pan the entire street, so enthralled spectators could be seen watching from the wooden sidewalks.

As Mrs. Tilghman recalled, one resident of the town rode in as Jennings and his men pounded down the street to pull up in front of the bank, their guns drawn.

"The bank is being robbed!" the startled man shouted. "The bank is being robbed! Get your guns!"

The movie had to be stopped while Tilghman quietly explained it was all make-believe. The chagrined citizen then joined the other spectators. Jennings and his men rode back up the street for another take, and Tilghman waved his hand for the cameras to start rolling again.

Four extraordinary stills taken from the pioneering movie directed by frontier lawman, Bill Tilghman, and starring Al Jennings, the overblown outlaw leader who had gained national recognition from the *Saturday Evening Post*'s serialization of his life story. Tilghman staged the "holdup" of the Cache Bank as accurately as he could. In this scene the outlaw band, in the best Hollywood tradition, had swept into town shooting on the gallop while the town's defenders attempted to drive them off. *Courtesy Library of Congress, Motion Pictures Collection*

The "heroine" of the film after her "rescue" by the sheriff's posse. *Courtesy Library of Congress, Motion Picture Collection*

Al Jennings, the "outlaw leader" in the movie, being "captured" by Bill Tilghman after the movie bank robbery. Note Jennings's fictitious wounds.

The film's hero being congratulated for defending the town and its bank from the outlaw band. *Courtesy Library of Congress, Motion Picture Collection*

Henry Starr, the real Oklahoma outlaw who robbed the bank at Stroud, Oklahoma, and interrupted Bill Tilghman's movie making. *Courtesy National Archives*

The People's Bank, Stroud, Oklahoma Territory, robbed by Henry Starr and his gang, March 27, 1915. Starr and one of his men were shot by a seventeen-year-old boy firing a sawed-off .30-.30 Winchester his father used for killing hogs. Described by newspapers of his time as "the greatest outlaw of them all," Starr told reporters: "A kid with a hog gun! That hurts my pride!" Tilghman uncovered the evidence that convicted several members of the gang. *Courtesy William Tilghman Collection, University of Oklahoma Library*

The 692 feet of film was entitled *The Bank Robbery* and was the first time in the history of American film that a production was directed by a former gunfighter and cow-town sheriff with the principal role played by a western outlaw.[13]

Tilghman became deeply interested in films. He got out of Kent all he knew—which wasn't too much—about cameras and films, and read what he could find on the subject.

"Bill had a fine mind and loved any new challenge," his wife Zoe said. "Film making was a new challenge and he wanted to know as much as he could about that industry, which was just beginning. Then in 1915 after talking to United States marshal E. D. Nix, he formed the Eagle Film Company to film *The Passing of the Oklahoma Outlaws*."[14]

The story was to portray the rise and fall of the Doolin gang and the Dick West gang, which now, through the many public appearances of Jennings and the *Saturday Evening Post* serial, was called "the Jennings gang." The idea for the movie came from a meeting Tilghman had with Nix, who was irritated at the publicity Jennings was receiving. He complained to Tilghman that the "true story" of the breakup of the gangs should be told with proper tribute given to the marshals for bringing law and order to a wild territory. Tilghman agreed and suggested a movie telling the story exactly as it happened. Nix enthusiastically endorsed the project and promised his cooperation. Tilghman then went to Heck Thomas and Chris Madsen, the other two "guardsmen," and they also pledged their assistance. J. B. Kent of the Cache movie became the cameraman.

Lute Stover, who had some experience in scriptwriting, put the scenario together with Tilghman's help. Tilghman's wife recalled her husband's remarkable memory, not only for dates and names but for minute details of the many manhunts and gunfights.

Theater poster for Tilghman's film. *Courtesy William Tilghman Collection, University of Oklahoma Library*

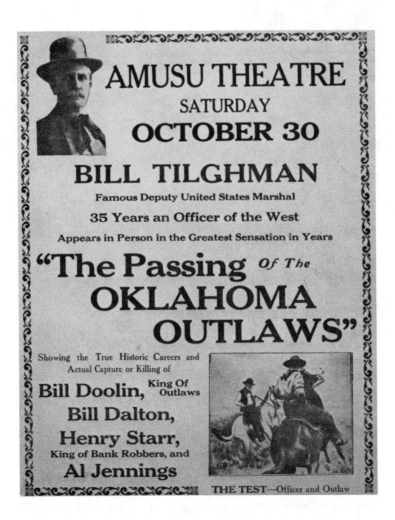

Cover of the press kit for Bill Tilghman's *The Passing of the Oklahoma Outlaws. Courtesy William Tilghman Collection, University of Oklahoma Library*

An aging Bill Tilghman "on tour" with his film. After the movie was over Tilghman would tell the audience of his experiences as a frontier lawman. *Courtesy William Tilghman Collection, University of Oklahoma Library*

"When he told a story he really made it come alive," she said.

Tom Smith, the deadly "Arkansas Tom" of the Battle of Ingalls, had just been released from prison. He was broke and had entered a strange world of telephones, fenced land, and Model T Fords bumping down the rutted back roads. The lean, cold-eyed killer was at first amazed when Tilghman asked him to play his own role in the movie, but he became interested when Kent showed him the workings of the camera and not only signed up with Tilghman's Eagle Film Company but provided details for Stover.

Tilghman was determined that every scene had to be authentic, so the company filmed the historic incidents precisely where they had taken place. Tilghman reenacted his capture of Bill Doolin in the Eureka Springs bathhouse, Marshal Ledbetter captured the Jennings and O'Malley brothers at the Spike S ranch, while Arkansas Tom led his band of wildly enthusiastic if fictitious outlaws into small towns to rob the banks, hold up a train, and reenact the bloody Battle of Ingalls.

While the movie was being filmed, life imitated art. Henry Starr, related to Sam Starr, husband of the notorious Belle Reed Starr, led a small band into Stroud, Oklahoma, and simultaneously robbed the town's two banks. When word of the robbery reached the film company on location, Tilghman temporarily abandoned his producer-director role and became a lawman.[15]

After he caught one of the band he returned to movie making. The film was finally completed, but Tilghman discovered making a movie was only half the project; the other half was harder to accomplish—showing it to the public. In a 1961 interview Mrs. Tilghman explained how they did it.[16]

The late Zoe Tilghman with the author in her Oklahoma City home in the winter of 1961. *Photo by Gertrude Horan*

Bill Tilghman: Movie Distributor

The making of *The Passing of the Oklahoma Outlaws* was interrupted by the robbery of two banks in Stroud, March 27, 1915. The crime took place in Lincoln County so it was in Bill's jurisdiction and he had to stop playing make-believe, strap on his guns, and go after Henry Starr and his gang. The outlaw carrying the stolen money had been shot and a posse of townspeople found him just outside of town.

Bill learned one of the robbers was a man named Joe Davis, who had gained the alias "Alibi Joe." Although Davis had a long criminal record he was seldom convicted because he always came up with an iron-bound alibi.

Bill knew that on previous occasions Davis had used a hotel register or a livery owner's log as alibi; on the frontier they were seldom questioned. As soon as he got to Stroud and questioned the captured and wounded robber and talked to the people in the banks, Bill went to the hotel and examined the register. When he noticed a blank entry for the day of the robbery he waited for Davis to appear. Bill grabbed him as he was about to sign his name. Later the hotel clerk and the liveryman confessed they had been paid by Davis to falsify their registers. Bill continued his investigation. Henry Starr was captured and brought to Lincoln County. Later all the members of the band received long prison sentences on the basis of the evidence Bill uncovered and turned over to County Prosecutor Robertson.

Meanwhile the movie was finally finished. Marshal Nix and Chris Madsen had to return to their law enforcement duties, which left Bill with the task of putting together the small details of promotion, publicity, and the major task of putting the movie on the road.

Jack Wall, an experienced promotion man in Oklahoma City, was hired and he outlined a route across the country where the movie could be seen. Bill put together a poster with scenes from the movie along with favorable quotes he obtained from the leading lawmen. One was from Chief Justice Davis of the Oklahoma Supreme Court. Everyone in law enforcement approved the picture. It wasn't fiction, it was real, filmed by and with men who had taken part in the building of Oklahoma and bringing law and order to the frontier. Following each showing Bill would give a lecture on the events.

In September 1915, after showing the movie in the territory, Bill had his first big showing at the Tabor Palace in Denver. He wrote me that every showing had a capacity house and the receipts were over $1,500. This was important because the production company had debts and Bill was never one to have unpaid debts. It bothered him.

All that fall and winter he was in and out of small and big towns showing the movie and talking until his voice had dwindled to a whisper. In the spring he returned home for a rest. Then we loaded our Model T and our boys and set out on a leisurely trip, camping, fishing, and showing the movie.

We were certainly pioneers in the movie distribution business. We slept out in the rain, had our Model T mired in mud—once it overturned in Colorado—but we always found halls and movie houses to show *The Passing of the Oklahoma Outlaws.*

Bill's presence was a major attraction. Wherever we went the local newspapermen would interview him about his early days in Dodge City and the gunfights he had with the Doolin gang. One of the major problems was the local censor boards, usually the police department. Some wanted a handout, but Bill firmly told all of them he never handed out graft and he didn't intend to start at this time. While we were on tour J. B. Robertson was finally elected governor and he wired Bill offering a state appointment. Bill and I discussed it but in the end he decided he would never be happy with an office job, so he turned down the governor's offer and we continued in the movie business. I believe it was about 1920 when we reached Los Angeles and played the old Palace Theatre. No one expected an audience, but in a week the movie was playing to crowded houses. One of the delightful days Bill had was visiting Wyatt Earp, who lived there. They spent hours reliving the old Dodge City days.

We temporarily stopped showing the "picture," as it was referred to in the family, when Bill joined our old friend, Governor Robertson, in his fight against the Klan and later when Bill ran for sheriff in Oklahoma County. The Klan never forgot how he stood up against their organization and when he turned down their offer to become a member, they campaigned against him and he lost. The Klan's candidates were swept into office. While I stayed at home with the children, Bill took the picture again on the road. By this time we had replaced the Model T with a truck and Bill crisscrossed the West with it. But the strain was beginning to tell on him. Also the governor's office was always calling on Bill to do some special job. No matter what his physical condition, he never refused.

Although his health was bad, Tilghman accepted an assignment to go to Mexico and hunt down a railroad embezzler. He located the man in the interior and notified the American ambassador, who introduced him to Porfirio Diaz at the presidential palace.

When the Mexican dictator insisted he take along a company of soldiers to help make the arrest, Tilghman refused. The best way, he told Diaz, was to go in alone.

A few weeks later he tailed the American fugitive to a restaurant. After arranging for a special train to stand by, he walked up to the man, put a gun to his head, bent over, and told him quietly he was under arrest.

For a few seconds the fugitive's hand inched toward a revolver hidden inside his jacket.

"Don't try it," Tilghman said mildly. "I'm pretty good with this thing."

The American dropped his hand and Tilghman walked him to the train. He was returned to the States, convicted, and sent to prison.

In 1924 when conditions in Cromwell, a boom oil town seventy miles east of Oklahoma City, became a statewide scandal, Governor M. E. Trapp begged Bill to accept the police chief's badge and clean up the community.

"Bill wasn't well and he had only started to enjoy retirement when the call came," Mrs. Tilghman recalled. "I had a premonition that night when the governor called, but I also knew Bill would accept. He had a rigid sense of honor and public duty, so once again he took down his guns."

Cromwell, a town of a single wooden main street against a backdrop of pulsing oil rigs, was wilder and more vicious than Dodge City or the other Kansas cow towns Bill Tilghman had known in another century.

The old-time gunmen usually followed a frontier code, but for the bootleggers, corrupt officials, drug pushers, and hired killers who infested Cromwell there was no code or law. Tilghman arrived in August. By late fall he had brought law and order to the roaring oil town.

In one episode two hijackers suddenly found themselves in a gun duel with an elderly sharpshooter who gave them a chance to surrender or be killed. They quickly came out with their hands up.

In another episode, a big city narcotics pusher arrogantly boasted how he would send the new police chief "back to the sticks" only to face an unwavering .45 caliber automatic pointed at his stomach by a soft-spoken man with graying hair and cold gray-blue eyes, who advised him to drop the package of cocaine he was carrying. The pusher quickly threw up his hands and dropped the drugs to the street.

That fall Tilghman arranged with his two deputies to arrest a man he identified as the head of a drug ring bringing narcotics into the state. A stakeout was set up. While his men watched the spot, Tilghman returned to Cromwell in the early hours of a Sunday morning. Eating in a restaurant he heard a flurry of shots, ran out, and disarmed a cursing drunk. As he was about to search the man, later identified as a federal Prohibition agent, he suddenly grabbed a pistol hidden inside his coat, shot Tilghman twice, and escaped.

A few minutes later Bill Tilghman died on a dusty couch in a nearby secondhand furniture store.[17]

The state was stunned by his murder; flags were ordered to fly at half mast and his body lay in state in the rotunda of the capital. The following April 22, anniversary of the Oklahoma Land Rush, a carefully groomed horse, with Bill's two six-shooters dangling from the saddle horn, led an Oklahoma City parade sponsored by the survivors of the 1889 land rush.

There was no rider; Bill Tilghman had gone home.

BEAR RIVER TOM SMITH

One of the best and certainly the most unique lawmen of the western frontier was "Bear River" Tom Smith, an ex-New Yorker who ruled Abilene in its wildest days with his fists instead of a gun. For the four months he wore the marshal's star, Smith never drew his six-shooter, never shot a man as he rode his giant, silver-gray horse, "Silverheels," up and down Texas Street day and night until the last cowhands staggered back to their camp and the last lamp in the brothels flickered out.

Smith, of medium height and weight, had auburn hair and a thick moustache of the same color. He had gray-blue eyes and, as a man who knew him in Abilene recalled, "His manner was gentle, his voice low-toned, his gray eyes of bluish tint were his most expressive feature when aroused."[1]

In a time when a man's virility was often judged by the amount of raw frontier whiskey he could consume, Smith was a teetotaler. Nor did he gamble. He sincerely liked children, respected women, even the rough whores of Texas Street, and firmly believed that communities in the West could survive only if law and order prevailed.

Smith was reticent about his early background but T. C. Henry, Abilene's first mayor, who hired Smith, told his brother, Stuart Henry, the novelist and historian, that Smith had been a New York City policeman, skilled in boxing and was a good shot despite his reluctance to use firearms. He had an extraordinary

°

background. In 1857 he was a survivor of Utah's Mountain Meadow Massacre. Later he became a wagon master hauling railroad material across Utah, Nebraska, and Wyoming to finally join the Union Pacific's construction gang as the line moved across the frontier.[2]

In 1868 he was living in Bear River City, Wyoming, when a band of vigilantes lynched three prisoners and made wholesale arrests of many railroad workers. A mob marched out of "construction city," released the prisoners, burned down the jail and the tent housing Lege Freeman's *Frontier Index*, which the mob claimed had fomented the vigilantes. A few days earlier Freeman had published a denial that he was "chief of the vigilantes." Freeman escaped, but his newspaper's press and type were tossed into the flames.

The mob then marched on a log cabin where the armed vigilantes had taken refuge. Smith appeared and tried to act as mediator but was shot. He recovered and later was appointed "marshal" of the rough construction towns established, then abandoned, as the Union Pacific moved across the frontier.[3]

Bear River Tom Smith, as he was known, first appeared in Abilene in early March 1870 "because he had heard a marshal was wanted." Mayor Henry, who knew Smith's reputation as a tough lawman, conferred with the town's four trustees, including Joe McCoy, pioneering drover and founder of Abilene. Henry and the trustees agreed that Smith's mild manner and soft voice would only leave him a bullet-riddled corpse, so Henry told Smith there were other applicants to be interviewed and they would let him know.

Henry then sent to St. Louis for two tough cavalrymen to appoint as marshals. The troopers viewed Texas Street that evening and hastily left the following morning. They told the mayor "any man would be a fool to associate with cowpunchers full of unrectified whiskey and tryin' to do a buck and wing in a dance house . . . Texans is used to Hades. . . . I ain't got money left to pay for my funeral and I ain't just ready to die yet."[4]

As days passed it was evident the wild Texas cowboys, pouring in with the herds, were taking over the community. A small stone jail was built in the center of Texas Street to the amusement of the hands, who waited until the carpenters had finished, then lassoed the roof and pulled it off to release a Negro cook arrested for firing a pistol while drunk. Other bands charged down the streets, bullets shattering glass windows—including the mayor's office—and riddling business signs. When Henry put up posters ordering the cowhands to turn in their guns, the posters became targets. Men oiled six-shooters and there was open talk of forming a vigilante committee. Henry, remembering Smith, suggested to the trustees that he be hired. The trustees agreed, and Henry telegraphed the New Yorker at a Union Pacific construction camp to tell him that he had been appointed Abilene's marshal.

On June 4, 1870, Henry picked up Smith in a wagon at Ellis, Kansas, and they drove to Abilene. Henry advised Smith that Abilene was "pretty tough" and he advised him to look over Texas Street before he accepted the post.

Smith, riding the giant silver gray, "Silverheels," returned the next day and told Henry that Abilene was no different from many of the western towns he had seen.

The mayor asked, "Do you think you can control the town?"

Smith's quiet reply was, "I think it can be done."

Smith was hired at $250 a month "and half the fines." When Henry told him

Bear River City, Wyoming Territory, where Tom Smith earned his nickname. This photograph was taken by Joseph Eiam Stimson, a nineteen-year-old Connecticut photographer who went west to become an official photographer for the Union Pacific. His studio was in Cheyenne. *Courtesy Wyoming State Archives Museum and Historical Department*

there was an ordinance against carrying firearms within the town's limits, and that the cowboys had used the warning posters for targets, Smith told him to immediately plaster the town with more posters.

"But how on earth would you—one man—disarm them and the drovers—and the professional 'badmen'? It's a little army, one against an army," Henry pointed out.

Smith shrugged. "It won't be a holiday," he admitted, "but that's the proposition as I see it."[5]

The posters ordered by Smith soon appeared in the lobby of the popular Drover's House, other hotels along Texas Street, and in saloons. Soon after he started his patrol riding Silverheels, Smith met a burly cowhand nicknamed "Big Hank" who had boasted in the saloons that no lawman would ever disarm him.

Smith quietly pointed to a poster and ordered the gunfighter to unbuckle his gun belt and deposit his weapons with the nearest bartender. Hank laughed and challenged Smith to do the task himself.

Smith leaped out of the saddle and before the cowhand could draw, hit him a powerful blow on the jaw. When Marshal Smith repeated his order, groggy "Big Hank" surrendered his guns. While the suddenly subdued residents and customers of Texas Street silently watched, Smith ordered Hank to leave Abilene and never come back. Without a word the cowboy mounted his horse and rode out of town.

A desperado named "Wyoming Frank," who had a minor reputation as a bully and a badman, was the next man to challenge Smith. The scene was repeated. When the Wyoming gunman started to draw on Smith, the marshal's blow knocked him out. After a few buckets of water brought him to, Smith took the cowboy's guns and ordered:

"Get out of town in five minutes and don't come back."

Abilene never saw "Wyoming Frank" again.

As an eyewitness reported: "That was the signal . . . pistols and rifles were offered but Tom quietly told them to give their weapons to the bartenders until they were ready to leave camp."

Tom Smith's "oil lamp fight" enhanced his reputation as a marshal who intended to maintain the law and order in his community. In a notorious saloon called "The Old Fruit" Smith waded into a crowd of hooting, jeering Texans to arrest a hand who had fired a shot at a sign and challenged Smith to come and disarm him.

While Smith was slugging cowboys one threw a lamp at him. He ducked and it smashed against a wall. The fighting broke off abruptly; everyone knew what fire could do to a tinder dry cow town. The cowboys poured out through the swinging doors but the oil didn't explode, possibly because it was low grade. Smith stamped out the burning wick, tossed the cowboy he had knocked out across his shoulder, and started down the street to the jail.

So many shots were fired without hitting Smith that the Texans swore the marshal wore a "steel plate under his shirt." The ludicrous legend still exists.[6]

After the saloon brawl Abilene remained fairly quiet under Smith. He was tough but fair, and the Texans came to respect and fear his iron fists. The grateful citizens presented him with a brace of ivory-handled six-shooters and Mayor Henry told him to stay on as marshal as long as he wished.

New herds from Texas arrived every day. More corrals were built and the brawling of the steers being forced into the narrow cattle cars to be butchered for the East could be heard until late at night. Clouds of dust hung over the staging area during the day and the town smelled of raw pine as new homes and business establishments were built. Housewives began to plant boxwood elders and cottonwoods in front of their houses and Havana cigars appeared in the more "elegant" saloons. In the "fancy houses" cowboys in woollen shirts and buckskin pants stuffed into boots danced with the girls "to whom virtue is an unknown and unexpected grace."

Shortly after he was appointed marshal of Abilene on June 4, 1870, Smith held a meeting of the town's businessmen and saloon owners. He advised them it was in their own interest to uphold the ordinance banning firearms in the community. He shrewdly pointed out that if the Texans were deprived of their weapons there would be less violence, and ranchers, farmers, and homesteaders would bring their families into the town and spend money. Cowboys from Texas were transients. Ranchers and farmers could be steady customers. To allow the wild cowboys to take over the streets would only end in disaster for the town. Smith's logic worked and Abilene's business community strongly supported the marshal's rules and ordinances.

That summer when Abilene was nearing its peak as one of the leading cow towns of the Wild West, Smith became a familiar figure on Silverheels, cool eyes under his sombrero searching the milling crowds of cowboys, dance-hall girls, pimps, saloon keepers, gamblers, and drovers for the face of a wanted man or a man carrying forbidden guns. The young, tough Texans cherished their weapons and their ability to "capture" a cow town, but word soon drifted along the cow camps on the trails leading north that ordinary bullets wouldn't kill this Yankee lawman whose fists could crack a man's jaw.

Smith ruled Abilene until that fall when ironically he was killed, not by a drunken cowhand or a gunfighter seeking to enhance his reputation, but by a pair of Scotch homesteaders.

Tom Smith's last fight took place on November 2, 1870, on Chapman's Creek, several miles from Abilene. Accounts of that bloody day vary but perhaps Mayor Henry's brief account in the Kansas Historical Society bulletin is the most accurate.

> On October 23, a Sunday, Andrew McConnell, a Chapman Creek homesteader shot and killed his neighbor, John Shea, in a fight over Shea's cattle eating the homesteader's corn crop. During the dispute Shea pulled his six-shooter and "snapped it twice" at McConnell but the gun failed to fire and McConnell killed him. An investigation confirmed McConnell's plea of self-defense and murder charges were dismissed. But Shea's neighbors were not satisfied and insisted the case be reopened. Warrants for the arrest of McConnell and his partner, Miles, were issued and turned over to Smith to be served.
>
> Smith, accompanied by a deputy named McDonald—some accounts name him the Dickinson County sheriff—rode to Chapman Creek. When McConnell was informed by Smith he was under arrest, he shot the marshal twice in the chest. Despite his wounds Smith grappled with McConnell and finally beat him to the ground. After a brief struggle he handcuffed his shouting, cursing prisoner.

Suddenly Miles, who had been chopping wood in the rear of the dugout, appeared, waving his ax. As Smith staggered to his feet Miles split his skull.

After what Mayor Henry described as a "furious fusillade," the deputy rode back to Abilene where a posse was formed. They returned to the dugout to find that McConnell and Miles had fled, leaving the almost decapitated body of Smith in front of the dugout.

In another account, published many years later in the *Abilene Chronicle*, J. B. Edwards described McDonald as a cowardly sheriff who had abandoned Smith after he had been wounded by McConnell. Edwards claimed a neighbor who had accompanied the lawmen witnessed the wounded Smith dragging McConnell across the yard when Miles appeared and "snapped" his rifle at McDonald, who fled. Then the two men overpowered the bleeding marshal and while McConnell held him down, Miles used the ax to kill him.[7]

A posse placed the marshal's body on a bed of straw in a wagon, covered it with branches, and returned to Abilene.

The cow town was dumbfounded: fearless Bear River Tom Smith, who ruled the wild Texans with his iron fists, killed by two bushwhacking grangers! Posses searched the prairie and some time later Miles and McConnell were captured and returned to Abilene for trial. They were found guilty and although there were lynching threats, the pair was sentenced to long terms in the state's prison.

Tom's funeral services were held in Abilene's little frame Baptist church. Saloons, gambling houses, and brothels were closed. Texas Street was quiet. Behind the hearse, banked with flowers, walked Silverheels, Smith's ivory-handled six-shooters and belt hanging from the pommel. The long file of men, women, and children, all with crepe on their arms, wound down Texas Street, then across the railroad tracks, and finally mounted the slope of the small hill to the simple grave and its wooden marker.

In 1904 a granite boulder from Oklahoma's granite mountain was placed at the head of a new grave site. When the metal casket was raised, spectators saw under the glass window of the casket, "Tom Smith as in every way as perfect as he was when he was put into the coffin."

As Abilene's former mayor, T. C. Henry, noted in his speech that day, Tom Smith had never drawn a gun or killed a man, although he had been shot at many times.[8]

A plaque on the boulder read:

THOMAS J. SMITH
MARSHAL OF ABILENE, 1870
DIED A MARTYR TO DUTY NOV. 2, 1870
A FEARLESS HERO OF FRONTIER DAYS
WHO IN THE COWBOY CHAOS
ESTABLISHED THE SUPREMACY OF LAW

CHARLES A. SIRINGO

IT IS FORTUNATE FOR HISTORIANS OF THE WILD WEST
that Charlie Siringo hung up his spurs and saddle after years of punching cows,
breaking wild horses, and making cattle drives from Texas to the northern beef
markets.

In 1883, after fifteen years as a cowboy, Siringo retired to Caldwell, Kansas, to
concoct "ice cream sodas and lemonade at almost any day or night" as his
advertisement in the *Caldwell Journal* informed its readers. A year later he added
an oyster parlor, boasting he could supply lunch accompanied by a cup of
coffee—"genuine cowpuncher coffee that will almost stand alone."[1]

Then the peaceful prairie community, always disdainful of its wild sister cow
towns, Abilene and Dodge City, had its own moment of notoriety when
Caldwell's marshal, Henry Brown, was killed in Medicine Lodge, Kansas, while
attempting to hold up a bank. A short time later the stunned citizens learned
Brown had been one of Billy the Kid's riders and had left Lincoln County, New
Mexico, a hoofbeat ahead of a sheriff's posse.

It is evident that about this time Siringo was becoming bored with preparing
lunches and ice cream sodas. The killing of Brown reminded him of the days
when he had ridden with Billy the Kid, so he wrote a brief memoir of the
legendary bandit as he remembered him.

The impact of seeing his own name in the *Caldwell Journal* must have stirred

182

Charles Siringo's ad in the Caldwell, Kansas, *Journal* of February 19, 1885, advising readers where they could get "Genuine Cowpuncher coffee." As a self-styled, "old stove-up cow puncher," Siringo had "retired" from the cattle business to run a combination ice cream parlor and restaurant in Caldwell. *Courtesy Kansas State Historical Society*

him, and he began writing *A Texas Cowboy: or Fifteen Years on the Hurricane Back of a Spanish Pony,* one of the most memorable books in western frontier literature.[2]

Siringo's book was first published in 1885 by a Chicago firm, then issued again a year later by Siringo and a partner. It had a healthy sale and Siringo sold his ice cream parlor to join the Pinkerton National Detective Agency and become the famous cowboy-detective of the Wild West.

For twenty-three years he lived an incredible, exciting life on the dying frontier as he trailed Butch Cassidy and the Wild Bunch, the deadly Harvey (Kid Curry) Logan, rustling gangs, horse thieves, bank and train robbers, and played undercover roles in the savage western mining and railroad strikes.

He retired a second time after the turn of the century to write of his experiences as a detective and to engage in a long and bitter court fight with the Pinkertons. The private detective agency held up his book for two years until he finally changed the title, substituted fictitious names, and cut some of his material.[3]

Henry Brown, marshal of Caldwell, and his gang, in handcuffs after they had been captured following an attempt to rob the Medicine Lodge, Kansas, bank on May 8, 1884. Brown and his men were later killed in a shootout with their captors. After reading the extra put out by the *Caldwell Standard* about the robbery, the shooting, and Brown's career as a member of the Billy the Kid gang, Siringo wrote "Sketch of Billy the Kid's Life," which was published in the *Standard.* *Courtesy Kansas State Historical Society*

Lithograph used as a frontispiece of the now very rare first edition of Charles A. Siringo's *A Texas Cowboy*, published in 1885. On September 17 and 24, that same year, the book's ad in the *Journal* advised readers that only limited copies were sold by subscription for $1. *The James D. Horan Collection*

Lithograph used in the first and second editions of Siringo's *A Texas Cowboy*, the first authentic cowboy autobiography. The book is now considered a classic of western literature. *The James D. Horan Collection*

Siringo wearing what he called "my cowboy uniform." *The James D. Horan Collection*

Charlie Siringo on the trail of Harvey Logan, tiger of the Wild Bunch. Siringo, as a Pinkerton detective, chased the notorious Kid Curry for thousands of miles across the West but never captured him. *The James D. Horan Collection*

Alavardo Hotel and the Santa Fe depot in the 1880s. During the Lincoln County War, Siringo stayed at the hotel with Ash Upton, the frontier newspaperman who gained frontier literary immortality as the man who wrote Pat Garrett's book on Billy the Kid. *The James D. Horan Collection*

Siringo's first success, *A Texas Cowboy*, distributed for forty years under five different publishers, was widely read in the range country. Like Tom Horn's memoirs and John Wesley Hardin's autobiography, the paperback edition was peddled on trains by "candy butchers."

Siringo constantly rewrote his experiences but *The Texas Cowboy* was the most authentic, beginning with his birth on February 7, 1855, at Dutch Settlement, a tiny settlement halfway down the Matagorda Peninsula, near old Indianola, Texas. His parents were immigrants, his father Italian, his mother Irish. He spent only a few months in a classroom and by age eleven was punching cows and breaking wild horses at $2.50 a head; it wasn't unusual for him to break five horses in a day. He became a teen-age wanderer, working as a bellboy in a St. Louis hotel and as a roustabout on the Mississippi's Morgan steamboat.

One night he fell into a hold and suffered severe injuries. But Siringo, who one westerner described as "tough as a hickory nut," survived to be taken in by the freight manager of a steamship line who lived in St. Louis.[4]

The former child-cowboy was awed by his new luxurious home. The steamship man and his wife were fond of the rough frontier boy, and dressed him up and enrolled him in a private school "to learn German, French and English."

Siringo tried his best to fulfill the hopes of the couple that he would become a polished young man. He worked hard at his school books and diligently avoided the class bully who had selected him as the butt for his abuse. The young Texan took his beatings meekly until one day when he turned on the bigger boy, nicked him with a small knife, and chased him out of the schoolyard.

Siringo left St. Louis to search unsuccessfully for his mother and sister, then decided to return to the couple, who gave him a prodigal's welcome. He went back to school "to take up my old studies, German, French and English," but in a few months he was "back on the rolling deep" aboard another Morgan steamboat bound for Galveston, Texas. He left the river for Shanghai Pierce's Rancho Grande, one of the largest ranches in Texas. Siringo recalled the spread was so immense that he and the other hands branded 25,000 calves that season.

For most of the 1870s, Charlie Siringo trailed the herds north. He drifted from ranch to cow camp as many carefree cowboys did in those days, and won a reputation as a wild bronc rider and a deadshot with a rifle and six-shooter. At twenty-two he was working for David T. Beals, owner of the huge LX ranch near Amarillo; he was soon Beals's most trusted hand.

Siringo knew the wild Kansas cow towns and did his share of hurrahing Dodge City's sheriffs. In his memoirs he described his first meeting with Bat Masterson, then owner of The Lone Star saloon and dance hall while he was sheriff of Ford County.[5]

Siringo, with his friend Wess, arrived in Dodge on July 3, 1877, "after sixty days with wild steers, wild Indians and wild rivers." Both cow hands decided to draw their pay and "celebrate the glorious Fourth in proper style in Dodge City."

A brawl started when a buffalo hunter began dancing with Wess's girl friend. When Siringo moved in to help his partner, Bat Masterson, who was behind the bar, began hurling heavy beer glasses with deadly aim at the brawlers. One caught Siringo in the forehead, opening a deep gash. With their guns drawn, the two cowboys slowly backed out of the saloon.

As Siringo told the story, he and Wess ran the town's marshal "up an alley" as they, "whooping and shooting," galloped out of town.

Siringo also got to know many of the badmen of the Wild West, including John Wesley Hardin and Billy the Kid. The tales he told about Hardin are familiar but he claimed to have met Billy the Kid at the LX ranch, where the famous Lincoln County outlaw showed Charlie "he could plant two bullets in the mark to my one."

Siringo's most intriguing story about the Kid has the outlaw giving him "a finely bound novel that he had just finished reading, autographing it for me with the date of the presentation" in exchange for a cigar holder!

In 1910 Siringo wrote *A Pinkerton Cowboy Detective* and his feud with the agency began. The private detective company's attorney went to court. The Superior Court of Chicago ordered Siringo to change the title of his book to *A Cowboy Detective* and to delete much of the material. In his book, Pinkerton became Dickenson and even such famous western names as Tom Horn became Tom Corn.

The cowboy-detective continued to battle his powerful enemy for years. In 1915 he privately published his *Two Evil Isms: Pinkertonism and Anarchism.*[6]

The text was a deadly denunciation of the Pinkerton Agency with little said about "anarchism." The former frontier detective accused the agency of fixing elections, bribing juries, kidnapping witnesses in major felony cases, corrupting public officials, and causing the execution of an innocent man.

Siringo self-righteously pointed out it had been a "great strain" on his conscience to have worked so long for the Pinkertons without a protest. In anticipation of criticism, he explained:

"The question might be asked why I did not show my manhood by resigning and exposing this crooked agency in the beginning. Exposing it to whom, pray? Not to the officers of the law, I hope. In my cowboy simplicity I might have been persuaded to do it at that time. But I am glad I did not, for, with my twenty-two years behind the curtains, I can now see the outcome. It would have resulted in many sleeps in the city bull-pen, and a few doses of the third degree to try and wring a confession for blackmailing this notorious institution.

"Up to the time of the Homestead riot, and since the moral wave has been sweeping over the land, the Pinkerton National Detective Agency was above the law. A word from W. S. Pinkerton or one of his officers would send any scrub citizen to the scrap heap or even the penitentiary."

When the book was issued, Pinkerton's attorneys returned to court. In March 1915, once again the Superior Court of Cook County ordered that Siringo's stock of books and plates be held within the jurisdiction of the court until further notice. That summer the court ruled that the books and printing material be turned over to the Pinkertons.

However Siringo refused to give up. In 1927 Houghton Mifflin published Siringo's *Riata and Spurs: The Story of a Lifetime Spent in the Saddle as Cowboy and Detective.*

A good part of this new book contained material which had appeared in the original *A Cowboy Detective*, now with actual names and the name of the Pinkerton Agency. According to a letter in this author's possession, written by Siringo to a magazine writer in 1924, the Pinkertons once again forced his publisher to delete material from his book. He wrote:

"They [Houghton Mifflin] have cut out all my detective experiences and in its place have added material from my 'Bad Man Cowboys' manuscript. The new book will contain the lives of many 'bad' killers such as John Wesley Hardin, Bill Longley, Ben Thompson, King Fisher, Jim Miller, Sam Bass and Clay Allison."[7]

In later printings of the book, pages 120–268 of the original text are omitted and other material substituted; no notice is given that more than half of the book is composed of material which is not in the original edition.

Eugene M. Rhodes recalled Siringo of those last years as a man with "faded brown eyes, but sharp eyes that never miss the slightest movement of any person or anything. Not nervous but always alert. A thin face, brown like saddle leather; wind and sun have tanned that face beyond all changing. Most expressive hands, a trigger finger that sticks out with every gesture . . . thin-lipped, a mouth that would be hard if it were not for an occasional quirk of humor. Quite a frank smile and often a chuckle. Not a tall man, slender, yes, frail. You note this with a shock . . . wears a small red silk handkerchief. A low-crowned Stetson, neat clothing and shoes, not boots, straight back; does not stoop, head carried like a Chanticleer."[8]

Siringo died in Hollywood, October 19, 1928.

2417 Grand Canal.
Venice, Calif.
Sep. 15th   1924 (7)

Dear Mr. Neil Clark:
                Your favor of
11th inst. to hand. In
reply will say that the
Houghton Mifflin Co.
of No. 2 Park Street.
Boston, Mass. had to
discontinue the publication
of my book "Riata and
Spurs" owing to threat
of the Pinkerton Agency
to bring court proceedings
on account of me
giving away secrets of
the agency. Hence
they have cut out
all my detective
experience, and in
its place have
added material

Here and next page: Extremely rare letters written by Siringo to Neil M. Clark, who wrote an article on Siringo for *American* magazine, January 1929. Siringo discusses his troubles with the Pinkerton Agency and the "two-gun" men he knew on the frontier. At the time, Siringo was seventy-two years old. *The James D. Horan Collection*

range.
        A blacksmith's son
in Jackson County, Tex.
could fire two powder
and ball Colt pistols
— one after the other —
and do great execution.
He once won a bet
of $250 that he could
kill six quails out of
a flock sitting on the
ground before they
could get away. Some
he killed on the
wing after they had
raised to fly. I was
near where this bet
was won — but didn't
see it.
        Sincerely yours
        Chas. A. Siringo

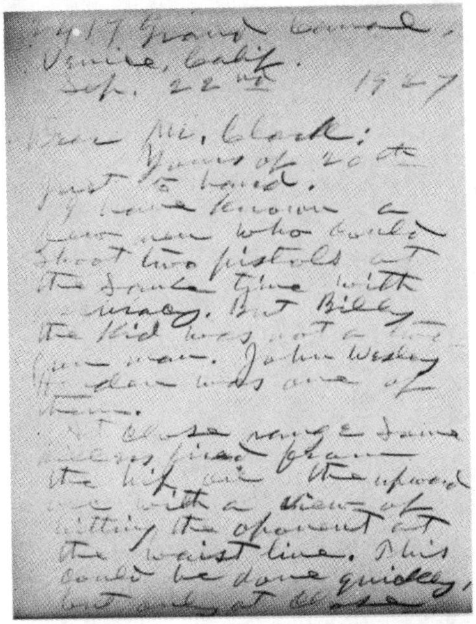

188

2417 Grand Canal,
Venice, Calif.
Sep. 22nd   1927

Dear Mr. Clark:
Yours of 20th just to hand.
I have known a few men who could shoot two pistols at the same time with accuracy. But Billy the Kid was not a two-gun man. John Wesley Hardin was one of them.
At close range a man always fired from the hip on the upward arc with a view of hitting the opponent at the waist line. This could be done quickly, but only at close

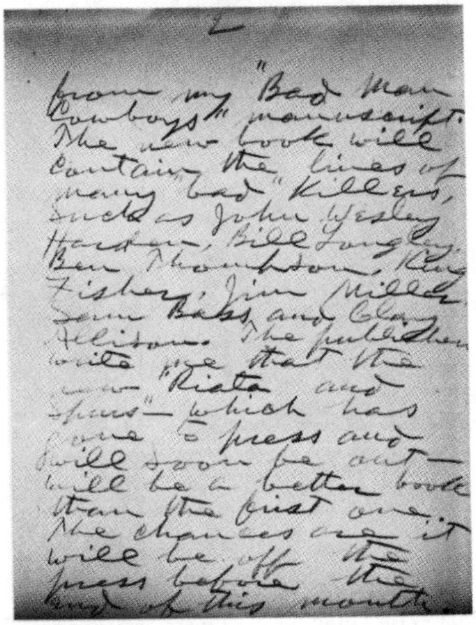

2

range from my "Bad Man Cowboys" manuscript. The new book will contain the lives of many bad "killers", such as John Wesley Hardin, Bill Longley, Ben Thompson, King Fisher, Jim Miller, Sam Bass, and Clay Allison. The publisher writes me that the new "Riata and Spurs" which has gone to press and will soon be out will be a better book than the first one. The chances are it will be off the press before the end of this month.

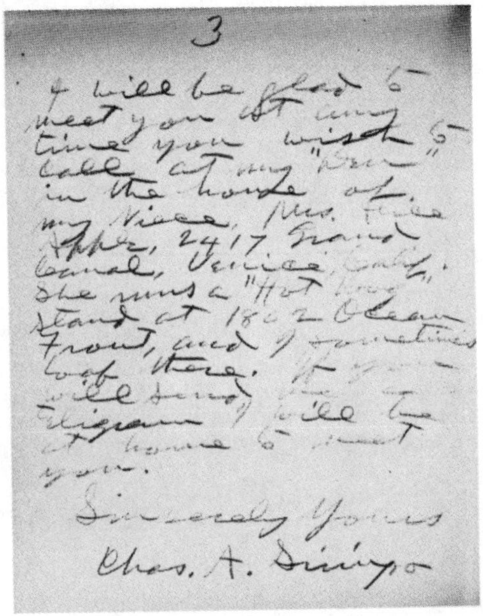

3

I will be glad to meet you at any time you wish to call at my "Den" in the house of my niece, Mrs. [illegible] Apple, 2417 Grand Canal, Venice Calif. She runs a "Hot Dog" stand at 1802 Ocean Front, and I sometimes loaf there. If you will send me a telegram I will be at home to meet you.
Sincerely Yours
Chas. A. Siringo

WYATT EARP
AND THE BATTLE
OF THE O. K. CORRAL

THE MOST ENDURING OF AMERICAN LEGENDS IS WYATT Earp. He was a dour, cold-eyed man whose fabrications and exaggerations, aided by a calculating biographer and television, our instant historian, transformed him from a minor frontier policeman and deputy into a Lancelot of the Wild West, equipped with a magic gun, who tamed the raw cow towns and faced down a band of killers at the gates of a dusty stable named the O. K. Corral.

Earp and his heroic roles are fakery, and his super revolver, the Buntline Special, never existed. Yet countless repetition of the lies and television's heroic figure playing out the fantasies and the fables of the Wild West convinced millions of Americans that Wyatt Earp was the premier lawman of the frontier.

Earp's early years parallel those of his contemporary peace officers. Like Bat Masterson and Bill Tilghman, he had been a farm boy, the teen-age head of family when his father went to war, a buffalo hunter, Indian fighter, railroad worker, and street brawler, skilled in the use of a six-shooter and a rifle.

The beginning of the Earp legend, mostly self-made, began in Ellsworth, Kansas, one of the early trail's-end cow towns, where he claimed to have disarmed Ben Thompson, the Texas gambler and one of the deadliest gunfighters on the frontier. Earp wasn't even there.

But Wyatt did serve a brief term as a policeman in Wichita. The official records reveal that Earp joined the two-man police force on April 21, 1875, serving under

A rare early photograph of Wyatt Earp at the time he was in Dodge City. This photograph was taken by William DeVinney of Ulysses, Kansas. *Courtesy Mazzulla Collection, Amon Carter Museum of Western Art*

Wyatt Earp about the time he arrived in Tombstone. *The James D. Horan Collection*

Virgil Earp, wounded in the gun battle of the O. K. Corral. George Whitwell Parsons, who kept a daily journal of his days in Tombstone, called the fight, "desperate men and a desperate encounter." On the night of December 28, 1881, gunmen ambushed Virgil, wounding him and crippling him for life. *The James D. Horan Collection*

James Earp who went to Tombstone with his brothers planning to open a corral and stage station. *The James D. Horan Collection*

Morgan Earp in 1881. He was wounded in the O. K. Corral gunfight and in March 1882 was shot and killed by gunmen as he was playing pool with Wyatt. The remaining Earps killed the men they believed responsible for the murder of Morgan. *The James D. Horan Collection*

192

The cow town of Ellsworth, Kansas, 1872, where the Wyatt Earp legend began. It was here, a year later, that Wyatt insisted he disarmed the deadly Ben Thompson, after the gambler's brother Billy had killed Ellsworth County Sheriff Chauncey Whitney on August 15, 1873. Earp was not even in town at the time of the shooting. *The James D. Horan Collection*

Ben Thompson, one of the deadliest gunfighters in the Wild West. *The James D. Horan Collection*

Billy Thompson, Ben's brother, who became a homicidal maniac when he was drunk. In March 1880 Bat Masterson rescued Billy Thompson from a Ogallala, Nebraska, lynch mob. *The James D. Horan Collection*

GOVERNOR'S PROCLAMATION.

WHEREAS, C. B. Whitney, Sheriff of Ellsworth County, Kansas, was murdered in the said county of Ellsworth, on the 15th day of August, 1873, by one William Thompson, said Thompson being described as about six feet in height, 26 years of age, dark complexion, brown hair, gray eyes and erect form; and Whereas, the said William Thompson is now at large and a fugitive from justice;

NOW THEREFORE, know ye, that I, Thomas A. Osborn, Governor of the State of Kansas, in pursuance of law, do hereby offer a reward of FIVE HUNDRED DOLLARS for the arrest and conviction of the said William Thompson, for the crime above named.

L. S.

IN TESTIMONY WHEREOF, I have hereunto subscribed my name, and caused to be affixed the Great Seal of the State. Done at Topeka, this 22d day of August, 1873.

THOMAS A. OSBORN.

By the Governor:
W. H. SMALLWOOD, Secretary of State.

An 1873 wanted poster for Billy Thompson. *The James D. Horan Collection*

Wichita, Kansas, at the time Wyatt Earp was a member of the cow town's two-man police force. *The James D. Horan Collection*

the town's marshal and assistant marshal. His major arrest took place the following month when he captured a horse thief who became entangled with a housewife's clothes line. The *Wichita Beacon* told the story. The editor, who wrote the tongue-in-cheek account, clearly regarded the arrest as a minor incident in a very busy frontier community; he relegated it to page five and misspelled Wyatt's name.[1]

An Aristocratic Horse Thief*

On Tuesday evening of last week, the Policeman Erp in his rounds, ran across a chap whose general appearance and getup answered to a description given of one W. W. Compton, who was said to have stolen two horses and a mule from Le Roy, in Coffee County. Earp took him in tow and required his name which he gave as "Jones." This didn't satisfy the officer who took Mr. Jones into the Gold Room on Douglas Avenue that he might examine him fully by lamplight. Mr. Jones, not liking the look of things, ran out, running to the rear of Denison's stables, Erp fired one shot across his poop to bring him to, to use a naughty-cal phrase, and just as he did so, the man cast anchor near a clothesline, hauled down his colors and surrendered without firing a gun. The officer laid hold of him and before he could recover his feet for another run, and taking him to the jail placed him in the keeping of the sheriff.

On the way to the jail "Jones" acknowledged he was the man wanted; the fact of the arrest was telegraphed to the sheriff of Coffey County who came down Thursday night and removed Compton to the jail of that county. A black horse and a buggy were found at one of the feed stables where Compton left them. After stealing the stock at Coffey he went to Independence where he traded them for the buggy, stole the black horse and came to this place. He will probably have the opportunity to do the state service for some years only to come out and go to horse stealing again, until a piece of twisted hemp or a stray bullet puts an end to his hankering after horse flesh.

A year later Earp assaulted William Smith, a candidate for Wichita's city marshal. The second man on the two-man police force found himself in custody, charged with "violating the peace and order of the city," as the *Beacon* reported. He was fined $30 by Judge Atwood and was ordered to turn in his badge.

Rumors in the community had Michael Meagher, the incumbent, asking Wyatt to put his opponent "hors de combat and thus remove an obstacle in the way of the reelection of the city marshal."

The *Beacon* hastened to assure its readers there was no truth to the gossip. Mike Meagher, the paper pointed out, was "noted for his manly bearing and personal courage."

The *Beacon* reported that the evidence produced before Judge Atwood proved that the marshal had "repeatedly" warned Earp not to have any "personal collision" with Smith and that Mike had separated the pair.

The story continued: "If there is any room to reflect on the marshal, it is that he did not order his subordinate out of Smith's room as soon as he entered, knowing that as he did, that Erp had fight on the brain."

The paper's editor concluded that "the good order of the city" had been vindicated when the city government had Wyatt arrested, found guilty, fined, and removed from the police force."

Meagher was reelected city marshal but despite Wyatt's friendship with Mike, the city commission, by a vote of six to two, refused to reappoint Wyatt to the police force. A few weeks later the city commission, now openly hostile to the Earps (Morgan had joined Wyatt in the hope of becoming a policeman), ordered that Wyatt's final policeman's pay be held up until he turned over all tax money he had collected to the city treasurer. The commission also ordered Meagher to enforce the "vagrancy act" against Wyatt and his brother.

Rather than be jailed as vagrants, the Earps headed for Dodge City.

*Original headline, May 12, 1875.

On last Sunday night a difficulty occurred betwen Policeman Erp and Wm. Smith, candidate for city marshal. Erp was arrested for violation of the peace and order of the city and was fined on Monday afternoon by his honor Judge Atwood, $30 and cost, and was relieved from the police force. Occurring on the eve of the city election, and having its origin in the canvass, it aroused general partisan interest throughout the city. The rumors, freely circulated Monday morning, reflected very severely upon our city marshal. It was stated and quite get generally credited that it was a put up job on the part of the city marshal and his assistant, to put the rival candidate for marshal *hors de combat* and thus remove an obstacle in the way of the re-election of the city marshal. These rumors, we say, were quite largely credited, notwithstanding their essential improbability and their inconsistency with the well known character of Mike Meagher, who is noted for his manly bearing and personal courage. The evidence before the court fully exhonorated Meagher from the charge of a cowardly conspiracy to mutilate and disable a rival candidate, but showed that he repeatedly ordered his subordinate to avoid any personal collision with Smith, and when the encounter took place, Mike used his utmost endeavor to separate the combatants. If there is any room to reflect on the marshal, it is that he did not order his subordinate out of Smith's room as soon as he entered, knowing as he did, that Erp had fight on the brain. It is well known that in periods of excitement people do not always act as as they would when perfectly collected and unexcited. The remarks that Smith was said to have made in regard to the marshal sending for Erp's brothers to put them on the police force furnished no just grounds for an attack, and upon ordinary occasions we doubt if Erp would have given them a second thought. The good order of the city was properly vindicated in the fining and dismissal of Erp. It is but justice to Erp to say he has made an excellent officer, and hitherto his conduct has been unexceptionable.

The *Kirwin Chief*'s report of the fight between Wyatt Earp and William Smith, candidate for Wichita's city marshal post. Earp (the paper misspelled his name) was fined $30 and court costs and ordered to leave with his brother, Morgan, or face arrest as vagrants. *Courtesy Kansas State Historical Society*

William Smith, who had the fist fight with Wyatt Earp. *Courtesy Kansas State Historical Society*

Topeka, Kansas, when it was a cattle town in the 1870s. This is a view of Kansas Avenue. *The James D. Horan Collection*

Dodge City, which the *Washington Star* dubbed "that wicked little city," appointed Earp a deputy or an assistant policeman in 1876. He served a year, was reappointed in May 1878, and finally left that raucous cow town in September 1879. He was a competent officer, praised by the *Dodge City Times*, who advised would-be badmen not to pull a gun on Earp "unless you got the drop and meant to burn powder without any preliminary talk."[2]

Wyatt not only confronted drunken cowhands in from a drive from Texas, but also a muscular dance-hall girl named "Miss Frankie Bell" who cursed out Wyatt so violently he slapped her and dragged her to the "dog house for a night's lodging and a reception at the police court next morning. The expense of which was about $20." Presumably the town fathers didn't like their policemen slapping women, even the muscular type, because Earp "was assessed the lowest limit of the law, one dollar."

Wyatt and his brother Morgan left Dodge to hunt gold in the Black Hills. On Earp's advice Bat Masterson ran for sheriff of Ford County and was elected in November 1877. He took office the following January. In April Bat's brother Edward, city marshal of Dodge, was shot and killed by a drunken cowhand. Charles E. Bassett, a veteran frontier lawman, was appointed in his place. On May 7 Earp returned to Dodge to replace John Brown as an assistant city marshal at $100 a month.

A short time later John Henry Holliday, the notorious "Doc" Holliday, who would be Earp's closest friend, arrived in Dodge to set up his dentist's office on the second floor of the Dodge House. As the advertisement in the *Dodge City Times* promised, "When satisfaction is not given money will be refunded."[3]

Stuart Lake, Earp's biographer, has the slender consumptive dentist putting aside his drill to save Wyatt's life shortly after he opened his office. Lake's version, using Earp's quotes, has Holliday coming to Earp's aid as he faced a mob of wild-eyed Texas cowboys. When Doc appeared with his guns, Wyatt pistol-whipped the leaders of the mob and dragged them off to jail.

The 300-pound Lawrence E. (Larry) Deger, city marshal of Dodge City. Wyatt Earp served under Deger as a deputy from 1876 to 1877. *Courtesy Mrs. Merritt L. Beeson; Kansas State Historical Society.*

A young Doc Holliday when he came to Dodge City. Holliday, born in Griffin, Georgia, gambled his way through almost every boom camp in the Wild West. He was Wyatt Earp's devoted friend and stood at his side in the O.K. Corral gunfight. He was a graduate of a dental school and for a time practiced in Dodge City. *Courtesy, Amon Carter Museum of Western Art, Fort Worth, Texas*

Doc Holliday's ad for his dental practice, *Dodge City Times*, June 8, 1878. *Courtesy Kansas State Historical Society*

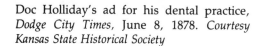

YARDS SOUTH OF RAILROAD TRACK.

DENTISTRY.

J. H. Holliday, Dentist, very respectfully offers his professional services to the citizens of Dodge City and surrounding country during the summer. Office at room No. 24, Dodge House. Where satisfaction is not given money will be refunded.

Mr. R. P. Edwards, boss herder for Henry Stevens, came up from the Canadian this week, where he has been

The *Times* doesn't mention the incident nor do any of the town's historians. Bob Wright, one of the founders of Dodge City, thought so little of Earp that in his autobiography he misspelled his name the few times he listed him as a member of a posse. But Wright and Billy Dixon, a young buffalo hunter who became a famous Indian scout, recalled Bat Masterson as the courageous sheriff of Dodge City who kept the town under control and won the admiration and respect of the Texas drovers.

In 1879 the Frank Loving and Levi Richardson gunfight took place. In the Earp-Lake version, Wyatt was the stand-up hero who coolly disarmed both men and escorted them to jail. The *Times*, prime source of what took place in Dodge City and Ford County during those years, told it differently. After Loving, a gambler, and Richardson, a freighter, began exchanging shots at point-blank range inside the Long Branch saloon, Charlie Bassett ran into the bar just as Loving finally hit Richardson—not all the residents of Dodge were crack shots. Bassett disarmed Loving while his deputy, William Duffey, relieved the wounded Richardson of his six-shooter. The freighter died soon after; a coroner's jury found the killing to have been justifiable homicide. Earp is not mentioned in the *Times* account.[4]

Later Earp was joined by his brother Virgil and Virgil's young bride, Allie. Wyatt and Allie never liked each other from their first meeting. In her memoirs, edited by Frank Waters, the western historian, Allie described how their covered

THE CAPTURE OF JIM KENNEDY,

THE SUPPOSED ASSASSIN OF DORA HAND alias FANNIE KEENAN.

THE PRISONER WOUNDED IN THE LEFT SHOULDER.

In last week's TIMES we detailed the circumstances of the killing of Dora Hand alias Fannie Keenan, at about half past four o'clock Friday morning. There were few persons up at this unseasonable hour, though all night walkers and loungers are not uncommon in this city, and the somber hours of that morning found one James Kennedy and another person gyrating in the dim shadows of the flickering light of the solitary opened saloon. Four pistol shots awakened the echoes in that dull misty morning, and aroused the police force and others. Pistol shots are of common occurrence, but this firing betokened something fatal. Assistant Marshal Earp and Officer Jim Masterson were soon at their wits' end, but promptly surmised the upshot of the shooting. Shortly after the firing Kennedy and his companion were seen in the opened saloon. The arrival of the officers and the movements of the two morning loungers threw suspicions in their direction. Kennedy mounted his

ing. There were some other reasons why the officers believed that Kennedy did the shooting, and accordingly a plan for his capture was commenced, though the officers did not start in pursuit until 2 o'clock in the afternoon. The party consisted of Sheriff Masterson, Marshal Bassett, Assistant Wyatt Earp, Deputy Duffy and Wm. Tilghman, as intrepid a posse as ever pulled a trigger. They started down the river road, halting at a ranch below the Fort, thence going south, traveling 75 miles that day. A heavy storm Friday night delayed the pursued and pursuers, but Saturday afternoon found the officers at a ranch near Meade City, 35 miles southwest of Dodge City, one hour in

The *Dodge City Times* story, October 12, 1878, of how Sheriff Bat Masterson's posse which included Wyatt Earp—"as intrepid a posse as pulled a trigger"—captured Jim Kennedy, the cowboy who killed Dora Hand, the popular dance-hall girl. *Courtesy Kansas State Historical Society*

Fanny Garretson (Garrettson) who narrowly missed being killed by cowboy Jim Kennedy's wild bullets. "I think I've had enough of Dodge City," Fanny concluded after the incident. *Courtesy Kansas State Historical Society*

Doc Holliday in his Tombstone days. *The James D. Horan Collection*

A view of Tombstone, the violent mining town, in the early 1880s. *The James D. Horan Collection*

wagon lumbered into Dodge City in the summer of 1879. They met Wyatt and Morgan, who were walking down a street. As Allie recalled, "It was just like a railroad train pulling into the depot on time with your friends waitin'."

Virgil joined his brothers, the three tall moustached men "looking like three peas in a pod."

Allie was barefoot and when Wyatt held out his hand she impulsively stretched out a bare toe.

"Wyatt gave me a cold and nasty look and turned away, but Morgan pinched my toes real friendly." [5]

This was not the first time the playful Allie would anger the fastidious, humorless Wyatt Earp. In the end she would bitterly denounce him as a fraud.

After the herds passed Dodge and the town settled down to becoming a slumbering prairie community, Earp and his wife, Mattie, moved on to Tombstone, Arizona Territory. He was joined by Virgil, Morgan, and Jim. Doc Holliday and his big-nosed mistress, Kate Elder, soon followed. Wyatt's first job was as a Wells Fargo shotgun messenger. Virgil was appointed a special policeman, and Jim, oldest of the brothers, who suffered for years from a Civil War wound, became a faro dealer. Warren, the youngest, would join them later. They all lived within a tight circle in small frame houses near First and Fremont streets. Now, as always, the clan was together.

In the fall of 1880 Wyatt was appointed a deputy by Sheriff Charles Shibell and Morgan took over his job as shotgun messenger. [6] At about the same time Wyatt was given a piece of the gambling concession in the Oriental saloon in return for driving out Johnny Tyler, a troublesome professional gambler.

By that fall Tombstone had become a thriving mining town of two thousand located in Pima County; within three years the population would jump to five thousand. Saloons were open twenty-four hours a day. The Oriental on Fifth and Allen was the most elaborate, but there was also the Alhambra, Campbell and Hatch's, and the Eagle Brewery, where free lunch was served. The whores paraded on the north side of Allen Street. Instead of whooping, thirsty cowboys there were miners and mud-caked boots and pokes of silver. Twenty-mule wagons with huge iron-rimmed wheels constantly rumbled down the street to the stamp mills. Dust, the bane of Tombstone, hung over the town from dawn to dusk. The evening breeze or violent thunderstorms would erase the shimmering dusty veils to reveal the Dragoon Mountains, majestic in the suddenly clear air.

Tombstone, like Dodge in its early days, was a violent town. Few days passed without a shooting or a killing. A sensational gunfight that summer when the Earps arrived was between Mike Killeen and "Buckskin" Frank Leslie, the Oriental's bartender, who openly courted the pretty Mrs. Killeen. When the cuckolded husband discovered that Leslie had taken his wife to a ball at the Cosmopolitan Hotel, he returned with a six-shooter "and found them sitting side by side on the porch of the hotel, his arm around her waist." Historians have insisted for years that in an exchange of shots Leslie killed Killeen, but in a deathbed statement published in Tombstone's *Epitaph* Killeen named George Perine, a Tombstone gambler, as the man who shot him. [7]

The dying man said he had "used up Leslie pretty well" in a fist fight when

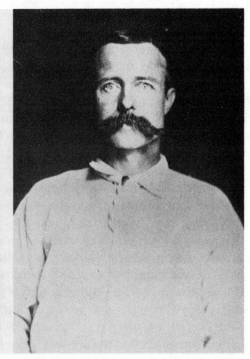

Celia (Mattie) Blaylock, Wyatt Earp's second wife—his first wife died in 1810—taken about the time they arrived in Tombstone. She was then about twenty-two. Earp abandoned her when he left for Colorado. She died destitute, a prostitute in the mining camp of Pinal, Arizona Territory, July 2, 1888. *Courtesy Arizona Historical Society*

Frank (Buckskin Frank) Leslie, the gunfighter who joined Wyatt and Bat Masterson in trailing the outlaws who held up the Tombstone stagecoach and killed the driver. In June 1880 Leslie killed Mike Killeen in a shootout over Killeen's wife. Later he killed Billy (Billy the Kid) Claiborne who had fled before the gunfight started at the O. K. Corral. *Courtesy Arizona Historical Society*

Buckskin Frank's letter to the Colt Company ordering a "first class pistol in every respect." *Courtesy Connecticut State Library*

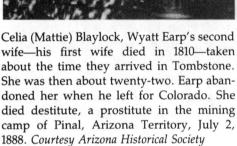

Perine, the gambler, appeared and shot him. A short time after he was acquitted for murder, Leslie married the widow.

At the time of Earp's appointment as Shibell's deputy, southeastern Arizona was terrorized by bands of rustlers, horse thieves, and desperadoes, loosely classified as "the cowboy element." Some used Charleston and Galeyville, two small settlements, as their headquarters. It was inevitable that when the cowboys came to Tombstone there would be gunfire.

The mining community had two newspapers, the *Tombstone Nugget* and the *Tombstone Epitaph*. The *Nugget* began publishing in October 1879 and the *Epitaph*, established by John P. Clum, who played a prominent role in the lives of the Earps, appeared the following year.

Clum was not unknown when he entered the newspaper business. A rather arrogant young man, he had been Indian agent at the San Carlos reservation until he resigned after a skirmish with Indian Bureau officials who didn't believe his boast that he could single-handedly solve the complex Indian problem in the Arizona Territory—a task the cavalry had been unable to cope with for years.[8]

The *Nugget* was a strong supporter of the county Democratic party. Its editor, Harry Woods, was friendly with Sheriff Johnny Behan and John Dunbar, treasurer of Cochise County and Behan's partner in Tombstone's Dexter Livery Stable. In turn, Clum's *Epitaph* was closely allied with the community's "law and order" faction, which would help to elect Clum Tombstone's mayor.

Both newspapers strongly disagreed over the "cowboys." The *Nugget* pointed out that not all were killers, rustlers, and stagecoach robbers; many were responsible ranchers in Sulphur Valley. But the *Epitaph* bluntly labeled them a curse to the frontier.

Neither paper printed what everyone knew—rustling was widespread with various bands plundering the Mexican herds. But this was accepted by "respectable" ranchers—some "law and order" men—who readily bought and resold the stolen cattle driven into Sulphur Valley through Skeleton Canyon.

The best known of the "cowboy element" was the Clanton clan, a large ranching family of hard-drinking riders led by N. C. "Old Man" Clanton, as he was known. With him were his sons, Peter, Joseph Isaac, or Ike; Phineas or Phin; and Billy, a teen-ager. Associated with them were the McLaury brothers, Tom and Frank, who had left their family's prosperous Iowa farm to start a ranch in Sulphur Valley.

The Clantons and the McLaurys were friendly with William Graham, known to frontier history as Bill Broscius or "Curly" Bill, and Johnny Ringgold or Johnny Ringo, whose catchy name has given birth to numerous movie roles and has attracted almost as many legends as Jesse James.

The most ludicrous of the legends pictures Ringo as a handsome, reckless "educated" cowboy, skilled with a gun. He is said to have attended college before drifting west to find adventure. In his travels he carried worn copies of the classics in his saddle bag. Of course he read them in the original Greek and Latin.

In reality Ringo was a morose alcoholic who moved from cow town to cow town, sometimes working as a hired gun. In the fall of 1875 he played a minor role in Texas' Mason County War or the "Hoo Doo War," one of the deadliest of the Texas feuds.

Newman H. Clanton, leader of the Clantons. He was killed in 1881 by Mexicans who ambushed him and his riders in a canyon in New Mexico. *The James D. Horan Collection*

In her history of Mason County, Stella Gipson Polk traced the feud's nickname, the Hoo Doo War, to the stammering of a frightened county black who cried out, "Who do it . . . who do it. . . .?"

The feud had its beginning in the Civil War when neighbor fought neighbor and the county was ruled by two factions, former German refugees who had gained large land holdings, and the native Texans. It simmered for years, until 1875, when Tim Williamson, a Mason County rancher, was arrested by Deputy Sheriff John Worley for rustling cattle. While they were on their way to the county jail, a mob drove off Worley and lynched Williamson.

A century later it is difficult to find the truth about the charge against Williamson. Captain Dan Roberts, in his book on the Texas Rangers, pictured Williamson as a trail boss for a big Mason County ranch outfit. On his drives north to Dodge and Abilene his herds swept up "wholesale" cattle belonging to the frugal German ranchers. When their complaints were ignored they lynched Williamson.

Scott Cooley, a former Texas Ranger and a close friend of Williamson, set out to avenge the rancher's killing. He first killed Deputy Sheriff John Worley, "who he believed should have afforded Williamson better protection," then gathered several friends of Williamson, including Johnny Ringo—then Ringgold—to start the Hoo Doo War. Men were shot on the streets of Mason, the county jail was stormed by a mob. Other men vanished, dead men were found on lonely roads. The violence mounted until the Texas Rangers under Major Jones were ordered into the county by the governor.

Ringo and several other gunmen were arrested and placed in the Burnet County jail, but they escaped. Ringo then left Texas for Arizona, "then considered a far-off land from Texas."

Four years later he made a violent appearance in Pima County when he shot a saloon customer who had insulted him by drinking beer instead of whiskey. Ringo had to delay his appearance before the county grand jury because, as he wrote the sheriff, he had shot himself in the foot.

Tombstone next heard of Ringo when he began riding with the Clantons on their Mexican beef raids.

Another associate of the Clantons was Frank Stilwell, brother of the well-known Indian scout, Simpson E. (Jack) Stilwell. Frank, who maintained a livery stable at Charleston and Bisbee, had an unsavory reputation when he arrived in Tombstone. A few years before he had shot and killed a Mexican cook who had served him tea instead of coffee. He had also been questioned in the brutal murder of an elderly miner.[9]

The townspeople of Tombstone were divided in their opinion of the "cowboys," or "the boys." The merchants welcomed their money while the law and order citizens agreed with Clum they were fit only for the gallows.

It is believed that Pete Clanton was the first of the clan to die violently. In the fall of 1877 he was riding with a band of what the *Weekly Arizona Miner* called "horse thieves and desperadoes who have become a terror to the people . . . they have their headquarters in Springfield from whence they raid in different directions."

The Citizen's Committee, a vigilante group, clashed with the gang, and in the wild gun battle two citizens were killed and one wounded while a "desperado named Pete" was killed. The army was asked for help, and Captain John N. Andrews of the Eighth Infantry from Fort Apache was sent to the scene. The *Miner* wrote, "The outlaws are becoming too numerous and should be shot on sight or turned over to the Apache scouts to use their improved methods of torture . . . anything is too good for such cattle."

The *Miner* reported that the vigilantes, "unable to cope with the outlaws, with their meagre supply of guns and ammunition," went to Fort Apache and demanded arms. Captain Andrews, the fort's commander, telegraphed Governor Hoyt for permission. Hoyt first agreed, then countermanded his permission, "until such time as he can be assured that they [the guns] are not going into the hands of the wrong party."[10]

Three years later the Earps clashed for the first time with Curly Bill Graham, whom Wyatt and the legend makers transformed from a young, happy-go-lucky, hard-drinking cowboy into one of the most ferocious killers on the Arizona frontier.

On a frosty October night in 1880, shortly after midnight, Curly Bill and several cowhands began "shooting at the moon" after a daylong tour of the saloons. Marshal Fred White hurried to Sixth and Allen streets and began scuffling with Graham. As White yanked at the six-shooter it fired, a bullet tearing through the sheriff's groin. Wyatt, hearing the earlier shots, had rushed to the spot just as White fell. He pistol-whipped Curly Bill and dragged the unconscious cowboy off to jail while White was carried to Doctor Matthews' office, possibly by Morgan and Virgil.

Curly Bill was arraigned and held for action of the county grand jury. When Doctor Matthews reported the next day that White was dying there was talk of vigilante action. The Earps removed the cowhand, nursing an aching head, to Tucson to await trial.[11]

Oddly, neither the *Nugget* nor the *Epitaph* reported White's deathbed statement exonerating Curly Bill of intentionally shooting him. White said the Colt revolver went off as he yanked it from the cowboy's hand. On the basis of this, Graham was later acquitted of the murder charge.

A short time later the Tombstone town council appointed Virgil to fill White's office, and a special election was scheduled for January 1881. Virgil ran but was defeated by Ben Sippy. Virgil, his pride bruised, resigned his deputy's post and ran against Sippy for the second time in the regular city elections the following year. Again he was defeated. Then the Earps's ambition to hold public office suffered another blow when Pima County Sheriff Shibell fired Wyatt as his deputy and assigned in his place John H. Behan, who had been sheriff of Yavapi County.

John H. Behan, sheriff of Cochise County and Wyatt Earp's bitter enemy. Behan later served as the superintendent of the Yuma Territorial Prison, fought in the Spanish American War, and was a government secret agent in China's Boxer Rebellion. He finally returned to Tombstone, where he died. *The James D. Horan Collection*

In the fall of 1879 when their covered wagons had rolled into Tombstone, Wyatt had assumed he and his brothers would soon be wearing tin stars and running the mining community. Now they were losers. But for them the fight wasn't over. The three brothers, grim and impressive in their long black coats, spotless white shirts, black string ties and broad-rimmed hats, studied Tombstone's dusty streets and revised their strategy. After all, a new county was about to be born.

The territorial legislature, sitting in Prescott, carved a new county out of Pima's 28,000 square miles and called it Cochise after the famous Apache war chief. Tombstone was designated as the county seat. The question of who would be appointed county sheriff was debated in the saloons, gambling halls, mining camps, and business houses.

The office was worth several thousand dollars a year. The sheriff also received ten percent of his collections as county assessor and tax collector of one of the nation's richest mining areas.

The Arizona Territory was run by the Republicans, but Pima and the newly established Cochise counties were controlled by a smoothly running Democratic machine. There were two logical candidates: Wyatt Earp, a Republican, and Behan, protégé of John Dunbar, the county treasurer and Behan's partner in a Tombstone livery stable.

Behan presented Wyatt with a proposition. If Wyatt would stand aside and make no campaign for the office, Behan would appoint him as his first deputy. Wyatt, who knew Arizona's Republican governor, John C. Fremont, to be unpredictable in his appointments, whereas Behan was supported by the powerful county Democratic organization, accepted the plan.

However, when Behan was appointed by Fremont, the Earps discovered political patronage ruled the frontier as firmly as it did New York's Tenderloin. Behan appointed as his deputies Frank Stilwell, associate of the Clantons; H. N. Woods, the *Nugget*'s editor; William Breakenridge, a local Democrat and later author of *Helldorado,* a lively if erroneous memoir of his days in Tombstone; and Dave Neagle, an honest, ineffectual, loyal party member.

Behan, an ambitious politician, tried to cultivate the clannish Earps but was rebuffed. On the surface they remained friendly for a short time but a smoldering rivalry began when Behan proudly pinned on his silver star.

William A. Breakenridge, who became deputy sheriff of Cochise County under John H. Behan during the time of the Earps. In 1928 Breakenridge wrote *Helldorado,* an account of his days in Tombstone. In it he pictures Wyatt as anything but a dedicated frontier lawman. *The James D. Horan Collection*

Doc Holliday openly showed his contempt for Behan. One day they quarreled over Doc's faro game, the consumptive, homicidal dentist taunting Behan in front of the crowded saloon that he was playing with money Holliday had "given his woman." As Holliday later recalled in a newspaper interview: "He always hated me after that, and would spend money to have me killed."[12]

But now there was another familiar frontier face in Tombstone. Bat Masterson had found Dodge City too tame, so he rode to Tombstone to join the Earps and to try his luck at gambling. He would stay only a short time before he drifted to Colorado, where in a few years his life would again be touched by Wyatt Earp and Doc Holliday.

On January 4, 1881, according to Stuart Lake's biography, Wyatt single-handedly held off a mob that tried to lynch Johnny ("Behind-the-Deuce") O'Rourke, a young gambler who had shot and killed W. P. Schneider, chief engineer of the Corbin Mine in Charleston.

There are conflicting stories of why O'Rourke killed the engineer. One has the gambler becoming enraged because Schneider refused to discuss the cold weather. O'Rourke swore the engineer came at him with a knife as the result of a gambling row.

O'Rourke first appeared in front of Vogan & Flynn's saloon in Tombstone riding a horse "reeking with sweat." He told a crowd he wanted protection because he had "killed his man." Allen Street was soon crowded. Marshal Sippy, who had gathered together a posse including Virgil Earp and Behan, commandeered a wagon to take the gambler to jail in Tucson.

The *Epitaph's* account of what happened proves that Wyatt lied to Lake. Instead of holding off a lynch-minded mob by himself, it was Sippy who calmed the crowd:

"Sippy's sound judgment prevented any such outbreak as would have been the certain result, and cool as an iceberg, he held the crowd in check. No one who was a witness of yesterday's proceedings can doubt, that for his presence blood would have flown freely. . . . Bowing to the majesty of the law, the crowd subsided, and the wagon proceeded on its way to Benson with the prisoner, who by daylight this morning was lodged in the Tucson jail."[13]

It should be recalled that Clum and his newspaper were strong supporters of the Earps. Had the incident happened as Wyatt described it to Lake, the newspaper would have lionized its favorite hero.

Before he could be brought to trial, Johnny Behind-the-Deuce escaped from the Tucson jail and vanished.

In March 1881 a series of events took place which eventually culminated in the Battle of the O. K. Corral, one of the most famous gunfights in the history of the Wild West. It started in mid-March when Kinnear & Company's stagecoach, carrying a Wells Fargo gold chest, left Tombstone for Tucson. There were eight passengers. One, Peter Roerig, decided that rather than spend the long journey inside the stuffy, crammed coach, he would cling to the rear top seat. The driver was Bud (Budd) Philpot. Bob Paul, fearless and a fine shot, rode shotgun.

They changed teams at Contention. The night was clear and frosty, the landscape lightly dusted with snow. It was near ten o'clock when the stage slowed down for a grade. Suddenly several men stepped out of the shadows; one shouted a command:

"Hold it, boys!"

Paul roared back, "I don't hold for no one!" and fired. He was answered by a barrage of rifle shots. Philpot slipped silently over the side and Roerig, the

The Wells Fargo stage office
in Tombstone. *The James D.
Horan Collection*

passenger, moaned and slumped into his seat. The frightened team bolted, the
heavy coach swaying dangerously from side to side, as it bounced along the
rutted road. Paul, risking his life, tethered for a long moment on the wagon
tongue, then slowly reached down and retrieved the reins. He finally controlled
the horses, drove to Benson, and telegraphed Tombstone. Roerig was pronounced dead on their arrival. The frozen body of Philpot was later found in the
snow; nearby were footprints and a number of shells.

Earp gathered a posse consisting of his brothers, Bat Masterson, Buckskin
Frank Leslie, and others and took off after the robbers. A small-time thief, Luther
King, was caught and confessed that he was the horse holder. He named the
robbers and killers as Bill Leonard, Harry Head, and Jim Crane, rustlers, thieves,
and friends of the Clantons.

King was turned over to Sheriff Behan, who returned to Tombstone with his
prisoner. When the Earps returned empty-handed, they were stunned to learn
that King had escaped "by quietly stepping out the back door of the sheriff's
office" while Deputy Woods—the *Nugget*'s editor—was witnessing the sale of a
horse to John Dunbar.[14]

Now Doc Holliday was the principal suspect. The impassive, coughing dentist
dismissed the charges as nonsense. He logically pointed out that if he had been
the field general of the holdup gang he would have ordered the stagecoach's
team shot so he could collect the bullion.

Doc's enemies produced evidence that Holliday had been Bill Leonard's friend
for years and had been seen near his shack in Charleston. Holliday admitted he
knew Leonard but explained that he had visited Charleston to take part in a
poker game. He produced the elderly driver of a water wagon who testified that
Doc had ridden back with him "from the walls."

Earp accused Behan of falsely accusing Holliday to help his reelection
campaign. Wyatt, who had hoped to capture the stagecoach robbers and walk
into the sheriff's office by a landslide vote, then devised a byzantine plot to find
and arrest the killers and be hailed as Tombstone's champion of law and order.

Earp went to Ike Clanton with his plan: the cowboy leader would lure his old
friends, Leonard, Crane, and Head into a rendezvous and then tip off Earp.
Wyatt would get the glory and Ike the Wells Fargo reward. Clanton later testified

that he turned down the plan; Earp insisted he accepted it. There was no way of determining who was telling the truth.[15]

In June 1881 another bizarre event took place. Marshal Ben Sippy, who had been in office only a short time, abruptly left Tombstone and never returned. Mayor John Clum promptly appointed Virgil in his place. Clum gave no explanation of why he had appointed a man to an office he could not win in two elections. Nor did anyone explain why the popular Sippy had suddenly abandoned his community and the post he had campaigned for and won.

Virgil pinned on his new star and the Earp clan was jubilant. Then came news that Bill Leonard and Harry Head, the stagecoach robbers, were dead. The *Arizona Star* reported the pair had been killed "in a fight to the death" with some cowboys after their abortive robbery of a store in New Eureka, New Mexico. In August, Jim Crane, last of the stagecoach robbery suspects, was also killed in New Mexico.

The next development was touched off when "Big Nose" Kate Elder, Doc Holliday's mistress, went on a drunk and told Sheriff Behan that Holliday had masterminded the robbery and killed Philpot, the driver. Behan quickly obtained a warrant for the dentist, who was arraigned on a charge of murder and robbery.

The owners of the Alhambra and Wyatt Earp put up the $5,000 bail.

Kate, hungover and remorseful, denied her statement. Shortly after the charges against Holliday were dropped, she left Doc and Tombstone for the last time.[16]

Holliday and the Earps accused Behan of tricking a drunken woman into signing the affidavit; Behan denied it but the feud between the sheriff and the Earps intensified.

On the evening of September 8, two highwaymen held up the Bisbee stage after it clattered out of Tombstone. The bullion box yielded $2,500 and the purses of the passengers another $500. Behan wasn't on hand but his deputies, Breakenridge and Neagle, rode out, followed by another posse composed of Wells Fargo Agent Marshal Williams, Fred Dodge, a Wells Fargo detective, Wyatt and Morgan Earp. In his book, *Helldorado*, Breakenridge tells how he and Neagle interviewed the passengers who told them one of the road agents had used the phrase, "Have we got all the sugar?" Both men were startled. They knew this was the favorite phrase of Deputy Sheriff Frank Stilwell.

When they returned to the scene of the robbery they found boot marks and followed the trail of the horses into Bisbee. There they discovered that Stilwell had had a shoemaker replace the high heels of his boots with low heels, which fitted the tracks at the scene of the holdup.

Stilwell and Pete Spence, Stilwell's partner in a livery stable, were arrested in a Bisbee saloon by Breakenridge and Neagle. Marshal Williams, Dodge, and the Earps arrived to be greeted by the two triumphant deputies who told them they were taking their prisoners to Tombstone.

The embarrassed Earps persuaded Williams to swear out a federal warrant, and both groups of lawmen, one on either side of Stilwell and Spence, rode back into Tombstone.[17]

Wyatt soon made it known that the "cowboys" were ready to gun him down because he had brought in Stilwell and Spence, friends of the Clantons.

In October, Ike Clanton was convinced Wyatt was "telling lies about me in town," making him an accomplice of the Wells Fargo robbers, ready to turn in his friends for the reward money. There is no evidence that Earp openly accused him but Clanton insisted to his brothers and the McLaurys that it was all part of a plan by the Earps not only to frame him but also to identify him as an informer to the erratic yet dangerous Johnny Ringo.

The feud between the two factions grew. All Tombstone knew it would soon result in a confrontation between the "cowboy element" and the Earps.

Clanton made his first move when he and his gang raided the Charleston jail to free Billy Claiborne, one of his riders who had been arrested for a killing. The young cowboy loved to swagger down Tombstone's Allen Street with two six-shooters on his hip as the ladies whispered: "There goes Billy the Kid." New Mexico's original Billy would have dismissed Claiborne as a coward and a braggart.

Shortly after midnight, October 25, Ike was in the lunchroom of the Alhambra when Doc Holliday came in, denouncing him for threatening the Earps and calling him, as Ike later repeated: "a s-- of a b---- of a cowboy and to get my gun out and go to work."

Clanton told Holliday he was not armed and denied he had made any threats against the Earps. As he left, he quoted Morgan Earp, who had come in behind Holliday, as telling him, "go heel yourself, you can have all the fight you want now." [18]

Curiously, half an hour later Clanton wandered into the Oriental and sat in a poker game with Morgan Earp, Tom McLaury, and Sheriff Behan. When this bizarre game broke up in the early hours of the morning, Holliday again threatened Clanton. However, Jim Flynn, a city policeman, appeared, and Holliday and the Earps left.

Guns in Tombstone were commonplace. There was an ordinance prohibiting the carrying of weapons but no one paid any attention to it. George Parsons, whose Tombstone diary presents a vivid picture of that wild mining camp, once complained, "Another man killed . . . too much loose pistol practice . . . the death roll since I came here—the violent deaths—foots up fearfully large."

The Earps had never enforced the weapons ordinance; they could have jailed half the town. But the morning after the poker game the three Earps disarmed Ike Clanton as he was standing on Fourth Street. All witnesses agree that Wyatt hit Clanton across the head with the barrel of his six-shooter, then disarmed him under his brothers' drawn guns. Ike was unceremoniously dragged off to Judge Wallace's court and fined for carrying firearms within the city limits. Battered and bruised, Ike paid the fine and promised Wyatt, "I will fight you anywhere."

A short time later Wyatt met and pistol-whipped eighteen-year-old, unarmed Tom McLaury, although the boy protested he had done nothing wrong. He protested he had "always been a friend of the Earps and had never done anything against him [Wyatt]."

A confrontation was near. In Hafford's saloon on the corner of Fifth and Allen streets, the Earps met Sheriff Behan and insisted that the Clantons and McLaurys be disarmed and jailed.

This was after Wyatt had battered young Tom McLaury, who had thrown open his coat to show Earp he was not carrying a gun. Later it would be revealed he had checked his six-shooters with a bartender.

Behan would deny under oath he had told the Earps, "They won't hurt me. They'll kill you, if you try and take their guns, Virge."

Then Behan left for the O. K. Corral, where by his own testimony, corroborated by other witnesses, he searched the Clantons and McLaurys for weapons and insisted they accompany him to his office.

He discovered the Clantons and the McLaurys to be unarmed. Billy Clanton and Billy Claiborne were carrying guns. All the cowboys had rifles in their saddle boots.

In Hafford's, the big clock over the bar slowly ticked away. Grouped around a table Wyatt, Morgan, and Virgil Earp discussed the issue; should they go down to the O. K. Corral and confront the Clantons, with the knowledge that only guns and bullets would end the tense day, or should they let the boasting cowboys ride out of town to certainly return another day?

Despite the legends and myths there was only one lawman at that table, City Marshal Virgil Earp, who had won his badge when Ben Sippy left Tombstone. There was little debate; it was not in the makeup of the Earps to turn away from a fight. After they loaded their guns, Virgil deputized his brothers. Joined by Doc Holliday, they walked toward the O. K. Corral.[19]

It was a chilly sullen day with snow capping the peaks of the Dragoons. Nothing stirred on shabby Fremont Street as Tombstone watched with a chilled heart. The three Earps, all big men, were dressed in their usual black coats, white

The entrance to the O. K. Corral. The famous "street fight," as Wyatt Earp called it, did not take place inside the corral as Hollywood and television has pictured it. The Earps and Holliday walked west on Fremont Street past this entrance for a short distance to a lot adjacent to the photographic gallery of Camillus Fly, the frontier photographer. As the firing began the Earps slowly backed into the street to join Holliday. The McLaurys died in the street, along with Billy Clanton. Fly disarmed the young Billy Clanton as he tried to get off a last shot. The gate in this photograph was erected after the gunfight. *The James D. Horan Collection*

shirts, string ties, and broad-brimmed black hats, the classic uniform of the western frontier gambler-lawman. The frail consumptive dentist wore a knee-length, saggy gray coat, which hid a shotgun and a nickel-plated .45 caliber Colt revolver. With Holliday on the inside they walked four abreast, their faces grim and set. They passed the Fremont Street butcher shop, where Mrs. M. King, just coming out, stepped back to let them pass.

"Let them have it," someone growled to Doc, and he tersely replied, "All right."

A gust of wind moaned up the street and pulled back Doc's coat; the horrified woman standing in the doorway saw Doc's shotgun and nickel-plated revolver.

At the corner of Fourth and Fremont the quartet saw Sheriff Behan standing with Frank McLaury. When someone cried, "Here they come," McLaury and Behan turned and walked back to the corral.

The livery consisted of open-air stalls, with the rear leading to an alley which crossed the block, east to west. North of the alley was an open yard.

Flanking the Fourth Street end was the studio of Camillus N. Fly, the pioneer photographer who took the pictures of Geronimo's council with General Crook. The Third Street side was the adobe wall of an assayer's office. It was here that Ike and Billy Clanton, the McLaury brothers, and Claiborne had taken their stand.

As the Earps and Holliday neared the corral, Behan ran up to them. What he said was disputed in court, the Earps insisting Behan told them the cowboys were disarmed, the sheriff just as vigorously denying it.

Suddenly a gun cracked and the Battle of the O. K. Corral had begun. As Sheriff Behan later testified, "It was over in twenty or thirty seconds." The McLaurys and Billy Clanton were dead. The loudmouth, Ike Clanton, and the boastful young gunfighter, Billy Claiborne, had fled. Virgil, Morgan, and Doc were wounded, only Wyatt and Holliday were standing when the heavy gunpowder smoke drifted away.

Countless stories, fiction and nonfiction, together with movie, radio, and television "documentaries" and dramas, have been written about this incident. Most of the versions have been exaggerated, distorted, and fictionalized.

The truth of what happened at two o'clock on that October day lies somewhere in the hearing which took place in the Tombstone courtroom of Magistrate Wells Spicer, described as a "great friend of Wyatt Earp." Not only did the surviving participants testify but more importantly disinterested witnesses, so beloved by

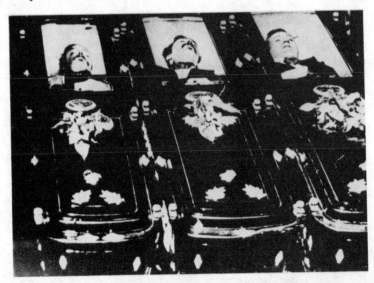

The McLaury brothers and Billy Clanton killed in what has been called by generations of Americans "The Battle of the O. K. Corral." *The James D. Horan Collection*

the law in homicide cases, told what they had seen and heard prior to the savage confrontation.

The *Nugget* and the *Epitaph* covered the hearings. Surprisingly, for all their partisanship, they reported the testimony clearly and without distortion. A majority of frontier historians generally favor the *Epitaph* as the better of the two newspapers. However, a study of both reveals that the *Nugget* was not as naive or incompetent as John Clum's editorials insisted it was. The *Nugget*'s editor, Harry Woods, for whatever part he played in the ludicrous escape of King, the suspected stagecoach robber, was an experienced mining reporter and knew how to cover breaking news.

This author, a metropolitan editor for many years, believes the *Nugget*'s coverage of the historic Earp-Clanton hearing was superior to the *Epitaph*'s. The *Nugget*'s precise and lengthy columns of testimony are a tribute to Woods's idea of hiring a shorthand reporter.

Here is the testimony the spectators heard in that tiny packed Tombstone courtroom between October 30 and December 1, 1881.[20]

Eyewitness Accounts of the Battle of the O. K. Corral, October 26, 1881

The first witness called by the prosecution was Sheriff Johnny Behan. He has long been pictured as the frightened, cowardly protector of the Clanton gang. However, there were men in Tombstone who regarded him as "a polished gentleman, who did not chum around with tin horns and gamblers [like the Earps]."

Political ambition rather than corruption appears to have been Behan's major flaw. The new county was ruled by a strong Democratic machine and Behan, its rising star, was always ready to compromise, placate, and cajole to please his leaders rather than play the role of a stone-faced lawman striding down the lonesome frontier street to meet his destiny in a blaze of gunfire. Johnny Behan could have found a comfortable niche in modern politics.

His courage cannot be questioned. Unlike the cowardly Ike Clanton, who started it all, and the boastful Billy Claiborne, who fled, he single-handedly tried to prevent the gun battle. He provided a vivid and surprisingly objective eyewitness account of the most violent seconds in the history of America's Wild West.

> Sheriff John Behan being sworn, says:
> The first I knew that there was likely to be any trouble, I was sitting in a chair getting shaved in a barbershop, it was about half past one or two, it may have been later, but not much, saw a crowd gathering on the corner between Fourth and Allen streets, someone said there is liable to be trouble between the Earps and the Clantons; there was considerable said about it in the shop; asked the barber to hurry up and get through as I intended to go out and disarm and arrest the parties; after I finished in the barber shop I crossed over to Hafford's corner; saw Marshal Earp standing there and asked him what the excitement was; Marshal Earp is Virgil Earp; he said there were a lot of s--s of b-----s in town looking for a fight; he did not mention any name; I said to Earp you had better disarm the crowd; he said he would not, he would give them a chance to make a fight; I said it is your duty as a police officer to disarm them, rather than encourage the fight; don't know what reply he gave me but I said I was going down to disarm the boys.

I meant any cowboys who had arms connected with the party; Marshal Earp at the time was standing in Hafford's door; several people were around him, I don't know who; Morgan Earp and Doc Holliday were then standing out near the middle of the street, near Allen and Fourth Streets; I saw none others of the defendants there; Virgil Earp had a shotgun with the muzzle touching the doorsill at his side; I did not see any arms on the others at the time; I then went down Fourth Street to the corner of Fremont and I met there Frank McLaury holding a horse and talking to someone; I greeted him and I said to him I would have to disarm him, that there was likely to be trouble in town and I proposed to disarm everybody in town who had arms. He said he would not give up his arms as he did not propose to have any trouble. I told him he would have to give up his pistol all the same; I may have said gun, as gun and pistol are synonymous terms. About that time I saw Ike Clanton and Tom McLaury down the street below Fly's Photograph Studio. I said to Frank: "Come with me."

We went down to where Ike and Tom were standing. I said to the boys, "you must give up your arms." Billy Clanton was there when I got to where Ike was. I found Tom McLaury, William Clanton and Will Claiborne. I said to them, "boys you have to give up your arms." Frank McLaury demurred. I don't know his exact language, he did not seem inclined to give up his arms. He told me he did not have any arms. I put my arms around his waist to see if he was armed but he was not.

Tom McLaury showed me by pulling his coat open that he was not. I saw five standing there and asked them how many there were of them. They said four of us; this young man Claiborne said he was not one of the party, he wanted them to leave town. I said, "boys you must go up to the sheriff's office and take off your arms and stay there until I come back."

I told them I was going to disarm the other party. At that time I saw the Earps and Holliday coming down the sidewalk on the south side of Fremont Street. They were a little below the postoffice. Virgil, Morgan and Wyatt Earp and Doc Holliday were the ones. I said to the Clantons: "wait here for a while, I see them coming down. I will go up and stop them."

I walked up the street, twenty-two or twenty-three steps, and met them at Bauer's butcher shop under the awning in front and told them not to go any further that I was there for the purpose of arresting and disarming the McLaurys and Clantons; they did not heed me, I threw up my hands and said, "Go back, I am sheriff of this county and I am not going to allow any trouble if I can help it."

They brushed past me and I turned and went with them or followed them two steps or so in the rear, as they went down the street, expostulating with them all the time; when they arrived within a few feet of the McLaurys and the Clantons, I heard one of them say, I think it was Wyatt Earp:

"You s--s of b-----s you have been looking for a fight and now you can have it."

About that time I heard a voice say: "throw up your hands."

About this time I saw a nickel-plated pistol pointed at one of the Clanton party, I think it was Billy Clanton—my impression at the time was that Doc Holliday had the nickel-plated pistol. I will not say for certain that Holliday had it. Three pistols were in the hands of the Earp party, when the order was given "throw up your hands."

I heard Billy Clanton say, "Don't shoot me, I don't want to fight."

Tom McLaury at the same time threw open his coat and said, "I have nothing," or "I am not armed."

He made the same remark and the same gesture he had made to me when he first told me he was not armed. I can't tell the position of Billy Clanton's arms when he said, "I don't want to fight," my attention at the time was directed to the nickel-plated pistol; the nickel-plated pistol was first to fire, and another followed instantly, these two shots were not from the same pistol, they were too nearly instantaneous to be fired from the same pistol; the nickel-plated pistol was fired by the second man from the right; the second shot came from the third man from the right; the fight became general.

Two or three fired shots were very rapidly [sic] after the first shot by whom I do not know; the first two shots were fired by the Earp party, by whom I do not know; the next three shots, I thought at the time, came from the Earp party; this was my impression at the time, from being on the ground and seeing them; immediately after someone said, "throw up your hands" the nickel-plated pistol went off immediately. I think it was Wyatt Earp who said, "throw up your hands."

There was a great deal of fighting and shooting going on. I saw Frank McLaury staggering on the street with one hand on his belly and his pistol in his right; I saw him shoot at Morgan Earp and from the direction of his pistol should judge the shot went into the ground; he shot twice there into Fly's building at Morgan Earp and he started across the street; heard a couple of shots from that direction, did not see him after he got halfway across the street; then heard a couple of shots from his direction, looked and saw McLaury running, and a shot was fired and he fell on his head; heard Morg say "I got him." There might have been a couple of shots afterward but that was the end of the fight; can't say I saw the effect of the first two shots; the only parties I saw fall were Morgan Earp and Frank McLaury; my impression was that the nickel-plated pistol was pointed at Billy Clanton; the first that I was certain had been hit was Frank McLaury as I saw him staggering and bewildered and knew he was hit; then shortly after the first five shots.

I never saw any arms in the hands of the McLaury party except Frank McLaury and Billy Clanton; saw Frank McLaury on the sidewalk within a few feet of the inside line of the street; did not see a pistol in the hands of anyone of the McLaury party until eight or ten shots had been fired; Frank McLaury was the first of his party in whose hands I saw a pistol; Ike Clanton broke and ran after the first few shots. Ike, I think, went through Fly's building; the last I saw of him he was running through the back of Fly's building toward Allen Street.

The court was adjourned and the following day Behan continued his testimony, picking up where he described Ike Clanton running away from the gun battle.

I could not tell exactly where Ike was going; he was trying to get out of the way; I saw him at the corner of Fly's, and he ran from them; never saw him after he passed the corner of the gallery.

I saw a shotgun before the fight commenced; Doc Holliday had it as he passed down the street, he had it under his coat. When I walked up to meet him he pulled his coat further over the gun; did not see the gun go off but I knew afterwards that the shotgun had been fired; did not distinguish the shotgun report; did not know what became of the gun after the fight; saw the bodies of the boys after the shooting; Clanton was then not dead; I said nothing to Clanton, heard him say when removed to the house, "get away from me and let me die."

I saw him lying on the side of the street and saw him shoot once while lying there; there was quite a number in the room where Clanton was carried but do not know who; saw Dr. Gilbertson, I remember in the crowd; Gilbertson said, "there is no use giving him anything, he is dying"; I was not in the house when Billy Clanton died, he was gasping when I left; Tom McLaury and Billy Clanton were carried into the same house; Billy Clanton's feet were toward the door, don't know the position of Tom McLaury.

Behan ended his direct examination and the defense began its cross-examination.

I was in town the entire day of the 26th; I was about half an hour out at night; know the night before there had been some trouble between Ike Clanton and Doc Holliday; my recollection is that it was in the barbershop that I received first intimation of the threatened difficulty; about 2:30 or 3 o'clock in the morning I heard of a difficulty between Ike Clanton and Doc Holliday; had not heard of any difficulty between Wyatt Earp and Ike Clanton on that day; I had not before this time heard of any difficulty between Wyatt Earp and Tom McLaury in the neighborhood of [Judge] Wallace's office; heard of this first in the barber shop; was in Hafford's saloon some ten or fifteen minutes before the fight started; crossed Allen with Mr. [Marshal Charles] Shibell; don't remember whether I saw Virge Earp there or not; I may have said to Virge Earp, "we are going to take a drink, will you join us?" I don't remember; I don't remember seeing Captain Murray come in while we were drinking and Virge Earp to the other side of the counter; don't remember when Virge Earp came back that I said to him: "what does that s-- of a b---- of a strangler [vigilante] want?" am satisfied I never said such words; I am friendly with Murray and no such words passed my lips; don't remember if I asked Virge Earp what he was going to do; Virge Earp did not say to me, "I am going to disarm them"; I did not reply to that remark, "don't undertake to do that or they will kill you, they were just down to my corral having a gun talk against you, threatening your life."

I made no such reply, no such conversation ever happened; had not been down to my corral at the time you speak; did not say to Wyatt Earp, "they will not hurt me, I will go down and disarm them"; after I was shaved I said to Virge Earp I would go down and disarm them; did not say to [Marshal] Charles Shibell anywhere in the city that it was "a square fight" and I could not tell who fired the first shot; I made no such remark to Wyatt Earp; have contributed nothing and promised nothing to the prosecution of this case; Wyatt Earp and I were applicants for the position of sheriff before Governor Fremont, at least I was and I hear Wyatt Earp was; when I knew I would get the appointment, I went to Wyatt Earp and told him I would get the appointment and would like to have him in the office with me, also told him I did not want him to cease in his efforts to get it if he could; he said if he got the office he had his brothers to provide for and could not return the compliment.

I left the place of battle and came up Fremont on the street near Hafford's and met Wyatt Earp; we had some little conversation.

I was in the hall between Fly's lodging house and the photograph gallery, a very few minutes or seconds I guess. Remember saying so to Mr. Fly or someone that I had seen it all and while he was trying to get someone out of the house I told him to let him remain there as he might get killed [perhaps Billy Claiborne]. I put the young man in the back room and left him there. I do not remember telling him that I was the only witness who had seen the fight.

After I followed the Earps down to the scene of the fight I did not hold the same position until the fight was over; I circulated around them pretty lively.

Behan then pointed out on a chart where the various participants stood, reiterating that he believed Holliday fired the first shot of the battle with his nickel-plated revolver. Behan denied Holliday fired the shotgun and then threw it down, drawing his revolver. A luncheon recess was called. After court reconvened, Behan resumed the stand.

Ike Clanton and Frank McLaury had the reputation of being men of determination and courage; never heard anything about the other two boys—that is Tom McLaury and Billy Clanton, as to their reputation for courage and determination; Doc Holliday had on an overcoat, shaggy, light colored gray, the coat came down, I think, below his knees; it was a long coat, don't know if he took it off after I saw him with the shotgun; don't think he changed it, did not have time; don't remember whether anyone of the Earp party had a similar garment; don't think the fight lasted over twenty or thirty seconds. When I put my arms around the waist of Ike Clanton and when Tom McLaury opened his coat and said, "I am not armed" I was satisfied that Ike Clanton and Tom McLaury were not armed; left them and went to the Earps, Ike could not have had a pistol in his pocket without me knowing it; I never heard any threats made by the Clanton party against the Earps party; I did not say to Wyatt and Morgan and Virge Earp, "I have disarmed the Clanton party"; the Earp party after "no" remark of mine put their pistols further back to their pants and Holliday put his coat over his gun; Holliday hid the gun before I said anything to them; I did not hear Wyatt Earp say to Ike Clanton while Ike had hold of Wyatt's left arm, "this fight has commenced, either fight or get away." I did not see Ike Clanton get hold of Wyatt Earp's arm.

When I left the Clanton party to meet the Earps the Clanton party was not making any noise or disturbance, I knew Billy Clanton, he was a boy, would not take him to be of [legal] age; I never knew of Billy Clanton being in any difficulty and don't know of having heard of his being in any.

The important witnesses for the state, B. H. Fallehy, and Mrs. M. King, both Tombstone residents and not connected with either politics, the Earps, or Clantons, laid the prosecution's groundwork for a charge of premeditated murder when they quoted the Earps's intentions to kill the cowboys on sight:

A very rare photograph of Frank McLaury. This picture was taken in Iowa in 1879, before he and his brother Tom left their father's prosperous farm to settle in Arizona. *Courtesy New-York Historical Society*

Tom McLaury, about eighteen when he was killed. Testimony at the magistrate hearing showed Tom had turned in his guns to a bartender and was unarmed when the fight began. As Wyatt Earp approached, McLaury threw open his coat and cried, "I'm not armed!" *Courtesy New-York Historical Society*

J. S. Clanton

Joseph Isaac (Ike) Clanton, leader of the "cowboy element" and a bitter enemy of Wyatt Earp and Doc Holliday. Ike, a braggart and a coward, fled from the street fight, leaving his younger brother Billy to die. This photograph was taken by Camillus Fly. *Courtesy New-York Historical Society*

B. H. Fallehey, sworn and testified: I heard some stranger ask Ike Clanton what is the trouble; he said there would be no trouble; then Ike Clanton went over to Dolan's saloon; I then looked over and saw the Marshal standing at Hafford's doorway; then saw the Sheriff going over to where the Marshal and Sheriff were talking; the Sheriff says, "What's the trouble"; the Marshal says, "Those men have made their threats; I will not arrest them but will kill them on sight"; Virgil Earp said this; the Sheriff asked the Marshal in to take a drink; did not see them afterward, as I crossed over the street to the other side; when I got over there I saw one of the Earp brothers, the youngest one, talking with Doc Holliday; looked across the street; saw the Marshal again; some one came up to him and called him aside; when this gentleman got through talking with the Earps, saw three of the Earps and Doc Holliday go down the street together; they kept on the left side of the street on Fourth; I was on the right side; when I got to the corner of Frémont and Fourth I started to go across to the southwest corner of Frémont; when I got midway between in the street I saw the firing had commenced; I kept my eyes on the Earps and Holliday until the shooting commenced; I saw Doc Holliday in the middle of the street; the youngest of the Earp brothers was about three feet from the sidewalk; he was firing at a man behind a horse; Holliday also fired at the man behind the horse, and firing at a man who ran by him on the opposite side of the street; then I saw the man who had the horse let go, and was staggering all the time until he fell; he had his pistol still when he fell; I never saw the two elder Earps; I did not know where they were situated; I then went to the young man lying on the sidewalk and offered to pick him up; he never spoke except the movement of his lips; I picked up a revolver lying five feet from him; then I saw Doc Holliday running towards where the young man was lying, still having a revolver in his hand, making the remark, "The s— of a b— has shot me and I mean to kill him"; could not say who fired the first shots.

The prosecution introduced as a witness Mrs. M. King, who, being duly sworn, testified as follows: . . . I was present in Tombstone on the day the shooting occurred; . . . I was in the butcher shop on Frémont Street when the shooting occurred; I heard the firing; while I was in the butcher shop remember of seeing some armed parties pass the door; could not say they were all armed; saw Mr. Holliday with arms; he had a gun; I mean a gun as distinguished from a pistol; can't tell the difference between a shotgun and a rifle; don't know whether this was a shotgun or a rifle; I can identify the man in this room who had the gun. [Witness here identifies Mr. Holliday as the person.]

He is the person I mentioned as Mr. Holliday; he had on an overcoat; the gun was on his left hand side, with his overcoat over the gun and his arm thrown over it; I knew it was a gun because his overcoat flew back and I saw it; there were three persons with him; I suppose they were; all four were right together, walking in the same direction, down Frémont Street from the post office towards Third Street; I only know what I have been told who these persons were; I do not know the Earp brothers only by sight, and as they have been pointed out to me; persons pointed out to me as the Earp brothers were with him; I could not positively point out in this room any of the Earp brothers; I can say there is one man here who looks like them; these four men were on the sidewalk walking leisurely along, as any gentleman would walk, not fast, or very slow; when they got to the awning where the butcher shop is, Mr. Holliday and the man on the outside were just a little in front of the middle two; they were walking nearly abreast of each other; Holliday was on the left hand side, next to the building; I heard remarks from the party as they passed; I heard the gentleman on the outside, as I stepped into the second folding door, as he looked around say to Mr. Holliday, "Let them have it"; Mr. Holliday said, "All right." I suppose he said it to Mr. Holliday, for he answered him; no names were used; I heard no other conversation, at this exact time; I saw nothing of the fight.

In their cross-examination of Mrs. King, Thomas Fitch, one of the best-known criminal lawyers in the West, who represented the Earps, concentrated on the physical layout of the butcher's front door, obviously trying to show she could not have overheard the conversation.

However, Mrs. King was very precise in her description of the front door and the location of the Earps and Holliday, "the nearest one was two or three feet from me."

Other witnesses called by the prosecution and defense testified to the Earps's beating of Tom McLaury, the corral shootout, and threats made by the Clantons against the Earps. At least two supported Mrs. King's testimony as to the determination of the Earps not to arrest the cowboys but to kill them. One witness, a prim dressmaker named Addie Bourland, demonstrated the difficulty of prosecutors of all ages in getting exact details from their witnesses; Miss Bourland called Holliday's pistol "large and bronze colored." Everyone else had described the weapon as nickel-plated.

W. S. Williams, a Tombstone attorney who had just been appointed as assistant prosecutor of the new Cochise County, told how Sheriff Behan had visited the wounded Virgil Earp shortly after the shooting. While he admitted hearing Behan saying the Clantons refused to be disarmed, Williams would not confirm Earp's statement that Behan had called the battle "a fair fight."

Another witness, Robert S. Hatch, a saloon keeper, told the court Tom McLaury had turned his guns over to him "for safe keeping" and that he could produce them because "they are in my safe," thus supporting Clanton's testimony that young McLaury had thrown open his coat to show he "had nothing."

Wes Fuller, a gambler, friend of the Clantons and hostile to the Earps, detailed the gunfight, demonstrating how Billy Clanton "throwed up his hands" and was gunned down despite his plea, "Don't shoot me, I don't want any fight." The Earps, he said, "fired the first shots, two shots almost together."

The two stars of the proceedings were Ike Clanton and Wyatt Earp; the wounded Virgil, Morgan, and Doc Holliday had been excused. Both gave their versions of the Benson stage robbery, the scheme to lure the three robbers and murderers of Philpot, and what took place at the O. K. Corral fight. It was one man's word against another.

Ike Clanton being sworn, says: My name is Joseph I. Clanton; reside four miles above Charleston, on the river; my occupation is that of a cattle and stock dealer. . . . Myself and the McLowry brothers and Wm. Clanton and a young fellow named Willie Claibourne were standing in a vacant lot on Frémont Street, between Fly's building and the one next west of Fly's, talking; Sheriff Behan came down and said he would have to arrest us. He said he would have to arrest us and disarm us; I asked Behan what for? He told me to preserve the peace; I told him I had no arms; then William Clanton told him he was just leaving town; the Sheriff then said if you are leaving town all right; he then told Tom and Frank McLowry he would have to take their arms; Tom McLowry told him that he had none; Frank said he was going out of town and did not want to give his arms up, while the party that hit his brother was still armed; the Sheriff told him that he should do it; and to take his arms up to the Sheriff's office and take them off; then he (Frank) said he had business in town that he would like to attend to, and would not lay off his arms and attend to the business, but that he would leave town if the Earps were not disarmed; the Sheriff put his arms around me to see if I was armed; Tom McLowry said to him, I am not armed, and opened his coat this way (showing each hand on lapel and coat thrown wide open); the Sheriff then looked up Frémont Street and ordered us to stay there until he came back . . . just as Behan started up the Earps and Holliday appeared on the sidewalk . . . he held up his hands to them and told them to stop, that he had our party in charge.

Q. State what they did when Behan told them to stop? A. They passed right on by him; did not stop but came on to where we were.

Q. How far was it from where you were standing to where Behan met the Earps and Holliday? A. I would judge it to be about twenty paces.

Q. You say they came on down to where you were, what did they do when they got there? A. They pulled their pistols as they got there and said: "You s—s of b—s, you have been looking for a fight, and now you can have it"; Wyatt and Virgil said it, and at the same time ordered us to throw up our hands; we threw up our hands, and they at the same time commenced shooting.

Q. Who commenced shooting? A. The first two shots were fired by Holliday and Morg Earp.

Q. Who fired the next? A. Wyatt Earp and Virg Earp, in quick succession; just after Morg and Holliday shot, Virg fired, before Wyatt did.

Q. How close together were the first two shots? A. They were fired so close together that I could not tell which fired first. . . .

Q. At the time the Earp party came up to where you and the McLowrys and Billy Clanton were standing, what if anything, did Wyatt Earp do? A. He shoved his pistol against my belly, and said, "throw up your hands"; and said, "you s— of a b— you can have a fight." I turned on my heel and took Wyatt Earp a hold of his hand and pistol with my left hand and grabbed him around the shoulder with my right hand and held him for a few seconds; while I was holding him he shot and I pushed him around the photograph gallery and jumped into the photograph gallery door; went right through the hall and out the back way, and went off across Allen Street and into the dance hall; as I was leaving and as I jumped into the door of the photograph gallery I heard one or two bullets pass right by my head; as I passed through an opening on my way from the gallery I heard another bullet pass me.

Q. State if there was any previous difficulty between you and the defendants or either of them, if so, when and where? A. Yes, sir, there was a difficulty between Holliday and Morg Earp and me the night before the shooting, at a lunch stand in this town, close to the Eagle Brewery saloon, on the north side of Allen Street; as near as I can remember it was about 1 o'clock in the morning; I went in there to get a lunch; while I was sitting down at the table Doc Holliday came in and commenced cursing me and said I had been using his name; that I was a s— of a b— of a cowboy, and to get my gun out and get to work; I told him I had no gun; he said I was a d—n liar and had threatened the Earps; I told him I had not, and to bring whoever said so and I would convince him that I had not; he told me again to pull out my gun and if there is any grit in me to go fighting; all the time he was talking he had his hand on his pistol in his bosom; I mean he had his hand in his bosom, and I believed on a pistol; I looked behind me and I saw Morg Earp with his feet over the lunch counter; he also had his hand in his bosom, looking at me; I then got up and went out on the sidewalk; Doc Holliday said as I walked out, "You s—n of a b—h, you ain't heeled; go heel yourself"; just at that time Morg Earp stepped up and said, "Yes, you s—n of a b—h, you can have all the fight you want now"; I thanked him and told him I did not want any of it; I am not heeled. Virgil Earp stood then about fifteen feet from me down the sidewalk. Just about this time, Wyatt Earp came out of the door; while we were still standing there. . . .

Wyatt did not say anything; Morgan Earp told me if I was not heeled when I came back to be heeled; I walked off and asked Morgan Earp not to shoot me in the back; I did not see Morg Earp or Doc Holliday that night to speak to them; well, that night I came back in half an hour to the saloon on the west, the Alhambra, I think; I sat down to play poker in the morning in that saloon; I think the name of it was the Alhambra; Tom Corrigan was tending bar there; those two saloons I have got the names mixed; the first row between me and Holliday was in the Alhambra, we were playing poker in the Occidental, Virg Earp, Tom McLowry, myself, John Behan and another gentleman, I don't remember his name; in the row with Holliday and Morg Earp on the sidewalk Virg Earp told them to let me alone while Jim Flynn was there, then again as I walked away; Jim Flynn is a policeman; there was no Jim other than Jim Flynn there at the time; when the poker game broke up in the morning I saw Virg Earp take his pistol out of his lap and stick it in his pants, I got up and followed him outdoors on the sidewalk; he was going down Allen Street in front of the Cosmopolitan hotel; I walked up to him and said from his actions the night before in regard to the policeman and what he said the night before, and playing poker with his six-shooter in his lap, I said I thought he stood in with those people who tried to murder me the night before; I told him if that was so I was in town; he said he was going to bed; I went and cashed my chips into the poker game.

Had no more talk with him that morning; well, think it was about half-past 12 o'clock on Fourth Street, between Frémont Street and Allen Street, Virg and Morg Earp came up behind me; do not know where they came from; Virg Earp struck me on the side of the head with a six-shooter from behind and knocked me up against the wall; Morg Earp cocked his pistol and stuck it at me, towards me; Virg Earp took my arms, my pistol and Winchester; I did not know or see that they were about there; did know who struck me until I fell against the house; then they pulled me along and said: "You damned s—n of a b—h, we'll take you up to Judge Wallace's office"; when I got there Wyatt Earp came in and cursed me, and said I could have all the fight I wanted; did not see Doc Holliday there; Wyatt Earp called me a thief and a son of a b—h, and said I could have all the fight I wanted, and said he could out-shoot me, or whip me, am not certain which he said; Virg Earp came up and said, "Yes, we will give it to you pretty plenty now"; Morg Earp told me he would pay my fine if I would fight him; I told him I would fight him; Wyatt Earp offered me my gun—rifle—by pointing it muzzle foremost, and told me to take it; as he presented me the gun I saw Virg Earp put his hand in his bosom (this way), [showing] Morgan Earp stood over me, on a bench behind me; Wyatt Earp stood to my right and in front of me; then I told them I did not want any of it that way, Wyatt Earp asked me when I wanted to fight, and where and how.

As well as I can remember, I said "I will fight you anywhere or any way"; this is all I remember of what occurred there; this all transpired while I was in Judge Wallace's court; I am inclined to think that Judge Wallace was not in court at the time; I was waiting there in court some time before the fine was imposed on me; there were a good many people at the door when this occurred; I was fined, paid my fine, and was released; this, I think, was about 10 o'clock; all this occurred on the day of the killing, about, as near as I can judge, about one hour and a-half before the shooting.

Q. At the time you were released, who had your arms? A. Virg, at least, he had taken them in charge when I was arrested, and had not given them to me.

Q. When and where did you get your arms? A. I got them I think a couple of days after that from Billy Soule, the jailer.

Q. You were asked in your cross-examination if Billy Leonard, Jim Crane and Harry Head were supposed to be connected with the attempt to rob the stage at the killing of Budd Philpot, and to which you answered: "I don't know anything about it but what Virgil Earp, Wyatt Earp, Morgan Earp and Doc Holliday and others told me." Please state what Doc Holliday told you, upon that subject, and when you have answered as to him, state what Morgan Earp told you, then state what Virgil Earp told you, and then what Wyatt Earp told you?

A. Doc Holliday told me, to the best of my recollection, this: I came up town a few days after Budd Philpot was killed; Doc Holliday asked me if I had seen William Leonard and his party; I told him I had; I had seen them the day before and they had told me to tell Doc Holliday that they were going to the San José Mountains. He then asked me if I had had a talk with them. I told him only for a moment. He told me then he would see me later in the evening. This was in front of the Cosmopolitan Hotel; later in the evening I met him at Jim Vogan's place and after talking with him a while he asked me if Leonard told me how he came to kill Budd Philpot. I told him Leonard had told me nothing about it. He [Doc Holliday] then told me that Bob Paul, the messenger, had the lines and Budd Philpot had the shotgun, and Philpot made a fight and got left. About that time someone came along and the conversation ended.

I told Doc Holliday not to take me into his confidence, that I did not wish to know any more about it. Doc Holliday told me he was there at the killing of Budd Philpot. He told me that he shot Philpot through the heart. He told me this at the same time and in connection with the sentence that, "Philpot made a fight and got left." He said he saw "Budd Philpot, the d—n s— b— tumble off the cart." That is the last conversation I ever had with Holliday in connection with that affair. He has often told me to tell Leonard, Head and Crane, if I saw them, that he was all right.

Sometime in June, about the 1st, I came into Tombstone and I met Wyatt Earp in the Eagle Brewery saloon; he asked me to take a drink with him; while our drinks were being mixed he told me he wanted a long private talk with me; after our drinks we stepped out in the middle of the street; he told me then he could put me on a scheme to make $6,000; I asked him what it was; he told me he would not tell me unless I would promise either to do it or promise never to mention our conversation to anyone; he told me it was a legitimate transaction. And then the conversation as detailed in my cross-examination ensued.

The next morning after this conversation with Wyatt Earp I met Morg Earp in the Alhambra saloon, and he asked me what conclusion I had come to in regard to my conversation with Wyatt; I told him I would let him know before I left town; he approached me again in the same place four or five days after this; we had considerable talk about it then at that time, but I only remember that he told me that ten or twelve days before Budd Philpot was killed that he had "piped off" $1,400 to Doc Holliday and Bill Leonard, and that Wyatt Earp had "given away" a number of thousand dollars (I think he said $29,000) the day Budd Philpot was killed—which sum was going off on the train that night; we talked a while longer, but I don't remember what was said, only I told him I was not going to have anything to do with it; I meant I would have nothing to do with killing Crane, Leonard and Head; Virg Earp told me to tell Billy Leonard at one time not to think he was trying to catch him when they were running him, and he told me to tell Billy he had thrown Paul and the posse that was after him off his track at the time they left Helm's ranch, at the foot of the Dragoon Mountains, and that he had taken them on to a trail that went down into New Mexico, and that he had done all he could for him, and he wanted Billy Leonard to get Head and Crane out of the country, for he was afraid one of them might be captured and get all his friends into trouble; he, Virg Earp, said in that conversation, that they had quit a trail of three horses and followed a trail of fifteen horses; he said I [should] send them this word to assure them that I have not gone back on them; he stated he knew the trail of Crane, Leonard and Head went south towards the San José Mountains, and the Sheriff and posse followed the other trail into New Mexico.

Q. Why have you not told what Doc Holliday, Wyatt Earp, Virgil Earp and Morgan Earp said about the attempted stage robbery and the killing of Philpot before you told it in this examination?

A. Before he told me I made him sacred, solemn promises that I would never tell it, and I never would if I had not been put on the stand, and another reason was that I found out by Wyatt Earp's conversation that he was offering money to kill his confederates in this attempted stage robbery, through fear that Bill Leonard, Crane and Head would be captured and tell on them, and I knew that after Crane, Leonard and Head was killed that some of them would murder me for what they had told me.

Testimony for the defense—Statement by Wyatt Earp . . . witness took the stand and commenced his statement by reading a carefully prepared manuscript. . . . My name is Wyatt S. Earp; 32 years old the 19th of last March; born at Monmouth, Warren County, Ill., reside in Tombstone, Cochise County, Arizona, and have resided here since December 1st, 1879, and am at present a saloon-keeper; also, have been Deputy Sheriff and detective.

The difficulty which resulted in the death of Wm. Clanton and Frank and Tom McLowry, originated last spring.

Shortly after the time Bud Philpot was killed by the men who tried to rob the Benson stage, as a detective I tried to trace the matter up, and I was satisfied that three men named Billy Leonard, Harry Head and James Crane were in that robbery. I knew that Leonard, Head and Crane were friends and associates of the Clantons and McLowrys, and often stopped at their ranch; it was generally understood among officers and those who have information about criminals, that Ike Clanton was a sort of chief amongst the cowboys; that the Clantons and McLowrys were cattle thieves and generally in the secrets of the stage robbers, and that the Clanton and McLowry ranches were meeting places and place of shelter for the gang.

I had an ambition to be Sheriff of this county at the next election, and I thought it would be of great help to me with the people and business men if I could capture the men who killed Philpot; there were rewards of about $1200 each for the capture of the robbers; altogether there was about $3600 for the capture.

I thought this might tempt Ike Clanton and Frank McLowry to give away Leonard, Head and Crane, so I went to Ike Clanton, Frank McLowry and Joe Hill when they came in town; I had an interview with them in the back yard of the Oriental Saloon; I told them what I wanted; I told them I wanted the glory of capturing Leonard, Head and Crane, and if I could do so it would help me make the race for Sheriff at the next election; I told them if they would put me on the track of Leonard, Head and Crane and tell me where those men were hid, I would give them all the reward and would never let anyone know where I got my information; Ike Clanton said he would like to see them captured; he said that Leonard claimed a ranch that he claimed, and that if he could get him out of the way that he would have no opposition in regard to the ranch.

Clanton said Leonard, Head and Crane would make a fight, that they never would be taken alive; that I must first find out if the reward would be paid for the capture dead or alive. I then went to Marshall Williams, the agent of Wells, Fargo in this town, and at my request he telegraphed to the Agent or Superintendent of Wells, Fargo at San Francisco to find out if the reward would be paid for the robbers dead or alive. He received in June, 1881, a telegram which he showed me promising that the reward would be paid dead or alive.

The next day I met Ike Clanton and Joe Hill on Allen Street in front of the little cigar store next to the Alhambra; I told them the dispatch had come; I went to Marshall Williams and told him I wanted to see that dispatch for a few minutes. He went to looking for it and could not find it just then; he went over to the telegraph office and got a copy and came and gave it to me. I went and showed it to Ike Clanton and Joe Hill and returned it to Marshall Williams, and afterwards told Frank McLowry of its contents. It was then agreed between us that they should have all the $3,600 reward, outside of necessary expenses for horse hire in going after them, and that Joe Hill should go where Leonard, Head and Crane were hid over near Eureka, in New Mexico, and lure them in near Frank and Tom McLowry's ranch, near Soldier Holes, 30 miles from here, and I would be on hand with a posse and capture them.

I asked Joe Hill, Ike Clanton and Frank McLowry what tale they would make to them to get them over here. They said they had agreed upon a plan to tell them that there would be a paymaster going from Tombstone to Bisbee shortly to pay off the miners, and that they wanted them to come in and take them; Ike Clanton then sent Joe Hill to bring them in; before starting Joe Hill took off his watch and chain and between two and three hundred dollars in money, and gave it to Virgil Earp to keep for him until he got back; he was gone about ten days, and returned with the word that he had got there one day too late, that Leonard and Harry Head had been killed the day before he got there by horse thieves; I learned afterwards that the horse thieves had been killed subsequently by members of the Clanton and McLowry gang; after that Ike Clanton and Frank McLowry claimed that I had given them away to Marshall Williams and Doc Holliday, and we began to hear of their threats against us.

I am a friend of Doc Holliday, because when I was City Marshal of Dodge City, Kansas, he came to my rescue and saved my life when I was surrounded by desperadoes.

About a month or more ago Morgan Earp and myself assisted to arrest Stilwell and Spencer on the charge of robbing the Bisbee stage; the McLowrys and Clantons have always been friends of Stilwell and Spencer, and they laid the whole blame of their arrest on us, though, the fact is we only went as a Sheriff's posse; after we got in town with Spencer and Stilwell, Ike Clanton and Frank McLowry came in; Frank McLowry took Morgan Earp into the street in front of the Alhambra, when John Ringgold, Ike Clanton and the two Hicks boys were also standing by, when Frank McLowry commenced to abuse Morgan Earp for going after Spencer and Stilwell; Frank McLowry said he would never speak to Spencer again for being arrested by us; he said to Morgan: "If you ever come after me you will never take me"; Morgan replied if he ever had occasion to go after him he would arrest him; Frank McLowry then said to Morgan: "I have threatened you boys' lives, and a few days ago had taken it back, but since this arrest it now goes." Morgan made no reply and walked off.

Before this and after this Marshall Williams, Farmer Daly, Ed Byrnes, Old Man Winter, Charley Smith and three or four others had told us at different times of threats to kill us made by Ike Clanton, Frank McLowry, Tom McLowry, Joe Hill and John Ringgold; I knew all those men were desperate and dangerous men; that they were connected with outlaws, cattle thieves, robbers and murderers; I knew of the McLowrys stealing six government mules and also cattle, and when the owner went after them—finding his stock on the McLowry boys' ranch—that he was driven off, and told that if he ever said anything about it they would kill him, and he has kept his mouth shut until several days ago for fear of being killed. I heard of Ringgold shooting a man down in cold blood near Camp Thomas; I was satisfied that Frank and Tom McLowry had killed and robbed Mexicans in Skeleton Canyon three or four months ago, and I naturally kept my eyes open, for I did not intend that any of the gang should get the drop on me if I could help it.

Ike Clanton met me at Vogan's old saloon five or six months ago and told me that I had told Holliday about this transaction concerning the "giving away" Head, Leonard and Crane; I told him I had never told Holliday anything; I told him that when Holliday came up from Tucson I would prove it; Ike Clanton told him that Holliday had told him so; when Holliday came back I asked him and he said no; I told him that Ike Clanton had said so; on the 25th of October—the night—Holliday met Ike Clanton in the Alhambra lunch room and asked him about it; Clanton denied it; they quarrelled for three or four minutes; Holliday told Clanton he was a damned liar if he said so; I was sitting eating lunch at the lunch counter, Morgan Earp was standing at the Alhambra bar talking to the bartender, I called him over to where I was sitting, knowing that he was an officer, and told him that Holliday and Clanton were quarrelling in the lunch room, and for him to go in and stop it; he climbed over the lunch counter from the Alhambra bar, went into the room, took Holliday by the arm and led him into the street; Ike Clanton in a few moments followed them out; I got through eating and walked out; as I opened the door I could hear that they were still quarrelling outside; Virgil Earp came up, I think out of the Occidental, and told them (Holliday and Clanton) that if they did not stop their quarrelling he would have to arrest them.

They all separated at that time, Morgan Earp going down the street, home; Virgil Earp going into the Occidental saloon, Holliday up the street to the Oriental saloon, and Ike Clanton across the street to the Grand Hotel. I walked into the Eagle brewery where I had a faro game which I had not closed. I stayed in there a few moments and then walked out on the street and there met Ike Clanton. He asked me if I would take a walk with him, he wanted to have a talk with me. I told him I would if he did not go too far, that I was waiting for my game in the brewery to close, as I had to take care of the money. We walked about half way down the side of the brewery building on Fifth Street and stopped. He told me that when Holliday approached him in the lunch room, that he was not fixed just right. He said that in the morning he would have man for man, and that this fighting talk had been going on for a long time, and he guessed it was about time to fetch it to a close. I told him I would fight no one if I could get away from it, because there was no money in it. He walked off and left me saying, "I will be ready for all of you in the morning." I walked over to the Oriental, he come in, followed me in rather, and took a drink, having his six-shooter on and playing fight and saying, "you must not think I won't be after you all in the morning." He said he would like to make a fight with Holliday now. I told him Holliday did not want to fight, but only to satisfy him that this talk had not been made. About that time the man who was dealing my game closed it, and brought the money to me. I locked it up in the safe and started home. I met Holliday on the street between the Oriental and Alhambra. Myself and Holliday walked down Allen Street, he going to his room, and I, to my house to bed.

I got up next day, October 26th, about noon. Before I got up Ned Boyle came to me and told me that he had met Ike Clanton on Allen Street, near the telegraph office, and that Ike was on it; that he said that as soon as those d—d Earps make their appearance on the street today the ball will open; that Ike said, "We are here to make a fight and we are looking for the s—s of b—s." I lay in bed some little time after that; got up and went down to the Oriental saloon. Harry Jones came to me after I got up and said, "What does all this mean?" I asked him what he meant. He says, "Ike Clanton is hunting you Earp boys with a Winchester rifle and a six-shooter." I said, "I will go down and find him and see what he wants." I went out, and at the corner of Fifth and Allen, I met Virgil Earp, the marshal. He told me how he had heard that Ike Clanton was hunting us. I went down Allen Street, and Virgil went down Fifth and then Frémont Street. Virgil found Ike Clanton on Fourth, near Frémont, in an alley way. He walked up to him and said, "I heard you were hunting for some of us." I was coming down Fourth Street at this time. Clanton then threw his Winchester around toward Virgil; Virgil grabbed it and hit Clanton with his six-shooter and knocked him down. Clanton had his rifle and his six-shooter in his pants. By that time I came up. Virgil and Morgan Earp took the rifle and six-shooter away and took them to the Grand Hotel after examination and took Ike Clanton before Justice Wallace. Before the examination Morgan Earp had Ike Clanton in charge as Virgil Earp was out.

A short time after I went to Wallace's court and sat down on a bench. Ike Clanton looked over to me and said, "I will get even with all of you for this. If I had a six-shooter now I would make a fight with all of you." Morgan Earp then said to him, "If you want to make a fight right bad I'll give you this," at the same time offering

Ike Clanton his own (Ike's) six-shooter. Ike Clanton started up to take it, and Campbell, the Deputy Sheriff, pushed him back in his seat, saying he would not allow any fuss. I never had Ike Clanton's arms at any time, as he has stated. . . .

I was tired of being threatened by Ike Clanton and his gang; I believed from what they had said to me and others and from their movements that they intended to assassinate me the first chance they had, and I thought that if I had to fight for my life with them I had better make them face me in an open fight, so I said to Ike Clanton, who was then sitting about eight feet away from me, you d—n dirty cow thief, you have been threatening our lives, and I know it, I think I would be justified in shooting you down in any place I would meet you, but if you are anxious to make a fight I will go anywhere on earth to make a fight with you, even over to the San Simon, among your own crowd; he replied, all right, I will see you after I get through here, I only want four feet of ground to fight;

I walked out, and just then, outside of the court-room and near the Justice's office, I met Tom McLowry; he came up to me and said to me, "if you want to make a fight I will make a fight with you anywhere"; I supposed at the time that he had heard what had just transpired between Ike Clanton and myself; I knew of his having threatened me, and I felt just as I did about Ike Clanton, that if the fight had to come I had better have it come when I had an even show to defend myself, so I said to him, "all right, make a fight right here," and at the same time slapped him on the face with my left hand and drew my pistol with my right; he had a pistol in plain sight, on his right hip, in his pants, but made no move to draw it; I said to him, jerk your gun and use it; he made no reply; I hit him on the head with my six-shooter and walked away down to Hafford's corner, went into Hafford's and got a cigar and came out and stood by the door. Pretty soon after I saw Tom and Frank McLowry and William Clanton. They passed me and went down Fourth Street to the gunsmith shop; I followed down to see what they were going to do; when I got there Frank McLowry's horse was standing on the sidewalk with his head in the door of the gunsmith shop; I took the horse by the bit, as I was deputy city marshal, and commenced to back him off the sidewalk; Tom and Frank McLowry and Billy Clanton came to the door; Billy laid his hand on his six-shooter, Frank McLowry took hold of the horse's bridle. I said "you will have to get this horse off the sidewalk." Frank McLowry backed him off on the street. Ike Clanton came up about that time and they all walked into the gunsmith shop. I saw them in the shop changing cartridges into their belts. They came out of the shop and walked along Fourth Street to the corner of Allen; I followed them to the corner of Fourth and Allen Streets, and then they went down Allen and over to Dunbar's corral.

Virg Earp was then City Marshal; Morg Earp was a special policeman for six weeks or two months, wore a badge and drew pay; I had been sworn in Virgil's place to act for him while he was gone to Tucson to Spencer and Stilwell's trial; Virgil had been back for a few days but I was still acting; I knew it was Virgil's duty to disarm those men; expected he would have trouble in doing so and I followed up to give assistance if necessary, especially as they had been threatening us as I have already stated.

About ten minutes afterwards, and while Virgil, Morgan, Doc Holliday and myself were standing on the corner of Allen and Fourth Streets, several persons said there is going to be trouble with those fellows, and one man named Coleman said to Virgil they mean trouble. They have just gone from Dunbar's Corral to the O. K. Corral all armed. I think you had better go and disarm them.

Virgil turned around to Holliday, Morgan Earp and myself, and told us to come and assist him in disarming them. Morgan Earp said to me, they have horses, had we not better get some horses ourselves so that if they make a running fight we can catch them, I said no. If they try to make a running fight we can kill their horses and then capture them.

We four then started through Fourth to Frémont Streets. When we turned the corner of Fourth and Frémont, we could see them standing near or about the vacant space between Fly's photograph gallery and the next building west. I first saw Frank McLowry, Tom McLowry, Billy Clanton and Sheriff Behan standing there. We went down the left hand side of Frémont Street, when I got within about 150 feet of them. I saw Ike Clanton, Billy Claiborne and another party. We had walked a few steps from there when I saw Behan leave the party and come toward us. Every few steps he would look back as if he apprehended danger. I heard Behan say to Virgil, "Earp, for God's sake don't go down there, for you will get murdered." Virgil replied, "I am going to disarm them"; he being in the lead. When I and Morgan came up to Behan, he said, "I have disarmed them." When he said this, I took my pistol which I had in my hand under my coat, and put it into my overcoat pocket. Behan then passed up the street, and we walked on down. We came upon them close, Frank McLowry, Tom McLowry and Billy Clanton standing all in a row against the east side of the building on the opposite side of the vacant place west of Fly's photograph gallery. Ike Clanton and a man I did not know was standing in the vacant spot, about half way between the photograph gallery and the next building west. I saw that Billy Clanton, Frank and Tom McLowry had their hands by their sides; Frank McLowry's and Billy Clanton's six-shooters were in plain sight. Virgil said, "Throw up your hands: I have come to disarm you."

Billy Clanton and Tom McLowry commenced to draw their pistols; at the same time Tom McLowry threw his hand to his right hip, throwing his coat open like that (showing), and jumped behind a horse. I had my pistol in my overcoat pocket, where I put it when Behan told us he had disarmed the other parties. When I saw Billy Clanton and Frank McLowry draw their pistols, I drew my pistol. Billy Clanton leveled his pistol on me, but I did not aim at him. I knew that Frank McLowry had the reputation of being a good shot and a dangerous man and I aimed at Frank McLowry. The first two shots which were fired were fired by Billy Clanton and myself, he shooting at me and I at Frank McLowry. I do not know which shot was fired first. We fired almost together. The fight then became general.

After about four shots were fired, Ike Clanton ran up and grabbed my left arm. I could see no weapon in his hand, and I thought at the time he had none, and so I said to him, "The fight has now commenced; go to fighting, or get away." At the same time I pushed him off with my left hand. He started and ran down the side of the building and disappeared between the lodging house and photograph gallery; my first shot struck Frank McLowry in the belly; he staggered off on the sidewalk, but first fired one shot at me; when we told them to throw up their hands Claiborne held up his left hand and then broke and ran, and I never seen him afterwards until late in the afternoon; I never drew my pistol or made a motion to shoot until after Billy Clanton and Frank McLowry drew their pistols; if Tom McLowry was unarmed I did not know it; believe he was armed and fired two shots at our party before Holliday, who had the shotgun, fired at and killed him; if he was unarmed there was nothing in the circumstances, or in what had been communicated to me, or in his acts or threats that would have led me even to suspect his being unarmed; I never fired at Ike Clanton, even after the shooting commenced, because I thought he was unarmed; I believed then, and believe now, from the facts I have stated and from the threats I have related, and other threats communicated to me by different persons, as having been made by Tom McLowry, Frank McLowry and Ike Clanton, that these men last named had formed a conspiracy to murder my brothers, Morgan and Virgil, Doc Holliday and myself; I believe I would have been legally and morally justifiable in shooting any of them on sight, but I did not do so, nor attempt to do so; I sought no advantage when I went, as Deputy Marshal, to help to disarm them and arrest them; I went as a part of my duty and under the directions of my brothers, the marshals; I did not intend to fight unless it became necessary in self-defense or in the rightful performance of official duty; when Billy Clanton and Frank McLowry drew their pistols, I knew it was a fight for life and I drew and fired in defense of my own life and the lives of my brothers and Doc Holliday.

On December 1, Magistrate Wells Spicer, Wyatt Earp's "good friend," handed down his decision that not enough evidence had been produced by the state to send the case to the county grand jury. The potential defendants were ordered released.

Spicer's shocking decision showed he was legally inept, had been influenced by his friendship and admiration for the Earps, or had been reached politically. His lengthy ruling ignored a number of important points scored by the state. Spicer casually dismissed the witnesses who testified Tom McLaury was unarmed "because it is not of controlling importance." Ike Clanton's story "falls short of being a sound theory" simply because he "was not injured at all." Spicer appeared to have forgotten Clanton's description of how he heard Doc Holliday's bullets whistling about his head as he fled through Fly's gallery.

Although the testimony of Mrs. King and the other impartial witnesses had proved a prima facie case of premeditated murder for a grand jury to consider, Spicer was not impressed. He dismissed the prosecution's charge that the Earps and Holliday "acted with criminal haste" because, as he wrote, "I cannot believe this theory."

The *Epitaph*, for once, opened their columns; Spicer's verbatim decision occupied five columns on page one. But it was the *Nugget*'s editorial that said it best:

"The remarkable document which appears in another column, purports to be the reasons which actuated the judge in his final action. But the suspicion of reasons of more substantial nature are openly expressed upon the streets, and in the eyes of many the Justice does not stand like Caesar's wife, "Not only virtuous but above suspicion."

The unsolved mystery of the hearing has been why an unidentified attorney attached to the prosecution's staff, had abruptly demanded on November 5 that Magistrate Spicer cancel the bail of Holliday and the Earps and remand them to jail.

Spicer granted the request, bail was revoked, and the defendants were turned over to Sheriff Behan. However, after the day's hearing was over the defense counsel obtained a writ of habeas corpus releasing the infuriated Wyatt Earp and Doc Holliday.

A series of letters ironically discovered in the archives of the New-York Historical Society solves the mystery.

They were written by William McLaury, oldest of the brothers, who arrived in Tombstone during a four-day late October recess. A Fort Worth lawyer, McLaury's letters make him appear to be a singularly independent man.

Four years before, he had hung up his shingle in Fort Worth and announced to that solidly Democratic and pro-Confederate town he was not only a Yankee but a Republican. He exposed a corrupt postal clerk, ran for postmaster, and became leader of Fort Worth's few Republicans or "Radicals," as they were called. In 1879 he established a partnership with former Confederate Captain S. P. Greene—"a sound Democrat," as a disgusted McLaury described him—and the incongruous pair became one of the best-known law firms on the Texas frontier.

When McLaury received word of the "murders of my brothers by these brutes," he immediately left for Tombstone determined, as he wrote relatives in Iowa, "to hang them." He depicts the town as "terrorized" and the prosecutor "cowed" by the Earps. McLaury joined the prosecution staff and made the bail motion. One of his letters to his father describes that day and discloses that his brother, Tom, was robbed of $1,600 as he lay dying.[21]

THE MCLAURY LETTERS

When he heard the news of the O. K. Corral shootout, William R. McLaury, oldest of the brothers, rushed from Fort Worth to Tombstone, where he joined the prosecution's staff. It was McLaury, a well-known Texas lawyer, who demanded that Wyatt Earp and Doc Holliday be held without bail for the duration of the hearing.

Because of the unique importance of the letters, they are used in full. More than twenty years ago, the letters and the photographs of the slain McLaurys and Ike Clanton were discovered by this author and late Sylvester Vigilante, in the files of the New-York Historical Society. Letters and photographs, courtesy of the New-York Historical Society.

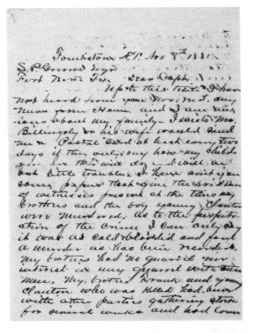

Letter of November 8, 1881

to 2.

I saw a man called out on the sidewalk ... he ... a team ... with us and took me down and I ... called ... getting better ...

... to the town are boarding ... and had been here about fifteen minutes, had transacted their business and were ready to ... Mount their horses, to have Brother Ike and Isaac Clanton were going out in a way ... the team being their ... Brother Ike and I Clanton had been in town from the morning of the day previous ... as ... we arrived. Frank & William Clanton were armed ... were completely surprised ... after ... was mortally wounded. He shot Holliday. Morgan & Virgil Earp wounding Morgan and Virgil slightly.

Robert I arrived him ... these who were able to be out were on the streets on Bail. And the people were many of them in dread of these men, they came into the Court room heavily armed. The Dist. Atty.

---

2 to 3

was completely ... and after promising her on the ... to move the Court to commit these men without bail. He would not do it, and after agreeing in the presence of all our attys to do so would not do it, and none of our attys. would do so and would not permit me to do so, and said they did not want to see me killed, and to prevent me from making the motion refused to ... if I ... not think they would make a move and did not fear them, the fact is I only hoped they would, as I would be on my feet and know the first go, and thought I could kill them both before they could get a start. On yesterday I told our folks I would make the motion ... I had consulted the court and knew he would grant it and told them to do as they pleased. I made the motion they were as quick as Lawbs, only looked a little scared. It was

---

Page 4

... greatest after a careful discussion. They ... got a writ of Habeas Corpus ... turned over ... that last night. The ... ... were dismissed. People were afraid to talk. Our witnesses were running away. No one but the ... and ... dared come forward to give any information unless brought ... by attachment ... Now considerable are in Jail and in bed. But my Oh! Capt. this don't bring back my dead brothers. If Dr. ... wants to know where Hades is I can inform him. Last night after it was known the murderers were in Jail the Hotel was a perfect Jam until nearly morning, everybody wanted to see me and shake my hand. I will remain here during this term of Court which will be in session Monday next. We

Letter of November 9, 1881

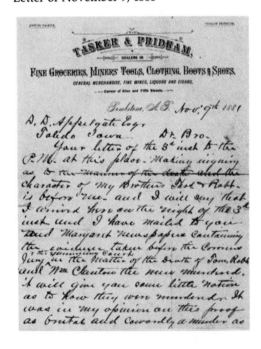

TASKER & PRIDHAM,

DEALERS IN

FINE GROCERIES, MINERS' TOOLS, CLOTHING, BOOTS & SHOES,

GENERAL MERCHANDISE, FINE WINES, LIQUORS AND CIGARS.

Corner of Allen and Fifth Streets.

Tombstone, A.T. Nov. 9th 1881

J. D. Applegate Esqr.
Toledo Iowa   Dr. Bro—

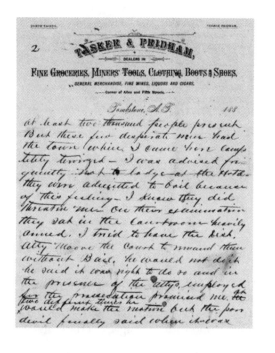

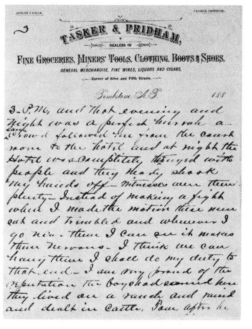

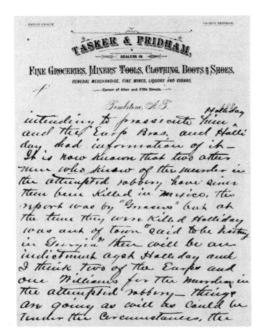

William H. McLaury on the Earp-Clanton Hearing in Tombstone

I will give you some little notion as to how they [his brothers] were murdered. It was in my opinion, as brutal and cowardly a murder as have ever been recorded. The men who committed the murders caused the sending out the [news] dispatches in the manner it was done. They also called upon the Acting Governor now for troops to protect the city.

Now I find my brothers stood as high with these people both in the city and in the county as you did in your county when I knew you there. In fact I find that with the exception of about thirty or forty men here whose business is gambling and stealing among whores [sic] are the Earp brothers and one J. H. Holliday. My brothers were universally esteemed as Honorable, Peaceable brave citizens, never having been charged or suspected of having committed any offense. They have lived here for four years. You will see by the papers I sent you that many people came, some twenty miles to attend their funeral. There was I should say, at least two thousand persons present.[22] But these few men had the town, when I came here, completely terrorized.

I was advised frequently when I came here not to lodge at the hotel. They were [admitted] to bail because of this feeling. I know they did threaten me. On their examination they sat in the courtroom heavily armed. I tried to have the district attorney move the court to remand them without bail. He would not do it. In the presence of the attorneys employed by the prosecution [he] promised me at two different times he would make the motion but the poor devil finally said when it was—someone would be killed.

I then consulted with our attorneys employed and none of them would do it. They said they did not propose to risk their lives. Things went on this way for nearly two days. These men are on the streets and at large. Seeing them free kept me on fire. Witnesses were scared and some ran away. None, with one exception, would come to the hotel or office.

I had mingled with the people and saw enough to know that if these men were jailed things would change at once. I went before the court and was admitted. I then got associated as counsel for the state in this case. I then stood where I could send a knife through their hearts if they made a move, and then made my motion and it was granted.

They did not make a move and perhaps it was good for me they did not for I was anxious to have an opportunity to send them over the bay.

The sheriff then took them into custody, this was around about 3 P.M. and the evening and night was a perfect hurrah. A large crowd followed me from the courtroom to the hotel and at night the hotel was completely thronged with people and they nearly shook my hands off. Witnesses were there plenty. Instead of making a fight when I made the motion these men sat and trembled and whenever I go near them I can see it makes them nervous. I think we can hang them.

I am very proud of the reputation the boys had around here. They lived on a ranch and raised and dealt in cattle. Tom, after he was shot, was robbed of about $1,600. I am trying to unearth it but while I don't think I can do it I shall make a strong effort. They had just sold off their stock and would have started for my place in a day or two and they calculated to have visited father and sisters in Iowa.

The cause of the murders was this situation: Holliday, one of the murderers, attempted to rob the express of Wells Fargo and Co., and in so doing shot and killed a stage driver and a passenger. The other parties engaged in the murder with him, the Earp brothers, were interested in the attempt on the exps. robbery, and young Clanton who was killed, a boy of eighteen years old, knew the facts about the attempted robbery and had told his brother, J. I. Clanton and Thos. and Robt. and they had got up facts, intending to prosecute him. The Earp brothers and Holliday had information of it. It is now known that two other men [Leonard and Head], who knew of the murder in the attempted robbery, have been killed in New Mexico, the report was by "Greasers" but at the time they were killed Holliday was out of town "said to be visiting in Georgia." There will be an indictment against Holliday and I think two of the Earps and one Williams for the murder on the attempted robbery. Things are going as well as could be under the circumstances, the people are backing me thoroughly. They have to be kept quiet. I think the men will be punished according to law and in the event they escape by any trick or otherwise, then if you read the papers there will be more "Press Dispatches." This has been a desperate matter to me. These boys were dear to me and would have walked through fire for me.

Robt. after he was mortally wounded and lying on the ground raised up on his elbow and fired several shots, wounding three of the murderers.[23]

I will send you newspapers.

W. R. McLaury

Unfortunately there are no letters of McLaury disclosing what he thought of Magistrate Spicer's verdict. Three years later he and his father were still corresponding about the case. Some sort of justice had been done, McLaury bitterly observed, with the death of Morgan and the crippling of Virgil, but the chief culprit, Wyatt Earp, was still "free on the streets," once arriving in Fort Worth "but staying only a few hours." The events in Tombstone, he advised his father, belonged in the past, "and we ought to think about [them] as little as possible."

The Last Days in Tombstone

The acquittal of the Earps and Doc Holliday was the beginning of their end in Tombstone. On October 29, 1881, three days after the deadly "street fight," as Wyatt always called it, the Tombstone City Council asked for a meeting to "consider grave charges" against Virgil Earp. Following a closed hearing he was suspended from office and relieved of his city marshal's badge. The nature of the "grave charges" was never revealed.

A short time later City Supervisor Mike Joyce forced Wyatt to give up his gambling concession in the Oriental saloon. After Joyce made a remark about stage robbers walking out of court, Wyatt leaned over the bar and slapped his face. Later Joyce got a gun, found Earp and Holliday in the Alhambra but before he could shout out his challenge to fight, he was disarmed by Sheriff Behan. Joyce was later fined $15 for carrying weapons within city limits.

Frank Waters, in his fine study of the life of the Earps, traced the transfer of property and mines by the Earps to their father in Colton, California, which indicated to Tombstone they were ready to leave.[24]

The evidence of the properties raises the question of how the Earps—bartenders, saloon keepers and part-time shotgun messengers—managed to accumulate the money to buy real estate and mines. It is evident from the businessmen who put up $42,000 in bail for Earp and Holliday—the wounded Morgan and Virgil were confined to bed and excused from bail—that they were friends of men who had power in the frontier community. Justice Wells, who had heard their case, was not only a mine broker but a lawyer; J. D. Kinnear and the Wells Fargo Company admired Wyatt. Earp was also a friend of U.S. Attorney Crawley P. Dake in Tucson and several rich mine owners. And John Clum, Mayor of Tombstone and owner of the *Epitaph*, supported the Earps.

Did these friends of the Earps arrange for them to appear before Magistrate Spicer to guarantee that the shooting case would never reach Tucson? Although the Earps had law and order supporters on the Pima County Grand Jury such as Marshal Williams, the Wells Fargo agent at Tombstone, and J. D. Kinnear, head of the mining company whose gold bullion had been guarded by the Earps, it is evident that someone in official Tucson did not admire the Earps for what they had done at the O. K. Corral.

The *Nugget* listed the grand jury members and reported an objection by the state to the "swearing of certain jurors to act as such because in the cases of Wyatt, Morgan and Virgil Earp and Doc Holliday, they were strong advocates of their action in cases wherein they would come before the grand jury."[25]

The motion was denied and the jurors were sworn in. In dismissing the Earps and Holliday, because he did not think the evidence presented was "sufficient to warrant a conviction," Spicer did leave the legal door open for the grand jury, with its tremendous power to ignore prosecutors and lower courts, to reopen the hearing, call witnesses, and hand up indictments. One wonders if there had been discussions behind the closed door of the Pima County Grand Jury after Spicer announced his decision. Did someone try to get the grand jury to act? Did Kinnear and the other law and order friends of the Earps kill such a motion?

Violence continued to stalk the Earps. A few days after Christmas, 1881, assassins gunned down Virgil Earp, crippling him for life. Wyatt gathered a posse to ride around the countryside and parade about Charleston until its citizens sent a telegram to Sheriff Behan charging that the Earps and Holliday were "leading the filth of Tombstone armed with rifles and revolvers" in terrorizing the community. They pleaded with Behan: "Come here and take them where they belong." [26]

Curly Bill was now one of Wyatt's principal targets. He hinted darkly that the tousled-haired cowboy was a cold-blooded killer preparing to put together a gang to replace the Clantons and McLaurys. But Wyatt apparently did not know Curly Bill had left Arizona the previous spring after he had been wounded in a drunken brawl. The *Arizona Star* of May 26, 1881, told the story on its page one.

Curly Bill, the Noted Desperado, Gets It in the Neck at Galeyville*

The notorious Curly Bill, the man who murdered Marshal White at Tombstone last fall, and who has been concerned in several other desperate and lawless affrays in South Eastern Arizona, has at last been brought to grief, and there is likely to be a vacancy in the ranks of our border desperados. The affair occurred at Galeyville Thursday. A party of 8 or 9 cowboys, Curly Bill, and his partner Jim Wallace among the number, were in town enjoying themselves in their usual manner, when deputy Sheriff Breakenridge of Tombstone, who was at Galeyville on business, happened along.

Wallace made some insulting remark to the deputy at the same time flourishing his revolver in an aggressive manner. Breakenridge did not pay much attention to this "break" of Wallace but quietly turned around and left the party. Shortly after this, Curly Bill, who it would seem had a friendly feeling for Breakenridge, insisted that Wallace should go and find him and apologize for the insult given. This Wallace was induced to do and after finding Breakenridge he made the apology and the latter accompanied him back to the saloon where the cowboys were drinking.

By this time Curly Bill who had drank [sic] just enough to make him quarrelsome, was in one of his most dangerous moods and evidently desirous of increasing his record as a man killer. He commenced to abuse Wallace, who, by the way, had some pretensions himself as a desperado and bad man generally and finally said, "You d—d Lincoln county s— of a b—, I'll kill you anyhow." Wallace immediately went outside the door of the saloon, Curly Bill following close behind him. Just as the latter stepped outside, Wallace, who had meanwhile drawn his revolver, fired, the ball entering penetrating the left side of Curly Bill's neck and passing through, came out the right cheek, not breaking the jawbone. A scene of the wildest excitement ensued in the town.

The other members of the cowboy party surrounded Wallace and threats of lynching him were made by them. The law abiding citizens were in doubt what course to pursue. They did not wish any more blood shed but were in favor of allowing the lawless element to "have it out" among themselves. But Deputy Sheriff Breakenridge decided to arrest Wallace, which he succeeded in doing without meeting any resistance. The prisoner was taken before Justice Ellinwood and after examination into the facts of the shooting he was discharged.

*The *Star*'s headline.

The wounded and apparently dying desperado was taken into an adjoining building, and a doctor summoned to dress his wounds. After examining the course of the bullet, the doctor pronounced the wound dangerous but not necessarily fatal, the chances for and against recovery being about equal. Wallace and Curly Bill have been partners and fast friends for the past 4 or six months and so far is known, there was no cause for the quarrel, it being simply a drunken brawl.

A great many people in South Eastern Arizona will regret that the termination was not fatal to one or both of the participants. Although the wound is considered very dangerous, congratulations at being freed from this dangerous character are now rather premature, as men of his class usually have a wonderful tenacity of life.

One rancher who said good-bye to Curly Bill reported he was still convalescing from the bullet wound and said he was leaving Arizona "forever because he couldn't expect anything but more trouble and notoriety from accidentally killing Marshal White in Tombstone." [27]

In March Morgan Earp was shot and killed while he was playing billiards with Wyatt in Campbell and Hatch's saloon on Allen Street. At the coroner's inquest, Marietta Spence, the Indian wife of Pete Spence, identified her husband, Frank Stilwell; Florentino Cruz, a woodcutter; Indian Charlie "and a German named Freis" as Morgan's killers. Spence and Stilwell had been arrested earlier for the Brisbee stage robbery but the charges had been dropped. Mrs. Spence testified that her husband had threatened to kill her if she ever told what she knew. The inquest's finding identified Earp's killers as Spence, Stilwell, Freis, and two Indian half-breeds—"one whose name is Charlie but the name of the other not ascertained."

The findings of the inquest were solely based on the testimony of the Indian woman, who many times had been beaten by her husband. Later it was determined that Frank Stilwell could not have been one of the killers crouching in the darkness; he was in Tucson at the time. The Earp murder had taken place at eleven o'clock at night. It was seventy-five miles between Tucson and Tombstone and Stilwell had been seen in Tucson early in the morning following the shooting. [28]

But Wyatt never considered the weak and circumstantial evidence presented before the inquest; his brother's killers had been officially named and he was determined to be their executioner.

Immediately after the findings of the coroner's jury were handed up, one of Sheriff Behan's deputies took Indian Charlie into custody. Pete Spence, who knew the Earps would be looking for him, quickly surrendered to Behan.

A few days later Wyatt and his younger brother Warren, Doc Holliday, Sherman McMasters and "Turkey Creek" Jack Johnson, two gunmen who had been part of Earp's Charleston posse, accompanied the still very weak Virgil Earp and his wife to Tucson. This was the first stop of the journey to Colton, California, where the parents of the Earps would bury their son.

They arrived at dusk. By a strange coincidence Frank Stilwell and Ike Clanton were in Tucson waiting to testify before a grand jury about the Bisbee stagecoach robbery. There are various explanations as to why Clanton and Stilwell were at the Tucson train depot when the Earps appeared; one report had them waiting to meet a man named McDowell, another grand jury witness. There is also a strong possibility they were both lured to the spot. Perhaps another arrangement made by the Earps's powerful friends in Tombstone?

As always when he smelled gunpowder, Ike ran and vanished into the darkness. Stilwell hurried down the tracks, fleeing from the Earps. An engineer later testified he momentarily caught a glimpse of Stilwell's frightened face in the glare of his locomotive's headlights. Then shots echoed above the chugging and snorting of the waiting engines in the yard.

Jack Stilwell, brother of the Indian scout, who was arrested by Wyatt Earp in September 1881 as one of the Bisbee stagecoach robbers. The charges were soon dropped for lack of evidence. Stilwell was killed by the Earps in March 1882, at the Tucson depot. *The James D. Horan Collection*

Stilwell died without drawing his six-shooter. In Lake's biography, Wyatt claimed he had been forced to fight Ike Clanton, Stilwell, and a band of "killers" at the depot and during the wild brawl Stilwell grabbed his gun and was killed when it went off! A special dispatch to the *Epitaph*, datelined March 21, describing Stilwell's "riddled" corpse, once again proved Earp had lied:

"Six shots went into his body—four rifle balls and two loads of buckshot. Both legs were shot through and a charge of buckshot in his left thigh and a charge through his breast, which must have been delivered close, as the coat was powder burned and six buckshot holes within a radius of three inches.

"Stilwell had a pistol on his person which was not discharged. He evidently was taken unaware as he was desperate in a fight and a quick shot."

Witnesses testified at the coroner's inquest that four men had "chased," then shot Stilwell. The Earps and Holliday were identified. Ike Clanton took the stand to testify that he saw Wyatt and Warren Earp, Holliday, McMasters, and Johnson follow Stilwell as he ran down the tracks.[29]

Pima County murder warrants were issued for the accused killers but they could not be found in Tucson. After saying good-bye to Virgil and his wife, the five had flagged a train beyond Tucson's limits and got off at Contention. There they hired horses and rode to Tombstone.

Later that night Sheriff Behan, notified by Pima County's sheriff that the warrants had been issued, went alone to the Cosmopolitan Hotel to find the Earps, Holliday, and their followers packed and ready to leave.

According to the *Epitaph*'s account, Behan stepped in front of Wyatt.

"Wyatt, I want to see you for a moment," he said.

Wyatt pushed him aside. "I have seen you once too often," he growled as he swung up on his horse.

Behan, who knew he was no match for five guns, watched in silence as the five horsemen vanished in the darkness of Allen Street.[30]

Before they left the area, Earp and his men visited Pete Spence's woodcutting camp looking for Florentino Cruz.

When Earp asked for Cruz, he was told by Theodore D. Judah, who worked in the camp, that the Mexican "was looking for some stock which had strayed away." Judah indicated the direction the Mexican had taken and the party immediately left as directed, passing over a hill which hid them from sight.

A few minutes later Judah heard "ten or twelve" shots. Shortly after he found Cruz's body "not far from camp, riddled with bullets."

After hearing the testimony of witnesses, still another coroner's inquest jury named Wyatt and Warren Earp, Doc Holliday, McMasters, and Johnson as the killers.[31]

Chris Bilicke's "fashionable Cosmopolitan Hotel" in Tombstone. When they first arrived in the mining camp, Doc Holliday and his sweetheart, "Big Nose" Kate Elder, stayed here. After killing Frank Stilwell, Wyatt and Doc Holliday, who were staying at the hotel, packed and left. They met Sheriff Johnny Behan in the lobby and Behan tried to talk to Earp, but Wyatt brushed him to one side. Minutes later the Earps and Holliday had left Tombstone forever. *Courtesy Arizona Historical Society*

The legend makers and Wyatt Earp claimed that Wyatt killed Johnny Ringo in a gun battle. Ringo committed suicide under this tree in July 1882 in Turkey Creek Canyon. His gun, with one shot fired, was found nearby. *The James D. Horan Collection*

On March 27 the *Epitaph* startled its readers with an account of "one of the most desperate fights that ever took place on Arizona soil" between the Earps and a band of cowboys headed by Curly Bill at Burleigh Springs, eight miles south of Tombstone.

After a fierce gun battle the cowboys were driven off, their leader shot out of the saddle. The body was identified as that of Curly Bill, "the man who had killed Marshal White on the streets of Tombstone, one year ago September."

Nine days later the *Epitaph* sheepishly published what it called "the second version" of the battle of Burleigh Springs. Two ranchers searching for strayed mules "west of Drew's Ranch below Contention" reported they came upon four cowboys who told them they had been camped by a spring when they saw Wyatt Earp and his riders approaching. The quartet told the ranchers, "not knowing how they stood in with them [the Earps] they thought they would give them a shot just for luck so they blazed away and shot off the pommel of Wyatt Earp's saddle and killed the horse Texas Jack [Johnson] was riding. They said that not one of the party charged upon them but Wyatt, the balance all running away. Wyatt dismounted and fired his gun at them without effect. Texas Jack jumped up behind one of the other boys à la Mexicana, as off they went as rapidly as they could."[32]

The *Nugget* scoffed at the *Epitaph's* account and offered $1,000 to anyone who could prove that Curly Bill was dead. The *Epitaph* angrily denounced the *Nugget* for offering the reward when it didn't pay its employees and offered $2,000 if Curly Bill "WILL PRESENT HIMSELF, thereby proving he is alive. . . . We will donate $2,000 to any DESERVING CHARITY he may mention."

The two papers battled each other in print, then were joined by a San Francisco daily which published a satirical account of how the Oakland Light Cavalry was "immediately put under arms" because its citizens had heard the Earp posse was ready to invade the city searching for Curly Bill and his band of desperate outlaws. "Lint, bandages and cots for the wounded" were prepared in the streets of Oakland, the deadpan account went on, but finally it was discovered that the advancing riders were "the Earl Brothers on their way to the city" and the alert was canceled.

With the Earps gone, John Clum decided he had had enough of frontier publishing and sold the *Epitaph*. In May 1882 he turned over his two-year-old newspaper to the publisher of the *Yuma Free Press*, who stated in an editorial the

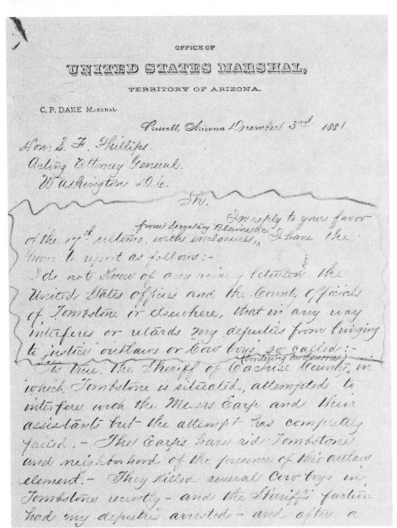

Prescott, Arizona December 3rd 1881.

Hon: S. F. Phillips.
Acting Attorney General.
Washington D.C.

Sir.

In reply to your favor of the 19th ultimo, from Secretary Blaine etc. with enclosures, I have the honor to report as follows:—

I do not know of any thing between the United States officers and the County officials of Tombstone or elsewhere, that in any way interfere or retards my deputies from bringing to justice outlaws or Cow boys so called:—

It is true, the Sheriff of Cochise County, in which Tombstone is situated, attempted to interfere with the Messrs Earp and their assistants but the attempt has completely failed.—The Earps have rid Tombstone and neighborhood of the presence of this outlaw element.—They killed several Cow boys in Tombstone recently—and the Sheriff's faction had my deputies arrested—and after a

Letter of United States Marshal C. P. Dake to the United States attorney general in Washington, praising the Earps for eliminating the "cowboy element" from the Arizona Territory. Dake was not only trying to save his job but was lying to Washington. The Earps left behind such a lawless county that President Chester A. Arthur threatened to send troops into the Arizona Territory by May 15, 1882, unless the territorial lawmen brought peace to their communities. *Courtesy National Archives*

John Heith, a thirty-two-year-old Texas bad man, lynched by Tombstone vigilantes in 1884. *The James D. Horan Collection*

following day that his new policy would be, "Facts stated as they exist, and not tortured into sensational romances." A short time later Clum was also removed as Tombstone's postmaster.[33]

After they left Arizona, Wyatt, Warren, and Doc said good-bye to the other riders and rode to Colorado. There, for the first time in their violence-tested friendship, Wyatt and Doc quarreled. Later Holliday would dismiss the cause as a minor "misunderstanding" but neither he nor Earp ever revealed why they separated—the Earps going on to Gunnison and Doc to Pueblo.[34]

After the Battle of the O. K. Corral

Another myth surrounding the Earps that refuses to be put to rest has them riding out of Tombstone, bloody but unbowed cavaliers who had finally restored

By the President of the United States of America.
A Proclamation.

Whereas it is provided in the laws of the United States that "whenever, by reason of unlawful obstructions, combinations, or assemblages of persons, or rebellion against the authority of the government of the United States, it shall become impracticable, in the judgment of the President, to enforce by the ordinary course of judicial proceedings, the laws of the United States within any State or Territory, it shall be lawful for the President to call forth the militia of any or all the States, and to employ such parts of the land and naval forces of the United States as he may deem necessary to enforce the faithful execution of the laws of the United States, or to suppress such rebellion, in whatever State or Territory thereof the laws of the United States may be forcibly opposed, or the execution thereof forcibly obstructed";

And whereas it has been made to appear satisfactorily to me, by information received from the Governor of the Territory of Arizona and from the General of the Army of the United States, and other reliable sources, that in consequence of unlawful combinations of evil disposed persons who are banded together to oppose and obstruct the execution of the laws, it has become impracticable to enforce, by the ordinary course of judicial proceedings, the laws of the United States within that Territory, and that the laws of the United States have been therein forcibly opposed and the execution thereof forcibly resisted;

And whereas the laws of the United States require that whenever it may be necessary, in the judgment of the President, to use the military forces for the purpose of enforcing the faithful execution of the laws of the United States, he shall forthwith, by proclamation, command such insurgents to disperse and retire peaceably to their respective abodes, within a limited time;

Now, therefore, I, Chester A. Arthur, President of the United States, do hereby admonish all good citizens of the United States, and especially of the Territory of Arizona, against aiding, countenancing, abetting, or taking part in any such unlawful proceedings, and I do hereby warn all persons engaged in or connected with said obstruction of the laws, to disperse and retire peaceably to their respective abodes on or before noon of the fifteenth day of May.

In witness whereof I have hereunto set my hand and caused the seal of the United States to be affixed.

Done at the city of Washington this third day of May, in the year of our Lord eighteen hundred and eighty-two, and of the Independence of the United States the one hundred and sixth.

Chester A. Arthur.

By the President,
Fred.k T. Frelinghuysen
Secretary of State.

Seal.

Proclamation of President Arthur threatening to send troops into the Arizona Territory. *The James D. Horan Collection* law and order and dignity to a grateful community long ruled by the forces of evil.

Letters found in the National Archives, written by President Chester Arthur; Secretary of the Interior S. J. Kirkwood; Acting Territorial Governor John Gosper; and United States Marshal Crawley P. Dake, a supporter of the Earps, completely shatters this myth.[35]

Dake, surely the most naive of frontier lawmen, started the flow of letters shortly after the O. K. Corral fight, when he wrote to Acting Governor Gosper asking *his* opinion of what had caused the violence in Tombstone!

Gosper's reply was a shrewd analysis of what had eroded the moral fibers of the mining town. He told Dake it was not only the "cowboys" who had betrayed their community but "all men of every shade of character" who had been so busy accumulating wealth, power, and position that they allowed the lawless to take over. The *Epitaph* and the *Nugget* were also scored in Gosper's cold and bitter reply. Both newspapers, he wrote Dake, had failed in their traditional duty as municipal watchdogs. Instead of presenting objective news they had become partisan organs willing to parrot the views of those political leaders who could guarantee the county's official advertising.

Behan and the Earps were also denounced by Gosper; in their fierce rivalry for the lucrative sheriff's office, they'd permitted a breakdown in law and order with their fellow citizens as the victims.

Gosper suggested that whoever was elected governor—and this was s hint of what he would do if elected—should remove Behan from office and force Dake to shake up his own administration by appointing new deputies.

But Gosper had his own flaws. His letter to Kirkwood is startling, not for his candid condemnation of his fellow citizens and their "half-heathenish mode of thinking and acting," but for his disclosure to a member of the presidential cabinet that he had visited Tombstone a month before the corral fight and had "suggested" and "encouraged" the formation of a vigilante committee. He also revealed to Kirkwood that he had hired a private detective to ascertain what was going on in the violent mining camp.

One wonders why Gosper did not order the higher territorial courts to review Magistrate Spicer's obviously prejudiced decision. He also failed to use a powerful legal weapon at his disposal. He could have ordered the Pima County Grand Jury to begin an immediate investigation of the street fight, the corrupt conditions existing in both Tombstone and the county, the raging town lot fraud, and what he called the "class who carries water on both shoulders"—the ranchers who denounced the "cowboys" but secretly bought and then resold their stolen cattle. From his statements, the county prosecutor appeared eager to conduct such a probe but had been prevented by politicians.

Gosper took none of these measures. Instead, he blatantly sought Kirkwood's favor, using the terrifying conditions in Tombstone to get the presidential appointment as the territorial governor.

Gosper also repeated the myth of a howling band of outlaws swooping down and sacking Tombstone, such as Quantrill did to Lawrence. But Quantrill had several hundred riders. Such a band existed only in the imagination of the Earps and the *Epitaph*. There were rustlers in Sulphur Valley but even Gosper admitted there were no more than twenty-five to fifty. Did he honestly believe such a number could have "raided" the hard-bitten mining camp? Also the rustlers were only loosely organized, mostly small groups who rode into Mexico. There was no charismatic leader or common cause to bring them together and follow him on such a foolhardy mission. The rustlers of Sulphur Valley were simply thieves, with none of the hard-riding bravado that was found in the Wild Bunch, then terrorizing Wyoming, Utah, and Nevada. In Washington, Secretary Kirkwood, shocked by Gosper's disclosures and Dake's irresponsibility in not taking action to prevent Tombstone's volatile conditions from exploding into tragedy, sent a letter to President Arthur suggesting that troops be sent immediately into Arizona Territory to help the civil authorities enforce the law. Kirkwood pointed out to the president what Dake, Gosper, and the "good people" of the county had ignored for so many years: the secret partnership between the rustlers and the ranchers had gradually eroded the relationship between Mexico and the United States.

This collection of official letters gives more of an insight to what really happened in Tombstone and why, in those violent days, than all the romantic fakery about the Earps which has been handed down from generation to generation of gullible readers.

The Letters of United States Marshal Dake, Secretary of the Interior Kirkwood, Acting Territorial Governor Gosper and the Proclamation of President Chester A. Arthur*

OFFICE OF THE EXECUTIVE,
Prescott, A. T., Nov. 28, 1881

Hon. C. P. Dake,
United States Marshal:

Dear Sir:

In your communication of this date asking me to give you my opinion of the causes of the frequent disturbances of the public peace at Tombstone and vicinity in this Territory, with such suggestions as might occur to me looking to a remedy for the unfortunate occurrences, based upon facts obtained by me on my recent visit to that section, permit me to say that the underlying cause of all the disturbances of the peace, and the taking of property unlawfully, is the fact that all men of every shade of character in that new and rapidly developed section of mineral wealth, in their mad career after money, have grossly neglected local self government, until the more lazy and lawless elements of society have undertaken to prey upon the more industrious and honorable classes for their subsistence and gains.

The civil officers of the County of Cochise, and city of Tombstone, partaking of the general restless spirit of rapid accumulation of money and property, is another cause of public disturbances, inasmuch as they have seen to "wink at crime" and to have neglected a prompt discharge of duty for the hope and sake of gain. The thoroughly abandoned class of men called highway robbers and cattle thieves called

*From the James D. Horan Collection.

"cowboys" cunningly taking advantage of the favorable state of affairs for themselves, have robbed from the wealthier class of citizens, and when apprehended and detected by the officers of the law, have in many cases no doubt *purchased** their liberty or have paid well to be left unmolested.

The peaceful and law abiding citizens of the section of the Territory are very generally of the opinion that the officers of the law are often themselves in league with the "cowboy" element to obtain legal gain.

Another cause of the troubles is the fact that the present sheriff of Cochise County and one of the Earp brothers, the latter being in some manner connected with the police force for the city of Tombstone, are candidates or aspirants for the sheriffship at the polls another season. The rivalry between them, having extended into a strife to secure influence and aid from all quarters, has led them and the particular friends of each to sins of commission and omission greatly at the cost of peace and property.

The two newspapers published in Tombstone are also censurable for the course they have pursued in relation to public and private matters. For the strife and jealousies between the sheriff and his deputies of the county and the Earp brothers of the city, the two papers have taken sides very largely through selfish motives of gain, the county printing being given to one of the papers for its hearty support and the city patronage to the other for its support.

Still another cause of the general lawlessness prevailing in that section of our territory is the fact that many of the citizens are dealing dishonestly, with one hand secretly behind them handling the stolen property of the "cowboys" while with the other hand openly before them they are disposing of the stolen property [mostly beef cattle] to honest citizens, afterwards dividing with the regular thieves. This class of criminals is the most difficult to reach and bring to justice. Hotels, saloons, restaurants, etc., where the rough "cowboy" element spend their money freely, are both weak and wicked in their sympathy for the protection of this lawless class.

From my last visit to Tombstone and vicinity, since the killing of the McLowery [McLaury] and Clanta [Clanton] on the streets of Tombstone by the Earps, I gathered the above and many other facts and beliefs.

Now as to the remedy to be applied. I would suggest that the Department of Justice, which you are serving, be requested to furnish you with funds sufficient to enable you to employ a man of well known courage and character, of cool, sound judgment, who, with a suitable posse of men, can first fully apprehend the true nature of the situation, and then with proper discretion and courage go forward with a firm and steady hand, bringing as fast as possible the leading spirits of this lawless class to severe and speedy punishment.

It might be a wise and successful measure for the executive of the Territory to cause the removal from office of the sheriff, while yourself, as United States marshal, remove your deputies to the end that each man possessing the confidence of the public, and who would work in harmony with each other in enforcing the law and keeping the peace, could be appointed to succeed them. At present, however, I do not think it would be prudent for me as acting governor, to resort to measures of that character. Simply as acting governor, I am not assured the time it would require to inaugurate and carry through the extreme or radical measures the situation certainly requires.

Hoping the knowledge and suggestions given above may become available to you

*Author's italics throughout.

in the matter of bringing about a better state of affairs, and pledging you all the aid and support possible to be given by this department,

I am most respectfully your obedient servant,

John J. Gosper,
Acting Governor

OFFICE OF THE EXECUTIVE,
Prescott, Arizona, November 29, 1881

Hon. S. J. Kirkwood,
Secretary of the Interior, Washington, D.C.:

Sir:

I am this day in receipt of your favor of November 21st instant, in which you refer to my letter to the Secretary of State, November 30, 1881 on the subject of lawlessness in the southeastern part of this Territory, and in which you ask several certain questions, which I am pleased to answer in the order in which they are asked, to the best of my ability.

"In what part of the Territory does this lawlessness prevail?"

In all parts to a greater or less degree, but especially in the county of Cochise, which forms the extreme south east part of the Territory, bordering for many miles on the line between Arizona and Mexico on the south, and New Mexico on the east. It is in this county that the "cowboy" element is concentrated because of the ease of escape into either Mexico or New Mexico.

2nd. "Do cowboys consist wholly of whites?"

They do not. A few Mexicans are mixed with them; but the Mexican element is very much in the minority. The American whites fully direct and control on the American side of the line. A bitter hatred exists between the "cowboys" and the Mexicans generally. Bands of cowboys have been severely punished now and then, while on the Mexican side of the line, cattle stealing and a spirit of revenge of one race against the other, seems to exist.

3d. No Indians are engaged in any manner to the particular troubles herein alluded to.

They, the Indians, are troublesome only when roaming at large, or on their way through settlements from their reservations to their "happy hunting grounds."

4th. My estimate of the whole number of "cowboys" [skilled cattle thieves and highway robbers] working together in the County of Cochise, is about 25 to 50. The estimate of the same class made to me by the sheriff when I was there is about 15 to 25. Some of the observing and easily frightened citizens of the county placed the number at a 100 or more. I am speaking of the *utterly abandoned class* now. There is a class, however, much larger in number than the above, of the "good Lord and good devil" kind who "carry water on both shoulders," perhaps as difficult to handle as the *extreme* criminal class. Please note a fuller description of the latter class in a copy of a letter addressed today to Marshal Dake which accompanies this.

5th. Can the Governor suspend or remove sheriffs?

He cannot in counties where they are elected by the citizens of their respective counties. In counties where they are appointed by the governor they can be removed after a hearing and for cause. The County of Cochise was organized by legislative enactment during the past winter, and the principal county officers were appointed by the Governor to serve until regular election which will be held in one year—or a little less—from this time. The sheriff of the said county was appointed by the governor.

In response in part to your kind request for me to make such suggestions I might deem proper, permit me to call your attention to a copy of a letter I wrote to United States

Marshal Dake, herewith enclosed, relating to the Tombstone and Cochise Counties troubles.

As therein suggested much aid can be rendered on the part of the general government through the Department of Justice. In a case of an extreme emergency, of course, we should look for aid and relief through the powers of the United States Army. At the time of the killing of three men (on account of difficulties existing between some of the civil officers and the rough element) on the streets of Tombstone, it was greatly feared the city would be raided, sacked and destroyed by the cowboy element, and telegrams from the mayor and others were sent to me, *urgently requesting troops.*

The general commanding the military department was also telegraphed to for aid. My knowledge of the existence in Tombstone of a *large and carefully* organized *"committee of safety"* on the part of the most *wealthy* and *responsible* business men thereof, whom I knew would be able to protect, generally, life and property, led me to send telegrams allaying unnecessary alarm.

With a view to declaring martial law in that County, if the extremity of the case should require it, I proceeded at once to Tombstone and used my best influence to bring about a more tranquil feeling, finding, as I did, the situation more wisely solvable by milder means. I found the "committee of safety," very ready and willing to fly instantly to the aid of civil officers, well armed to act as a *posse comitatus* to protect and keep the peace.

At the moment the unexpected and alarming discharge of firearms took place in the city above alluded to, at the sound of a *"signal whistle"* nearly a hundred men sprang into the streets from their offices and stores, *fully armed* and determined to meet and conquer any band of robbers and cowboys bent on terrorizing and raiding the town, as had been done in many other places in that county. Finding no occasion for action, they as quickly mysteriously disappeared, each to his quiet avocation.

When the Earps were arrested and imprisoned, it was greatly feared the cowboys would overpower the sheriff and keeper and kill them; therefore and for further reason that the sheriff and the Earps were not on harmonious terms, a committee of a few men of the general committee of safety stood guard, day and night, around the jail. I am speaking and shall speak at length of this committee of safety because of the fact it will give yourself and other officers of the general government charged with enforcing the law, a sense of relief in the light of one efficacious means of an ultimate settlement of this vexed question.

On my first visit to Tombstone, September last, on account of the cowboy trouble, finding no immediate assurances of full safety to life and property from the civil authorities, and finding the law-abiding citizens uneasy and distressed, I *suggested* and *encouraged* the organizing of this said committee, in a *secret manner*, not for the purpose of taking the law into their own hands, but for the purpose of protecting their lives and property from destruction by the murderers and robbers entering in that section. In connection with a trusted member of that committee, for a time I employed a *private detective* to operate in that section to ascertain facts no other way obtainable.

Since the organization of this committee—the fact of the organization after a while leaking out—a number of the worst cowboys have left the vicinity fearing they might be "lynched" or "stretched up by the neck" without judge or jury.

Since the better class of the citizens of Tombstone are not giving more attention to the civil affairs, a more hopeful aspect presents itself. However, the situation is *very far from being satisfactory.*

It will take *time* and *severe* measures to bring about a reign of peace and a quiet sense of security in that section of the Territory. I am strongly of the opinion there should be a change of civil officers in that county.

Two important suggestions touching upon the means of enforcing the law and keeping the peace in the Territory, and I will close this somewhat lengthy communication. Congress should by all means repeal the *posse comitatus* act prohibiting the military from aiding and making arrests or pursuing fugitives from justice, *especially* as far as this Territory is concerned, along the borders of Mexico.

If the military could legally be put in pursuit of these bands of outlaws terrorizing our peaceful citizens in isolated places and elsewhere, they would be soon broken up and compelled to follow the pursuit of peace or be brought to punishment. The second suggestion I have to make should be direct to the President through yourself.

The Federal officers appointed by the President to serve the *country at this time and in this Territory*—more especially the *governor and the United States Marshal*—should be appointed with a *special* view to the peculiar class of duties devolving upon them. They should be *men of experience in public affairs, resolute* and *active* in their temperaments.

This last suggestion is made in the face of the fact that my friends at this time are pressing my name for the governorship, and modesty might have directed me to have omitted making it, but I have no *selfish* motive whatever in so doing. I shall take this liberty of addressing you pointedly upon that subject by the next mail. That is, the subject of the governorship.

In my opinion the law of the Territory is broad enough to encompass the question of keeping the peace if a *sufficient* number of general and local officers can be appointed and elected with *character* and *courage* sufficient to enable them to go forward in a *prompt* and *faithful* discharge of duty.

The next Territorial legislature, meeting one year and one month from this time, should be called upon to change the old law in some respects and enact new laws touching upon the question of *city* and *county* police. The people of this Territory are of the true Yankee type, active and aggressive, and generally without sufficient regard for public morals, with their minds preoccupied with matters almost exclusively private.

The signs of the times, however, are more hopeful for a better public opinion. Missionaries and railroads are sowing the seeds of a better civilization for the citizens of this Territory, and with improved home-rule, backed and managed by the general government, we shall soon emerge from our half-heathenish mode of thinking and acting. As a citizen of the Territory fully appreciating the earnest interest you are taking in our affairs,

I am, most respectfully, your obedient servant,

John Gosper,
Acting Governor

OFFICE OF THE EXECUTIVE
Prescott, Arizona, December 19, 1881

Hon. S. J. Kirkwood,
Secretary of the Interior, Washington, D.C.

Dear Sir:

As an additional reason to urge upon Congress the propriety of repealing the *posse comitatus* act relating to the use of the United States Army in the direction of aiding the civil authorities in keeping the peace, permit me to call your attention to the enclosed clippings taken from the *Tucson Citizen* of issue, the 16th instant.

Ten companies of United States Cavalry are in camp within a brief distance of Tombstone, the center of those outrages upon public peace and frequent attempts to take the lives of peaceful citizens, and yet their arms are paralyzed.

If members of Congress, even the extreme Democrats who procured the passage of the act, could be made to even in part comprehend the character of the unfortunate situation in the southeastern part of this Territory, they would, without any hesitancy, vote to repeal the act in question, so far at least as it relates to the Territory.

The most prompt and certain means of ridding the Territory of this reckless and utterly abandoned class, is to cause the cavalry branch of the United States Army to follow them to the bitter end.

The Territory of New Mexico should be included within the repeal of the act, inasmuch as the cowboy element could very easily cross the line from Arizona into New Mexico and thus evade the troops.

As soon as I can with propriety, be permitted to visit Washington, I shall do so and shall feel duty bound—whether in or out of office—to appeal to individual members of Congress to give the Territory relief from the reckless rule now cursing the peace and liberty of otherwise favored portions of the Territory.

Trusting that you will earnestly urge upon Congress the passage of some law of relief to our crime-burdened people,

I am, most respectfully,

John Gosper,
Acting Governor

DEPARTMENT OF THE INTERIOR,
Washington, January 20, 1882

Sir:

I have the honor to enclose copies of two communications from the Acting Governor of Arizona concerning the disturbances in the southeastern portion of that Territory, and to suggest that same be referred to Congress for consideration in connection with the recommendation contained in your annual message that the law be so amended as to permit the use of the military to assist the civil Territorial authorities in enforcing the laws. The repression of lawlessness in Arizona and New Mexico is important as bearing not only upon the prosperity of these Territories, but upon the preservation of peace between the United States and Mexico, as the operations of the lawless bands referred to, extend into Mexico.

It appears from the letters of the Acting Governor, that a difficulty in the way of repressing the lawlessness arises from the fact that the sheriffs are intimidated, or that from personal motives they desire to curry favor with the disorderly element of society. It is therefore suggested whether it would not be expedient and proper that authority should be conferred by law upon the governor of any Territory to remove or suspend a sheriff for neglect of duty and to appoint a person in his place.

Very Respectfully,

S. J. Kirkwood,
Secretary

THE PRESIDENT
TO THE SENATE AND HOUSE OF REPRESENTATIVES:

I transmit herewith a letter from the Secretary of the Interior, with accompanying papers, relative to the lawlessness which prevails in parts of Arizona, and [in] connection therewith call attention to that portion of my message of the 6th of December last, in which suggestions were made as to legislation which seems to be required to enable the general government to assist the local authorities of the Territory in restoring and maintaining order.

Chester A. Arthur

EXECUTIVE MANSION
February 2, 1882

The struggle to bring law and order to Tombstone and Cochise County continued through that winter and spring. Finally, on May 3, 1882, President Chester A. Arthur threatened to declare martial law within two weeks unless the outlaw bands were disbanded and the vigilantes hung up their guns. More effective than a presidential threat was the newly elected sheriff, John Slaughter, a wealthy rancher, former Texas Ranger, and Indian fighter. After he had served two terms the county was regarded as one of the most peaceful in the territory—and without John Gosper's "committee of safety."

John Slaughter, the quiet-spoken rancher who cleaned up Tombstone and Cochise County after the Earps had left. *The James D. Horan Collection*

Doc Holliday Bucks the Tiger for the Last Time

After Wyatt and Warren Earp had left him to go to Gunnison, Doc Holliday slipped easily into the gambling fraternity of Pueblo, a booming Colorado coal and iron town. He got the gambling concession at the Cominque Club and soon became a fixture in the gaming room, a dignified man with gray-streaked ash blond hair and piercing blue eyes who idly riffled the cards as he waited for a gambler. Doc was beginning to cough more, the spotlessly clean linen handkerchief he pressed against his lips came away with flecks of blood.

Larimar Street, Denver, in Doc Holliday's time. The frail but fast-shooting dentist was arrested in Denver in 1882 by a self-styled "deputy" who was later discovered to be an extortionist. This photograph is attributed to William Jackson, the frontier photographer. *The James D. Horan Collection*

Deadwood, South Dakota, the mining camp where the faro banks set no limit in Wyatt Earp's time. This print was made from the original glass plate. *The James D. Horan Collection*

Deadwood mining scene.
The James D. Horan Collection

Most of the gamblers, whores, bartenders, saloon owners, and police knew the part Doc had played in the O. K. Corral "street fight" and he became something of a celebrity in Pueblo.

On the afternoon of May 16, 1882, Holliday and two gamblers attended the races at Denver's Fair Grounds. He was walking down a street when suddenly he heard footsteps behind him. Before he could whirl about, two six-shooters pressed in his back and a voice gleefully ordered: "Throw up your hands!"

Holliday coolly raised his hands. "Who are you?" he asked.

The man behind him hooted triumphantly: "Doc Holliday, I have you now!"

When Deputy Charlie Linton appeared, Doc's captor identified himself as Perry Mallan, "a deputy sheriff from Los Angeles."

Linton hurried both men to Sheriff Spangler's office, where Mallan charged Doc with the murders of Stilwell, Clanton, Curly Bill, and several others.

Holliday ignored Mallan and told Linton, "I can prove this man is not a sheriff and in fact no officer in Cochise County. I can show you his reason for bringing me here—"

Linton interrupted him. "This is no place to make a statement."

Meanwhile Mallan kept shouting that Holliday, "this cold-blooded coward, killed my partner," and waving his two six-shooters. There was a small telephone exchange in Pueblo, and Linton was trying to raise the operator so he could order a hack to take all of them to the county jail. He finally grew weary of Mallan waving his guns about and ordered him to put the weapons back in their holsters or he would take them away.

While Doc looked on, amused, Linton and Mallan began a shouting match over Mallan's right to wave his guns. Finally, Mallan grudgingly holstered his weapons while Linton continued to ring for Pueblo's telephone operator. When

Denver's nightlife as Doc Holliday knew it. Various advertisements from Denver's "Red Book."
Courtesy Fred M. Mazzulla

In one ad Ella Wellington promises her customers, "everything first class."
Courtesy Fred M. Mazzulla

the hack finally arrived Linton, with Doc between him and Mallan, walked out to the street.

Holliday told a reporter he hoped his good friend "Bob" (Bat) Masterson, then sheriff of Trinidad, Colorado, would be told of his arrest.

The reporter raced after the trio in another hack and spoke to Doc as he was being jailed. Again Holliday mentioned Masterson's name; he repeated that Mallan was not a law officer, at least not from Cochise County, Arizona.

Later the reporter interviewed Mallan, who claimed Doc had killed his partner, Harry White, seven years before and that he had been following him for years "out of revenge." The reporter never asked Mallan why he had failed to catch up with Doc in Tombstone.[36]

The following day Bat Masterson appeared in Pueblo with a writ of habeas corpus. He told a reporter for the *Pueblo Chieftain* that Doc was "not as black as he is painted, that he is a United States officer and that he is simply being persecuted and run down in order that he may be placed in the power of the cowboys of Arizona, who hate him and desire his death."

After Doc was released by the writ, he assured the *Chieftain*'s reporter "he had nothing to fear from that quarter [Arizona], as he had received full pardon from the governor for his bloody work in consideration for the effective work he had rendered the authorities."[37]   It was evident Doc and Masterson were pulling the long bow but the reporters for the Denver and Pueblo papers solemnly used all they were told.

Gradually, the Pueblo police discovered that Doc's charges against Mallan were correct; he was simply a bounty hunter. The *Chieftain* identified him as a former confidence man who earlier had tried to sell Doc the tale that Jack Stilwell, the famous scout and Frank's brother, was in town waiting for the chance to kill him. Doc asked him to point out Stilwell but Mallan insisted he would also be killed.

Holliday knew it was a crude extortion plot but rather than go to the police "and have trouble," he left for Denver hoping to shake off Mallan, who instead followed him there and made the "arrest."

Now Mallan found himself in trouble. A number of Denver businessmen identified him as a crook from Akron, Ohio, who had swindled them in fraudulent business deals. The *Chieftain* described him as a "small man with reddish face and beard, small ferrety eyes and not an inviting cast of features. He is much the inferior of Holliday in every particular, in appearance at least."

Holliday, the *Chieftain* boasted, was a man of "considerable culture."[38]

Meanwhile, Sheriff Spangler had wired to Sheriff Behan in Tombstone that he had both Doc and the Earps in custody. Why he added the Earps, who were still in Gunnison, is a mystery.

There was one last touch of irony in this strange series of events. Arizona's Governor Tritle assigned Pima County's Sheriff Bob Paul to go to Colorado and collect the prisoners. Paul was the shotgun messenger who had fired at the outlaws and saved the Tombstone stage as it raced down the frozen road—in the robbery which eventually led to the famous "street fight" and the decline of the Earps in Arizona.

While Paul rode to Prescott to get the governor's official order, Masterson

256

"DOC" HOLLIDAY,

An Alleged Desperado, Well Known, Here, Captured in Denver.

Belief the Prisoner is Being Persecuted and Greatly Sinned Against.

Yesterday the news came to this city of the arrest of John H. Holliday, better known as "Doc," who was taken on the charge of being a desperado and a "hard man" generally. The arrest was made by one Perry Mallen, who claimed to be a United States officer, and who made the arrest by taking "Doc" unawares, holding two revolvers and causing him to hold up his hands. Mullen was accompanied by Deputy Sheriff Charlie Linton, and the arrest was made at half-past nine o'clock on one of the principal streets. Shortly after the arrest was made, Bat Masterson, the marshal of Trinidad, then in Denver, heard of the affair, and soon secured a writ of habeas corpus, upon which the prisoner was released, but still placed under surveillance, until he could be tried by Judge Elliott some time yesterday afternoon. Masterson, who is generally known as "the man who smiles," and whose words are weighty in official circles, says Holliday is not so black as painted, that he is a United States officer, and that he is simply being persecuted and run down in order that he may be placed in the power of the cowboys of Arizona, who hate him and desire his death. Holliday was a member of the corps, in fact, a leader, and took an active part in fighting the cow-boys last fall, when the latter made their memorial raid upon Tucson and Tombstone, where a large number of men were killed.

The arrest has great local interest because the prisoner and his captor spent considerable time in this city before they went to Denver, and both became quite well known.

passed through this city nearly two weeks ago, remaining here one or two days, and it is supposed that they are now in Gunnison City, toward which place they were then headed. Some few days after the brothers had departed, "Doc" Holliday appeared in the city, and remained here until last Sunday, when he departed for Denver. He made no effort to conceal his identity, and when questioned as to his doings in Arizona, said he had nothing to fear from that quarter, as he had received full pardon from the governor for his bloody work, in consideration of the effective services he had rendered the authorities. In conversation here he said that he had never killed any one, except in protecting himself, and that all he asked was to be let alone; he had left Arizona for the single purpose of being at peace with every one around him, and he hoped his enemies would allow him that privilege.

please. His home is in Ogden, Utah.

"Doc" Halliday is a man of light weight, rather tall, smoothly shaven, and is always well dressed. Streaks of gray can be seen in his hair, which grows from a head a phrenologist would delight in examining. His eyes are blue, large, sharp and piercing. He is not over thirty five years of age, and as straight as an arrow. He gained his title of "Doc" in a legitimate manner, as he once practiced medicine, in Los Angeles, California notably. He is well educated, and his conversation shows him to be a man of considerable culture. That he has killed a number of men in the southern territories, and that he is regarded as a hard, dangerous man there is no disputing, but his friends claim that extenuating circumstances existed in every case of murder with which he is charged. If he had been taken by the proper officials, his arrest might be hailed with delight by a great many who now look upon it as an outrage, because they believe Mallen is an imposter, and that he made the arrest simply to gain a little blood money and turn his prisoner over to the "tender mercies" of his enemies. The interference of the marshal of Trinidad in Holliday's favor, and his assertion that the man is not the fiend he is represented, would certainly indicate that he is being persecuted, and that the captor is no better, if as good, as his prisoner.

The arrest of Doc Holliday as reported in the *Pueblo Chieftain*, May 17, 1882. *The James D. Horan Collection*

worked furiously to keep Doc in the jurisdiction of Colorado. Bat, who had "excellent connections," as one paper reported, arranged for Doc to be charged with robbing a man of $300 in a confidence game. It was a fraudulent charge but Doc was arraigned and held in jail. While Bat raised the bail, Holliday charmed the press with interviews and blood and thunder stories of his past.

The reporter for the *Denver Republican* noted that Doc's hands were "small and soft like a woman's but the work they have done is anything but womanly. . . . The slender forefinger which has dealt the cards has dealt death to many a rustler with equal skill and quickness and the slender wrist has proved its muscles of steel in many a deadly encounter."

Doc spun his tales without a smile and told the reporter as he sadly gazed out into the rain, that if he was returned to Arizona, "that will be the end of Holliday. . . . We hunted the rustlers and they all hate us. Johnny Behan, Sheriff of Cochise County, is one of the gang and a deadly enemy of mine, who would give any money to have me killed."

In his interview with the *Republican* Doc also revealed that he had a "little misunderstanding with the Earps before they had departed for Gunnison but it didn't amount to much and they would do all they could to help me."

When Sheriff Bob Paul arrived in Colorado he was infuriated to find that the Earps were not in custody. His official orders had to be returned to Arizona to be revised. This gave Masterson more time. On May 23, the *Pueblo Chieftain* proudly announced that Mallan had confessed he was a fraud. Three days later Colorado's Governor Frederick W. Pitkin received Arizona's request to return Holliday. Pitkin kept delaying his decision while Bob Paul fumed with impatience.[39]

Meanwhile, Masterson made sure Doc was arraigned again and again for the fake robbery charged. Finally Doc was released in $300 bail but faithfully—almost eagerly—appeared each time in court to humbly request a postponement. Finally Arizona gave up and Bob Paul returned to Pima County and the charges eventually were dropped. Only then did the Pueblo court dismiss the fake robbery case.

In June 1883 Wyatt briefly returned to Dodge City to join Bat Masterson, Mysterious Dave Mathers, and Neil Brown to help Luke Short, part owner of the Long Branch saloon, when Ford County Prosecutor Mike Sutton tried to drive the gamblers from the now very calm prairie town.

Sutton had pushed through an ordinance which prohibited gambling within the city's limits. The ordinance was not strictly enforced and Short told his friends he was being discriminated against by the police and by Sutton.

When the band of gunmen appeared, the frightened city officials, who still heard echoes of the gunfire in Dodge when the Texas cowboys rode in after a drive, immediately telegraphed Colonel Thomas Moonlight, the adjutant general of Kansas. Moonlight arrived and acted as chairman of a "peace commission" for several days. Bat, Wyatt, and the others told Colonel Moonlight they intended to remain as long as Sutton and the police tried to deprive Luke Short of his rights as a citizen of Dodge.

Moonlight decided that Short had been wronged and as the *Ford County Globe* announced, "the gambling gentry smiles and are again happy, since they are allowed to spread their layouts again. All games were in full blast early yesterday morning."[40]

The members of the "Dodge City peace commission" solemnly had their picture taken for posterity, shook hands, and disbanded. Meanwhile, Doc Holliday continued to live in Colorado, drifting from town to town. He knew he

The "Dodge City Peace Commission," 1883. *Back row, left to right:* W. H. Harris, Luke Short, Bat Masterson. *Front row, left to right:* Charlie Bassett, Wyatt Earp, W. F. McLain, and Neil Brown. In some photographs of the "commission," William (Billy) Petillon, a reporter for the *Dodge City Democrat,* is standing next to Masterson. *The James D. Horan Civil War and Western Americana Collection*

was dying from tuberculosis. The racking coughs were getting worse, the blood was thicker on his handkerchiefs. When he took over the faro bank in Leadville's Monarch saloon, there were plenty of customers eager to boast they had bucked the famous Doc Holliday.

Allie Earp, who nursed her wounded husband Virgil back to health, told Frank Waters that Wyatt saw Doc in the gambler's last days. It is unfortunate there was no one to record this strange meeting of two men who had shared so many dangerous hours. Did they talk of the old days, of Tombstone when they first saw that raw dusty town in 1879? Of the feud with Johnny Behan? The bloody seconds of the O. K. Corral "street fight," now part of frontier history? Or did they mostly stare out at the darkness of Denver, Pueblo, or Leadville, no words needed to be spoken as they sipped the raw whiskey.

In August 1884 there was one last act of violence. Holliday shot Billy Allen, the Monarch's bartender, in a dispute over a $5 loan. Doc knew from his marksmanship he was slipping—it took two shots to bring Allen down. And the bartender suffered only a flesh wound in the upper arm.

Holliday surrendered his single action .45 to a Captain Bradbury with a request that he not let anyone shoot him in the back.[41]

The following March Holliday went on trial for shooting Allen. After two days of testimony Doc was acquitted, but the Leadville sheriff gently suggested to Holliday he had worn out his welcome in Leadville. That night Doc was escorted to the stage station and left for Colorado Springs. He next appeared in Denver running the faro game at the Metropolitan. After another restless year of wandering, he returned to Leadville, where he won some money at the tables.

In the spring of 1887 he was very frail, his body shaken by constant coughing spells. Someone told him the hot baths at Glenwood Springs were beneficial for TB patients, so one day in May 1887 Doc slowly descended from the stage in front of the Glenwood Springs Hotel and registered.

The series of hot bath treatments only aggravated his condition. A local doctor told him he had advanced tuberculosis and would die within a few months. He finally became bedridden, then delirious for two weeks, and finally slipped into a coma. He died at 10 A.M., November 8, 1887. He was thirty-seven years old. His only survivor was a cousin, a Sister of Charity in Atlanta, Georgia.

In its obituary, the local newspaper pointed out that Holliday had many faults, "but who shall be the judge of these things?"

Doc would have liked that.

Death of J. A. Holliday.

Died, in Glenwood Springs, Colorado, Tuesday, November 8, 1887, about 10 o'clock a. m., of consumption, J. A. Holliday.

J. A. Holliday, or "Doc" Holliday as he was better known, came to Glenwood Springs from Leadville last May, and by his quiet and gentlemanly demeanor during his short stay and the fortitude and patience he displayed in his last two months of life, made many friends. Although a young man he had been in the west for twenty-five years, and from a life of exposure and hardship had contracted the consumption, from which he had been a constant sufferer for many years. Since he took up his residence at the Springs the evil effects of the sulphur vapors arising from the hot springs on his weak lungs could readily be detected, and for the last few months it was seen that dissolution was only the question of a little time, hence his death was not entirely unexpected. From the effects of the disease, from which he had suffered probably half his life, Holliday, at the time of his death looked like a man well advanced in years, for his hair was silvered and his form emaciated and bent, but he was only thirty-six years of age.

Holliday was born in Georgia, where relatives of his still reside. Twenty-five years ago, when but eleven years of age, he started for the west, and since that time he has probably been in every state and territory west of the Mississippi river. He served as sheriff in one of the counties of Arizona during the troublous times in that section, and served in other official capacities in different parts of the west. Of him it can be said that he represented law and order at all times and places. Either from a roving nature or while seeking a climate congenial to his disease, "Doc" kept moving about from place to place, and finally in the early days of Leadville came to Colorado. After remaining there for several years he came to this section last spring. For the last two months his death was expected at any time; during the past fifty-seven days he had only been out of his bed twice; the past two weeks he was delirious, and for twenty-four hours preceding his death he did not speak.

He was baptised in the Catholic church, but Father Ed. Downey being absent, Rev. W. S. Rudolph delivered the funeral address, and the remains were consigned to their final resting place in Linwood cemetery at 4 o'clock on the afternoon of November 8th, in the presence of many friends. That "Doc" Holliday had his faults none will attempt to deny; but who among us has not, and who shall be the judge of these things?

He only had one correspondent among his relatives—a cousin, a Sister of Charity, in Atlanta, Georgia. She will be notified of his death, and will in turn advise any other relatives he may have living. Should there be an aged father or mother they will be pleased to learn that kind and sympathetic hands were about their son in his last hours, and that his remains were accorded Christian burial. —*Nov. 9, 1887* x   J. L. R

Doc Holliday, after one of the most violent careers in the history of the Wild West, died quietly and alone in a Colorado Springs sanitarium, November 8, 1887. His "sole correspondent" was a cousin, a Sister of Charity living in Atlanta, Georgia. *Courtesy James Riland Collection, State Historical Society of Colorado*

The Last Years of Wyatt Earp

In his last years Wyatt Earp continued to exaggerate the role he had played on the frontier. By his own accounts he had tamed the cow towns, chased the outlaws from Arizona, and generally brought law and order to the Wild West. At the O. K. Corral he pictured himself as fighting off a gang of outlaws who had set a price of $1,000 on his head.

In Tombstone Earp had left his wife, Mattie, who died a sad and lonely suicide in Pinal, Arizona, in the spring of 1888. He then married Josephine (Josie) Sarah Marcus, daughter of a San Francisco department store owner. During the Klondike gold rush they went to Alaska, where Wyatt opened the Dexter saloon in Nome. He still pictured himself as a two-gun sheriff from the days of the Wild West, but one night U.S. Marshal Albert Lowe slapped his face, took away his guns, and sent him off to bed.[42]

Wyatt Earp at Nome, Alaska, during the gold rush. *Left to right:* Ed Engelstadt, Earp, and John Clum, his old friend and supporter during the violent Tombstone days. *The James D. Horan Collection*

Wyatt always needed money; the only jobs he knew were chasing outlaws, gambling, running a saloon, or riding shotgun for a stagecoach. Now highwaymen were captured by posses recruited over the telephone, and trolley cars had replaced stagecoaches. In Wyoming and Utah the Wild Bunch was playing out the last role of outlawry in the West; even fraudulent Jesse Jameses were appearing on stage. It seemed that no one remembered Wyatt Earp, the greatest lawman of the West.

In the summer of 1896 he sold two articles to the *San Francisco Examiner* which were published on August 2 and August 9. Both were illustrated with woodcuts and obviously written by a rewrite man on the *Examiner*'s Sunday side. One was about the Tombstone stage robbery and the killing of Bud Philpot; the other described the O. K. Corral fight.

261

SUNDAY Examiner MAGAZINE

FACT FICTION ART DRAMA MUSIC SOCIETY FASHION SPORT AND THE NEWS OF THE WORLD

EVERY SUNDAY THE EXAMINER CONTAINS MORE READING MATTER THAN ANY THREE MAGAZINES

PAGES 21 TO 36   SAN FRANCISCO: SUNDAY MORNING, AUGUST 9, 1896.   PAGES 21 TO 36

WYATT EARP TELLS TALES OF THE SHOTGUN-MESSENGER SERVICE.

"It's Lame Bradley. Throw Out That Box."

Headline for Wyatt Earp's article the following week in the *Examiner*'s Sunday magazine section. *Courtesy General Library, University of California at Berkeley*

Poor Budd Philpot Lurched Forward and Fell Under the Wheels.

Woodcut showing the stagecoach driver falling after he had been killed. *Courtesy General Library, University of California at Berkeley*

In each one Earp emerged as the hero successfully fighting off the forces of evil. The articles, filled with distortions, half truths, and lies were the beginning of the Earp-manufactured legend.

How Wyatt Earp Routed a Gang of Arizona Outlaws*

It may be that the trail of blood will seem to lie too thickly over the pages that I write. If I had it in me to invent a tale I would fain lighten the crimson stain so that it would glow no deeper than a demure pink. But half a lifetime on the frontier attunes a man's hand to the six-shooter rather than the pen, and it is lucky that I am asked only for facts, for more than facts I could not give.

Half a lifetime of such turbulent days and nights as will never again be seen in this, or, I believe, in any land, might be expected to tangle a man's brain with memories none too easy to sift apart. But for the cornerstone of this episodic narrative I cannot make better choice than the bloody feud in Tombstone, Ariz., which cost me a brave brother and cost more than one worthless life among the murderous dogs who pursued me and mine only less bitterly than I pursued them.

And so I marshal my characters. My stalwart brothers, Virgil and Morgan, shall stand on the right of the stage with my dear old comrade Doc Holliday; on the left shall be arrayed Ike Clanton, Sheriff Behan, Curley Bill and the rest. Fill in the stage with miners, gamblers, rustlers, stage robbers, murderers and cowboys and the melodrama is ready to begin. Nor shall a heroine be wanting, for Big Nose Kate was shaped for the part both by nature and circumstances. Poor Kate! Frontier whiskey must have laid her low long since. And that gives me an opportunity to introduce the reader to both Doc Holliday and Kate by telling of an episode in their checkered lives two years before the action of my melodrama begins.

It happened in '77 when I was city marshal of Dodge City, Kansas. I had followed the trail of some cattle thieves across the border into Texas, and during a short stay in Fort Griffin I first met Doc Holliday and the woman who was known variously as Big Nose Kate, Kate Fisher and, on occasions of ceremony, Mrs. Doc Holliday. Holliday asked me a good many questions about Dodge City and seemed inclined to go there, but before he had made up his mind my business called me over to Fort Clarke. It was while I was on my way back to Fort Griffin that my new friend and his Kate found it necessary to pull their stakes hurriedly. Whereof the plain unvarnished facts were these:

Doc Holliday was spending his evening in a poker game, which was his custom whenever faro bank did not present superior claims on his attention. On his right sat Ed Bailey, who needs no description because he is soon to drop out of this narrative. The trouble began, as it was related to me afterward, by Ed Bailey monkeying with the deadwood or what people who live in the city call discards. Doc Holliday admonished him once or twice to "play poker"—which is your seasoned gambler's method of cautioning a friend to stop cheating—but the misguided Bailey persisted in his furtive attentions to the deadwood. Finally, having detected him again, Holliday pulled down a pot without showing his hand, which he had a perfect right to do. Thereupon Bailey started to throw his gun around on Holliday, as might have been expected. But before he could pull the trigger Doc Holliday had jerked a knife out of his breast pocket and with one sideways sweep had caught Bailey just below the brisket.

*Original headline.

"I'm Going to Arrest You, Boys," Said Virgil."   For Answer Their Six-Shooters Began to Spit.

Headline from Wyatt Earp's article on the O. K. Corral fight, in the *San Francisco Examiner*, August 2, 1896. Earp gave a distorted version of the famous shootout. *Courtesy General Library, University of California at Berkeley*

How Wyatt Earp Routed a Gang of Arizona Outlaws.

Well, that broke up the game, and pretty soon Doc Holliday was sitting cheerfully in the front room of the hotel guarded by the City Marshal and a couple of policemen, while a hundred miners and gamblers clamored for his blood. You see, he had not lived in Fort Griffin very long, while Ed Bailey was well liked. It wasn't long before Big Nose Kate, who had a room downtown, heard about the trouble and went up to take a look at her Doc through a back window. What she saw and heard led her to think that his life wasn't worth ten minutes' purchase and I don't believe it was. There was a shed at the back of the lot and a horse was stabled in it. She was a kind hearted girl, was Kate, for she went to the trouble of leading the horse into the alley and tethering it there before she set fire to the shed. She also got a six-shooter from a friend down the street, which, with the one she always carried, made two.

It all happened just as she had planned it. The shed blazed up and she hammered at the door yelling "Fire." Everybody rushed out except the marshal, the constable and their prisoner. Kate walked in as bold as a lion, threw one of her six-shooters on the Marshal and handed the other to Doc Holliday.

"Come on, Doc," she said with a laugh.

He didn't need any second invitation and the two of them backed out of the hotel keeping the officers covered. All that night they hid among the willows down by the creek, and early next morning a friend of Kate's brought them two horses and some of Doc Holliday's clothes from his room. Kate dressed up in a pair of pants, a pair of boots, a shirt and a hat, and the pair of them got away safely and rode the 400 miles to Dodge City, where they were installed in great style when I got back home.

Which reminds me that during my absence the man whom I had left behind as a deputy had been killed by some cowboys who were engaged in the fascinating recreation known as "shootin' up the town." This incident is merely mentioned as a further sign of the time, and a further excuse for the blood which cannot but trickle through the web of my remembrance.

Such then, was the beginning of my acquaintance with Doc Holliday, the mad, merry scamp with heart of gold and nerves of steel, who, in the dark years that followed stood at my elbow in many a battle to the death. He was a dentist, but he preferred to be a gambler. He was a Virginian but he preferred to be a frontiersman and a vagabond. He was a philosopher but he preferred to be a wag. He was long, lean, an ash-blond and the quickest man with a six-shooter I ever knew. It wasn't long after I returned to Dodge City that his quickness saved my life. He saw a man draw on me behind my back. "Look out, Wyatt!" he shouted, but while the words were coming out of his mouth he had jerked his pistol out of his pocket and shot the other fellow before the latter could fire.

On such incidents as that are built the friendships of the frontier.

In 1879 Dodge City was beginning to lose much of the snap which had given it a charm to men of reckless blood and I decided to move to Tombstone, which was just building up a reputation. Doc Holliday thought he would move with me. Big Nose Kate had left him long before—they were always a quarrelsome couple—and settled in Las Vegas, N. M. He looked her up en route, and the old tenderness reasserting itself, she resolved to throw in her lot with his in Arizona. As for me I was tired of the trials of a peace officer's life and wanted no more of it. But as luck would have it I stopped at Prescott to see my brother Virgil, and while there I met C. P. Dake, the U. S. Marshal of the Territory. Dake had heard of me before and he begged me so hard to take the deputyship in Tombstone that I finally consented. It was thus that the real troubles of a lifetime began.

The boom had not struck Tombstone then but it did a few months later when the mills for treating the ore were completed, and tales about the fabulous richness of the silver mine were bruited abroad. Before long the town had a population of 10,000 or 12,000, of whom about 400 were cattle-thieves, stage robbers, murderers and outlaws.

For the first eight months I worked as a shotgun messenger for Wells Fargo & Co. and beyond the occasional excitement of an abortive holdup and a few excursions after cattle thieves and homicides, everything was quiet as a grave. Then the proprietors of "The Oriental," the biggest gambling house in town, offered to take me into partnership. One of the owners was unpopular and a coterie of tough gamblers were trying to run him out of town. The proprietors had an idea that their troubles would cease if they had a Deputy U.S. Marshal for a partner and so it proved for a time at least, so I turned over my position with Wells Fargo & Co., to my brother, Morgan, who held it for six months after which I gave him a job in "The Oriental." My brother Virgil had also joined me. When the town was incorporated he was appointed Chief of Police.

About this time was laid the foundation of the vendetta which became the talk of the frontier and resulted in no end of bloodshed.

A band of rustlers held up the stagecoach and killed the driver and one of the passengers. Virgil and I, with another man, followed them into the mountains for seventeen days but our horses gave out and they got away from us.

When we got back to town I went to Ike Clanton, who was sort of a leader among the rustlers, and offered to give him all the $6,000 reward offered by Wells Fargo & Co., if he could lead me to where I could arrest the murderers. After thinking about this deeply he agreed to send a partner of his, named Joe Hill, to lead me to where they were hiding, within twenty-five miles of Tombstone. But in case I killed his partners he wanted to make sure the reward would be paid dead or alive. In order to assure him I got the Wells Fargo agent, Marshal Williams, to telegraph San Francisco about it and the reply was affirmative.

So Clanton sent Hill off to decoy the men I wanted. That was to take several days. In the meantime Marshal Williams got drunk and suspecting I was using Ike Clanton for some purpose, tried to pump him about it. Clanton was terrified at the thought of any third person knowing our bargain and he accused me of having told Williams. I denied it. Then he accused me of having told Doc Holliday. Fear and whiskey robbed Clanton of any discretion and he let his secret out to Doc Holliday who had known nothing about it. Doc Holliday, who was the soul of honor, berated him vigorously for his treachery and the conversation was heard by several people.

That was enough for Clanton. He knew his only alternative was to kill us or be killed by his own people. Early next morning Virgil and I were told he was out with rifle and six-gun looking for us. So we went outside looking for him, taking a different route. Virgil was going down Fourth Street when Clanton came out of a hallway looking in the opposite direction.

"I want you Ike," Virgil said, walking up behind him. Clanton threw his gun around and tried to take a shot but Virgil knocked it away, pulled his own and arrested this man.

He was fined $25 for disturbing the peace.

Ike Clanton's next move was to telegraph to Charleston, ten miles away, for Billy Clanton, Tom McLaury, Frank McLaury and Billy Clayton [Claiborne]—hard men everyone.

They came galloping into town, loaded up with ammunition and swearing to kill us off in short order. Thirty or forty citizens offered us their help but we said we would manage the job alone.

"What had we better do?" Virgil asked.

"Go and arrest 'em," I said.

The four newcomers and Ike Clanton stationed themselves on a fifteen-foot lot between two buildings in Fremont Street and sent us word if we did not come down and fight they would waylay and kill us. So we started down after them—Doc Holliday, Virgil, Morgan and I. As we came to the lot they moved back and got their backs against one of the buildings.

"I'm going to arrest you boys," said Virgil.

For answer their six-guns began to spit. Frank McLaury fired at me and Billy Clanton at Morgan. Both missed. I had a gun in my overcoat pocket and I jerked it out at Frank McLaury, hitting him in the stomach. At the same time Morgan shot Billy Clanton in the breast. So far we had the best of it, but just then, Tom McLaury, who had got behind his horse fired under the animal's neck and bored a hole right through Morgan sideways. The bullet entered one shoulder and came out at the other.

"I got it, Wyatt," said Morgan.

"Then get behind me and keep quiet," I said—but he didn't.

By this time bullets were flying so fast I could not keep track of them. Frank McLaury had given a yell when I shot him and made for the street, one hand over his stomach. Ike Clanton and Billy Clayton [Claiborne] were shooting fast and so was Virgil, and the two latter made a break for the street. I fired a shot which hit

Tom McLaury's horse and made it break away, and Doc Holliday took the opportunity to pump a charge of buckshot out of a Wells Fargo shotgun into Tom who promptly fell dead. In the excitement of the moment, Doc Holliday didn't know what he had done and flung away the shotgun in disgust, pulling his six-shooter instead.

Then I witnessed a strange spectacle. Frank McLaury and Billy Clanton were sitting in the middle of the street, both badly wounded, emptying their six-shooters like lightning. One of them shot Virgil through the leg and he shot Billy Clanton. Then Frank McLaury started to his feet and staggered across the street, though he was full of bullets. On the way he came face to face with Doc Holliday.

"I got ye now, Doc," he said.

"Well, you're a good one if you have," said Holliday with a laugh.

With that they both aimed. But before you can understand what happened next I must carry the narrative back half a minute.

After the first exchange in the lot Ike Clanton had gotten into one of the buildings from the rear and when I reached the street he was shooting out of one of the front windows. Seeing him aim at Morgan I shouted: "Look out, Morg, you're getting it in the back!"

Morgan wheeled around and in doing so fell on his side. While in that position he caught sight of Doc Holliday and Frank McLaury aiming at each other. With a quick drop he shot McLaury in the head. At the same instant McLaury's pistol flashed and Doc Holliday was shot in the hip.

That ended the fight. Ike Clanton and Billy [Claiborne] ran off and made haste to give themselves up to the sheriff, for the citizens were out a hundred strong to back us up.

I have described the battle with as much particularity as possible, partly because there are not many city dwellers who have more than a vague idea of what such a fight really means, and partly because I was rather curious how it would look in cold type. It may or may not surprise some readers to learn that from the first to the last shot fired, not more than a minute elapsed.

Of the exciting events which followed, I can give no more than a brief account. The principal factor in all that happened was Sheriff Johnny Behan, my political rival and personal enemy. Doc Holliday and I were arrested on a charge of murder. My two brothers were exempt from this proceeding because they were both disabled. We were acquitted at the preliminary hearing and rearrested on another warrant charging the same offense. This time the hearing was held at Contention, nine miles from Tombstone, and we would have been assassinated on the road had not a posse of the best citizens insisted on accompanying the Sheriff as a guard. The hearing was never completed because Holliday and I were released on writ of habeas corpus. In the meantime the Grand Jury persistently refused to indict us.

But the determination to assassinate us never relaxed. Three months later Virgil was returning home to the hotel, and when he was half-way across the street, five double-barreled shotguns were discharged at him from an ambushcade. One shot shattered his left arm; another passed through his body. I arrested several of the assassins but twenty or thirty rustlers swore to an alibi and they were acquitted.

Three months later, before Virgil had recovered from his wounds, Morgan was shot dead through the glass door of a saloon, while he was playing a game of pool. I sent his body home to Colton, California, and shipped off Virgil—a physical wreck—on the same train from Tucson. But even at the depot I was forced to fight Ike Clanton and four or five of his friends who had followed us to do murder. One of them named Frank Stilwell, who was believed to be Morgan's murderer, was killed by my gun going off when he grasped it.

When I returned to Tombstone Sheriff Behan came to arrest me but I refused to surrender and he weakened. For a long time thereafter I maintained the anomalous position of being a fugitive from the county authorities, and performing the duties of Deputy United States Marshal, with the sanction and moral support of my chief. With Doc Holliday and one or two faithful comrades I went into camp among the hills and withstood more than one attack from outlaws who had been implicated in the death of one brother and the disablement of another—attacks which resulted fatally to some of my enemies and left me without a scratch.

One such encounter I will describe because it illustrates as well as anything could some of the exigencies of a frontier vendetta.

We had ridden twenty-five miles over the mountains with the intention of camping at a certain spring. As we got near the place I had a presentiment that something was wrong and unlimbered my shotgun. Sure enough nine cowboys sprang up from the bank where the spring was and began firing at us. I jumped off my horse to return the fire, thinking my men would do the same, but they retreated. One of the cowboys who was trying to pump lead into me with a Winchester was a fellow named Curly Bill, a stage-robber whom I had been after for eight months, and for whom I had a warrant in my pocket. I fired both barrels of my gun into him, blowing him all to pieces. With that the others jumped into a clump of willows and kept on firing so I retreated keeping behind my horse.

He was a high-strung beast and the firing frightened him so that whenever I tried to get my Winchester from the saddle, he would rear up and keep it out of my reach. When I had backed out about a hundred yards I started to mount. Now it was a hot day and I had loosened my cartridge belt two or three holes. When I tried to get astride I found it had fallen down over my thighs, keeping my legs together. While I was perched up thus, trying to pull my belt higher, with one hand, the horn of my saddle was shot off. However, I got away all right, and just then my men rallied. But I did not care to go back at the rustlers so we sought out another hole for camp. The skirt of my overcoat was shot to pieces on both sides, but not a bullet had touched me.

Sheriff Behan trailed us with a big posse composed of rustlers, but it was only a bluff, for when I left word for him where he could find us and waited for him to come, he failed to appear.

My best friends advised me to leave the Territory, so I crossed into Colorado. While I was there they tried to get a requisition for me but the Governor refused to sign it.

It's an old story now. I have been in Arizona in recent years—as near Tombstone as Tucson in fact—but no one sought to molest me. The outlaws who were my worse enemies are most killed or in the penitentiary.

Poor Doc Holliday died of consumption three years ago in Colorado. My brother Virgil is running a stock ranch in Texas. A large section of his upper arm is entirely without bone and yet he can use his fingers.

On reading it over it seems to me there is not only too much blood but too much of myself in the story. However, a man gets in the habit of thinking about himself when he spends half a lifetime on the frontier.

                                                                    Wyatt Earp

In his second article Earp described the Tucson stagecoach robbery and the killing of Bud Philpot (Earp spelled Philpot with two t's).

Curiously, Earp praised Bud Paul, the shotgun messenger and later sheriff of Pima County, who was sent to Colorado to bring back the Earps and Doc Holliday to Tombstone to stand trial for the murders of Stilwell and Cruz. Perhaps Earp was thanking Paul for not forcing the Colorado authorities to arrest him and his brother Warren in Gunnison.

Once again Earp took credit for a feat accomplished by other lawmen: he wrote that he and his brother Morgan trailed the robbers of the Tombstone stage into Bisbee, where they arrested Frank Stilwell and Pete Spence.

Stilwell and Spence, owners of a livery stable in Bisbee, were actually arrested by Deputy Sheriffs William Breakenridge and Neagle, who trailed the pair to Bisbee after they had interviewed the stage's passengers who told them one of the masked robbers had called out, "Have we got all the sugar?" a favorite expression of Stilwell. They also learned Stilwell had his high heels replaced by low ones. Breakenridge found the original high heels in the shoemaker's shop and they fitted the tracks at the scene of the holdup.

Wyatt Earp: Referee without a Six-shooter

That winter Wyatt played a leading role in one of the most controversial fights in America's ring history. The year's big event was the Sharkey-Fitzsimmons heavyweight fight held at Mechanics' Pavilion in San Francisco, December 2, 1896. Earp was chosen as referee on the day of the fight when it became apparent the managers of Sharkey and Fitzsimmons could not agree on any of the city's best-known referees.

Earp and the fight established a number of precedents. It was the first time a fight referee had to be relieved of his six-shooter; women were permitted to attend for the first time, and it was the first fight publicly patronized by San Francisco's blue blood society.

Before the fight Fitzsimmons's brother-in-law and manager, Martin Julian, charged that Earp had been "fixed" and he delayed the fight by arguing with an impatient, jeering crowd.

Earp finally was summoned from a nearby restaurant. When he took off his coat Police Captain George W. Whittman noticed Earp was carrying a single action .45 with an eight-inch barrel. Whittman told Wyatt he could not enter the ring carrying a gun, so Earp asked him to step into a private office so he could unbuckle his holster and turn the weapon over to him. For some unexplained reason Whittman refused to have a private meeting with Earp, so Wyatt unbuckled his holster and surrendered his gun to Whittman, who in turn gave it to Chief Patrick Crowley, chief of the San Francisco Police Department.

For seven rounds Fitzsimmons hit Sharkey at will but during the eighth Sharkey suddenly clutched his groin and, writhing with pain, fell to the canvas.

While the bewildered audience looked on, Earp gave the bout to Sharkey because of Fitzsimmons's "foul blow."

One of the best accounts of that fight, still debated by ring historians, was written by Edward H. Hamilton, a reporter for the *San Francisco Examiner*.[43]

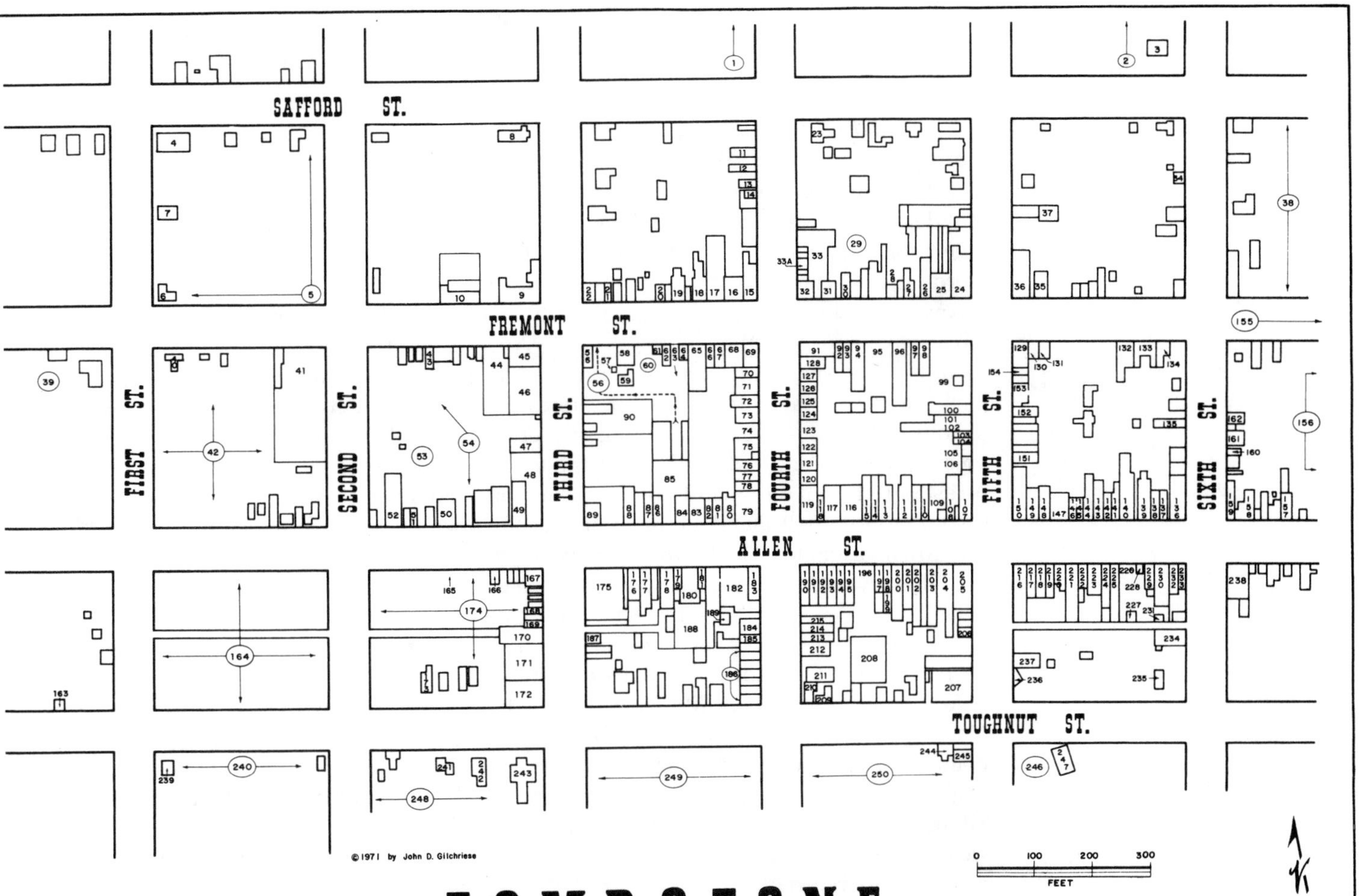
SAFFORD ST.
FREMONT ST.
ALLEN ST.
TOUGHNUT ST.
FIRST ST.
SECOND ST.
THIRD ST.
FOURTH ST.
FIFTH ST.
SIXTH ST.
0 100 200 300
FEET

TOMBSTONE

ARIZONA TERRITORY

CIRCA 1881 - 82

This map is the result of Robert N. Mullin's original sketch made in 1916. Robert N. Mullin, distinguished Western authority, researcher and writer, in collaboration with John D. Gilchriese has made available his final research for this publication of Tombstone's most reliable historic map.

Historical research by Robert N. Mullin and John D. Gilchriese
Cartography by Steve Bahre

1. Robert Eccleston's home
2. First permanent public school building (3 blocks north, in residential district)
3. Catholic Church (under construction)
4. Harris Foundry
5. Dwellings
6. House owned by Wyatt Earp
7. T.E. Gray's home
8. ST. PAUL'S EPISCOPAL CHURCH (Under construction; completed June '82)
9. AZTEC HOUSE (Mrs. Mugan) (Also known as "Bachelors' House"; Arizona Trading Co.)
10. W.H. Tuttle's TOMBSTONE CORRAL (Formerly John Dunbar's Stable; later, Sandy Bob's)
11. S.W. Clawson
12. Reed & Williams, Att'ys.
13. H.G. Maxson, Surveyor
14. B.C. Quigley, City Auditor
15. Gird Block , ORIGINAL COURT HOUSE; Summerfield Brothers
16. Dry Goods Store; Recorder's Office; Exchange Bldg.
17. COURT ROOM (Later Mining Exchange Dance Hall and Modoc Stage Office) Above offices of Justice Wallace, Judge J.H. Lucas, Marshall Williams, W. Lindsey's Employment Agency. M.M. Corella, H.G. Howe, mining engineer; A.J. Mitchell, civil engineer; attorneys J.B. Southard, John W. Murphy, P.T. Colby, Ben & Briggs Goodrich, Marsh & Stiles. (Later, Nobles Hotel)
18. TOMBSTONE EPITAPH (Furnished rooms above) (Later, the Prospector)
19. W.A. Eastman's Carpenter Shop
20. MRS. ADDIE BOURLAND'S MILLINERY & DRESSMAKING SHOP
21. Sandy Bob's home
22. Addie Bourland's (after mid-summer 1882)
23. Turnverein Hall
24. SAN JOSE HOUSE, "Neat Rooms With or Without Fire"
25. LEXINGTON LIVERY STABLE ("Jack Crabtree's)
26. AMERICAN HOTEL (MISS NELLIE CASHMAN & MRS. T.S. CUNNINGHAM, April-June 1882)
27. J.V. Vickers' Real Estate Office
28. Hart's Gun Shop
29. Arizona Iron Works (R. G. Westerman)
30. Chinese Laundry
31. New York Variety Store
32. LXL Auction House
33. SCHIEFFELIN HALL. Theater on ground floor; Masonic Lodge rooms above

33
A. Dr. Nelson S. Giberson

34. G. Hill Howard, Counselor at Law
35. G.T. Henderson, M.D.
36. Woodhead & Gay's Cash Store (F.N. Wolcott)
37. Hill & Jones' Carpenter Shop
38. Cribs and "Female Boarding Houses"
39. Residences of VIRGIL and JAMES EARP (Until March, '82) Also WYATT and MORGAN EARP (July 8 to October 26, '81)
40. PETE SPENCE
41. Charles N. Thomas' WEST END CORRAL
42. Mexican quarter
43. Ham Light's Place
44. TOMBSTONE LIVERY & FEED YARD
45. Graff & Schoenholzer Blacksmith Shop
46. WELLS FARGO CORRAL
47. Blacksmith Shop (Later Billy King's)
48. Arizona Corral
49. San Francisco Lodging House (later, 1883-4, the LeVan House)
50. Atlantic Restaurant
51. Miss Birdie Parker
52. Smith's Private Lodging House
53. Mountain Maid Mine
54. "Hop Town", Chinese quarter
55. W. A. HARWOOD'S HOUSE (Occupied by Assay Office in Spring '82)
56. "BATTLE OF THE O.K. CORRAL". Route followed by the Clantons and McLaurys to the vacant lot where they met the Earp-Holliday group.
57. "Mr. & Mrs. Olsen, Paintings & Hair Goods" November 1881
58. FLY'S LODGING HOUSE
59. C.S. FLY'S PHOTOGRAPHIC STUDIO
60. Vacant lot
61. Everhardy's Butcher Shop (Bauer's, 1882)
62. Bauer's Grocery, 1882
63. Vacant; sometimes used as back entrance to O.K. Corral; a later photograph of this site (Lot #6, owned by Montgomery & Benson) sometimes erroneously identified as scene of O.K. Corral Battle
64. PAPAGO CASH STORE (Frank B. Austin, prop.)
65. CITY HALL (under construction; completed December '82)
66. A.O. Trantrum, Recorder and City Attorney
67. L.W. Blum & Co.
68. TOMBSTONE NUGGET (Until May 1, '82)
69. Capitol Saloon (Tom Moses) (Maurice E. Clark property)
70. E.T. Keatney's Drug Store (formerly Emmal & Ross)
71. J.G. Brown, Grocer (formerly H.E. Hill's Cash Grocery)
72. New Orleans Restaurant (R. C. Campbell) (formerly, Mrs. P. Jones)
73. New Orleans Saloon (J. Manendez)
74. Vacant lot (J. Manendez)
75. Zeckendorf Building; Schoenfeld & Hayman Furniture Store; after May 2, '82, TOMBSTONE NUGGET and W. Heyes, Watchmaker
76. E.W. Brinckman & J.C. Tappeiner, Assayers
77. Langenberger's Tin Shop
78. N.Y. Coffee Saloon (4th Street Coffee Shop) (T.J. McCullough; later, G.G. Berry)
79. QUONG KEY'S CAN CAN RESTAURANT (original location; later Walsh's)
80. Golden Eagle Beer Depot (formerly Moses & Mehan's Saloon)
81. Headquarters Saloon (Leigh Bros.)
82. W.W. Ross, Patent Medicines (formerly J.H. Greer)
83. Elite Restaurant
84. D.R.M. Thompson's Saddle Shop
85. O.K. CORRAL STABLE (Montgomery & Benson)
86. C.W. Pinkham's Stage Line Office
87. Dragoon Saloon (Pat Lynch; once operated by Dolan, later by Billy King)
88. Stage Barn (J. Mandef) (Later, Cummings' Butcher Shop)
89. U.S. CUSTOMS OFFICE
90. P.H. Harrington's yard (adobe wall on three sides)
91. Post Office
92. St. Louis Restaurant
93. Chandler & Forsythe's C.O. D. Store, 1881
94. A.D. Otis Hardward & Furniture Store (Robert Eccleston)
95. Vacant lot (Vickers & McCoy) (later, lumber yard)
96. Melrose Restaurant (Edmund Saul)
97. City Market (T.P. Ward; later Fred Castle)
98. Charles M. Smith, Commission Merchant
99. WELLS SPICER, Justice of the Peace, "Att'y & Counselor at Law, Mining Broker, Notary Public, U.S. Commissioner, Commissioner of Deeds for California", etc. and L.F. Blackburn, Deputy U.S. Marshal (until May 10, '82)
100. Club room; also officer of W.M. Ritchie and B.L. Peel, Attorney
101. Store building later occupied by furniture store
102. Store building later occupied by furniture store
103. C.J. Duval, Assayer
104. Uncle Meyers' Pawn Shop
105. Rockaway Oyster House
106. H.W. Hasselgren's Commercial Printing Shop (April-May '82; formerly at 210 Fremont, Nov. '81; 225 5th, Jan.-March '82)
107. B. Wehrfritz bldg. Fredericksburg Brewery Depot and Free Lunch. (Formerly, 1881, GOLDEN EAGLE BREWERY SALOON & LUNCH; originally, 1880, THE CRYSTAL PALACE) Above: offices of George F. Goodfellow, H.M. Matthews, F.C. Dunn, physicians; E. P. Ryder, dentist; M. Kelleher, City Surveyor; Virgil W. Earp, U.S. Deputy Marshal)
108. Dave Cohen's Cigar Store and Card Room (Wm. Spruance property)
109. Joe Hoefler's General Store (formerly, '81, WELLS FARGO) (J.S. McCoy)
110. Smith & Dyar's Stationery Store (later barber shop and baths)
111. Jewelry & Watch Repairing
112. Campbell & Hatch Saloon, "BOB HATCH's BILLIARD HALL"
113. ALHAMBRA SALOON (Nichols & Mellgren)
114. Goldbaum Bros. (formerly M. Rosendorff)
115. OCCIDENTAL SALOON (Doling) (Later, Can Can Restaurant) (Above: Isaacs' Keno Room, later in rear room of Oriental)
116. COSMOPOLITAN HOTEL (Albert C. "Chris" Bilicke)
117. Maison Doree, formerly Cosmopolitan Restaurant, J.W. Cameron; Fortlouis Cigar Store)
118. Sultana Cigar Store & Card Room (N.H. Wolf)
119. HAFFORD'S CORNER SALOON
120. Robertson's Book Store
121. J. Fontana, Watchmaker; Above 119, 120, 121, BROWN'S HOTEL
122. GEORGE F. SPANGENBERG'S GUN SHOP
123. Vacant lot (L.A. Atchison)
124. Col. Dean, Auctioneer (D.C. Davis Property)
125. Dr. McSwegan's office
126. Union News Depot (Sol Israel)
127. Ice Cream Parlor
128. A Bauer's residence (later Bauer's Butcher Shop)
129. Dillon & Kenealy's General Store. (Richey's Building, sometimes called the Candy Factory, extended on 5th Street to 152; the 2nd floor housed the offices of attorneys Earll, Smith, Campbell & Robinson; formerly County Offices, Goodrich & Goodrich, etc.)
130. Abbott House
131. Delmonico House; T.H. Southard, Atty.
132. Lydia Clark
133. Mrs. A.S. Gray
134. Wm Herring, Counselor at Law
135. Lodging house (M. Calisher)
136. B. Wellman Building. McKean & Knight's General Store; Palace Barber Shop
137. Leary the Cobbler (Pat O'Neil shot here by John Fleming, May 2, '82)
138. Rafferty's Saloon
139. Belle LeVan
140. E.T. Hardy & Co. (prior to April, '82: M. Calisher's General Store)
141. Vincent & Braden's Music Hall
142. Raferty's Saloon
143. Key West Cigar Store (E. Brophy)
144. Lion Brewery
145. Arcade Restaurant
146. ARCADE CIGAR STORE & SALOON (Alexander & Thompson) (where fire of June '81 originated)
147. City Bakery
148. H. Kayser's Boot & Shoe Store (formerly Meyers Bros.)
149. American Clothing Store (J. M. Vizina) (Formerly Charles H. Glover's One Price House, June '80--February '82)
150. Vizina & Cook Block. THE ORIENTAL SALOON (Mike Joyce); Cigar Store (J.B. McGuiness); Oriental Oyster House in rear; offices and Rickabaugh Club above. (On sidewalk here, Charlie Storms killed by Luke Short; Billy Claiborne by Frank Leslie)
151. HUDSON & Co.'s BANK (formerly Safford, Hudson & Co.); Milton S. Clapp, insurance. (Later: 1884, Spangenberg's Gun Shop; 1880, WELLS FARGO OFFICE)
152. Fitzhenry & Mansfield's Grocery
153. Frank Yaples Store & Sewing Machine Agency (Rook killed here)
154. Mrs. A.P. Trarey's Millinery Shop
155. East: Mrs. E.R. Worth, Furnished Rooms, 1 block; Mrs. A.P. Frary, 1 block; Mrs. O.E. Roberts' Gardens, 3 blocks; Madam Brosce, 3 blocks.
156. Female Boarding Houses
157. A.J. Ritter, Undertaking, Pictures & Chromos
158. Soma Winery
159. Cribs
160. Female Boarding House
161. House; later Dutch Annie's
162. House; later Blonde Marie's
163. Miss Josephine Harcourt
164. Mexican dwellings and places of entertainment
165. China Mary's
166. Charley Lee Kong
167. Wm. Dee
168. Quong On Chong
169. Quong Ching Hing
170. Chinese Lodging House
171. Garel & Page Wagon Shop
172. Charcoal Yard
173. Webster Street's house
174. "Hop Town" Chinese Quarter
175. P.W. Smith's Corral
176. Heyes Jewelry Store (until May 2, '82)
177. U.S. Restaurant (Mrs. Lena Crawley & Mrs. Fenig) (A. J. Ritter property) (Later Arlington Hotel)
178. J. Lenoir's Furniture Store (Oberfelder property) (later in '82, opposite at 317-21 Allen)
179. J.J. Patton's Saddle Shop
180. Dexter Stable (John Dunbar & John Behan until May 15, '82; thereafter, John Dunbar)
181. Dividend Saloon (Formerly The Fashion) (Lynch & O'Neil)
182. P.W. Smith's Store, "Dry Goods, Amazon Bourbon and Rebstock's St. Louis Beer" (After May 2, '82, Cochise Hardware & Trading Co.) (182-183 known as the ALLEN BLOCK)
183. Agency; Pima County Bank (1880-81) (Later Pima County Bank)
184. Lodging house (formerly COMMERCIAL HOTEL, 1880)
185. COURTROOM, Justice of the Peace, A.O. Wallace
186. Offices, principally lawyers'
187. Wing Woo Lung Laundry
188. Dexter Corral
189. Location of Tombstone's first temporary public school
190. Andy's Club Saloon
191. S.C. Bagg's Pawn Shop (later, fruit store) OCCIDENTAL HOTEL above 190-3 in 1883 (Pascholy & Tribolet)
192. OCCIDENTAL HOTEL
193. OCCIDENTAL HOTEL
194. Occidental Chop House (Pete Clandianos)
195. Parlor Barber Shop & Baths
196. Vacant lot (Z.H. Taylor) used as entrance to Pioneer Livery Stable
197. Sandy Bob's Stage Office (later a saloon)
198. San Francisco Jewelry Store (P. Heitzelman)
199. Western Union Telegraph Office
200. GRAND HOTEL (Archie McBride until May 12, '82; originally Mrs. Holly, '80; Mrs. J.E. Brown, '81) (ground floor: hotel office and C. L. Mellgren's Dining Hall; above: hotel rooms and Tombstone Club quarters; basement: Fountain Saloon and Jake's Lunch Room)
201. I. Levy, Musical Instruments & Stationery
202. Watt & Tarbell's Undertaking Parlor (later: saloon)
203. Miller & King
204. Furniture Store, previously location of JIM VOGAN'S BOWLING ALLEY and the Sample Room Bar (Later: Frank Yaple's Store)
205. Adolph Cohen's Clothing Store
206. J.H. McKee, M.D.
207. RUSS HOUSE (J. Pascholy & Nellie Cashman until April '82; thereafter, J. Pascholy; Miss Cashman and Mrs. Cunningham '83-'84)
208. Pioneer Livery Stable (Z.H. Taylor) (Headquarters, Sandy Bob Stage Line)
209. Private dwellings. (later site of ARCADE HOTEL, today's ROSE TREE INN)
210. Private dwellings
211. Private dwellings
212. Mrs. Pauline Jones' Restaurant & Lodging House. (prior to April '82: Mrs. Peters')
213. Hawkins & Boarman, "Wholesale Liquor, Oil & Cigars" (after mid-summer '82: law offices)
214. B. Laventhal's Clothing Store (later: carpenter shop)
215. Furnished rooms
216. Jacob Meyers' Clothing Store (Huachuca Water Co., property) (formerly: Palace Saloon) (from which building, under construction, VIRGIL EARP was shot December 28, '81)
217. Tasker & Pridham, Gen. Mdse. (George Pridham, Public Administrator)
218. J.J. McClelland, Wholesale Liquors
219. E.P. Voisard, Assayer. (premises shared with A.E. Hartmann, Watchmaker, August '81-April '82; and with S.C. Bagg, Auctioneer, April-August '82) (Harness Shop after August '82)
220. WELLS FARGO OFFICE (Until mid-summer '82) (Aldenson & Williams property)
221. Cadwell & Stanford, General Merchandise
222. French Restaurant (G.G. Berry; formerly Ed Terrol)
223. Hartmann's Jewelry Store
224. Frederick & Hill, Metalware (formerly Goodrich's Tin Shop)
225. Arizona Brewery
226. Vacant lot, title undetermined
227. Mrs. Briggs Goodrich's house
228. Cobbler Shop (J.R. Adams)
229. B. Hattich's Tailor Shop
230. BIRD CAGE THEATER (Billy & Lottie Hutchinson) (later known as "The Elite" and "Olympic Opera House") (Opened Dec. 21, '81) (This site occupied by Mr. Fry's house until July 28, '80, and was vacant when Fred White was shot by Curly Bill here, Oct. 27, '80)
231. Cabin occupied by FRED DODGE
232. Palace Lunch Room
233. Palace Livery Stable office. (corral in rear) (prior to June '81: E. Fontana Dance House; after mid-summer '82: saloon)
234. Female Boarding House
235. Chinese Laundry (Early Tombstone Calaboose)
236. Combination Shaft Hoist
237. Palace Lodging House
238. R. Cohen & Co.
239. H.E. Hills & Co., Commission Merchants
240. Blinn's Lumber Yard
241. American Lodging House (Mr. & Mrs. Grant)
242. Mrs. Morton's Lodging House
243. NEW COCHISE COUNTY COURTHOUSE under construction (completed Fall '82, except south wing)
244. Office, T. & C. Ice Co.
245. Gird's Ice Plant (Present site WYATT EARP MUSEUM)
246. Tombstone Mining & Milling Co. hoist ("Million Dollar Stope")
247. FIREHOUSE
248. Cabins
249. Miners' cabins
250. Miners' cabins

Yes, It Was a Great Fight, But . . .*

Did Fitzsimmons hit Sharkey a foul blow? This is a question which will be asked and debated for years to come whenever San Franciscans are gathered together. A quiet, mild-mannered man named Wyatt Earp says he did. He was referee. His word "goes." The purse and the bets go with it.

Anybody who wishes to dispute the matter with Mr. Earp is invited to take the job off my hands. For they do say down in Arizona that the swivel play with which he brings his battery into action is a marvel in gunnery, and when he negligently fans the trigger there are few who care to remain in the neighborhood and take lessons in ballistics. He is something of a prototype of that "quiet Mr. Brown who on several occasions had cleaned out the town," so when Mr. Earp, referee on the occasion last evening when Robert Fitzsimmons and Thomas Sharkey fought with each other for $10,000 and all the honors of the prize ring, told in the eighth round that Mr. Fitzsimmons had struck Mr. Sharkey a low blow, and that consequently Mr. Sharkey had won the fight, no one cared to rise and say, "you're a perjured villain" or make any other remark indicating doubt or reproach. But once Mr. Earp had passed from view all sorts of people began saying all sorts of things, and they'll keep on saying them for many years to come.

And you ought to hear Mr. Fitzsimmons himself on that subject, and also Mr. Martin Julian, brother-in-law and manager. They are doing enough talking for a political campaign and making statements which are quite rash enough for the angry aftermath of a presidential election. Surely they are entitled to talk, for $10,000 is a lot of money to lose on one man's word, not to count the honor of victory and the sting of defeat. But the referee's word "goes," there is no getting behind those returns.

Certainly there was no reason why Fitzsimmons should have struck the foul blow. He had all the better of the fighting. He had punished Sharkey until the Sailor was wobbly and seemed "Going." He was himself strong on his legs and had a deal of driving power left in his arms. Without a foul he almost certainly would have won.

Those who cavil will say that Sharkey, himself a foul fighter, tricked the referee, having been taught by his experiences just how to claim a foul. Then again, before the fight, Martin Julian had said he had been informed that the referee had been "fixed."

But no one was running around last night to tell Mr. Earp these arguments: There was no wild rush at him to make the innuendoes. He was entirely free from those who bubbled over with suspicions. Somehow or other Mr. Earp was not remonstrated with.

And he didn't have his "gun."

That gun was in the inside pocket of Captain Whittman during all the exciting period after the decision was rendered. The incident of the disarming was really an "event of the evening." When Mr. Earp took the stage at the call of Billy Jordan, master of ceremonies, he was fortified on barbette.

Then Mr. Jordan made his remarks about having heard the referee was "fixed." He didn't make these remarks personal. In fact he expressed the highest regard for Mr. Earp personally. He had heard these disquieting rumors, however, and consequently felt called upon to protest. He seemed to squint over apprehensively to where the Earp artillery might at any moment begin volleying and thundering. It would be a poor sort of a shot who would miss Martin Julian.

*Original headline.

ADVERTISING GAIN,
2155 More Ads
During November, 1896.
During November, 1895.

The Examiner.

CIRCULATION GAIN,
903 Copies Daily
NET PAID AVERAGE CIRCULATION,
OCTOBER increase over
SEPTEMBER, 1896.

VOL. LXIII. SAN FRANCISCO: THURSDAY MORNING, DECEMBER 3, 1896. NO. 155.

"SHARKEY WINS BY A FOUL," SAID REFEREE EARP.

Although Declared the Victor He Was Writhing on the Floor When the Decision Was Given in His Favor.

FITZSIMMONS ACCUSES EARP OF FRAUD.

I was simply robbed out of $10,000 by that decision, and what is more, I knew I was going to be robbed before I entered the ring.

When I made that speech to the crowd telling them that I accepted Earp as referee notwithstanding the information that had been brought to me that he had been fixed to throw the fight to Sharkey, I knew that I was a goner. But what else could I do? If I had refused to fight the whole country would have said that I was afraid to meet the man who nearly put Corbett out.

My reputation as champion of the world was at stake and I could not afford to lose it for three times $10,000. The articles of agreement were that if Sharkey and I could not agree on a referee the club should have the selection of one. I suspected when Sharkey's people refused to agree to any of the men that I named that something was wrong, but I was not sure, so I told Julian to go on naming them until he got tired.

During all that time we couldn't get the other side to name anybody but a few unknown sporting men who couldn't get anybody to vouch for them. I didn't want to take anybody that didn't know anything about fighting, so we were left in a hole. Under the articles of agreement the naming of the referee went to the club and they picked Earp.

The way I came to know that he had been fixed was this: In the lobby of the Baldwin Hotel to-day, or, to be more exact, about 2 o'clock this afternoon, several men told Martin Julian not under any circumstances to accept Wyatt Earp, because he had agreed to throw the fight to Sharkey for a good sum of money. I am not at liberty to give the names of all the men who told that to Julian, but I can give you three of them, and they are men whose word will be accepted by sporting men all over the country. They are Riley Grannan, the racetrack plunger; Tom James, the man whom the whole house called for to act as timekeeper to-night, and M. A. Gunst, one of the Police Commissioners of this town. They all told Julian that they knew Earp had been "fixed."

Major Frank McLaughlin also told me that I would be foolish to accept Earp, because he had heard him say that Earp had been "fixed." He didn't say he knew it, though, as the others did. That is the reason why both Julian and I held out so long against Earp at the ring side. But appearances were against us and with the whole house jeering at us we were left in a hole that we could not crawl out of any other way.

Earp knows, and so does Sharkey, that I didn't hit the sailor where they say I did. My left landed straight in his stomach, where I had a right to hit him, and no other place. His lying down and groaning was all a part of the game. There was no need for me to foul him, because I had him whipped anyway and could have finished him before the end of the round. It don't make any difference, though. As I telegraphed Dan Stuart to-night I am willing to meet both Sharkey and Corbett in the same ring any night Stuart wants to pull the fight off. I will say one thing for Corbett, and that is that I don't blame him for saying that he was robbed out of the Jackson fight in this town. No pugilist can get a square deal from the thieves who handle fighting in this city and it is a safe bet that the last big fight San Francisco will ever see was pulled off to-night.

ROBERT FITZSIMMONS.

"YES, IT WAS A GREAT FIGHT, BUT---"

That Is Just About as Far as Anybody Cares to Go in Questioning Referee Wyatt Earp's Decision.

By Edward H. Hamilton

Did Fitzsimmons hit Sharkey a foul blow? That is a question which will be asked and debated for years to come whenever San Franciscans are gathered together. A quiet, mild-mannered man named Wyatt Earp says he did. He was referee. His word "goes." The purse and the bets go with it.

Anybody who wishes to dispute the matter with Mr. Earp is invited to take that job off my hands. For they do say down in Arizona that the swivel play with which he brings his battery into action is a marvel in gunnery. And those doing enough talking for a political campaign and making statements which are quite rash enough for the angry aftermath of a Presidential election. Surely they are entitled to talk, for $10,000 is a lot of money to lose on one man's word, not to count the honors of victory and the sting of defeat. But the referee's word "goes." There is no getting behind those returns. Certainly there was no reason that Fitzsimmons should have struck the foul blow.

(Continued on Page Three.)

WYATT EARP, WHOSE DECISION MEANT $10,000.

When I decided this contest in favor of Sharkey I did so because I believed Fitzsimmons deliberately fouled him, and under the rules the Sailor was entitled to the decision. I would have been willing to allow half fouls—that is, fouls that might be considered partly accidental—to pass by with only a reprimand, but in such a case as this I could only do my duty.

Julian approached me before the contest and said he had heard stories to the effect that I favored Sharkey. We talked a few moments and he went away apparently satisfied that everything was on the square.

Any talk to the effect that I was influenced in any way to decide wrongly against Fitzsimmons is rubbish. I saw Sharkey but once before in my life and that was when he boxed with Corbett. I had no reason to favor him. If I was to have allowed my feelings to govern me, my decision would have been the other way.

I am a pretty close observer and under most conditions I think I am cool. I went into the ring as referee to give a square decision, and so far as my conscience speaks I have done so. It made no difference to me who won, the victory should be to the best man. As I have already said, I met Sharkey only once before to-night, and that was when he fought Corbett. To-night I was standing in the enclosure near the ring when I met him again.

I have met Fitzsimmons several times, the first, I believe, being four or five years ago, when one of the best friends I have in the country and one of the truest supporters Fitzsimmons ever had, Bat Masterson, introduced us. I am very sure that Bat Masterson has lost a great deal of money on this fight, but I have always been able to decide against my own money and my friends can stand the consequences of such a decision.

I feel that I did what was right and honorable and feeling so I care nothing for the opinion of anybody. I saw the foul blow struck as plainly as I see you, and that is all there is to the story. In the fourth or the fifth round I warned Fitzsimmons that he was fouling in wrestling. In every clinch the tall man would force himself down upon Sharkey, who was fighting low, and attempt to smash him.

Fitzsimmons replied that he was not fighting foul. I answered that I wanted no more of it and demanded that he quit it and be square. I told him that I would warn Sharkey as I had warned him and that I would do something more than reprimand if the foul fighting continued.

There is one thing I regret. I should have given Sharkey the fight earlier in the contest. In the fourth round, I think it was, Fitz landed a left-handed blow and returned with his elbow, cutting Sharkey's eyebrow open. The Sailor should have had the fight then.

The foul blow of the right was seen plainly by me. Fitz smashed with his right on Sharkey's shoulder and then with an uppercut with the left he struck the Sailor below the belt. Sharkey was leaning over and the blow knocked him down. It was clearly a foul and before the Sailor moved I mentioned that the fight was over. The first blow had been weak and I believe that the second was intended for an uppercut, but it struck foul. No man until now has ever questioned my honor. I have been in many places and in peculiar situations, but no one ever said, until to-night, that I was guilty of a dishonorable act. And I will repeat that I decided in all fairness and with a judgment that was as true as my eyesight. I saw the foul blow.

WYATT EARP.

SHARKEY DESCRIBES THAT DECISIVE BLOW.

With the exception of an awful pain in my groin I cannot say that I feel any the worse for my encounter with Fitzsimmons. I did my very best during the contest to put him to sleep and am satisfied that I had the best of it in every round.

Fitzsimmons pretends to be a very fair fighter and has a knack of making himself appear as such, before the public. But the truth of it is he uses the foulest tactics of any man I ever met.

His principal fouling is done with his elbow. He used his elbow on me dozens of times and in that way cut that deep gash over my left eye, which caused me to bleed so freely during the last four rounds.

Outside of that cut and the injury to my groin I am all right and am willing to meet him again at any time. I can whip him to a certainty and I believe he knows it himself.

At no time during the contest was I fatigued or in trouble until I received that foul blow. In fact I felt that I was getting stronger as the fight progressed.

Fitzsimmons' blows did not hurt me—not one of them except that foul swing he made which laid me out.

While I was growing stronger and more confident of winning he was certainly losing in strength and quickness right along. This may not have impressed the spectators, but I could see it and I was taking advantage of his approaching collapse when he fouled me to save himself.

He has a trick of laughing and pretending that he is at ease, which deceived the crowd all through the fight.

Those punches I gave him around the ribs and abdomen distressed him. Had I not been quite so short in the reach I could have punched him out of the contest in about four rounds.

By keeping so far away from me he forced me to throw away many well meant blows.

I am certain that Fitzsimmons fouled me deliberately. He did it to save himself from defeat.

It was getting too plain to him that I was gaining in strength while he was going down hill, so to speak, and rather than be knocked out he thought he would lose on a foul. Had he not delivered that nasty blow which crippled me I would certainly have finished him in that round—the eighth, I believe it was.

I was for the moment paralyzed when I received that blow, and was wholly unable to protect myself. I felt myself sinking to the floor and I was doubled up in such a way that I could not guard myself from the last upper-cut which he sent in. I suppose as a finisher.

I am sorry that the question of supremacy was not settled on its merits rather than on a foul.

I can beat Fitzsimmons and I would far rather have knocked him out than win the purse on a foul. I don't think he will be anxious to meet me again, however, but if he does well, I am open to all engagements. I am in the boxing business as a profession.

I intend to win the world's championship if the decision in this contest has not already given me the right to that title. I am not going to pose as a talking fighter either. If anybody wants to meet me they will always find me willing.
THOMAS J. SHARKEY.

THE FIGHT AS VIEWED BY AN EXPERT.

Sharkey Showed Improvement and Fitzsimmons Seemed More Than Ordinarily Cautious.

By W. W. Naughton.

THE EXAMINER, SAN FRANCISCO: THURSDAY MORNING, DECEMBER 3, 1896.

'TIME!'

SWINNERTON'S ATTENTION WAS TAKEN BY THE PEOPLE WHO LOOKED ON.

A SURPRISE AND A DISAPPOINTMENT.

The Better Man Did Not Win, and If a Foul Was Committed It Was Certainly an Accident.

By T. Y. Williams

AGNEW WHIPS MULLER.

This Contest Was the Chief Feature of the Preliminaries Last Evening.

"YES, IT WAS A GREAT FIGHT, BUT—"

(Continued From Page One.)

THE FINAL BLOW AFTER THE ALLEGED FOUL WAS COMMITTED.

Cartoons by Swinnerton, famous cartoonist of his time, who was at ringside, and the sketch by the *Examiner*'s artist showing the "final blow." *Courtesy General Library, University of California at Berkeley*

"Have you got your gun?" asked Captain Whittman of Earp, noting Julian's uneasiness.

"Yep," was Earp's remark.

"You'd better let me have it."

"All right."

So for the first time in the history of the ring in California, it was necessary to disarm the referee. Possibly if the surrender of the weapon had been more generally observed there would have been more willingness to debate with Mr. Earp over the correctness of his views about that foul.

Apart from the unsatisfactory ending, the fight was good enough for anybody's money. There were blows which thudded so hard as to send a shiver over all the packed humanity in the great Mechanics Pavillion. There was enough uncertainty to keep the nerves on edge. Most of the time it was anybody's fight, and the give and take was always fast and full of possibility.

Sharkey was as his friends had said he was—a hard man to hurt and an earnest fighter. Fitzsimmons fulfilled all expectations of being a great ring general and a hard puncher. Certainly his superiority as a boxer was manifest throughout.

BUT——

That "But" ruins all the fun of the thing. Men will never feel certain that the fight was on the square, and that the best man was not tricked out of it. They will continue to say that the referee was misled and Sharkey "faked the foul."

There were people enough for a national convention. They were not those of whom Fitz James O'Brien sang, "their faces beaten in by the iron hoof of sin." That may have been the sort of people who gathered at the ring side on the turf in O'Brien's day when "two young men, lusty and tall with nothing between them of strife or wrongs" got together to slug and swat and maul each other, "hammer and tongs."

But last night's company began with the man who passes the plate in church and ended with a Justice of the Supreme Court. The clubs were crowded before the event. Many's the man whose wife went to bed last night commiserating with him on the fact that he had to work so hard "at the office." Many's the lawyer who had to meet "an important client." Many's the leader of the city's thought and action who softened his conscience with tales of the necessity of ascertaining whether or not those boxing contests are really brutal.

Over in Oakland the good matrons came near to postponing a cotillion at the request of the dancing men.

As it was, I fear many an Oakland belle experienced all the woes of a Wall-flower at that cotillion, for there were Oakland dancing men in droves at the fight.

Police commissioners were there, and superior court judges, and their eyes danced at the sight of blood, and their breath came hard when the fortunes of battle swayed—for they are very human, these police commissioners and superior judges. The produce exchange, the board of trade, the merchant's association, even the professionally good people of the civic federation, were all represented there, and none of the representatives seemed a bit ashamed. For Theodore Roosevelt and Dr. Parkhurst have said that this ring fighting is not brutal and surely they should know.

Women were there—some with veils and some without. I don't suppose that even Mr. Roosevelt or Dr. Parkhurst would say that it was just the place for women. Certainly the men who howled and yelled about ring didn't think so. Men don't care to have women see them when they take the bit of morality in their teeth and let their passions run away with them.

Chinamen were there sitting in common brotherhood with the whites. That may be called a step into the direction of social equality—and they all yelled just the same.

There wasn't much yelling when the fight went on, but once or twice there rose that low, tense dangerous sound.

"Woo-oo! Woo-oo! Woo-oo!"

That's the sound of the mob—the menace of the broiling human stream when it threatens to break the dam of order and roll on destroying. It greeted Julian when he protested the selection of Earp as referee. It rolled up against Sharkey everytime he struck Fitzsimmons in the clinches or tried his wrestling tactics which had proved so effective against Corbett.

But when the decision came there was no sign of riot. It took the crowd some time to ascertain just what had happened. Those who did know were not eager to mix things with Earp, and the information became general by a slow trickling process, passing from mouth to mouth and tier to tier. So by the time the full significance of the situation had reached the throng, Earp had gone. Sharkey had been carried away and there was no one left to mob but the police and Fitzsimmons, who left the ring protesting like one possessed.

Consequently it will be said that San Francisco accepted the decision gracefully, and the men who had staked fortunes on Earp's few fatal words won and lost their money with christian fortitude and gentlemanly forbearance.

The money won and lost on Sharkey's staying power was honest money, no matter who may be bold enough to question the final results. Most bets had gone up that the stocky Sailor would not last six rounds or seven rounds. But up to the eighth round he was "there all the while."

At the end of the third, Fitzsimmons leaned over to those in his corner and said: "I'll finish him in the next round."

But he didn't finish him.

In fact, at the end of the fourth it looked very much as though Sharkey could stay in the ring with the Australian a week or more.

In the fifth it was different though. Fitzsimmons got his arms into action and Sharkey was battered more than he had ever been battered by the seas. But in the sixth he braced wonderfully and won the cheer which greeted him when the gong sounded that the sixth-round money was all for the Sharkey man. Then in the seventh he kept fairly strong though few they were who had any notion that he could possibly win anything more than the seventh-round bets.

And then——

Then came a mix-up and a swirl of arms and Sharkey went down to claim his foul. If the fight had ended with the seventh round, few would have had a twinge or regret. But as it is, Fitzsimmons has placed his case into the hands of Colonel Henry I. Kowalsky in an effort to prevent the payment of the $10,000 check, which was the price for which they fought, and the big Australian's friends are crying fraud— crying in places where the quiet Mr. Earp will be certain not to hear them.

But it was a great occasion. If you don't think so, you should have seen Chief Crowley in his full uniform. He couldn't have done more had the President of the United States arrived. And you should have seen the crowd, which was fit to receive any president, even the "Advance Agent of Prosperity."

And you should have seen the fight.

But——.

Wyatt was indignant when he read Hamilton's story and sent a letter to the *Examiner* denying he had "favored Sharkey" and describing as "rubbish" the rumors he had fixed the fight. He claimed he had seen Sharkey only once before and that was when the Sailor had fought Corbett. Bat Masterson, he revealed, had introduced him to Fitzsimmons some time ago.

He wrote: "I am sure Bat Masterson bet a lot of money on the fight, but I have always been able to decide against my own money and my friends can stand the consequences of such a decision.

"I feel that I was right and honorable and feeling so, I care nothing of the feeling of anybody. I saw that low blow struck as plainly as I saw you and that is all there is to the story . . ."

Wyatt Earp's troubles continued after the fight. A court hearing was held to question Earp's verdict and to determine the legal winner of the $10,000 purse. Cross-examination stripped away Wyatt's facade of a "wealthy sporting man" who operated a string of racehorses. It was brought out that the horses were only leased, he did not own any stables and his assets were minimal.

The reporter for the *San Francisco Chronicle* described Earp as testifying "with a general air of meek resignation about his face."

He continued: "His announcement of his absolute poverty seemed to affect him greatly, and as he made this statement his voice sank to a whisper and he leaned his head back in a melancholy manner on the four carat diamond ring that adorned his little finger."[44] The attorneys for Fitzsimmons charged that Earp was part of a "foul, preconceived plot" and revealed that they found four of the city's busiest bookmakers who had switched their bets from Fitzsimmons to Sharkey at the last moment.

Wyatt's appearance in court drew the attention of the attorneys for H. S. Crocker & Company, the San Francisco firm which had given loans to Earp while he was preparing to leave Tombstone. A judgment for $2,121.21 was filed against Earp by the loan company. The *Chronicle* reporter shrewdly observed that once outside the courtroom Wyatt dropped his air of "meek resignation." As the reporter wrote: "He enjoys hugely the curiosity of the people wherever he appears in a public place by parading in localities where the biggest crowds congregate."[45]

Wyatt next appeared in print in May 1900 when he got into a brawl, probably at a local racetrack, with Tom Mulqueen, a professional fighter and "well known horseman." The *Arizona Citizen* reported that Wyatt "attempted to do the horseman but the latter knocked him glassy eyed in the first round."[46]

The Nevada gold fields of Tenopah and Goldfield, in 1902 and 1905, also knew Earp as a saloon keeper. Later he settled in Los Angeles. In 1911, at sixty-three, he was arrested for taking part in a bunco game to cheat a businessman out of $25,000.

The *Arizona Star*, no friend of Wyatt's, picked up the original story from the *Los Angeles Times*. However, an examination of both the *Star* and the *Times* reveals that this time Earp was a victim of sloppy reporting.[47]

The *Times* had Earp arrested after a Los Angeles real estate man complained to the police that "three professional sharpers and con men" were ready to fleece them out of $2,500—not $25,000 as the *Star* had reported. Police raided the hotel room where the game was scheduled to be held and arrested three men, one they identified as "Wyatt Earp, a well known sporting man."

Three days later the *Times* disclosed that the charge against Earp and his companions "is simply conspiring to violate the law prohibiting gambling." An earlier vagrancy charge was dropped at the request of the city prosecutor. On July 28, Earp pleaded not guilty. On September 11 all charges against him were dismissed. The *Los Angeles Times* story ended:

"Earp was in the room when the police entered but contended that he was not connected with the game and had simply dropped in by accident. No evidence against him was secured."

Stuart Lake and Wyatt Earp

John Newman Edwards, author and Missouri newspaper editor, created the image of Jesse James as America's Robin Hood. Stuart Lake, a free-lance magazine writer, established Wyatt Earp as the premier lawman of the Wild West, who cowed the gunfighters of the Kansas cow towns, drove the outlaws from Arizona, and faced down a band of killers at a dusty stable named the O. K. Corral. Lake's book, *Wyatt Earp: Frontier Marshal,*[48] published in 1931 and serialized in the *Saturday Evening Post,* has been the inspiration for movies and the basis for the television series of the 1950s which made Earp one of the best-known figures of Western frontier history.

Curiously, with few exceptions, it took historians and serious students of the West a long time to discover Lake's book was mostly romantic fiction. Perhaps it was because Lake seemed to intimidate other writers. He claimed a monopoly on Earp's life, insisting he was the only one who had interviewed his subject at length and independently corroborated Earp's statements after his death. When the TV series, seen by millions, began to implant Earp as a super-hero in popular American imagination, historical investigators began to seriously question the many thrilling incidents Lake claimed were dictated to him by Earp.

Among the earliest writers to be suspicious of the Earp "biography" was Burton Rascoe, author and nationally known literary critic. In his 1944 biography of Belle Starr, the notorious Oklahoma bandit queen, Rascoe wrote: "It seems extremely improbable to me that Wyatt Earp, an almost illiterate gunfighter, whose adult life was spent in strenuous action, could have written a book about his career in a style worthy of Ernest Hemingway."

About the time Rascoe had completed his manuscript, he received a letter from Lake. Apparently this was in reply to Rascoe's query of how the Earp book had been constructed.

In a footnote Rascoe summarized what Lake had written to him:

"I have heard from Stuart Lake admitting that my skepticism is justified. Earp, he says, was inarticulate. In speech he was at the best, monosyllabic. Lake plied him with questions for months on end and therefore he felt journalistically justified in inventing the Earp manuscript."[49]

Wyatt Earp in his last years.
Courtesy National Archives

What was behind this historical fakery? Was Lake's book the product of Earp's lies or the author's imagination? A partial answer can be found in the little known exchange of letters between Lake and Earp from December 1927 to just before Earp's death at the age of eighty, in 1929.

Some letters were typed by Earp's close friend John H. Flood; others were written in pencil and signed by Earp. They tell of Lake's initial determination to make his book a historical account of Earp's life, not only by interviewing the subject but also by independent research in Kansas and Arizona newspapers and court documents and by seeking pioneers for their memories.[50]

At the time, Earp was sick, broke, and discouraged. He and Josie, whom Lake later described as "the most shrewish female he had ever the misfortune to encounter," lived in a small bungalow on North Seventh Street, Los Angeles. They also spent time at Earp's mines near Vidal, California.

The collection of letters makes clear that Earp cooperated with Lake to the best of his frail health, searching old boxes in storage for photographs, clippings, court documents, and supplying the names and addresses of old frontiersmen for Lake to interview. A few letters hint at Earp's enormous ego. When Lake suggested he have a picture taken for the book, Wyatt wrote endlessly about the photograph. It appeared that the print was more important to him than the contents of his biography.

The letters disclose that Lake caught Earp lying when he pictured himself dramatically disarming Ben Thompson, the Texas gunfighter, in Ellsworth, Kansas, and then defied a mob to force Cad Pierce, Thompson's friend and fellow gambler to turn over his guns. But Lake quickly soothed the sick old man, urging him to "forget the slip" and promised he would "catch 'em all."

Josie appeared to be a constant threat to Lake; she was suspicious of him from their first meeting. When she insisted upon consulting a Los Angeles attorney to review the "agreement" Lake had given her husband to sign, Lake hurriedly assured Earp that his offer to split equally all profits was fair and "hog-tight." But Josie was never far from her husband when Lake did the interviewing.

Lake recalled for Robert N. Mullin, a superb researcher of the American West, how Josie would sit in a chair alongside the bed, carefully reviewing every question Lake asked the weary, bedridden man. There were times, Lake told Mullin, when she insisted upon supplying the answers. Lake desperately tried to reach Earp when his wife wasn't at home but the grim-faced woman always appeared at the bedside. Lake described the man who had pictured himself as the toughest lawman on the western frontier as "hen pecked," yielding meekly when his wife reviewed the accounts he gave to Lake. Finally Lake brought his wife along on his interviewing visits; it appears from some of his syrupy letters to Earp mentioning Josie, that he was able to talk alone to Earp while the two women chatted.[51]

Lake's critics question his statement that he had persuaded Earp to "devote the closing months of his long life to the narration of his full story." However, the letters indicate that Lake did just that, visiting Earp in Los Angeles and Vidal as often as Wyatt's health permitted.

At least one writer had suggested that Earp "did not wish to discuss in great detail his many adventures on the frontier."[52]

Lake's letters to Earp incorporating questions about their last interview show that Earp talked freely, was deeply interested in the book—he once chided Lake for not keeping in touch with him—and was anxiously waiting to read the manuscript. He never did. In January 1929, three days after he ordered Lake not to let his New York agent see the manuscript for a possible prepublication magazine sale, desiring to make further changes, Earp died.

In his first letter to Earp on Christmas Day, 1927, Lake, then living in San Diego, revealed that it was Bat Masterson's stories of Earp which had inspired him to write "your biography, your memoirs if you prefer." Lake recalled how he had worked with Masterson on the *New York Morning Telegraph*, "and heard Bat talk about you . . . I heard him talk enough to be sure that the story of Wyatt Earp was one very much worth telling." Lake outlined his idea of the book, "to start at the beginning, take in the early days of Dodge City and Wichita, so on to Tombstone and the years that have followed. . . . You to do the telling and I the writing." Lake disclosed that the idea of an Earp biography had been on his mind for the six years he had lived in California. He had tried to reach Earp without success, then obtained his address from the Arizona Historical Society.[53]

Earp replied on January 16, 1928. In a letter typed by his friend Flood, Earp advised Lake that he had been confined to bed for the last six months and was "just beginning to get on my feet again." He was planning a trip to the country, possibly his place in the desert near Vidal, "to build my health up and after that I shall be able to interest myself in other things, I hope." He invited Lake to visit him when he returned.[54]

Six days later Lake wrote to Earp hoping that his recovery would be "speedy and complete." Now there was a possessive air in Lake's letters. He advised Earp, "after a discussion of preliminaries, we might arrange to spend a certain amount of time together each day until I have to hand in the material required."[55]

Earp returned to the desert in early June and notified Lake that he was ready to meet with him. On June 11 Lake replied that he was "ready to talk over the idea of going right ahead with your biography."[56]

On June 15 he advised Earp that he was coming to see him on the nineteenth, "and then in a talk of an hour or so, we can settle all necessary preliminaries about what you decided to do about the suggested undertaking, and that if your decision is favorable, I can, in turn, outline my work for the future in according with your desire and convenience."[57]

Apparently they came to an agreement. Earp gave Lake a copy of an autobiography he had dictated to Flood but the writer returned it as unpublishable. He recommended they start from the beginning and Earp agreed. Then Lake asked for all photographs, clippings, copies of court documents, and articles dealing with Earp's life and the old man promised he and his wife would search their trunks and contact relatives.[58]

That summer they met whenever Earp's fragile health permitted. After one interviewing session, Lake wrote to Earp outlining the theme for their book:

"We are going to tell a fact story, are going to correct for the first and for all times, a great many misstatements that have crept into print. We must give our story a ring of truthfulness and of absolute frankness about all that has transpired."[59]

But Lake's lofty theme—he would abandon it—didn't impress Josie Earp. She continued to view with suspicion Lake and the "horse-high" agreement her husband had signed. Finally she consulted a lawyer and this irritated Lake. He wrote to Earp:

"You tell her I appreciate her feelings in the matter and know that she must be fully satisfied before anything else. Frankly, I would not want to go on with anything unless she was satisfied. What I tried to do in the agreement I brought up, was to state the whole business in simple language. The more you wind red tape around a deal of this sort the more you hamper your chances of realizing on it to the fullest possible extent. And I know that unless one has been through the mill, the details of this so-called literary business are baffling and confusing. I tried to look ahead to forestall any possible misunderstanding in the future.

"To my mind, the agreement I offered was horse-high, bull-strong, hog-tight, with each of us getting an even break. There was no possible loop-hole, we were in on a fifty-fifty basis."

Lake shrewdly appealed to Earp's ego, pointing out there was "more than money" to be considered. There was "prestige to be gained in only one way, the character of the publication in which your life story appears." Lake was referring to his plan to serialize his book in a national magazine.[60]

Their next session evidently was a long one. On August 31 Lake wrote to Earp posing some questions he had not asked earlier "because you were pretty well tired with all the work we had done."[61]

Earp had told Lake he killed the young cowboy Hoyt in Dodge City, as well as the two McLaurys, Florentino Cruz, Frank Stilwell, and Curly Bill.

Lake was anxious to know if that was Earp's total of dead men. He urged Earp to search his memory, "because if there were others and I do not include them, then there will be many people who do recall them to say my whole book is in error because I have not told the whole story." He also wanted Earp to list "any killings which were charged against you for which you were not responsible."

Ten days later, after a long interviewing session, Lake sent Earp another list of questions. He wanted "details" of the hunt for the gunmen who had shot Virgil Earp, "because you did not do this when I was taking notes and Flood's account is fragmentary."

He pressed Earp to go into all the events of his life, "or it will give them an opportunity to discredit the whole story." Lake didn't identify "them" but obviously he was referring to Earp's old Tombstone enemies, such as William Breakenridge and Lorenzo Walters, who had written their own books in which Earp emerged as anything but a shining frontier knight.

He ended this letter with another request for Earp to recall the name of the milliner who had testified in the O. K. Corral hearing and how many men were connected with the shooting of Virgil Earp.[62]

Earp replied three days later. The name of the Tombstone milliner escaped him, Earp confessed, but he stated flatly that Billy Clanton and Frank McLaury "had four or five bullets in their bodies, and of course it would be impossible to declare who was responsible for the shots."

Earp also disclosed that Josie had visited Allie Earp, Virgil's widow, in an attempt to dig up material for Lake but was told by Allie that everything had been destroyed in a hotel fire in Oklahoma. Earp also included a list of the birthdays and deaths of his father, mother, and brothers.[63] Josie Earp refused to go away. They argued about the type of book Lake intended to write. Finally Lake wrote to Earp begging him to assure Josie he would write a "nice clean story" of her husband's life.

"Please assure her it will be the type of a story which will satisfy her," he wrote. "You will have to excuse all my questions but I am a hound for accuracy, not altogether out of place in a work of this sort."[64]

In another letter Lake disclosed to Earp he had finally located a number of Tombstone pioneers who were contributing their memoirs. Although he agreed with Earp that Lorenzo Walters's *Tombstone Yesterdays* was filled with errors, Lake wrote that he intended to ask Walters for permission to use his photographs.[65]

All that fall Josie Earp's doubts and suspicions hung like a shadow over Lake. He again wrote to Earp asking him to assure Josie she would get the book she wanted.

"It will be a nice clean story," Lake wrote, "rather than any wild tale of bloodletting and whooping gunplay."[66]

When she finally read the manuscript months later Josie Earp would bitterly remember Lake's promise.

In one letter Lake revealed he had arranged for a library to send the works of Ned Buntline, the early pulp writer, to his home. He gave no reason nor did he ever discuss any of Buntline's stories or the writer's historical accuracy. Lake never mentioned Buntline's name again in any letter to Earp.[67]

This terse announcement of Buntline's name is the only clue to Wyatt Earp's fictitious Buntline Special, the super-gun created by Lake to further glamorize the romantic and fanciful lawman of the Wild West he had created.[68]

That fall Lake sent a steady flow of letters to Earp, informing him of how the book was progressing.

Once, after painting a rosy glow of high royalties, he confessed to Earp he did this, "to bolster up Mrs. Earp's confidence in me." He also apologized for the many questions he insisted Earp answer in detail, pointing out, "I wanted to get everything with absolute certainty. That is the only kind that counts and I thought that with a little time away from the steady questioning to which I subjected you, you might have called to mind other incidents that should be included."[69]

Lake's letters show that he was continuing to conscientiously search for old frontiersmen who had known Earp, and was interviewing them either in person or by letter. Once, he questioned Earp about the mysterious Freis, named by the coroner's inquest as one of the killers of Morgan Earp and Pony Deal, a minor Tombstone character.

Freis, whom Pete Spence's wife had identified as "the German," may or may not have been a gambler who took away the Oriental's gambling concession from Morgan. He is the only one of the four men named by the coroner's jury as Morgan's killers whom Earp and his posse did not seek out. There is no letter from Earp supplying Lake with information on Freis.

Then in October 1928 Lake uncovered evidence that Earp was lying.

Wyatt had given him a fabricated story of how he had disarmed and arrested Ben Thompson, the notorious Texas gunfighter and gambler, after Ben's brother, Billy, had killed Chauncey Whitney, sheriff of Ellsworth. Earp had also described a dramatic incident of how, when he was "marshal" of Wichita, he had defied a mob of angry Texas cowhands to disarm Cad Pierce, a popular drover, gambler, and Ben's friend.

Lake wrote to Earp that an account he had found in the *Ellsworth Reporter* described how Pierce had been killed in Ellsworth by Edward Crawford, a local policeman, the year before Earp's imaginary incident.

"It couldn't have been Cad Pierce you disarmed," Lake suggested. "Could it possibly have been Abel "Shanghai" Pierce, a big cattleman and a lofty drinker, so to speak, and mean when drunk, I've been told. . . ? If you can recall the name, I'd wish you send it down to me. . . . If you can't, we can get around it some way or other but I would like the name."

Then he added: "Don't let this little slip of memory disturb you. We all get 'em and I'll catch most of them, all of any importance."[70]

Earp promptly replied, admitting that he was wrong in naming Cad Pierce as the man he had disarmed. He agreed with Lake that it was "a mistake on my part. . . . It was Shang Pierce [sic]."[71]

Earp wanted to meet Lake and suggested that he come to Los Angeles "so we can have another talk" but Lake, with one eye still on Mrs. Earp, wrote, "It would be better that we do as Mrs. Earp suggested, drive over to Vidal just after Thanksgiving and spend a few days. At that time I will have the manuscript close enough to the end to make intelligent criticisms and revisions."

"Don't let *Helldorado* bother you," Lake concluded. "We'll call the turn on Breakenridge in the proper place."[72]

A furious Earp replied in a shaky scrawl advising Lake that he had discovered his photograph had been copyrighted in the Breakenridge book. He wrote: "I have lived a good many years and in all my life have never heard of such a nerve. . . . This has upset me more than anything for some time."

Earp was not only angry over the copyrighted photograph, but by the way he was pictured in the Breakenridge book. "All lies," he wrote Lake. Breakenridge was a "sly fox of the worst kind."

The picture and Breakenridge's book occupied most of Earp's thoughts that fall. One can only pity the sick old man brooding away the time in his small bungalow not far from where other men were playing out make-believe stories on film of the West he knew so well. Perhaps he remembered the days when some men were terrorized by the very sound of his name.

"Everything is keeping me from just giving him [Breakenridge] a chance to defend himself. . . . A man like him needs to be called down . . . and make him show what a lowdown coward he is," he wrote Lake in a barely legible note.

Then the picture he had taken in a Los Angeles commercial studio did not suit Lake. Earp wrote back in a huff, "I am sorry you cannot use my picture as it is a very true likeness of me. . . . But I will go Saturday and sit for a new picture."

Earp's next few letters to Lake discussed the new pictures and the one he liked showing him in "repose." When Lake suggested that he ask the Authors League's attorneys to take action against the publishers of *Helldorado* for using Earp's picture, Wyatt agreed and sent him power of attorney.[73]

In mid-November Lake finally got the pictures he wanted of Earp and hastened to tell Wyatt, "Mrs. Lake says to tell you that you are a handsome man." The book, he wrote, "is coming along swimmingly, almost too good to be true." Lake also revealed to Earp that his literary agent was predicting they would get up to a $10,000 advance on the book.

From his letters Lake was still interviewing Arizona pioneers who had known Earp. Among the contributors to Lake's file was Doctor T. L. McCarty, the Dodge City physician who had treated most of the cow town's gunshot wounds; Frank Warren, the bartender in the Long Branch saloon, "and a hundred others . . . all of whom write beautifully about you . . ."[74]

About this time Lake found Charles Hatton, who had been a young attorney in Wichita when Earp was a policeman. Hatton described two thrilling incidents for Lake. One was how Earp had silently, steadily walked about thirty feet toward a dangerous killer and relieved him of his six-shooter. The second incident related by Hatton was how Earp took off his badge and unstrapped his gunbelt to accept the challenge of a burly cowboy to use fists instead of guns. The pair went to the rear of a clothing store where Earp knocked out the cowboy. This was exciting material and Lake demanded more details.

He wrote to Earp: "Whose store was it? And even more important, what was the tough fellow's name? Give me anything else you recall of the affair."

In a reply typewritten by Flood, Earp modestly recalled how he had disarmed Sergeant Melvin A. King—later killed by Bat Masterson—without firing a shot or raising his voice. He identified the fellow he had beaten up in the rear of the store as a Texas gambler "who had twitted me considerably about arresting Ben Thompson in Ellsworth."[75]

Earp's arrest of Thompson, of course, was a fabrication. The King incident had taken place, but not as Earp described it for Lake.

Earp, backed up by two men holding shotguns, beat King over the head with the barrel of his six-shooter, then Earp and his two companions dragged the cavalry sergeant to the office of Justice of the Peace Edward Jewett, pulled down the shades, "and almost beat the defenseless man to death. Pretending to fine him, they went through his pockets and robbed him of everything he had."[76]

Earp identified George Peshaur as the Texan he had beaten in the back room of Cogswell's cigar store for taunting him about the "arrest" of Ben Thompson.[77] But there is no account of the incident in the *Ellsworth Reporter*. It was just another tall tale spun by Earp and swallowed by Lake.

Lake didn't finish the first draft of Earp's biography on Thanksgiving, 1928, as he had planned. Influenza swept across the West Coast and he was stricken. It wasn't until January 1929 that he was able to return to his typewriter. On January 7 he was reporting to Earp that his New York agent had urged him to send in half the manuscript. "He thinks he can sell the whole business from that."

Earp also wrote Lake on the seventh and their letters crossed in the mail. Wyatt was growing weaker and both he and his wife had been confined to bed. He had not heard from Lake for some time and wondered "what progress you have been making with the story?"

Wyatt disclosed that William S. Hart, the cowboy movie star, had suggested that Lake send his manuscript to Houghton Mifflin, the Boston publisher, whose West Coast representative had expressed interest in the book.

Lake, still wobbly from the flu, laboriously typed a two-page reply, suggesting that the publisher's representative get in touch with him to set up a meeting. He emphasized to Earp the importance of retaining their prepublication magazine rights which "would mean several thousand dollars, cash in advance, which a publisher does not pay."[78]

Earp's last letter to Lake was typed by Flood three days later. In it Wyatt urged Lake to see him in Los Angeles as soon as he could. He seemed disturbed about Lake's proposal to show some of the manuscript to his agent. He wrote:

"I would not want the manuscript to be seen or examined by any other person than yourself until it is absolutely complete—that would not be fair to me—there may be changes or corrections that I would want to make, and nobody should know its contents until I have read it over thoroughly."[79]

Earp died a few days later. As Lake had predicted, his book was serialized in the *Saturday Evening Post* and then published in October 1931 by the Houghton Mifflin Company. It became a national best seller and was highly praised by leading reviewers as an outstanding contribution to the literature of the frontier.

For some reason Lake abandoned his research after Earp's death and changed his "nice clean story" into a well-written fictional romance. One could go on for pages listing the book's errors, lies, distortions, omissions, and fraudulent events. To mention a few:

Lake stated that his book was the "first time" Earp had told his experiences on the frontier. Lake conveniently overlooked Earp's articles in the *San Francisco Examiner* of 1896.

Lake's version of the O. K. Corral gunfight is ludicrous. Lake has Earp disarming Ike Clanton and then Clanton sending a messenger to Earp advising Wyatt that if he left Tombstone, "they wouldn't harm your brothers but that if you stayed, you'd have to come down and make your fight or they'd bring it to you."

The leader of the vigilantes stoutly pleaded with Earp that he had "thirty-five men, waiting, ready for business" but Wyatt tersely thanked him and added, "this is our job."

Lake ignored Earp's 1896 article which had Frank McLaury firing at him while Billy Clanton shot Doc Holliday. In the book's version both McLaury and young Clanton "turned loose on Wyatt Earp the shots with which they opened the famous battle of the O. K. Corral."

In the *San Francisco Examiner* article Wyatt had Ike Clanton running into Fly's studio and firing at him from one of the windows! Lake has the young cowboy firing seventeen shots at the Earps and Holliday, but Ike actually fired none.

Eyewitnesses at the hearing testified that Doc Holliday fired the first shot with his nickel-plated revolver after Tom McLaury threw open his coat, crying out that he was not armed.

In his letters to Earp, Lake boasted how he had consulted Tombstone's newspaper accounts of Earp's role in the gunfight "to get at the truth." Nowhere in his account is Mrs. King testifying that she heard Holliday and the Earps agreeing to kill the Clantons and McLaurys. Here was an independent, unprejudiced witness offering prima facie evidence that the O. K. Corral fight was premeditated murder.

In 1896 Earp described how he was forced to fight Ike Clanton and four of his friends at the Tucson railroad yard. Lake quotes him: "One of them, Frank Stilwell, who was believed to be Morgan's murderer, was killed by my gun going off when he grabbed it."

Lake has Wyatt recognizing Stilwell and chasing him across the tracks. When he caught Stilwell he slowly pointed his gun at Stilwell's heart, then pulled the trigger.

If Lake consulted the record of the Tucson coroner's inquest, he totally ignored the findings of the jury, which told how Stilwell's body had been riddled with rifle and six-shooter bullets, including bursts of buckshot.

In his newspaper articles Earp wrote that he killed Curly Bill, his perennial enemy, with a shotgun, "blowing him to pieces." Lake has Wyatt killing Curly Bill after a raging gun battle which left Earp's hat, coat, and one boot pockmarked with bullet holes although he never sustained a scratch.

Curly Bill, of course, had left Arizona long before this fake gun battle, slightly bewildered as to why he had gathered such an awesome reputation simply because he had accidentally killed a sheriff.

Lake's description of the Ellsworth gun battle in which Billy Thompson accidentally killed Sheriff Whitney is a complete fraud. Although he had the *Ellsworth Reporter*'s account of that violent scene, Lake failed to point out to Earp that the *Reporter* had Ben Thompson surrendering his guns to Ellsworth's mayor, James Miller, and not Earp. There is nothing in any newspaper account or court document to substantiate Earp's story that he coolly walked up to the Texas killer and calmly persuaded him to turn over his gun. In reality Ben would have killed Earp within seconds.[80]

Lake also never questioned Earp's quick acceptance of his suggestion that the man he had "disarmed" in Wichita was Abel "Shanghai" Pierce and not Cad Pierce, Thompson's friend and fellow gambler, who had been killed the year earlier in Ellsworth by one of the cow town's policemen. Again there is no newspaper account or official document to support Earp's story of his confrontation with Shanghai Pierce, one of the best-known cattlemen in the Southwest.

Lake also has stories of Earp clobbering the Clements brothers, close relatives of John Wesley Hardin, and relieving them of their guns. But by the time this encounter is supposed to have taken place, Mannen Clements and Hardin, occupied with the Sutton-Taylor feud in Gonzales and DeWitt counties, Texas, were a hoofbeat ahead of the Texas Rangers.

The mystery of Lake's book is: What prompted him to substitute the "nice clean story" he had promised Mrs. Earp for his outrageous fiction? Did he regard Josephine Earp as a potential troublesome partner and censor who was no longer a threat after her husband's death, so he scrapped his original book for a slam-bang action tale of the Wild West that he knew would sell?

The question can't be answered a half century later, but Lake's letters show he sincerely admired Earp and accepted his exaggerations and fakery as historical fact even after he had uncovered evidence the sick old man was either lying or his memory, praised so highly by Lake, had slipped badly.

The Buntline Special

Out of Stuart Lake's fictional biography of Wyatt Earp came the enduring American legend of the Buntline Special revolver, an awesome eighteen-inch Colt equipped with a shoulder-stock attachment. Lake had Wyatt using the heavy barrel to club badmen into submission in the Kansas cow towns and to wipe out his self-styled band of desperadoes at the O. K. Corral.

In popular imagination the Buntline Special is Wyatt Earp's trademark. It has won him a reputation as a singular lawman of the Wild West, a knight without plumes who conquered evil with this grotesque but deadly weapon. This was fervently accepted by Hollywood and television. In the 1950s the television series based on Stuart Lake's book had countless little Americans swaggering about their backyards, brandishing plastic Buntline Specials and killing off their enemies in the dusty O. K. Corrals of their childish imaginations. One of the sins of television is that these children would retain this image of Earp for the rest of their lives.

The Lake-Earp tale of how Ned Buntline, the pulp writer, presented the guns to Earp and four other Dodge City lawmen, has been repeated for generations until the endless repetition has made it a historical fact for millions of Americans.

Lake's story has Earp's reputation in the 1870s as a fast-drawing, courageous lawman spreading across the country until it attracted Buntline's attention and the writer came to Dodge City. In 1876, to show his appreciation to Earp and the others for supplying him with "material for hundreds of frontier yarns . . . and the color," Buntline presented them with the special guns.

A survey of the prolific Buntline's works reveals he never used the background of outlawry and gunfighters and never used Earp or any of the western lawmen as his heroes. Like the pulp writers of his time, he preferred Indian raids, war chiefs of the Revolution, stirring sea tales, or scouts like Buffalo Bill.[81]

Buntline's link to the Wild West is based on his Buffalo Bill romances, beginning with "Buffalo Bill, The King of the Border Men!" which was serialized in Street & Smith's *New York Weekly* in the winter of 1869. Three years later crowds were enthralled by the incredibly bad dialogue of his play *The Scouts of the Prairie! And Red Deviltry as It Is!* and Buntline, in a fringed buckskin jacket, bound to a stake ready for torture, delivering a lecture on the curse of drink.

Lake has Buntline presenting the guns to Wyatt, Bat Masterson, Charlie Bassett, Neil Brown, and Bill Tilghman, sometime in the spring or early summer of 1876. He had Colt manufacture "five special forty-five calibre six-guns of regular action style, but with barrels four inches longer than standard—a foot in length—making them eighteen inches overall. Each gun had a demountable walnut rifle stock with a thumbscrew arrangement to fit the weapon for a shoulder piece in long-range shooting. A buckskin thong held the stock to a belt or saddle horn when not in use. The walnut stock of each gun had the word 'Ned' deeply carved in the wood and each was accompanied by a hand-tooled holster modeled for the weapon."[82]

Lake has Earp claiming the Buntline was his "favorite" over any other gun. "I could jerk it as fast as I could my old one and I carried it at my right hip throughout my career as a marshal. With it, I did most of the six-gun work I had to do."[83]

Lake's grandiose description of Earp's spreading reputation along the frontier of the 1870s as an undaunted lawman, skilled in the use of a six-shooter, is startling when compared with the facts. At the time Wyatt was simply known in Wichita and Dodge City as a policeman and a deputy. His only recorded feat in Wichita was the arrest of the horse thief.[84]

Robert Wright, the Dodge City pioneer, certainly would have mentioned Wyatt at length in his history of the cow town as he did Bat Masterson—if Earp had overshadowed or at least equaled the exploits of Masterson, Neil Brown, or the other lawmen. He recalled just about everyone who had played a role in the growth of the frontier community: buffalo hunters, outlaws, gunfighters, sheriffs, pranksters, bankers, and businessmen. He misspelled Earp's name the few times he mentioned him.[85]

In Lake's distorted description of the O. K. Corral gunfight he has Billy Clanton's bullets tearing through Earp's coat sleeves. Then, in a flash, Wyatt draws his Buntline Special and his bullet hits "Frank McLaury squarely in the abdomen, just above the belt buckle."[86]

Nowhere in the detailed newspaper accounts of the event, in Earp's own testimony, or in the testimony of witnesses, friends, and enemies of Earp, is there a mention of the Buntline Special.

In his own statement which he read at the hearings, Earp said that after Johnny Behan reported he had disarmed the cowboys, "I took my pistol, which I had in my hand under my coat and put it in my overcoat pocket. Behan then passed up the street and we walked on down."

One can imagine Earp struggling with an eighteen-inch revolver as he transferred the gun from under his coat to his pocket. Minutes later Billy Clanton, who was armed and considered a deadshot, could have changed the outcome of that historic frontier incident if Earp had really tried to draw such an awkward weapon.

The Dodge City and Ford County newspapers never mentioned the arrival of Ned Buntline, a celebrity of his time, or his "presentation" of the weapons to Earp and the other lawmen, although the newspapers recorded just about every event which took place in the cow town or the county.

The Colt Patern Manufacturing Company, which kept precise records of the sale of its guns to the frontier, has no records of Buntline Specials being manufactured or sold.

Lake identified Bat Masterson as a recipient of that fictional gun. In all the stories he told or wrote—and many included errors and myths—Bat never mentioned the Buntline Special.

In 1907 Bat wrote a series, "Famous Gun Fighters on the Western Frontier" for *Human Life,* a popular magazine of his time. His article on Wyatt Earp is long and detailed but does not include a Buntline Special.

More than twenty years ago Zoe Tilghman, widow of the celebrated western marshall, Bill Tilghman, told this writer the Buntline Special was a myth.

"There was no such thing as a Buntline Special," she said. "It came from the imagination of either Wyatt Earp or Stuart Lake. In all the years we were together and in all the stories I heard from Bill, he never mentioned that weapon—and there was a good reason; the Buntline Special never existed."

But if the famous guns *did* exist, what became of them? Lake abruptly dropped the Buntline Special after he had Wyatt Earp referee the Sharkey-Fitzsimmons heavyweight fight in San Francisco, December 1896. Lake has an Associated Press "ringside dispatch" describing how the crowd packing the Mechanics' Pavilion "howled for Earp." After Wyatt spoke to the suddenly hushed crowd, assuring them, "I'll call things as I see them," he stripped off his coat and vest.

He quotes Earp: "I had completely forgotten how I was dressed, and there on my right hip, the old Buntline forty-five, with its twelve inch barrel and the walnut butt, stuck out like a cannon. I know I turned red to my heels as I unbuckled the gun and handed it to Police Captain Whitman, who sat at the ringside."[87]

In the newspaper accounts of the fight no crowd "howled" for Earp nor was there any mention of the Buntline Special. The *San Francisco Examiner* simply described the weapon Earp surrendered to Police Captain George W. Whittman, at the officer's request, as a .45 caliber revolver with an eight-inch barrel.[88]

Neither Lake nor Earp mention the weapon in their exchange of letters. However, in his letter of September 30, 1928, Lake wrote to Earp that one of his "accomplishments" was to have the "works of Ned Buntline" sent to him from Washington, D. C. Presumably he had made an arrangement with the Library of Congress.

"Buntline, as you can imagine, had a great deal to say about Wichita and Dodge in their early days," he informed Earp. "Reading him should help me greatly."

Why did Lake want to read the fiction of a celebrated pulp writer when he claimed he was doing serious research among the Kansas and Arizona newspapers and official court documents? Was it because Earp had told him the fictitious story of the Buntline Special, or did Lake seriously believe this celebrated blood-and-thunder novelist could supply legitimate background of the cow towns? And was it from Buntline's novels that Lake finally got the idea to equip Wyatt with a mythical gun, the Caliban of the Wild West?

Television turned Stuart Lake's hero and his hero's extraordinary weapon into one of our beloved legends, accepted and admired by generations of Americans who played out their fantasies with him in the far-off cow towns of the Wild West, where hitched horses never urinated in the dusty streets, where savage vigilante mobs never choked their victims to death, where sheriffs were never corrupt, whores always had hearts of pure gold, and Curly Bill came from Central Casting.

Wyatt Earp and his Buntline Special are enshrined forever in the illustrious company of American myths, which include the cherry tree Washington never cut down, the bag of stolen gold Jesse James never gave to the weeping widow to pay off the greedy landlord, the flag Barbara Fritchie never waved, and the last words Lincoln never said. . . .

A wire service story from the old International News Service, July 8, 1958, of how thieves had stolen the tombstone from Wyatt Earp's grave. *The James D. Horan Collection*

COLMA, CALIF., JULY 8--(INS)--A SEARCH IS ON TODAY FOR A GRANITE TOMBSTONE MARKING THE PLACE WHERE THE CREMATED REMAINS OF FAMED WESTERN GUN FIGHTER WYATT EARP WERE BURIED IN A CEMETERY AT COLMA, JUST SOUTH OF SAN FRANCISCO.

MORRIS COLTON, SUPERINTENDENT OF THE HILLS OF ETERNITY MEMORIAL PARK, REPORTED THE TOMBSTONE, WEIGHING MORE THAN FIVE HUNDRED POUNDS, WAS STOLEN EARLY SUNDAY.

COLTON SAID HE SUSPECTS THE TOMBSTONE MAY TURN UP IN AN ARIZONA TOWN CALLED TOMBSTONE WHERE EARP MADE HIS REPUTATION ON THE WESTERN FRONTIER AS AN OUTLAW-KILLING UNITED STATES MARSHAL.

EARP WHO MADE A FORTUNE IN SOUTHERN CALIFORNIA REAL ESTATE AFTER RETIRING FROM HIS PEACE OFFICER CAREER CAME TO SAN FRANCISCO IN 1891.

HE LIVED IN SAN FRANCISCO UNTIL 1897 AND DURING THAT TIME MARRIED JOSEPHINE SARAH MARCUS, DAUGHTER OF A PIONEER STORE OWNER.

THEY WENT TO LOS ANGELES TO LIVE AND EARP DIED IN THE SOUTHERN CALIFORNIA CITY IN 1929.

HIS REMAINS WERE CREMATED AND HIS WIDOW HAD THEM PLACED IN THE COLMA CEMETERY.

AUTHORITIES SAID THERE WAS EVIDENCE THE PERSONS WHO STOLE THE TOMBSTONE TRIED TO GET THE URN CONTAINING EARP'S ASHES, DIGGING A HOLE FIVE FEET DEEP, BUT FAILED TO FIND IT.

NOTES

BAT MASTERSON

1.   Early in 1953 I started researching a biography of Bat Masterson, gathering material from the files of the now defunct *New York Morning Telegraph,* interviewing old newspapermen who knew Masterson, exchanging letters with Floyd Streeter, who sent me copies of valuable items from his own collection and seeking out sources in Kansas, Colorado, Arizona, and Texas. A short time later, Richard O'Connor joined the rewrite staff of the New York City newspaper of which I was an editor. When I learned Dick was halfway through his Masterson biography, I gave him my file which included a package of yellowing, brittle clippings I had carefully pasted together, copies of the *Telegraph*'s clippings including Masterson's columns, my interviews, etc. Fortunately I had taken notes from some of the major items and copied others. Hereafter cited as *The Masterson File.*

Dick O'Connor died several years ago, much before his time. Unfortunately, his Masterson biography, *Bat Masterson,* New York, 1957, hereafter cited as O'Connor, later the basis for that silly television series which left a plastic image of Masterson with the TV generation, was inferior, possibly due to haste and deadline pressure. O'Connor's economically minded publisher must share the blame for that poor book; it has no illustrations, sources, bibliography, or even a simple index.

2.   When Bat was on the *Telegraph*'s staff he was hounded by an admirer—I believe it was Fred Sutton, author of that very unreliable book *Hands Up!*—who begged Bat for one of his guns. It was a well-known story in the *Telegraph*'s city room—also told to Dick by the late Louella Parsons, who had worked with Bat on the *Telegraph*—how the irritated Masterson bought a six-shooter in an Eighth Avenue pawnshop, filed a number of notches on the gun's butt, and gave it to the pest. The story has been enlarged to Bat buying a number of guns,

289

filing the notches, and giving them away. There was only one.

3.   Records of St. Georges of Henryville Parish, County of Iberville. Down through the years I have received bits and pieces of historical information from readers of my books, some merely repeats of old legends and myths, but there are also pure nuggets. One old gentleman who had a hobby of searching through old newspapers directed me to the *New York Times* where Billy the Kid's name was correctly given as McCarty and not Bonney. One reader suggested Bat Masterson was a Canadian by birth and had been baptized in a church identified as St. George, County of Rouville. At the time I made an unsuccessful search and assumed the information was erroneous. Years later when I tried again I learned there was a St. Georges of Henryville. And that is where the baptismal records of the Mastersons are located. Chris Penn of Norfolk, England, first published this startling bit of historical information in *The Brand Book of the English Corral of the Westerners*, April 1967.

      Masterson was often called "Bart" by a few close friends, such as Theodore Roosevelt.

4.   *Bat Masterson: The Dodge City Years* by George G. Thompson, Fort Hays, Kansas, State College Series, Floyd B. Streeter, editor, 1943, pp. 4–11. Hereafter cited as Streeter. In 1937, Thompson obtained an invaluable interview with Bat's brother, Tom, who described their early years. Curiously, Masterson never mentioned to Thompson that Bat and Edward had been born in Canada. Masterson possibly wanted to maintain the all-American family image.

5.   *Life of Billy Dixon* (revised) by Olive Dixon, Dallas, Texas, 1927, p. 115. Hereafter cited as Dixon.

6.   Ibid., p. 135; *The Buffalo Hunters* by Mari Sandoz, New York, 1954, p. 182.

7.   Ibid., p. 135.

8.   Accounts of Nancy, infuriatingly meager, and the Battle of Adobe Walls, can be found in *Dodge City, The Cowboy Capital* by Robert Wright, Wichita, Kansas, 1913, pp. 198–203, hereafter cited as Wright; Dixon, pp. 158–189; "Buffalo Days" by James Winfred Hunt, *Hollands, Magazine of the South*, March 1933; "The Comanche Indians at the Adobe Walls Fight" by R. N. Richardson, *Panhandle Plains Review*, vol. 1, 1931, pp. 24–38; Streeter, pp. 6–100. All sources have various estimates of Parker's warrior army but Fred Leonard's figures in the *Leavenworth Times* are undoubtedly the most reliable.

9.   *Handbook of the American Indian*, Bureau of Ethnology, Bulletin 30, vol. 11, edited by Fred Webb Hodge, Washington, D.C., 1907, p. 204. Quana is from the Comanche *Kwaina* or "fragrant."

10.   *Leavenworth Times*, July 10, 1874.

11.   Dixon, Masterson quoted, pp. 163–164.

12.   Ibid., p. 168.

13.   Wright, pp. 198–203.

14.   Dixon, p. 192; *Out of the West* by Rufus Rockwell Wilson, New York, 1913, p. 424.

15.   Dixon states he was hired as a scout by General Miles on August 6, 1874, and joined Lieutenant Baldwin's command. He has Baldwin sending Bat Masterson "on ahead to tell the boys the troops are coming." Dixon, p. 192. Presumably Dixon and Masterson were Baldwin's two scouts who were in charge of the "six Delaware trailers." Streeter has Miles appointing Masterson, "second in command of the scouts."

      Dixon also places himself with Baldwin's troopers when they rescued the two girls . . . "pulling aside the hides, we were astonished at finding two small white girls who proved to be Julie and Adelaide." Streeter does not mention the incident. It is doubtful if Masterson was with Dixon; at the time Baldwin's command was rescuing the girls, Bat was working as a freighter, hauling supplies to Camp Supply.

16.   In his interview with Thompson, Tom Masterson described the Sweetwater gunfight, which he had undoubtedly heard from Bat.

      Masterson made no mention of Ben Thompson. George Thompson, in a footnote, cautiously described the version of the King killing in Stuart Lake's biography, *Wyatt Earp: Frontier Marshal*, Boston and New York, 1931, hereafter cited as Lake, "as much more exciting and colorful" than Masterson's more prosaic account, but he hastened to add: "But we cannot vouch for the part Ben Thompson played in this episode, there is no further evidence then what Earp says is true." It should be recalled that George Thompson wrote his pamphlet in 1943 when Lake's biography was still regarded as reliable and not the distorted, fictionalized tale it really is.

17. *Dodge City Times*, June 9, 1877.

18. Ibid., October 13, 1977.

19. Ibid., November 10, 1877.

20. Wright, p. 299.

21. *Dodge City Times*, April 13, 1878; Streeter, p. 26; Wright, p. 305; *Queen of the Cowtowns* by Stanley Vestal, New York, 1952, pp. 126–128; hereafter cited as Vestal.

22. *Clowning Through Life* by Eddie Foy and Alvin F. Harlow, New York, 1928, pp. 97–98.

23. *Dodge City Times*, July 27, 1878.

24. Sirigo tells this story in his *Lone Star Cowboy*, Santa Fe, New Mexico, 1919. Father Stanley (Stanley Crocchiola), the New Mexico historian, follows Lake's version as does Dane Coolidge in his *Fighting Men of the West*, New York, 1932, and O'Connor, pp. 110–111. Vestal, pp. 133–143, has a much more factual account. See also "Clay Allison vs. Dodge City Legend" by Gary L. Roberts, in *The Brand Book of the New York Corral of the Westerners*, vol. 8, no. 2, New York, 1961, pp. 32–34. The Clay Allison–Bat Masterson confrontation is a Wild West classic legend, colorful but invented.

25. *Dodge City Times*, July 17, 1880, reported that Bat returned with Billy Thompson from Nebraska and "he [Billy] has recovered from his wounds." See also *The Complete and Authentic Life of Ben Thompson—Man With a Gun* by Floyd Streeter, Introduction by William A. Kelleher, New York, 1957, pp. 125–126.

26. *Ford County Globe*, October 8, 1878; *Dodge City Times*, October 5, October 12, 1878; Wright, pp. 173–175; Lake, pp. 218–220; O'Connor, pp. 145–149.

27. *Dodge City Times*, January 11, 1879.

28. Ibid., March 29, June 14, 1879; Streeter, pp. 119–150; an account of the "railroad war" can also be found in Ben Thompson's obituary, *San Antonio Express*, March 3, 1884; "Capturing a Railroad in Colorado" by Cy Warman, *Denver Republican*, October 4, 1896, p. 21. Robert K. DeArment's *Bat Masterson: The Man and the Legend*, Norman, Oklahoma, 1979, has a fine account. His biography is excellent. See also *The Story of the Railroad* by Cy Warman, New York, 1898.

29. *Dodge City Times*, November 15, November 22, 1879.

30. *Ford County Globe*, May 10, April 19, 1881; Streeter, pp. 37–40.

31. Ibid., November 22, 1881.

32. Ibid., February 20, June 5, 1883.

33. Ibid., November 4, 1883.

34. *Human Life*, edited by Bat's friend, Alfred Henry Lewis. The article on Luke Short was one of the series under Bat's by-line.

35. See George Bolds's account of the County Seat Wars and the Siege of Cimarron in the Bill Tilghman chapter.

36. *The Masterson File; Colorado Sun*, February 25, 1892.

37. For a humorous account of the fight between Masterson and Floto see Gene Fowler's *Timberline*, New York, 1930, p. 118.

38. *New York Times*, April 27, 1908, has Bat in the White House urging TR to run for another term.

39. *The Sunset Trail* by Alfred Henry Lewis, New York, 1905.

40. President Theodore Roosevelt to W. B. Masterson, February 4, 1905, *Theodore Roosevelt Papers*, Library of Congress. Hereafter cited as Library of Congress.

41. Library of Congress. Masterson to Roosevelt, December 7, 1905.

42. References to the termination of Masterson's duties as a U.S. deputy marshal, Southern District of New York, can be found in the *General Records of the Department of Justice (Record Group 60, Judicial District File, No. 33, S 31, Section, 3,5,6, National Archives)*.

43. Library of Congress. Roosevelt to Masterson, Oyster Bay, Long Island, July 15, 1908.

44. Apparently the feud between Masterson and Ufer was longstanding. The *New York Herald*, May 17, 1907, carried a story about Bat and Ufer trading blows under the Belmont Race Track grandstand.

45. Library of Congress. Masterson to Roosevelt, December 21, 1911.

46. Wright, pp. 306–307.

47. Library of Congress. Roosevelt to Masterson, December 23, 1911.

48. Ibid. Masterson to Roosevelt, June 1, 1912.

49.   Ibid. Roosevelt to Masterson, June 3, 1912.

50.   Ibid. Masterson to Roosevelt, July 9, 1912.

51.   Ibid. Franklin Bernard, Denver, Colorado, to Masterson, August 25, 1913; Masterson to Roosevelt, March 1, 1913; Roosevelt to Masterson, March 4, 1913.

52.   Ibid. Masterson to Roosevelt, September 1, 1913.

53.   Ibid. Roosevelt to Masterson, September 2, 1913.

54.   Ibid. Masterson to Roosevelt, September 2, 1913.

55.   Ibid. Roosevelt to Masterson, June 26, 1914.

56.   Ibid. Roosevelt to Masterson, April 19, 1917.

57.   Ibid. Masterson to Roosevelt, May 14, 1917.

58.   Ibid. Roosevelt to Masterson, May 15, 1917.

59.   There are many fine books on the life of Theodore Roosevelt but perhaps the most outstanding is Pulitzer Prize-winning *The Rise of Roosevelt* by Edmund Morris, New York, 1979. However, any writer on TR is indebted to the indefatigable Hermann Hagedorn who interviewed anyone who had been associated with Roosevelt in New York and Washington politics and in the Dakota Territory for his books on TR and his family. Hagedorn might have been worshipful but he was also a prodigious researcher.

60.   *The Masterson File.* Interview with Sam Taub in 1953. Sam was active to the day he died in 1979.

WILLIAM WALLACE

1.   Wallace in the dedication of his now very rare book, *Speeches and Writings of William Wallace*, with autobiography, Kansas City, Missouri, 1914. Hereafter cited as *Wallace*.

2.   An indication of the bitterness existing between the two factions was indicated in a May 12, 1882, dispatch from Jefferson City describing how the legislature reacted to a resolution praising "the law abiding character of the citizens of Western Missouri, commend the vigilance and success of the peace officers of Clay and Jackson Counties for bringing the outlaws to Justice. . . ." The man who offered the resolution was bombarded with spittoons, jeers, and catcalls.

3.   *Wallace*, p. 247.

4.   Wallace's family history is taken from his autobiography and the many obituaries which appeared in Kansas and Missouri newspapers after his death.

5.   *Wallace*, pp. 254–255.

6.   *Wallace*, p. 258.

7.   Countless books have been written about Jesse James. Recommended are: *Jesse James Was His Name* by William A. Settle, Jr., Columbia, Missouri, 1966; *Jesse James Was My Neighbor* by Homer Croy, New York, 1949; *The Rise and Fall of Jesse James* by Robertus Love, New York, 1926; and, immodestly, my own, *The Authentic Wild West: The Outlaws*, New York, 1978, hereafter cited as *Outlaws*.

8.   See *Wallace* for his own story of the capture, indictment, and trial of Billy Ryan. The Kansas City newspapers covered it extensively.

9.   *Wallace*, pp. 139–194.

10.   *Kansas City Times*, August 22, 1940.

11.   *Kansas City World*, November 6, 1898, pp. 4–5. Hereafter cited as *World*.

12.   Wallace was only repeating the popular spelling of William Clarke Quantrill, the guerilla leader, and the folklore surrounding him. He was born in Canal Dover, Ohio, in 1837 and settled in Kansas, where he was known as "Charley Hart," a notorious horse thief and antislavery Jayhawker. He briefly taught school, then joined a small group of Quakers stealing slaves in Missouri. He betrayed the Quakers who were killed in an ambush and invented the tale of how he avenged his brother's death.

13.   James H. Lane was a former senator and a powerful figure in Washington when the Civil War broke out. Lane's Redlegs were as brutal as Quantrill's and Bloody Bill Anderson's troops. Lane narrowly escaped in the Lawrence massacre. Charles R. Jennison and Captain Pardee were veterans of the bloody border wars and were thoroughly hated by the Confederate sympathizers.

14.   The reporter who took down and wrote Wallace's story misspelled Dick Liddil's name throughout his article. I found this flaw common in newspaper accounts of outlaws. Liddil turned state's evidence and testified against Frank James in the Gallatin murder trial. His fascinating testimony, revealing for the first time the inner workings of the James-Younger gang, can be found in the now very rare *The Trial of Frank James for Murder* edited by George Miller, Kansas City, Missouri, 1898. It was reprinted by the Jingle Bob Press, New York, 1977. Liddil's full name was James A. Liddil; he was called ".Dick" by the gang.

15.   *Outlaws*, pp. 64–78; *Robber and Hero* by George Huntington, Northfield, Minnesota, 1894; *The Story of Cole Younger* by Himself, Chicago, 1903.

16.   The original statement of Greenup Bird, cashier of the Liberty Bank, can be found in *Outlaws*, pp. 36–37. Bird claimed $57,072.64 was taken in the robbery. George Wymore, a student at William Jewell College, was killed by the gang as they rode out of the town. Settle, in his book of Jesse James, claimed that "in time Jesse and Frank came to be acknowledged as the leaders" of that bank raid but Wallace states flatly the James gang staged the raid with his information coming from Liddil.

17.   Ironically, Henry (not Harry) W. Younger, father of Cole, was a staunch supporter of the Union. He owned a livery in Harrisonville, farms in Cass and Jackson counties, and was murdered after his son joined Quantrill.

18.   W. S. Earthman of Davidson County, Tennessee, a tax collector, lived on Whita's Creek, seven miles north of Nashville. Curiously, he not only helped to capture Bill Ryan but was also a witness in the murder trial of Frank James. He testified he met Jesse using the name of Tom Howard at a racetrack and knew Frank James as B. J. Woodson. Both men, he said, vanished from the area after Ryan's arrest.

19.   Tucker Basham or Bassham had been sentenced to ten years in the Missouri penitentiary for taking part in the Glendale train robbery. He was a resident of "Cracker's Neck," a heavily wooded area several miles east of Kansas City and populated by ex-guerillas and friends of the James gang. Basham, Ryan, and George Shepherd, another James rider who once claimed he had killed Jesse, all lived there.

20.   Mattie Collins was either Dick Liddil's wife or mistress.

21.   Mrs. Martha (another Mattie) Bolton was the sister of Charles and Robert Ford. Robert was the man who had killed Jesse James in St. Joseph. The gunfight between Liddil and Robert Woodson (Wood) Hite in which Hite was killed was probably over Mrs. Bolton.

22.   The lack of liaison between Wallace, the Jackson County prosecutor trying so hard to break up the James gang, and Governor Crittenden was incredible. Wallace had to go to Crittenden to obtain immunity for Liddil but neither Crittenden nor his secretary, Finis C. Farr, kept Wallace abreast of developments in what was then a notorious manhunt.

23.   Annie Ralston, daughter of Samuel Ralston, a wealthy Jackson County farmer, eloped with her bandit sweetheart in 1874.

24.   Frank James was greeted like a conquering hero after his surrender to Governor Crittenden. Crowds flocked to the depots hoping to catch a glimpse of the fabled outlaw and hundreds greeted him in Independence. James knew jurors came from newspaper readers and shrewdly granted an extensive interview with Frank O'Neil, a well-known political reporter for the *St. Louis Republican*. O'Neil, a city room veteran, failed to write objectively; his interview was sympathetic toward James, who pictured himself as living in constant fear of a bounty hunter's bullet. One wonders why O'Neil did not point out to his readers how Frank had lived in Tennessee. According to witnesses, the outlaw was an accepted member of the community, raced horses, played pool, discussed his favorite subjects of Robert Ingersoll and Shakespeare, and worked as a grain buyer for the Nashville Company.

It appears that Frank, the most wanted man in the country, had lived a perfectly contented life without the great fear he expressed to O'Neil—until he heard the news Bill Ryan had been captured. It was all part of the image-making process and certainly had an influence on the *Republican*'s many readers.

25.   Edwards created the Robin Hood myth for Jesse James. He was adjutant to Brigadier General Joseph (Jo) Shelby, renowned as the Confederate who never surrendered. Born in Virginia in 1839, Edwards was a skilled newspaperman and author of that unreliable history of the guerilla movement in the Civil War, *Noted Guerillas or the Warfare of the Border*, St. Louis,

1877. His newspaper articles, editorials, and books always pictured Jesse and his men as helpless victims of a cruel, relentless North.

26.   Wallace, perhaps because he realized Shelby was revered by many of the Confederates, treated the old soldier with a great deal of kindness. At the Frank James trial Shelby acted outrageously and should have been cited for contempt. He was drunk when he appeared in court as a character witness for James, had to be pointed to where James sat, tried to shake the defendant's hand, which would have been highly prejudicial to the state's case, and generally acted as a boor. The judge finally excused him.

27.   *Wallace*, p. 294.

28.   Ibid., p. 299.

29.   Ibid., pp. 305–306.

30.   Ibid., pp. 305–306.

THEODORE ROOSEVELT

1.   *Roosevelt's Dakota Ranches* by Roy Mathson, Bismarck, North Dakota, pp. 1–3, n.d. See also *Roosevelt and the Stockmen's Association* by Ray H. Mattison, *North Dakota History*, vol. 17, no. 2, April 1950; vol. 17, no. 3, July 1950.

2.   Hagedorn, pp. 58–60. See also "The Career of the Marquis de Mores, in the Bad Lands of North Dakota," *North Dakota History*, January–April 1946. See also *The Marquis de Mores, Dakota Capitalist, French Nationalist*, Fargo, North Dakota, 1972.

3.   *The Rise of Theodore Roosevelt* by Edmund Morris, New York, 1979, quoting Roosevelt's diary entry, February 14, 1884, p. 241. Hereafter cited as Morris. Roosevelt's wife, Alice, died of Bright's disease.

4.   *Utica Morning Herald*, April 30, 1884.

5.   Hagedorn, pp. 148–149.

6.   Ibid., pp. 150–154.

7.   Ibid., pp. 207–208.

8.   Ibid., pp. 348–349.

9.   Ibid., p. 366.

10.   *Bill Sewall's Story of TR* by William Wingate Sewall, New York, 1919, p. 60. Hereafter cited as Sewall; Hagedorn, p. 367; Morris, p. 322.

11.   Hagedorn, p. 368.

12.   Ibid., pp. 371–372.

13.   Ibid., p. 372.

14.   *Ranch Life and the Hunting Trail* by Theodore Roosevelt, New York, 1897, pp. 111–129. Hereafter cited as *Life*. The book is also illustrated by Remington.

15.   Hagedorn, p. 385.

16.   Ibid., pp. 385–386.

17.   *Life*, pp. 128–129.

18.   Ibid., pp. 401, 402.

19.   Ibid., p. 411.

20.   Ibid., p. 427; Sewall, p. 92.

WILLIAM TILGHMAN

1.   A great deal of my material on Bill Tilghman came from his widow, the late Zoe Tilghman, hereafter cited as Tilghman. This writer interviewed her at length in her Oklahoma City home and had considerable correspondence with her since 1951, when she did research for me on Rose of the Cimarron, Tilghman, the Doolin gang, etc., for my *Desperate Women*, published in 1952.

It was Mrs. Tilghman who revealed to me for the first time the identity of Rose of the Cimarron. For background on the Tilghman family see Mrs. Tilghman's now very rare *Marshal of the Last Frontier*, Glendale, California, 1949, pp. 24–60, hereafter cited as *Marshal*.

2.   In January 1961 Mrs. Tilghman showed me the rifle, which my wife photographed. Bill, she disclosed, had kept a careful daily log of the number of buffalo he killed. The chief, Roman Nose, was not the celebrated Indian warrior killed in the Battle of Beecher's Island. There were at least three warriors with the same name. One was killed in the Battle of the Rosebud.

Another extraordinary, if grim, feat of marksmanship was Billy Dixon's shot which killed a mounted Indian brave on a bluff on the third day of the Adobe Walls fight. Dixon, "using my big 50, took careful aim and fired," killing the brave at 1,538 yards. See *Life of Billy Dixon* by Olive Dixon, Dallas, Texas, 1927, pp. 180–181. Dixon, a friend of both Tilghman and Bat Masterson, received the Congressional Medal for his bravery as an Indian scout in the Buffalo Wallow fight, September 12, 1974.

3.   Unnamed newspaper account of Tilghman's life, Tilghman Collection, University of Oklahoma Library. Hereafter cited as Tilghman Collection.

4.   This writer first met George Bolds in 1955 and periodically taped his memories of Dodge City, Wyatt Earp, Bat and Jim Masterson, Bill Tilghman, Neil (also spelled Neal) Brown, and Bolds's participation in the County Seat Wars. I wrote his biography in *Across the Cimarron*, New York, 1956. After his death independent research authenticated many of the incidents he had described. The *New York World*, in its account of the Battle of Cimarron, reported that Bolds, as one of the participants, "received a ball in the leg." Another big city newspaper described George as "the leader of a band of outlaws from Ingalls."

5.   Tilghman.

6.   *Marshal*, pp. 178–191.

7.   Tilghman.

8.   Ibid.

9.   Ibid.

10.   Ibid.

11.   Ibid.; *Marshal*, pp. 240–243; various clippings in the Tilghman Collection.

12.   Tilghman. See also *The Law, the West and the Wilderness* by Kevin Brownlow, New York, 1979, p. 275. Abernathy was a colorful character in the Wild West. At eleven he was working as a hand on a cattle drive. At fifteen he was breaking wild broncs on the J-A ranch, part of the famous Goodnight spread. At sixteen he was a wolfer, catching the big animals with his bare hands and selling them to zoos, fairs, traveling shows, and parks. He was appointed U.S. Marshal of Oklahoma by President Roosevelt in April 1906. In the early days of American films he starred in a movie shot in Oradell, New Jersey, with seven wolves loaned to the movie company by Doctor W. T. Hornaday, director of the Bronx zoo. One night the wolves escaped. Abernathy recaptured the animals, as he recalled, "within twenty-five miles of the greatest city in the world. . . ."

He resigned his marshalship to join the Secret Service. His most memorable assignment was "Chinatown and the New York subways," trailing narcotic dealers.

13.   Tilghman; *Motion Pictures from the Library of Congress Paper Print Collection*, 1894–1912, by Kemp R. Niver, edited by Bebe Bergsten, California, 1967, p. 169; *Marshal*, pp. 310–315.

14.   Tilghman.

15.   Ibid.; *Marshal*, pp. 317–318. Henry Starr was killed trying to hold up a bank in Harrison, Arkansas, in February 1921. His relatives were prominent in the history of Oklahoma outlawry. The notorious Belle Reed Starr was married to Sam Starr, a full-blooded Cherokee, on June 5, 1880, according to official Cherokee Nation records. Sam was 23, Belle 27. As Belle Shirley of Carthage, Missouri, she had been the sweetheart of Cole Younger, who, legend insists, fathered her daughter, Pearl. Later Belle named her outlaw headquarters in the loop of the South Canadian River, "Youngers' Bend." Belle's first husband, Jim Reed, a Texas outlaw, was killed near Paris, Texas, while trying to hold up a train in January 1874. *The Galveston Daily News*'s terse report of the funeral ended: "He was a noted but desperate character and the citizens are truly glad at the riddance." Sam Starr was shot and killed by a cousin in December 1886.

Three years later Belle was shot and killed from ambush near Eufaula, Indian Territory. In her last years Belle liked to wear a long red velvet gown and two holstered guns. She had been arrested twice for horse stealing by rangers from "Hanging Judge" Parker's federal court. The first time she was acquitted; the second, she and Sam were sentenced to a year. In 1951 Cohn Rector, the last of Judge Parker's famed rangers, wrote to this writer describing his experiences with Belle. Once when he brought her into Fort Smith she offered to cook supper for him and the other deputies. Only when they reached Fort Smith did Belle tell them she had served fried rattlesnake.

16. Tilghman.
17. Ibid.; *Marshal,* pp. 349–367.

TOM SMITH

1. *Stuart Henry's Conquering Our Great American Plains,* New York, 1930, p. 159, quoting his brother, T. C. Henry, the first mayor of Abilene. Stuart, then in his twenties, was appointed mayor in September 1869, when the forty-nine residents of Abilene received incorporation as a community from Probate Judge Cyrus Kilgore. Stuart Henry, a well-known novelist and historian of the 1920s, used his brother's papers, interviews with pioneers, and his own boyhood memories when Smith was marshal, to write his reliable and well-written book. Hereafter cited as Henry.

In 1923–1924, Stuart Henry created a celebrated controversy over his criticism of Emerson Hough's *North of '36,* a novel of the frontier which was serialized in the *Saturday Evening Post.* Henry insisted that although the book was fiction, Hough had distorted historical dates and events. Hough simply replied that he was writing fiction and not history. Before the dust had settled the controversy had involved the daughter of Joe McCoy, the novelist and short story writer, Eugene Rhodes, Kansas newspapers, and W. P. Webb, later to be the author of the renowned *The Great Plains* but at the time identified by Henry as "a young adjunct professor" in the University of Texas History Department.

2. Mayor T. C. Henry described Smith as having "served at one time on the police force in New York City." Apparently this had come from Smith in their initial interview.
3. "The Press on Wheels: A History of the Frontier Index" by John A. Lent, *Annals of Wyoming,* vol. 43, no. 2, Fall 1971.
4. Henry, pp. 124–125.
5. Ibid., pp. 132–137.
6. Ibid., pp. 151–156.
7. *Abilene Chronicle,* 1896.
8. Memorial services for Thomas Smith, marshal of Abilene, May 31, 1904, Kansas State Historical Society.

CHARLES A. SIRINGO

1. *The Caldwell Standard,* June 5, 1884, February 19, 1885.
2. The first edition of Siringo's book was copyrighted by Siringo with the imprint of "M. Umbdenstock & Co., Publishers, Chicago, Illinois, 1885." The book is very scarce. The second edition, copyrighted a year later, appeared under the imprint of "Siringo and Dodson, Publishers, Chicago, Illinois." This edition has an addenda which contains advice on how to make money or go broke in the cattle business and describes the brutal treatment cowboys gave their horses.
3. The attempts by the Pinkertons to hold up Siringo's book by court action appears petty and puzzling. As Siringo protested, he "wasn't revealing any Agency secrets," the events he had written about were "done and over with." The Pinkertons—the "Dickensons" in the revised book—emerged looking foolish when the names of such celebrated gunfighters and killers such as Tom Horn became "Tom Corn." Siringo finished his book in 1910. It took him two years battling with the Pinkertons before he could get it published. This was a decade after Horn's autobiography and countless newspaper articles—many inspired by the Pinkertons themselves—had been published about their activities in the West. The Wild Bunch had drifted into legend and events Siringo had written about were part of frontier history.

4. Siringo's early experiences are from his *A Texas Cowboy* (reprint), New York, 1950, pp. 31–39.

5. From Siringo's *Riata and Spurs*, Boston and New York, 1927. Siringo constantly rewrote his own story, a fault overlooked by his admirers. In *A Texas Cowboy* he simply told how he and "Wess Adams" had a "gay time" in Dodge City with the night ending when Adams was "severely stabbed in a free for all." He made no mention of the Masterson incident in this one.

In Siringo's *A Lone Star Cowboy*, Santa Fe, New Mexico, 1919, p. 64, Wess Adams was again stabbed, this time by a Buffalo hunter, but when City Marshal Joe Mason came on the scene, "we ran him to cover in an alley." Still no mention of his encounter with Masterson. Siringo finally got to Masterson. I believe Siringo had material for only two books, one his experiences as a cowboy, the other as a frontier detective. His stories of outlaws and gunfighters are mostly unreliable.

6. Siringo sent the manuscript of this angry diatribe to the Pinkerton office in Chicago. In a covering letter he charged the agency "caused me a loss of $2,000" when his *Cowboy Detective* book, Chicago, 1912, was held up by the courts. He also revealed he intended to sell his new book, which he published himself "at 25¢ at the San Diego and San Francisco Expositions." See *Two Evil Isms* by Charles A. Siringo, introduction by Charles D. Peavy, Austin, Texas, 1967.

7. Two letters, written in pencil, 1924. The James D. Horan Civil War and Western Americana Collection.

8. "He'll Make a Hand" by Eugene M. Rhodes, *Sunset* Magazine, June 1927.

WYATT EARP

1. *Wichita Beacon*, May 12, 1875; *The Trail Guide: Kansas Frontier Police Before TV* by Nyle H. Miller, vol. 3, March 1958, pp. 2–3.

2. *Dodge City Times*, July 7, 1877.

3. Ibid., June 8, 1878.

4. *Ford County Globe*, April 8, 1878.

5. *The Earp Brothers of Tombstone: The Story of Mrs. Virgil Earp* by Frank Waters, New York, 1960, p. 30. Hereafter cited as Waters. See also *The Frontier World of Doc Holliday* by Pat Jahns, New York, 1957. Hereafter cited as Jahns. Also *Doc Holliday* by John Myers Myer, Boston and New York, 1955. They are the best biographies of the Earps and Holliday.

6. *Tombstone Epitaph*, October 20, 1880.

7. Ibid., August 12–25, 1880. Killeen's deathbed statement was published on the 24th. Leslie lived a violent life. On November 24, 1882, he shot and killed William (Billy the Kid) Claibourne, who had fled from the O. K. Corral gunfight with Ike Clanton. Leslie also killed his mistress, Millie Williams, on July 10, 1889, and wounded a young neighbor, James (O'Neil) Neal, after a drinking spree. He was sentenced to life imprisonment in Yuma Territorial Prison but was released in May 1897 to marry Mrs. Belle Stowell of Warren County, Illinois, who had become infatuated with Leslie after reading an account of his life on the frontier. As the *San Francisco Chronicle* of May 2, 1897, noted, a courtship began in their letters, "then fruit and flowers followed." Leslie last appeared in Oakland, California, in 1925, virtually a derelict. He stole a revolver from a merchant who had befriended him and was never seen again.

8. For an account of Clum's life in Tombstone, see "It All Happened in Tombstone," *Arizona Historical Review*, April 1929, and his son's biography, *Apache Agent: The Story of John P. Clum* by Woodworth Clum, first published in Boston, 1936, and then republished in 1978. Hereafter cited as *Apache Agent*.

9. *Weekly Arizona Miner*, October 19, 1877; *Nugget*, March 18, 1880.

10. *Weekly Arizona Miner*, November 2, 1877.

11. *Tombstone Epitaph*, October 28 and 29, 1880.

12. *Denver Republican*, May 22, 1882. Hereafter cited as *Republican*. Doc gave the *Republican* a long interview. Unfortunately the reporter did not question some of Doc's stories.

This writer has found most frontier newspapermen to have been incredibly gullible when it came to interviewing politicians, outlaws, lawmen, and public figures.

13.   *Tombstone Epitaph*, January 17, 1881; Waters, pp. 113–116.

14.   *Tombstone Epitaph*, March 15 and 19, 1881.

15.   See the testimony of Wyatt Earp and Ike Clanton in the O. K. Corral gunfight hearing before Magistrate Spicer.

16.   The *Nugget*, July 6–10, 1881; Jahns, pp. 177–179; Waters, pp. 130–132, 140–141. Some pioneering residents of Tombstone and Pima County claimed in their memoirs they "knew" Doc Holliday was one of the robber-killers but their names do not appear as witnesses against the frail but very dangerous dentist.

17.   The *Nugget*, September 10, 1881; *Epitaph*, September 11, 1881. See also William M. Breakenridge's version in his *Helldorado*, Boston and New York, 1928.

18.   See the testimony of Earp and Clanton for the events which led to their confrontation.

19.   In the countless versions of the O. K. Corral gun battle, Wyatt Earp many times has been described as a "marshal." A search of the Department of Justice files in the National Archives to finally settle this claim failed to produce any documentary evidence that Wyatt was a federal officer at the time of the fight. His brother was Tombstone's city marshal. In a letter to Acting Attorney General S. F. Phillips, December 6, 1881, United States Marshal C. P. Dake praised the Earps for their action in the gunfight for "having rid Tombstone and the neighborhood of this outlaw element." Dake, obviously fighting for his job, was severely criticized by both Washington and Acting Governor Gosper for lack of action on his part to prevent the street fight. Dake once referred to the Earps as "my deputies" but if he had deputized them there are no confirming records in Washington.

20.   The names of the witnesses and the dates their testimony appeared in the *Nugget* in 1881: Sheriff Behan, November 3, 4, 5; Mrs. M. King, November 5; Wes Fuller, November 6; motion by the prosecution to revoke the bail of the Earps and place the defendants in jail and the magistrate's opinion, November 6.

Also, William Claibourne, Dr. Gardner, Miss Addie Biutland, J. H. Licas, William Soule, November 9; Ike Clanton, November 10–11; J. B. Hatcher, A. Bauer, Thomas Keefe, November 11; Wyatt Earp, November 17 and 26; Magistrate Wells Spicer's decision, December 1.

The *Nugget*'s editorials, "Fortunate Gifts" and "Glad to Know," both commenting on the testimony appeared October 30. The *Nugget*'s files are in the archives of the Arizona Historical Society and were made available to this writer by Margaret Bret Harte, Research Librarian.

21.   McLaury was writing before the coroner's report had been issued which disclosed $2,923.45 had been taken from the body of his brother Tom. Frank McLaury's body yielded, "one Colt six-shooting pistol, with belt and cartridge. . . . From the body of William Clanton, one Colts [sic] six-shooter with belt and cartridge and one nickel watch and chain."

The unusual amount of money found on Tom McLaury's body appears to support the claim the McLaurys were working ranchers who had come into town to buy supplies and were not the band of rustlers as the Earps and the *Epitaph* pictured them. Certainly no rancher looking to take part in a gunfight would ride into Tombstone carrying such a large sum of money. *Coroner's Report to the Board of Supervisors of Cochise County, Arizona, Listing the Inquest Performed and Personal Property Found on the Bodies, November 8, 1881.* Hereafter cited as *Coroner's Report*.

22.   McLaury was writing with emotion and not from facts. Both the *Nugget* and the *Epitaph* reported Allen Street was "densely packed" but certainly not near McLaury's estimate of two thousand spectators.

23.   McLaury calls his brother "Robert" in his letters although in the official documents he was listed as "Frank." The killing of Leonard and Head was never attributed to "Greasers" but to the Haslett brothers, owners of a New Mexico general store the bandits tried to hold up. Later Jim Crane and a posse killed the Hasletts.

24.   Waters, pp. 179–180.

25.   It is doubtful if Marshal Williams voted with the county grand jury. Some suspected he had been the inside man tipping off the holdup gangs when the stage would be carrying bullion. A few days after the O. K. Corral gunfight, Williams borrowed $600 from H. S. Crocker & Company in San Francisco and left Tombstone. He was never seen again. On the same day Wyatt Earp borrowed $370.74 from the same company. Fifteen years later the *San*

Francisco Chronicle reported the Crocker Company had obtained a judgment against Earp for that amount of money.

26.   Waters, p. 188, quoting the *Nugget* and the *Epitaph* of January 25, 1882.

27.   Ibid., quoting the *Epitaph*, March 23–24, 1882; Waters, pp. 192–196.

28.   The *Epitaph*, March 23–24, 1882; Waters, pp. 192–196.

29.   *Coroner's Report; Arizona Daily Citizen*, March 27, 1882.

30.   The *Epitaph*, March 22, 1882.

31.   Ibid., March 23, 1882. Some accounts identify Cruz as "Indian Charlie." However, the *Epitaph* of March 27, 1882, called him "Florentino, a native of Mexico"; the coroner's jury used the same identification.

32.   The *Epitaph*, April 3, 1882.

33.   There are several versions of why Clum left Tombstone. Those writers who offer the maudlin motive of Clum leaving the mining town because his wife had died apparently never read Clum's biography written by his son, Woodworth, who quotes his father in *Apache Agent* that a week after his daughter was born in December 1880: "I encountered a major tragedy in my life when on December 18, my wife passed away." This was almost a year before the gunfight had taken place when Clum was vigorously supporting the Earps. Another reason offered for his departure was Clum's fear of being killed. This fear was valid. On December 15, 1881, outlaws attacked the Tombstone stage carrying Clum to Tucson. After an exchange of shots the driver discovered Clum was missing.

The following day Sheriff Behan's posse, including C. D. Reppy, Clum's business partner, learned Clum had escaped in the darkness and found his way to a mill where he borrowed a horse and rode to Benson.

It should be pointed out that Clum sold the *Epitaph* at the time the mining community was rapidly becoming one of the richest camps in the West. Certainly economics was not part of his decision to sell his newspaper and leave the community he professed to love so deeply.

Woodworth Clum's book is a son's tribute to a fascinating, colorful father but it also includes the myths and legends of the Earps, including the tall tales of Earp rescuing Johnny-Behind-the-Deuce, disarming Curly Bill, and killing the Clantons and McLaurys. John P. Clum, of course, is pictured as the only white man capable of handling the fierce Apaches—a job the U.S. Cavalry had failed to do for so many years.

In addition to the cowboys-versus-the-law-and-order-men feud, a flourishing land fraud had added to the tensions slowly building up in the community—tensions which helped to bring on the O. K. Corral battle.

Uncertain titles to town lots on which business houses had been built led to land jumping, drunken brawls, and gunfights in saloons and on the streets. The *Nugget* and *Epitaph* became part of the violent dispute when Clum charged the *Nugget* was the voice of the land fraud group. When the *Nugget* demanded that Clum produce proof of his charges, Clum sent the *Nugget* editor a copy of an unsigned letter written by a Tombstone resident!

Secretary of the Interior Carl Schurz; the United States Supreme Court; and Arizona's governor, state, and county officials, all became involved before the title-holding cases were finally resolved. See the excellent article "Arizona Land Fraud; Model 1880, The Tombstone Townsite Company" by Henry P. Walker, *Arizona and the West*, Spring 1979.

34.   *Republican.*

35.   The dates of the exchanges of the letters are: Acting Governor John J. Gosper to U.S. Marshal C. P. Dake, Prescott, Arizona Territory, November 28, 1881; Gosper to Secretary of the Interior S. J. Kirkwood, November 9, 1881; Gosper to Kirkwood, December 19, 1881; President Chester A. Arthur's message, May 3, 1881, "Lawlessness in Parts of Arizona," 47th Congress, 1st Session, House of Representatives, Executive Document, No. 58, all The James D. Horan Civil War and Western Americana Collection.

36.   *Denver Tribune*, May 16, 1882.

37.   *Pueblo Tribune*, May 16, 1882.

38.   Ibid.

39.   Ibid., Jahns, pp. 246–254.

40.   *Ford County Globe*, June 5, 1883.

41. *The Leadville Daily Herald,* August 20 and 26, 1884.

42. Waters, p. 218, quoting Anton Mazzonvitch, former cavalryman and author of *Trailing Geronimo,* Hollywood, California, 1931, who wrote an article on Earp in the *Brewery Gulch Gazette,* Bisbee, Arizona, April 29, 1932.

43. *San Francisco Examiner,* December 3, 1896.

44. *San Francisco Chronicle,* December 9, 1896.

45. Ibid.

46. Waters, quoting the *Arizona Daily Citizen,* May 22, 1900.

47. *Arizona Star,* July 26, 1911; *Los Angeles Times,* July 22, 1911.

48. *Wyatt Earp: Frontier Marshal* by Stuart Lake, Boston and New York, 1931. Hereafter cited as Lake.

49. *Belle Starr: The Bandit Queen* by Burton Rascoe, New York, 1941, p. 334.

50. The collection of letters is in the Huntington Library, San Marino, California. Hereafter cited as Letters. Permission to use the letters was graciously given by Miss Mary L. Robertson, Curator of Manuscripts.

51. Robert Mullin to the author, July 30, 1979.

52. *Wyatt Earp & the Buntline Special Myth* by William B. Shillinberg, Tucson, Arizona, 1976, p. 58. Shillinberg believes Earp did not wish to "discuss" his life story with Lake. This is in contrast to the contents and tone of the letters. They show Earp eagerly cooperated with Lake to the best of his health and provided Lake with what material he had. Shillinberg also described Mrs. Earp as the "chief prod" behind the book; that was Lake's role from the very beginning. As Lake told Robert N. Mullin, he and Josie had an abrasive relationship. The letters reveal she was skeptical of Lake's intentions and his agreement.

To those who insist on believing Wyatt Earp was one of the giants of the American West, Stuart Lake will always be the glib entrepreneur who fashioned a wild tale from the few crumbs Wyatt grudgingly gave him. And for the detractors of the Earp legend, Lake remains the skillful magazine writer who scorned all historical truth to write a sensational book, more fiction than fact.

The collection of the Lake-Earp letters, I believe, tells the real story; Wyatt Earp lied and glorified himself to Lake, who really didn't care. As a professional writer he knew what would sell and that is what he wrote. There will always be one unanswered question: What if Earp had lived to read Lake's manuscript? In my opinion he would have loved it, lies and all.

See also "The Colt Buntline Special .45" by George E. Virgines, *The Brand Book of the Chicago Corral of the Westerners,* May 1973; "The Buntline Special Colt" by John S. Dumont, *American Rifleman,* April 1955; "The Colt Buntline Special: A Rare Item" by Andy Palmer, *Great Guns,* August 1955.

It should be pointed out that *The Life and Adventures of Ned Buntline* by Fred E. Pond published in 1919, the first biography of the pulp writer, did *not* mention the fabulous gun.

53. Letters. Lake to Earp, December 25, 1927.

54. Ibid. Earp to Lake, January 16, 1928.

55. Ibid. Lake to Earp, January 22, 1928.

56. Lake's letter of June 11 refers to one he received from Earp, on the 8th. A copy is not among the collection.

57. Letters. Lake to Earp, June 15, 1928.

58. Ibid. Lake to Earp, June 26, 1928.

59. Ibid. Lake to Earp, June 15, 1928; Lake to Earp, June 26, 1928; Earp to Lake, July 22, 1928; Lake to Earp, July 25, 1928; Lake to Earp, August 5, 1928.

60. Ibid. Lake to Earp, August 9, 1928.

61. Ibid. Lake to Earp, August 31, 1928.

62. Ibid. Lake to Earp, September 10, 1928.

63. Ibid. Earp to Lake, September 13, 1928.

64. Ibid. Lake to Earp, September 14, 1928.

65. Ibid. Lake to Earp, September 18, 1928.

66. Ibid. Lake to Earp, September 22, 1928.

67. Ibid. Lake to Earp, September 27, 1928.

68. Ibid. Lake to Earp, September 30, 1928.
69. Ibid. Lake to Earp, October 2, 1928.
70. Ibid. Lake to Earp, October 19, 1928.
71. This is a scrawled note to Lake, n.d. Earp also advised Lake in this note that of all the guns he had seen, he knew "positively" that none had notches. Apparently this was in answer to one of Lake's questions. Also Letters, Earp to Lake, October 15 and November 2, 1928, both handwritten.
72. Ibid. Lake to Earp, November 2, 1928.
73. Ibid. Earp to Lake, November 6, 9, 14, 19, 1928, all handwritten.
74. Ibid. Lake to Earp, November 24, 1928.
75. Ibid. Earp to Lake, November 30, 1928.
76. Waters, pp. 38–39.
77. Letters. Earp to Lake, November 30, 1928.
78. Ibid. Earp to Lake; Lake to Earp, both January 7, 1929.
79. Ibid. Earp to Lake, January 10, 1929.
80. It is puzzling why some writers on Earp fail to consult *The Life and Advetures of Ben Thompson* by William M. Walton, first published in Austin, Texas, in 1884. Hereafter cited as Walton. Judge Walton was an old friend of the Thompson family and Ben gave him detailed interviews for his biography. Many of the incidents have been independently confirmed by newspaper accounts and court documents.

Ben Thompson gave Judge Walton a truthful account of the Whitney killing and he never mentioned Wyatt Earp. See Walton, pp. 124–135. Also *Ben Thompson: Man With a Gun* by Floyd Streeter, New York, 1957, pp. 92–106. Most historians, including Streeter, have Billy Thompson telling his brother after the shooting: "I do not give a ——. I would have shot if it had been Jesus Christ!"

But Ben quoted Billy to Walton: "Christ! What a misfortune! I tried to shoot Happy Jack [a deputy] but I stumbled and shot Whitney!" These quotes sound more logical; Whitney was an old friend of the Thompsons, not an enemy.

81. An example of some of Buntline's titles for his 400 dime novels: *Love's Desperation: Or the President's Daughter; Thayendanega, the Scourge of the War Eagle of the Mohawks; Stella Dorme: Or the Comanche's Dream; The King of the Sea: A Tale of the Fearless and the Free.* When he died in 1886 the *New York World* credited the "Colonel," as he liked to be called—his real name was Zane Carroll Judson—with carrying more battle wounds in his body than any other American. Some, the *World* forgot to point out, came from the guns of outraged husbands. Ned had never been an officer nor was he ever wounded in battle.

Jay Monaghan's *The Great Rascal*, Boston and New York, 1952, is a rousing, well-written biography of the "king of the dime novels." Monaghan briefly mentions Lake's versions of the Buntline Special, p. 259.
82. Lake, pp. 145–146.
83. Ibid., p. 146.
84. *Wichita Beacon*, May 12, 1875.
85. *Dodge City, the Cowboy Capital* by Robert M. Wright, Wichita, Kansas, 1913.
86. Lake, p. 292.
87. Ibid., p. 368.
88. *San Francisco Examiner*, December 4, 1896.

TOMBSTONE MAP: Robert N. Mullin, the author of the map used in this book as endpapers, is a fine research historian and writer of the American West. He writes that at the time of his map research he discovered that the deed records "had not been made from a surveyor's accurate measurements" and he had to depend on the statements of two pioneer Tombstone citizens. He also found that fire insurance maps, accepted as accurate, contained errors as to shapes of buildings, "the form of which is still discernible by old foundations. The *Nugget* and the *Epitaph* (ads) were not accurate sources in all cases because merchants and professional men advertised in the papers, and the type, once set, seems to have remained unchanged even after there is positive evidence of change in the business locations. I once accumulated some correspondence written on printed letterhead and placed more confidence in the locations on the stationery than on any one source."

BIBLIOGRAPHY

Books

AIKMAN, DONALD. *Calamity Jane and the Lady Wildcats*. New York, 1927.
———. *The Taming of the Frontier*. New York, 1929.
BENNETT, ESTILLINE. *Old Deadwood Days*. New York, 1928.
BOTKIN, BEN (ed.). *A Treasury of Western Folklore*. New York, 1944.
BOURKE, FRANCIS. *Great American Train Robberies*. New York, 1909.
BRADLEY, T. T. *Outlaws of the Border*. Cincinnati, Ohio, 1929.
BREAKENRIDGE, WILLIAM M. *Helldorado*. Boston and New York, 1928.
BROWNLOW, KEVIN. *The War, the West, the Wilderness*. New York, 1979.
BURNS, WALTER. *Tombstone: An Illiad of the Southwest*. New York, 1929.
COOLIDGE, DANE. *Fighting Men of the West*. New York, 1932.
CRITTENDEN, HENRY HUSTON (comp.). *The Crittenden Memoirs*. New York, 1939.
CROY, HOMER. *Jesse James Was My Neighbor*. New York, 1949.
CRUMBINE, S. J. *Frontier Doctor*. Philadelphia, 1948.
CUNNINGHAM, EUGENE. *Triggernometry*. New York, 1934.
DAVID, CLYDE BRION. *The Arkansas*. New York, 1940.
DEARMENT, ROBERT K. *Bat Masterson: The Man and His Times*. Norman, Oklahoma, 1979.
DICK, EVERETT. *The Sod House Frontier*. New York, 1937.
DIXON, OLIVE. *The Life of Billy Dixon*. Dallas, Texas, 1914.
DODGE, COLONEL RICHARD IRVING. *Our Wild Indians*. Hartford, Connecticut, 1883.
EDWARD, J. B. *Early Days in Abilene*. Abilene, Kansas, 1940.
FOWLER, GENE. *Timberline*. New York, 1930.
FOY, EDDIE and ALVIN F. HARLOW. *Clowning Through Life*. New York, 1928.
GARD, WAYNE. *Frontier Justice*. Norman, Oklahoma, 1949.
———. *The Chisholm Trail*. Norman, Oklahoma, 1954.

GREESSLEY, GENE. *Bankers and Cattlemen*. New York, 1966.

HAGEDORN, HERMANN. *Roosevelt in the Bad Lands*. Boston and New York, 1921.

HARMAN, S. W. *Hell on the Border*. Fort Smith, Arkansas, 1898.

HENDRICKS, GEORGE W. *The Bad Men of the West*. San Antonio, Texas, 1941.

HENRY, STUART. *Conquering Our Great American Plains*. New York, 1930.

HODGE, FREDERICK WEBB. *Handbook of the American Indians*. Washington, 1907.

HORAN, JAMES D. *Desperate Men*. New York, 1949.

———. *Desperate Women*. New York, 1951.

———. *The Authentic Wild West: The Gunfighters*. New York, 1977.

———. *The Authentic Wild West: The Outlaws*. New York, 1978.

HUNT, FRAZIER. *The Long Trail from Texas*. New York, 1940.

JAHNS, PAT. *The Frontier World of Doc Holliday*. New York, 1957.

LAKE, STUART. *Wyatt Earp: Frontier Marshal*. New York, 1931.

LEADVILLE CITY DIRECTORY. *Ballenger and Richards*. Leadville, Colorado, 1882–1887.

LEWIS, ALFRED. *The Sunset Trail*. New York, 1905.

LOVE, ROBERTUS. *The Rise and Fall of Jesse James*. New York, 1926.

McCOY, JOSEPH. *Historic Sketches of the Cattle Trade in the West and Southwest*. Kansas City, Missouri, 1874.

McNEAL, THOMAS. *When Kansas Was Young*. New York, 1922.

MARTIN, DOUGLAS D. *Tombstone's Epitaph*. New Mexico, 1951.

MILLER, GEORGE, JR. (ed. and comp.). *The Trial of Frank James for Murder*. Columbia, Missouri, 1898.

MONAGHAN, JAY. *The Great Rascal: The Life and Adventures of Ned Buntline*. Boston and New York, 1952.

MORRIS, EDMUND. *The Rise of Theodore Roosevelt*. New York, 1979.

MYERS, JOHN MYER. *The Last Chance*. Boston and New York, 1950.

———. *Doc Holliday*. Boston and New York, 1955.

NIX, EVETT. *Oklahombres*. St. Louis and Chicago, 1929.

O'CONNOR, RICHARD. *Bat Masterson*. New York, 1957.

PARSONS, GEORGE WHITWELL. *The Private Journals of George Whitwell Parsons*. Phoenix, Arizona, 1929.

RAINE, WILLIAM McLEOD. *Famous Sheriffs and Western Outlaws*. New York, 1929.

———. *Guns of the Frontier*. New York, 1940.

RASCOE, BURTON. *Belle Starr: The Bandit Queen*. New York, 1941.

ROOSEVELT, THEODORE. *Ranch Life and the Hunting Trail*. New York, 1897.

SETTLE, WILLIAM A. *Jesse James Was His Name*. Columbia, Missouri, 1966.

SEWALL, WILLIAM. *Bill Sewall's Story of TR*. New York, 1919.

SHILLINBERG, WILLIAM B. *Wyatt Earp and the Buntline Special Myth*. Tucson, Arizona, 1976.

SIRINGO, CHARLES. *A Texas Cowboy: Or Fifteen Years on the Hurricane Deck of a Spanish Cow Pony*. New York, 1885.

———. *A Cowboy Detective*. Chicago, 1912.

———. *A Lone Star Cowboy*. Santa Fe, New Mexico, 1919.

———. *Riata and Spurs*. New York, 1927.

SPRING, AGNES WRIGHT. *The Cheyenne Black Hills Stage and Express Routes*. Glendale, California, 1949.

STARR, HENRY. *Thrilling Events: The Life of Henry Starr*. Colorado, 1914.

SUTTON, FRED. *Hands Up! Stories of the Six Shooters of the Old West*. New York, 1927.

THOMPSON, GEORGE G. *Bat Masterson: The Dodge City Years*. Fort Hays, Kansas, 1943.

TILGHMAN, ZOE. *Outlaw Years*. Oklahoma City, Oklahoma, 1928.

———. *Marshal of the Last Frontier*. Glendale, California, 1949.

———. *Spotlight*. Oklahoma City, Oklahoma, 1960.

TURNER, FREDERICK JACKSON. *The Frontier in American History*. New York, 1920.

VESTAL, STANLEY. *Dodge City: Queen of the Cowtowns*. New York, 1952.

———. *Warpath and Council Fire*. New York, 1948.

WALLACE, WILLIAM H. *Speeches and Writings of William H. Wallace with Autobiography*. Kansas City, Missouri, 1914.

————. Closing Speech for the State by William H. Wallace, Prosecuting Attorney of Jackson County, Missouri, in the trial of Frank James for Murder, held in Gallatin, Missouri, Daviess County, in August and September of 1884. Kansas City, Missouri, 1884.

WALTERS, LORENZO. *Tombstone's Yesterdays*. Tucson, Arizona, 1929.

WALTON, WILLIAM M. *Life and Adventures of Ben Thompson*. Austin, Texas, 1884.

WELLMAN, PAUL. *Dynasty of Outlaws*. New York, 1961.

WILSON, RUFUS. *Out of the West*. New York, 1913.

WOOD, M. V. (ed.). *History of Alameda County, California*. Oakland, California, 1883.

W.P.A. *Colorado: A Guide to the Highest State*. New York, 1941.

————. *Kansas: A Guide to the Sunflower State*. New York, 1940.

————. *South Dakota: A Guide to the State*. New York, 1952.

WRIGHT, ROBERT M. S. *Dodge City: The Cowboy Capital*. Wichita, Kansas, 1913.

YOUNGER, COLE. *The Story of Cole Younger*. Chicago, 1903.

Periodicals

BRITE, LUKE (as told to Virginia Ridout Klaus and Opal Cranor Wilcox). "The Bob Fitzsimmons-Peter Fight." *The El Paso County Historical Society*, Summer 1965.

CLUM, JOHN C. "It All Happened in Tombstone." *Arizona Historical Review*, April 1929.

CUSHMAN, GEORGE L. "Abilene: First of the Kansas Cowtowns." *Kansas State Historical Quarterly*, August 1940.

EARP, WYATT. "How Wyatt Earp Routed a Gang of Arizona Outlaws." *San Francisco Examiner Sunday Magazine*, August 2, 1896.

————. "Wyatt Earp Tells Tales of the Shotgun Messenger Service." *San Francisco Examiner Sunday Magazine*, August 9, 1896. University of California, Bancroft Library, Berkeley, California.

HAYNES, A. A. "The Cattle Ranches of Colorado." *Harper's Magazine*, 1879, republished, Pueblo Regional Library, 1979.

HORAN, JAMES D. "Photographs That Are Pure Gold." *Parade Magazine*, January 6, 1980.

HUTTON, PAUL. "Little Big Horn to Little Big Man: The Changing Image of the Western Hero in Popular Culture." *The Western Quarterly*, January 1976.

JONES, C. A. "The Good Bad Man." *Atlantic Monthly*, 1934.

LAKE, STUART. "Tales of the Kansas Cowtowns." *Saturday Evening Post*, 1930.

MATHESON, ROY. "Roosevelt's Dakota Ranches." Bismarck, North Dakota, n.d.

MICHELSON, CHARLES. "Stage Robbers of the West." *Munsey's Magazine*, July 1901.

MILLER, NYLE H. "Kansas Police Officers Before TV." Topeka, Kansas, 1958.

MOOAR, JOSIAH WRIGHT. "Buffalo Days." *Hollands, the Magazine of the South*, 1933.

RASCH, PHILIP P. "Farewell to the Clantons." *New York Brand Book*, vol. 5, no. 2, New York, 1958.

RICHARDSON, RUPERT N. "The Comanche Indians at the Adobe Walls Fight." *The Panhandle Plains Historical Review*, vol. 1, 1931.

ROBERTS, GARY L. "Clay Allison vs. The Dodge City Legend." *Brand Book, New York Westerners*, vol 8, no. 2, 1961.

SHINN, CHARLES HOWARD. "Pacific Outlaws." *New York Sun*, Sunday, September 4, 1890.

SIMPSON, H. O. "Early Day Gunmen Give Color to the Picturesque Setting of Dodge City." *Topeka Daily Citizen*, December 9, 1934.

SNELL, JOSEPH W. "Painted Ladies of the Cow Towns." *The Trail Guide*, Independence, Missouri, 1965.

SONNICHSEN, C. L. "The West That Wasn't." *The American West: The Magazine of Western History*, November–December 1977.

STARR, HENRY. "Story of the Crime Life of Henry Starr as Told by the Famous Bandit." *Wichita Eagle*, February 27 to March 4, 1921.

WALLACE, WILLIAM. "How the James Gang Was Wiped Off the Face of the Earth." *Kansas City World*, November 6, 1898.

Memoirs, Manuscripts, Journals, Letters, Tape Recordings, Official Documents, and Private Collections

Coroner's Report to the Board of Supervisors of Cochise County, Arizona, Listing the Inquest Performed and Personal Property Found on the Bodies. November 8, 1881. Arizona Historical Society.

LAKE, STUART. Letters to Wyatt Earp and Earp's Replies, 1927–1929. The Huntington Library, San Marino, California.

Motion Picture Prints from the Library of Congress Motion Picture Collection Paper Print Collection.

O. K. Corral Testimony. *Tombstone Daily Nugget.* Arizona Historical Society.

TILGHMAN, WILLIAM, Collection. University of Oklahoma Library.

FROM THE JAMES D. HORAN CIVIL WAR AND WESTERN AMERICANA COLLECTION

ARTHUR, CHESTER, President. Message to Congress on Outlawry in the Arizona Territory, 1882.

BOLDS, GEORGE. "The County Seat Wars of Kansas: The Battle of Cimarron with the Mastersons." Series of tape recordings made with Bolds, frontier deputy, Ford County surveyor and early pioneer of Ingalls, Kansas.

CRITTENDEN, THOMAS THEODORE, Governor. Messages and Proclamations on Outlawry in the State of Missouri and the Breakup of the James-Younger Gang, 1883.

CROOK, GEORGE. Annual Report of Brigadier General George Crook, U.S. Army, Commanding, Department of the Platte, Omaha, Nebraska, 1876.

———. Military Operations, Department of the Platte, 1879.

MASTERSON, BAT. Miscellaneous clippings, interviews, and notes.

———. "Famous Gunfighters of the Western Frontier." *Human Life*, 1907.

Outlaws and Lawmen. A collection of newspaper clippings, magazine articles, letters, memoirs, and original photographs of outlaws and peace officers.

RAWSON, H. O. Original sketches of outlaws and lawmen and material dealing with their lives and times.

ROOSEVELT, THEODORE. Collection of original mounted photographs made by Roosevelt and captioned by him, of the hunt for the horse thieves on the Little Missouri, Dakota Territory, March 30 to April 11, 1886.

SIRINGO, CHARLES. Letters on the techniques and characters of famous western gunfighters, 1929.

TILGHMAN, ZOE. Letters and interviews, 1950s to 1960s.

U.S. Cavalry journals, 1892.

WALLACE, WILLIAM. "He Was Not with Frank James!" A pamphlet, privately printed by Wallace, denying he ever accompanied Frank James on a hunting trip.

Newspapers consulted are listed by name and date in the text and footnotes.

INDEX